JEWS WITHOUT POWER

American Jewry During the Holocaust

Ariel Hurwitz

JEWS WITHOUT POWER
American Jewry During the Holocaust

Newly Updated Edition

©2015 by Ariel Hurwitz

All Rights Reserved

Published by **ISRAEL ACADEMIC PRESS**

(A subsidiary of MultiEducator, Inc.)

553 North Avenue • New Rochelle, NY 10801

Email: nhkobrin@Israelacademicpress.com

ISBN # 978-1-885881-44-1

© 2015 Israel Academic Press

❖ ❖ ❖

To my wife Cipora (z"l),

To my children Shlomit, Galia (z"l) and Shaul,

And to my grandchildren

Shir, Amir, Liri, Noam and Noga

With all my love and appreciation

TABLE OF CONTENTS

Acknowledgements

When I began to research the subject of this book, I had, as all historians have, some amorphous views concerning the subject. When I had finished researching and began to write I was actually pleased to see that I had changed many of my previous views – some had taken a turn of 180 degrees. The facts of the case, as I had learned them from the archival material, had altered my views on many issues. My views are quite different from those held by most of the Jewish community today, as well as those of many historians.

This book, *Jews Without Power,* deals with the policies of the American government, the American public and the American Jewish organizations in regards to the destruction of European Jewry by Nazi Germany. Most specifically I have attempted to concentrate on the role played by the American Jewish leadership during this crucial period.

Though a number of books have appeared on this topic, I believe that this work sheds new light on many aspects of the subject and will contribute to a better understanding of the period. I have attempted to indicate the dilemmas facing the American Jewish leadership during the Holocaust and to present their action in light of the conditions existing at that time, on the backdrop of the Second World War and the growing antisemitism in the United States.

In the past few years both historians and popular writers have been highly critical of the role played by the American Jewish organizations in the attempts to rescue European Jewry during the Holocaust. The Bergson group (the Irgun delegation in the United States) alone has been held up as an example of how other Jewish organizations should have acted. Rabbi Stephen Wise (president of the World and American Jewish Congress) has often been singled out for criticism, despite the fact that he was one of the first, and most vociferous, leaders who warned of the dangers of Nazism, and called for world Jewry to organize in order to meet the challenge. This book presents the role of the Jewish leadership and the many efforts of their organizations to rally support for rescue. Alas to no avail!

This book relies heavily on archival sources and I wish to thank the many archivists and librarians all of whom were so helpful and pleasant to deal with and always prepared to assist. I would like to single out especially Dr. Abraham Peck, formerly Director of the American Jewish Archives at the Hebrew Union College in Cincinnati, Ohio, who hosted me for a month at the College where I was able to delve through the monumental archives of the World Jewish Congress and the immense files of Rabbi Stephen Wise.

In the United States I researched at the American Jewish Historical Society Archives at Brandeis University, Waltham, Mass.; Franklin Delano Roosevelt Library, Hyde Park, New York; Lehman Library, Columbia University, New York; Library of Congress, Washington, D.C.; National Archives, Washington, D.C. (State Department Archives; Treasury Department Archives); Sterling Library, Yale University, New Haven Conn.; VMI Archives, Lexington, Va. (Marshall Archives); YIVO Archives, New York; Zionist Archives, New York.

In addition I also explored the archives of varied Jewish organizations: American Jewish Committee Library, New York; American Jewish Congress Library, New York; American Jewish Joint Distribution Committee, New York; B'nai Brith Library, Washington, D.C.; Hadassah Archives, New York; Jewish Labor Committee Archives, New York; Vaad Hahatzalah, Yeshiva University Archives, New York, In Israel I worked at the Central Zionist Archives, Jerusalem; Labor Archives, Tel Aviv; Moreshet Archives, Givat Haviva; Jabotinsky Archives, Metzudat Ze'ev, Tel Aviv; Oral History Department, Institute of Contemporary Jewry, Hebrew University, Jerusalem; Yad Va'shem Archives, Jerusalem.

I was also very fortunate to have the opportunity to conduct personal interviews at length with Maurice Perlzweig (Head of the World Jewish Congress' Political Department during the period of the Holocaust), and with Hillel Kook (Peter Bergson), who led the delegation of the Irgun Zvai Le'umi (the so-called Bergson Boys) in the United States during the Second World War.

I am deeply indebted to my teacher and mentor for many years, Professor Yehuda Bauer, who encouraged and developed critical thought among his students and demanded accuracy in writing, down to the smallest details.

My special appreciation goes to my wife, Cipora z"l, herself a child survivor of the Holocaust, for her patience, assistance and guidance in understanding that period of history, which is so difficult to deal with and to comprehend.

List of Abbreviations

AJC	American Jewish Committee
AJConf	American Jewish Conference
AJCong	American Jewish Congress
ARC	American Red Cross
AZEC	American Zionist Emergency Committee
CJA	Committee for a Jewish Army
ECSJE	Emergency Committee to Save the Jews of Europe
ECZA	Emergency Committee for Zionist Affairs
GJC	General Jewish Council
ICRC	International Committee of the Red Cross
IGCR	Inter-Governmental Committee on Refugees
IRC	International Red Cross
JDC	American Jewish Joint Distribution Committee
JEC	Joint Emergency Committee for European Jewish Affairs
JLC	Jewish Labor Committee
OSS	Office of Strategic Services
OWI	Office of War Information
PACPR	President's Advisory Committee on Political Refugees
WJC	World Jewish Congress
WRB	War Refugee Board

Preface

"To imagine the past as if it were still only present"
— Johan Huizinga

In the year 2014, as I complete this preface, there are presently serving in the United States Congress 12 Jewish Senators (12%) and at least 22 Jewish Members of the House of Representatives (5%), whereas the Jewish population of the U.S. stands at less then 2%. The daughter of the former President of the U.S., whose wife was the Secretary of State, has married a Jewish man in a semi-Jewish ceremony, and the only ones who seem to care are the Orthodox Jews. In contrast, the Secretary of State during the Second World War, Cordell Hull, did not include his wife's name in the Congressional Record, as was the custom, quite possibly due to the attacks that had been leveled at her Jewish ancestry. Today it is difficult to look back at the time of the Holocaust and imagine a Jewish community that lacked influence and feared a growing antisemitism. Looking back from a vantage point of more than 60 years, at a time when the American Jewish community is well organized, having one of the most successful lobbying groups, AIPAC, a central organization – the Presidents Conference – and when even xenophobic politicians speak of the Judeo-Christian heritage of America, it is easy to blame the inaction of American Jewry for at least part of the fate of European Jewry.

It is commonly accepted today, both among the general public interested in the subject, and among historians who have studied the matter, that the United States did very little to aid or rescue European Jewry during the Holocaust. There is much less agreement as to what could actually have been done, either by the American government or by American Jewry, to save those people singled out for extermination. America proclaimed that it was fighting a war not only against German aggression, but against the world outlook of National-Socialism as well, yet it generally remained silent and unmoved by the unprecedented tragedy that was overtaking the principal victims of that very Nazi ideology.

Not only was the period of World War II conspicuous by the silence, which surrounded America's meager response to the destruction of European Jewry, but the silence continued long after. For more than two decades following the war neither the American intellectual community, nor American Jewry, tried to confront the United States' failure to rescue.[1] America and American Jewry did not examine their role during the Holocaust. Had they really stood almost totally passive before the most barbaric act in human history, or had they attempted to rescue as best they could under the conditions existing during that savage war?

The first major endeavor to deal with this issue came, pointedly, not from a historian, nor from any Jewish leader, but from a journalist, Arthur Morse. In his pioneering book, 'While Six Million Died,'[2] Morse detailed the role of the U.S. government in thwarting any attempts to bring Jewish refugees during the Nazi period to America's shores. He exposed the callousness and conspiracies of State Department officials in their handling of the so-called 'refugee problem' (the common euphemism used in referring to the Jewish victims). Morse succeeded, as well, in demolishing the halo that had surrounded Franklin Delano Roosevelt, who had been perceived by American Jews as a devoted friend. Since Morse's book first appeared in 1967, we have been virtually deluged with an immense number of books,[3] articles, reviews, dissertations[4] and papers attempting to deal either with particular aspects of the subject, or with the question in its entirety.

It is important to note the time-frame in which these works have been written. Aside from Arthur Morse's book, they first began to appear in the period right after Israel's victory in the Six Day War. The threat to destroy Israel and the 'hands-off' policy of the Western nations that preceded the war appeared analogous to the fate of Jewry during the Holocaust creating a renewed interest in that period and a tendency to compare it to the Six Day War.

However, much had changed in the status of Jews in the intervening years. Then, Jews in Europe had been led, unarmed and unable to resist, to the gas chambers of Treblinka. After the creation of the State of Israel in 1948, the Jews had a sovereign nation of their own which, in the Six Day War, had amazed the world with its military prowess. Not only was Israel able to defend its borders against vastly larger Arab armies, and it had proved itself able to reach into the very heart of Africa to save Jews from the hands of terrorists. Earlier, American Jewry had been unable to induce their government to provide the barest aid to their brethren who were being systematically massacred in Europe. During the 1970s and 1980s they were able to mobilize the U.S. to provide massive support for the State of Israel and to assist in the struggle to free Soviet Jewry. The general political atmosphere in the U.S. has also changed. In the 1930's, public opinion in the U.S. was opposed to involvement in Europe, and the U.S. became embroiled in the war only after being attacked. A generation later the U.S. abandoned its isolationist policies, and now sees itself as the standard bearer of democratic society, with thousands of American soldiers involved in Afghanistan and Iraq.

It is not surprising, therefore, that many people today find it difficult to understand, what seems to be the almost total lack of power of American Jewry during the Holocaust and their inability to move the American government toward rescuing the victims of Nazism. They project the conditions of the generation of their fathers to the circumstances of American Jewry today, and they ask: "How could it have been?" Books and articles began to appear in the United States accusing the large and wealthy American Jewish community of having abandoned their kinsmen in Europe and, in effect, reconciling themselves to the 'do-nothing' policy of their government. The mutual recriminations and self-accusations reached such a point that a prestigious commission, chaired by former Supreme Court Justice Arthur Goldberg, was created to examine the role of American Jewry during the Holocaust.[5]

It was Elie Wiesel, the novelist and 'conscience' of the Holocaust, who was among the first to challenge the methods and actions of the leaders of the American Jewish community during the Holocaust. In an article, "Telling the Tale,"[6] written only a few months after the Six Day War, Wiesel attacked the American Jewish community, and especially its leadership. He accused them of having stood aloof and therefore of being partners in the shame of abandoning their people. "And so we must share the guilt" he maintains, "We did not do enough." Wiesel seems to believe that had they just "proclaim[ed] hunger strikes to the end"; had "shaken heaven and earth" European Jewry would have been rescued.[7] "If our brothers had shown more compassion, more initiative, more daring [...] Who knows, the enemy might have desisted."[8] This view, which almost totally condemns the previous generation for remaining silent while six million died, is probably shared by most Jews today. They unambiguously state that they would have acted differently. In discussing the response of the American Jewish community to the Holocaust, Alan Dershowitz writes in his best-seller *'Chutzpah'* that: "I know that I and my generation of Jews would not have [...] gone about business as usual while Jewish lives were at stake."[9]

A number of books have appeared developing the same theme: Had the American Jewish community, and especially its leadership, confronted the American government, specifically the President, in a more challenging, aggressive, even threatening manner, European Jewry, or at least a much larger part of it, could have been saved.[10] They counterpose what they see as having been the ineffective, pleading approach of the establishment leadership, to the energetic, public struggle of the so-called 'Bergson Boys'' members of the Irgun Zvai Leumi (the Revisionist Zionist underground in Palestinian) delegation to the U. S., whom they credit with the only achievements worthy of mention.[11]

Is it true that the American Jewish community did not attempt to rescue European Jews? Did they really not demonstrate, not act, not do anything, as some state? What were the considerations of the Jewish leadership in determining their rescue policy? Were they correct in their reasoning?

There are many authors who describe the climate of antisemitism in the U.S. at that time, but only few consider this factor when evaluating the response of the Jewish organizations to the Holocaust. What were the dimensions of that antisemitism? How much did it actually influence the policy of the Jewish organizations? Did it prevent American Jews and their leadership from demanding that their government aid in rescuing their fellow Jews in Europe? That problem raises the thorny question of the possibility of a minority affecting the policies of the America government when it is not, at least as the government perceives it, in the direct interests of America. This question is especially relevant when it relates to time of war, and even more so when the matter does not concern American citizens, but rather some populace overseas.

We have to explore what American Jewry did to aid their brethren, and what results could they have reasonably attained as a small minority trying to place on the war-time agenda, proposals to rescue foreign subjects.

The condition of powerlessness is not the only factor incomprehensible to Jews today. At present, most Jewish groups have united quite effectively under the umbrella of the Conference of Presidents of Major Jewish Organizations. Many Jews, now, are unable to comprehend the inability of the Jewish community to unite, at the time of the Holocaust, in order to achieve, what was (or should have been) the most crucial goal on their agenda – the rescue of the Jews of Europe. Many authors decry the deep divisions that rent the American Jewish community at that time and treat it as though had the Jewish leadership shown just a little more statesmanship, all these rifts would have disappeared overnight.

The facts were that the Second World War found the Jewish community in the United States with a vacuum in leadership and profound divisions. On what methods of rescue action could they unite? That question alone created nearly insurmountable problems. It was not enough just to demand action. What form these actions should take was no less a problem. Should they appeal to the President? Should they demonstrate, and pressure the Administration? Should they work only within the accepted frameworks, or did the realities of the Holocaust require undertaking illegal actions as the only practical method of achieving results?

In dealing with the role of American Jewry and the Holocaust, there is no point in ruing the lack of unity in the community that was part of the realities of the time. As will be shown later it probably could not have been very different. What should be asked is what was done to create some joint and coordinated action? There also remains the question, that none has asked (though it was often posed by various Jewish leaders during the Holocaust): Would unity have promoted or impeded, rescue efforts?

Many writers condemn the American Jewish community for its support of President Roosevelt, which deterred them, out of a mistaken loyalty as they see it, from bringing pressure upon his Administration. Some imply that it was the Jewish leadership, more specifically, Rabbi Stephen Wise, who led the community down this blind alley. Elie Wiesel claims that American Jewry did not act because it was "taken in by Roosevelt's personality."[12] Rafael Medoff in his book *'The Deafening Silence'* blames the Jewish leadership for not having used the 'Jewish vote' as a stipulation – that in exchange for Jewish support Roosevelt would provide rescue.[13]

One must, however, delve deeper into the period and the person, to understand the basis for the reverential endorsement that Roosevelt received from the American Jewish community. It is crucial for us to understand this attitude because the loyalty of American Jewry to Roosevelt played a key role in determining the actions and reactions of Jewish groups to the attempts to save European Jewry. Were the Jewish leaders really capable, if they so determined, to bring the Jewish masses to 'revolt' against the leadership of the President?

Nor is it enough for us to understand the reasons for American Jewry's fealty to the President. We must also understand the constraints and the animosity confronting Roosevelt if we are to evaluate his response to the Holocaust. All biographers of Roosevelt agree that he was a consummate politician, finely attuned to the feelings of the public, and careful not to expend political capital on matters that he felt would create opposition if they were not central to his immediate goals. Though his worshippers were numerous, so too, were his detractors. During the years crucial to the rescue of Jews Roosevelt had to contend with the most contentious Congress of his entire presidency. How much did political considerations influence Roosevelt's response to the Holocaust? How much did they limit his maneuverability as regards the rescue of Jews?

Whereas earlier, Arthur Morse, Henry Feingold, and Saul Friedman had chronicled the callous attitude of Administration officials in squelching rescue efforts, David Wyman's book, *'The Abandonment of the Jews'*[14] was the first major work to give us an extraordinary picture of the attitudes, the indifference and insensitivity of the general American public, the press, and the Church, to the fate of European Jewry. If such was the situation we should ask why there was no understanding then – not even by the intellectual nor by the religious leadership – of what was unique in the Jewish suffering. Nor was there any perception of what the Holocaust meant in terms of the broader aspects of the war – as a struggle against the Nazi *weltanschaung*. Was there really no humanitarian spirit in the United States to which Jews could appeal?

We will deal later with the questions: What did they know? When did they know it? During the war, most Americans, including American Jews, were generally not aware of the Holocaust.[15] However, the actual question that has to be asked is not what they knew, but how did they comprehend it? This inability to comprehend, at times an unwillingness to accept, the news of what was transpiring in Europe must also be considered as a factor in studying and evaluating the American response to the Holocaust.

The last question we shall broach, important to consider if we are to develop a proper historical perspective, is the problem of judging what could reasonably have been obtained from Nazi Germany to alleviate the suffering of the Jews of Europe. This question is not only a hypothetical conjecture, the second-guessing of historians and laymen today. That same question was also asked during the Holocaust by those who dealt with rescue and affected the decisions of the proponents of rescue.

It is necessary to place this study in the proper perspective of its time; to bring into play, as best possible, the many factors in the background that affected those in the position to respond to the Holocaust. Only if we succeed in understanding the climate that existed in the United States at that time; the attitude of Americans towards the war; the worries that troubled Americans in their daily life; and the attitude of the American public to what was happening during the Holocaust, will we be able to understand what affected the actions of those who endeavored to save European Jewry. There is no point, in a historical analysis, to bewail the given circumstances. We should depict the situation as it was; interpret the evidence as we have it; and attempt to see what, under those conditions, was done, or could possibly and effectively have been done. There are many authors who describe the actions of the American government and of the Jewish organizations. There are only few who attempt to show us the backdrop of these responses, and how the existing situation effected the determination of policies at the time. This I seek to bring in this work.

Placing the problems of rescue within the true context of the time, does not absolve one from asking some of the existential questions that need to be asked. What is the value of acts done not to achieve an immediate, concrete purpose, but acts of conscience; acts meant to speak to future generations; acts carried out because "they simply had to be done"? Perhaps, the Warsaw Ghetto revolt falls into this category? Perhaps that is what the Nobel laureate, Elie Wiesel meant when he said "they should have gone on hunger strikes until the end[16]"? Those questions beg a reply not only from historians, but from all people. Those questions too, should be dealt with, and I shall attempt to address myself to them in the conclusion.

CHAPTER 1
The Jewish Community in America

(a) The Growing Divide: *"Your Huddled Masses"*
(from the poem by Emma Lazarus inscribed on the Statue of Liberty)

American Jewry has no history of ever being a unified community. In the years preceding World War I there was an attempt by Rabbi Judah Magnes to establish an organized Jewish community, but this effort was limited only to New York City, and after a period of ineffective action the 'kehilla' was disbanded[1]. By the Second World War most American Jews were native born and did not have any remembrance of having been part of a structured community, such as the 'kehilla' which had existed in most countries of the Diaspora. The American Jewish community was, and has remained, a voluntary, pluralistic body. Nor would American Jewry have it otherwise, no matter how much they may decry today the lack of unity at the time of the Holocaust. It is a natural development of their living in a free, open and multi-ethnic society. A voluntary, pluralistic community does not necessarily preclude the possibility of achieving some degree of unity and cooperation, as can be seen in the success of the present-day 'Conference of Presidents of Major Jewish Organizations'. However, in all its existence as a loosely connected community, there is no doubt that the period, which paralleled the Nazi era, found American Jewry at the very nadir of its communal ties.

It is usual to speak of the American Jewish community during the Second World War as having been composed of three distinct layers of immigration. The first was composed largely of Sephardic Jews who had arrived in America during the Colonial period. Their numbers were so small, and their dispersion so vast that by the 1930's they were almost all assimilated into American society and were not a factor in the Jewish community.

The upheavals in Europe in the 1840's, brought another wave of Jews to America. These consisted, predominantly, of German Jews. They, too, spread throughout the country, though mainly to the developing Mid-West and the West Coast which presented them with opportunities for their entrepreneurial spirit. Their numbers were larger, and they brought with them the new forms of Jewish worship of the German Reform movement. They found Reform Judaism well-suited to the soil of America, and it became their preeminent religious expression. By the time the third wave of Jews from Eastern European arrived in America at the turn of the century, the German Jews were well-established, and well-acculturated in American society. They took the new immigrants under their tutelage, and despite their considerably smaller numbers, provided the American Jewish community with leadership for many years. Nevertheless, by the time of the Second World War, not only had the German Jews lost much of their power in the community, but many of their children, as with the Sepharadim before them, were slipping away from Judaism.

More than two million Eastern European Jews arrived in the United States between 1881 (the time of pogroms in Russia) and 1914 (the outbreak of World War I). Unlike their predecessors, they congregated in the slums of the big cities, primarily on the eastern seaboard. Their sheer numbers; their living together in the 'urban ghettos'; their Jewish values so deeply entrenched in the Orthodox, closely-knit communities from whence they had come – all gravitated to slowing down their acculturation to American life. The established German Jews (the 'Uptown Jews' as the new immigrants labeled them) did their best to facilitate the absorption of the new immigrants (the 'Downtown Jews') into their new country. They were motivated not only by the traditional concern of Jews for the welfare of their fellow-Jews but also by a desire to protect their own status in the eyes of their fellow-Americans, who looked upon the new arrivals as a strange, uncouth, and criminal element.

Society exerted powerful pressures for these new immigrants to become 'Americans', which meant to adopt the language, the life-style and the culture of the dominant 'WASP' society. Nothing was more shameful than to be labeled 'a greener' – a newcomer who clings to his Old World ways. The United States was not prepared, as yet, to accept the doctrine of 'cultural pluralism' so prevalent in present day America. It was the 'melting pot' theory that then held sway – that all the variegated immigrant groups would be fused in a crucible to form a new nation and a new culture.

Living in a free society, in which there was a clear separation of Church and State, and pressed to give up their singularity, American Jews neither saw a need, nor had a desire, to create an organized community, certainly not on a national basis. The individual Jew was not required by state authority to remain a member of the community. His participation within Jewish life was only on the basis of his own free choice. Lacking any authority to impose unity, diversity flourished. A multitude of institutions and organizations sprang up among American Jewry that reflected the diversities of backgrounds, ideologies, and religious preferences now flourishing in this free society.

Nor were these the only factors that led to the cleavage in Jewish community life. Voluntary organizations are heavily dependent upon large donors for their budgets. These donors, in turn, are attracted by the many titles and honors heaped upon them. The more organizations, the more honors could be granted these contributors. Without an outside threat to force unity on the community, every major disagreement, or clash of personalities carried the possibility of further splits within the group. By the eve of World War II there were more than 300 national Jewish organizations in the U.S. and tens of thousands of local ones.[2]

The First World War, and the immigration laws passed in the early 1920's, brought to a virtual halt the admission of Jews into the U.S. Only in the 1930's, and especially at the end of that decade when persecution threatened the Jews in Germany, did a new wave of immigration begin arriving in America. Though hampered in their efforts to enter the U.S. by strict immigration laws and ordinances, tens of thousands of Jewish refugees succeeded, nonetheless, in entering America by the time of Pearl Harbor. Though their numbers were proportionally not large, these immigrants have a special place in our study. Having experienced Nazi antisemitism; possessing close, personal ties to Jews who remained in Europe; it is not surprising to find an unduly large proportion of rescue advocates among this group. It may be questionable whether some of the leaders among these new immigrants, as yet un-Americanized, can be truly classified as being part of the American Jewish community. During the period of the Holocaust none of them were American citizens; some had arrived in America with no intent of remaining; and, indeed, a few eventually settled in Israel. Nonetheless, they were in the U.S. at the time, and did interact with the American Jewish community, and therefore should be considered as germane to this study.

Though the mass wave of Eastern European Jews had totally changed the demographic makeup of American Jewry, the German Jews maintained their hegemony in the community for many decades. They had the wealth, they had the contacts within the American establishment, and it was they, totally Americanized, who were to be emulated if one was not to remain 'a greener.' In contrast stood the millions of newly-arrived immigrants, many still penniless, lacking in general education and, therefore, lacking in influence. The German-Jews extended their paternalistic aegis upon the Jewish 'masses'. As longtime American citizens they 'knew' what was best for Jews, and how best to 'care' for their needs. "The problems with which we have to deal are of such a delicate nature that the mob can not grapple with them", explained Louis Marshall, a leader of the German-Jewish community in the first decades of the 20th century.[3]

By the thirties the situation was changing. On the one hand, the wealth of German Jews was hard hit by the depression and their position weakened,[4] while on the other, a new generation of American-born and educated Jews of Eastern European extraction was seeking to assert itself. In a country in which they breathed the air of democracy, they were no longer prepared to allow a small plutocracy to control the Jewish community. The values and culture of the two Jewish communities were dissimilar, and as long as German Jewry felt it held a prerogative to speak for and to lead the entire American Jewish community, the clash was inevitable. The result was an atmosphere of mutual distrust and animosity, as well as the creation of a vacuum of power, as no group was able to speak for the community in its entirety. This bid by Eastern European Jewry to achieve hegemony over the community, and their German counterparts trying to hold on to the reins of power, was as yet unresolved by the start of World War II. Several attempts were made to achieve unity among the Jewish organizations, or at least to forge some degree of cooperation, but these proved ineffectual, and in the end they all failed.

Such was the situation of organized American Jewry when the Jews of Europe stood before the Nazi onslaught that threatened their annihilation and looked to American Jewry for aid. The American Jewish community found it difficult to unite on a program of action to influence its government to rescue Jews on the verge of extinction. The disagreements that existed between the different organizations were intrinsic, and not only on the basis of prestige, and therefore it was difficult to bridge the gap. The crisis of European Jewry; the need to find ways to aid them; and the awareness that they were dealing with the saving of lives, where an intemperate step might only worsen the situation, only deepened the gulf that existed between the diverse Jewish groups in the U.S.

By the eve of the Holocaust, the 'Uptown Jews' were becoming assimilated, and the 'Downtown Jews', who had begun moving out of their 'ghettos', were becoming Americanized so that both saw themselves as Americans first, and only secondly as Jews. In addition, in the wake of the depression, and the subsequent radicalization of a large segment of American Jewry, a new, deracinated Jew was also appearing, especially among the young. Faithful to Marxian ideology, they believed that in the modern world, salvation lay in a universal struggle, in which all oppressed people would unite for the common good. To think in the narrow terms of national or ethnic interests appeared to them as reactionary and particularistic, and did not suit the new man of the Twentieth Century. For them Fascism was a threat to all mankind, and there was no point to harp only on the Jewish aspect of suffering, unless it could provide an issue for rallying the Jewish masses to their banner. When Fascism threatened in Spain, hundreds of these young Jews enlisted to fight and die for a country that for centuries had been ostracized by Jews, yet later very few young Jews were enthused by a call to join a Jewish Army to defend the Jews of Palestine threatened by an Axis invasion. The fact that this universalistic outlook was embraced especially by the dynamic young and the intellectuals jeopardized the coherence of the American Jewish community far out of proportion to the actual numbers this attitude encompassed.

This was the picture of the American Jewish community on the eve of the Second World War. The vast majority of American Jews, while still holding on to their Jewishness, were in the process of becoming, first and foremost, Americans, eagerly seeking acceptance into a society that was increasingly viewing them with distrust and distaste. The American Jewish community was atomized, split into numerous competing and antagonistic organizations. The old German-Jewish leadership was trying to maintain its reign over the community and the upcoming Eastern European segment was seeking to achieve, what it believed to be, its rightful place as leader of American Jewry. Some had already become totally assimilated; others were swept up in a radical wave of universalism. If such was the situation existing in the American Jewish community on the eve of the great trials they were about to confront, one can understand that the struggle was both formidable and complex, for at that very same time, the position of Jews in the U.S. was being challenged in an increasingly threatening manner.

(b) Antisemitism in the United States:
"The Jews have too much power"
(from U.S. public opinion polls in the 1930's)

The wave of antisemitism that swept the world in the '30's and swelled with the Nazi rise to power in Germany, did not bypass the United States which had been imbued in a tradition of tolerance and democracy. Antisemitism now became a profound factor in determining the response of American Jewry to all that was happening to the Jews of Europe.

What was the scope of that antisemitism, and what was its effect? Bigoted opinions about Jews were fairly prevalent in America at that time. Various surveys taken in the U.S. during the 1930's and 1940's showed that about half of all Americans believed that Jews were unscrupulous in business; a third declared that Jews were too pushy; and many claimed that Jews were clannish, ill-mannered etc.[5] Nearly two thirds indicated at least one objectionable trait among the Jews, and nearly half stated that there were good reasons for the prevailing negative perceptions about Jews.[6] However offensive and degrading these views were, they were not unfamiliar. Jews had always known that they had never been much liked by their neighbors, though they had expected a different attitude in the United States.

As long as antisemitism did not injure the Jews directly, they lived with it as with a frightening shadow. But when actual discrimination began to mount they became very concerned. Public opinion polls showed that many gentiles were not prepared to have Jews live in their neighborhoods, and they objected to having Jewish children in schools together with their own. In a public opinion poll taken in April, 1940, 43% of those asked "would it make any difference to you [to hire] a Jew?" replied in the positive.[7]

The Jews did not need public opinion polls to perceive these realities. From their own daily experience they were aware of the attitude towards them. Jewish engineers had great difficulty finding jobs in the private sector. Jews were unable to obtain managerial positions in banks; Wall St. law firms did not hire Jewish lawyers and many prestigious universities maintained 'numerus clausus' quotas for Jewish applicants. In July, 1939, 10.1% of Americans in a public opinion poll stated that the U.S. should expel the Jews of America.[8] There were also many physical attacks upon Jews, and more than one Jewish boy had his nose bloodied because "he had killed Christ."

But what truly frightened the Jews most were groups on the Radical Right that began to emerge during the depression era, and who gathered strength throughout the thirties. Some attempted to qualm these fears and claimed that those groups represented only a small minority. True, they were only a minority, but not an insignificant one. There also existed a feeling that the views of this minority were slowly seeping into the cognizance of broader circles, and forming a firm base in American society. Perhaps only three and a half million Americans listened regularly to Father Coughlin's antisemitic sermons on the air, but 15 million listened occasionally, and the insinuations of the Catholic priest from Michigan slowly penetrated their consciousness.[9]

Surveys taken in the U.S. in 1939 and 1940 indicated that 37% of the American public concurred with Coughlin's views.[10] It was therefore not easy to allay the fears, and to claim that they were only a small antisemitic minority and that "It can't happen here." American Jews knew that the Nazis were also an insignificant minority when they had started out, and that within a very short time their racial theories sprouted in Germany, the European country where Jews had felt the most 'beloved'.

Father Coughlin Speaks

What had washed up this ugly wave on the shores of America, a nation that only a generation before had inscribed on the Statue of Liberty the words of the Jewish poetess, Emma Lazarus: "Give me your tired, your poor, your huddled masses yearning to be free"? After the First World War a surge of xenophobia had engulfed the country. Congress passed a number of immigration laws that deliberately discriminated against refugees from Southern and Eastern Europe, among them the Jews. The economic depression that brought poverty and much suffering to America sought channels for pent up feelings and among other ways, burst out in an animosity against the Jews. As had happened more than once in their long history, Jews were accused of being both many things and their opposites: The 'Jewish Bankers' were blamed for the economic depression and the resulting unemployment; while those who feared the economic and social displacement created by Roosevelt's New Deal, saw it as a Jewish, Communist plot aimed at destroying 'real' Americans. They labeled FDR's policies the 'Jew Deal' and some even hinted that Roosevelt himself was a Jew who had changed his name from Rosenfelt. And even if Roosevelt was himself not a Jew, some claimed he certainly was a captive of the Jews. Ironically (as we shall see), during the years 1938-1946 between 41-58% of the American public believed that Jews had too much power in the U.S., and the number believing it to be true was constantly growing. [11]

Another cause of antisemitism during that period was the growing tension between Jews and Catholics as a result of the Spanish Civil War. In that war the Catholic Church supported General Franco, whom they perceived as fighting to maintain 'Christian Civilization'. Most Jews, on the other hand, supported the Republican government, and viewed the struggle against Franco as the spearhead of the battle against Fascism. Young Jews volunteered for the International Brigades to fight in Spain. Others contributed money, and many Jews petitioned the U.S. government to provide aid to the legal government of Spain. The Catholics in the U.S. did not easily forgive the Jews for this stand. [12]

As the decade drew to its end and the world drew closer to war, another factor was added to the antagonism towards the Jews. America of the 1930's dug firmly into an isolationist stand and vowed not to be drawn, once more, into a European conflict. In opposition to most Americans, the majority of Jews favored an internationalist foreign policy and once the war broke out in Europe they advocated extending aid to Britain. This attitude enraged the isolationists who accused the Jews of dragging America into the war. The Jews, they said, were prepared to sacrifice 'American boys' (it appeared they did not view American Jews as belonging to this category) for the benefit of the Jews of Europe.

In a well-publicized speech, the famous aviator and public idol, Charles Lindbergh, claimed that "The three most important groups who have been pressing the country towards war are the British, the Jewish and the Roosevelt Administration. If any one of these groups [...] stops agitating for war [there would be] little danger of our involvement." [13] These were views held not only by critics outside of the American establishment. Hiram Johnson, one of the most influential Senators on Capitol Hill wrote in 1939 that the lines were drawn 'with all the Jews on one side, wildly enthusiastic for the President and willing to fight to the last American [...] and those of us [...] who are thinking in terms of our country, and that alone.'[14] And there were demagogues, such as Congressman John Rankin, who believed that "if you tell the people that its the Jews who want war, then you have half the battle [against intervention] won."[15]

Senator Hiram Johnson

Many Americans were more fearful of the danger presumably posed by the Jews than they were of Nazi aggression. When Americans were asked in a public opinion poll in 1940 which group constituted a menace to the U.S., more people answered that it was the Jews more than any other ethnic group (Jews-17%; Germans-14%; Japanese-6%;).[16] Even during the war years, when the U.S. was battling the Axis powers, still more people perceived the Jews as a threat than they did the Germans or Japanese (Jews-24%; Japanese-9%; Germans-6%).[17]

It is no wonder, therefore, that American Jews were distressed by these views, and that the Jewish defense organizations devoted much time at their meetings to discussing the issue. They contributed energy and money to confront antisemitism and to educate the general public to tolerance. The Jewish groups attempted, more than once, to minimize the role of the Jews in order to counter the accusations that Jews were dominating America. Instead of being proud of the unique Jewish contribution to the development of the film industry the Jewish organizations were quick to prove that the oft-made assertion (heard even in the chambers of the Senate) that Jews were taking over Hollywood had no foundation. In order to counter the claim that Jews had too much political power, articles were written showing how meager Jewish representation was in Congress, as indeed it was.[18] The articles sounded in an apologetic tone, and projected a strong desire to be accepted.

The fear that antisemitism would spread was so great that the Jewish organizations did everything in their power to prevent it. They hesitated taking any steps that might strengthen this phenomenon. If, at times, the Jews were not sufficiently aware of the dangers inherent in their requests to aid the Jews of Europe, there was always someone certain to remind them what might result from such attempts. Such was the case when the Jews tried to convince the U.S. to boycott the Berlin Olympics in 1936 if Jewish athletes were not guaranteed equal treatment. General Sherrill, a member of the U.S. Olympic Committee warned the Jews that

> We are almost certain to have a wave of antisemitism among those who never before gave it a thought, and who may consider that about 5,000,000 Jews in this country are using the athletes representing 120,000,000 Americans to work out something to help the German Jews.[19]

When, in the 1930's, the Jewish organizations, unassertively, proposed allowing a small number of Jews to find a haven in the U.S., they were warned by the press not to ask for 'special privileges' for the Jews of Europe, because it did "neither their country, nor themselves, nor their kin a service."[20]

That very same atmosphere of antisemitism also influenced those Jews serving in high governmental positions. They did their utmost to avoid showing their Jewishness because they were constantly being suspected that they were too much concerned with Jewish interests. Therefore they did not move to place

Jewish issues on the agenda of the Administration, and at times even served as a brake on Jewish action. They feared endangering both their own position, and the position of the Jewish community, by activities that would 'justify' the claim that Jews had too much power in Washington. Nor did they wish to burden President Roosevelt, whom they ardently supported.

There was no lack of self-hatred among some Jews in the Administration. Laurence Steinhardt, himself a Jew, who was U.S. Ambassador to Moscow, asserted that those (Jewish) organizations supporting the admission of refugees "obviously are more interested in finding a haven for these unfortunates than they are of safe-guarding the welfare of the United States." He also described the Jewish refugees asking for visas to the U.S. as "The same as the criminal Jews who crowd our criminal dockets in New York."[21]

President Roosevelt and the members of his Administration were also aware of the public's attitude to the Jews, and in all their dealings in Jewish matters always took this into consideration. On the one hand, they did not want to do anything that might intensify the popular animosity to Jews. On the other, they feared taking any actions that the public would interpret as granting special privileges to Jews, which would provoke the public against the Administration.

In the years preceding America's entry into the war Roosevelt attempted to support a policy of containing German aggression, despite the massive opposition to this in the U.S. To achieve this goal, which he considered preeminent, Roosevelt, the astute politician, was not prepared to waste his political capital on controversial matters that seemed to be of secondary importance. A confrontation with Congress on the question of opening up the U.S. to Jewish refugees belonged in this category. Roosevelt told his wife, Eleanor, when she approached him as an advocate for the Jewish refugees, that "First things come first and I can't alienate certain votes I need for measures that are more important at the moment for measures that would entail a fight."[22]

President Roosevelt also shared those biases prevalent in his gentlemanly circle, which perceived a flaw in the behavior and manners of the Jews, and therefore attempted, in a paternalistic way, to rectify them. In the diary of Vice-President Henry Wallace we find a conversation between Roosevelt and Churchill concerning the Jews. Roosevelt spoke in favor of dispersing the Jews in small groups throughout the world. He boasted that he had added four or five Jewish families to the communities in which he lived (Hyde Park and Marietta) and that "the local populace will have no objection if there were no more than that."[23] He viewed that as an appropriate solution. That is, not that Jews had the right to live wherever they pleased, but rather one must consider the fact that they were not wanted and, therefore they should be scattered (for their own benefit) in small doses among the populations of America, and of the world.

At the Casablanca Conference in 1943, Roosevelt revealed that he, too, acknowledged the claims of antisemites that the Jews were themselves, in part, to blame for the gentile's attitude towards them. At that conference Roosevelt proposed limiting the number of Jews in liberated North Africa, and reducing the number of Jews in the medical and legal professions in those countries. He explained that such a step "would further eliminate the specific and understandable[!] complaints which the Germans bore towards the Jews in Germany."[24] And when King Ibn-Saud refused having a Jew participate in the American delegation to Saudia, Roosevelt did not hesitate to remove Under-Secretary of Interior Abe Fortas from the delegation, leading to his resignation.[25]

That very same climate of antisemitism which was so prevalent in America of the 30's continued to grow throughout the years of the war, and peaked only in June, 1944. It became a problem that troubled and preoccupied the Jewish community in the U.S. during all those years and it was a formidable barrier to all attempts to organize aid to the Jews of Europe. On the one hand, the Jews of America feared taking any steps that would increase the hatred towards themselves. On the other hand, the Administration was careful not to distance itself from the non-Jewish population by acts that could be interpreted as favoring the Jews. And if large segments of the American populace did not even savor the Jews of their own country, how could they be asked to make an effort, and perhaps even sacrifices, for the benefit of the Jews of Europe?

CHAPTER 2
America and The Rise of Nazism

"If the climate of acceptance does not exist, no strength of personality can force it into being [...] No brilliance, no eloquence, for good or for evil, can in a democracy force a position until the people, as a whole are ready to embrace it." – Congressman Emanuel Celler

(a) "We can not remain silent"
(Rabbi Stephen Wise at Madison Square Garden Rally-March, 1933)

On March 19, 1933, two weeks after the Nazi 'victory' in the March 5th elections in Germany, the leadership of the major national Jewish organizations in the U.S. met in emergency session to discuss how best to respond to the pogroms that had begun against the Jews of Germany.[1] At that meeting the thinking of the various organizations was already clearly defined, as well as the course of action that each was prepared to follow. The policies, enunciated then, guided the response of the diverse groups to the threats of Nazism up until 1938.

There existed marked differences between the stands of the different Jewish organizations. On one side stood the American Jewish Congress (AJCong) and the organizations representing, in the main, Jews of Eastern European origin. The American Jewish Congress called for organizing Jewish life on a democratic base, and championed a policy of open confrontation to achieve Jewish rights. "Privileges must be sought in secret, rights may be demanded in open" declared Rabbi Wise.[2] They demanded that demonstrations be arranged and that a rally be held in Madison Square Garden. Rabbi Wise, who headed the AJCong, asserted that

> The time for caution and prudence has past. We must speak up like men. How can we ask our Christian friends to raise their voices in protest against the wrongs suffered by Jews if we remain silent [...] What is happening in Germany today may happen in another land on earth unless it is challenged and rebuked.[3]

Rally at Madison Square Garden

On the other side, the American Jewish Committee (AJC) and B'nai Brith opposed public demonstrations, and proposed concentrating on quiet diplomacy and approaches to the Administration.[4] The American Jewish Committee represented the wealthy leadership of the German-Jewish community in the U.S. It was an elitist organization with great influence, though at that time it numbered only a few hundred members. B'nai Brith, the oldest and largest Jewish fraternal order, was a dependable ally in the policy of quiet diplomacy of the AJC, and loyal to the world outlook of the German-Jewish community from which it too had emerged.

At that same emergency session Judge Lehman, one of the leaders of the AJC, pleaded with the participants to avoid taking hasty steps. "In the name of humanity", he implored, "don't let anger pass a resolution that will kill Jews in Germany."[5] Wise, who after the Holocaust was often blamed for supposedly maintaining silence, was accused then of being overly insistent in his desire to demonstrate publicly, and that his confrontational tactics would be responsible for Jews being killed in Germany.[6] However, Wise saw the dangers inherent in Nazism, and believed that the threat had to be confronted head on. "It is a battle against all of us, against world Jewry, and if we lose the battle on the German front, world Jewry will be shattered," he declared.[7]

Stephen Wise was the foremost leader of American Jewry during the 1930's and 1940's. An outstanding orator, and a man of immense energy and drive, Wise was an outspoken liberal who did not fear clashing with the views of many in his wealthy German-American Reform congregation. He was among the few who saw that the Nazis were not just a passing phenomenon, and that Hitler's intent was to dominate all of Europe and destroy the values of western civilization. "Let it not be imagined that Hitlerism is, as so often claimed, Germany's business alone", he warned. "Hitlerism is the world's business [...] and the sooner mass-mankind discovers that Hitler is its problem, the sooner humanity may end the agony that it faces and already has begun to suffer."[8] He was one of the first to grasp the meaning of the 'New Order' of the Third Reich, and resolved to head a struggle to alert the world to the dangers of Nazism.

Immense pressure was put upon Wise by the American Jewish Committee, B'nai Brith, and the State Department, as well, not to hold a public rally. Wise began to waver and show doubts, but when Supreme Court Justice Louis Brandeis advised him to go ahead with the plans the rally was held, as proposed, on March 27th, 1933. Brandeis had been a leading Zionist and one of the founders of the AJCong. Brandeis saw no disparity between being a proud Jew and being a loyal American, and did not flinch at placing Jewish demands before the American public or government.[9]

Supreme Court Justice Louis Brandeis

The demonstration went off successfully and its message made an impression upon the public. 20,000 people jammed Madison Square Garden and another 35,000 who attempted to enter, listened to the proceedings outside.[10] After that rally similar ones were held in various cities across the U.S. and on May, 10th the day that the Nazis burnt 'decadent' books, tens of thousands of angry demonstrators marched in the streets of New York in protest against the Nazi regime.

In those days, Wise was like an angry prophet in his warnings and protesting, but he acted in that way mainly when appearing before Jewish groups. In his dealings with the Administration a different Wise often emerged. There he vacillated, either from fear of creating a confrontation between the Jewish community and the Administration, or because Wise, the liberal, was reluctant to burden the President, whom he felt was too much occupied with the difficult internal problems then facing the country. More than once Wise threatened that he would have "to do the lamentable thing of crying out against the President who hasn't, by a single act or word, intimated the faintest interest in what is going on."[11] This threat was never carried out, not because at that time Wise was a lackey of Roosevelt, as he was later accused of being. On the contrary, in the year preceding Roosevelt's election to the presidency the two of them were at odds with one another. For four years after being elected, the President and his circle boycotted Wise, because he had not supported Roosevelt's presidential bid. Despite this clash, Wise was captivated by the courage and drive displayed by FDR during that turbulent period in American history.

Albert Einstein and Rabbi Stephen Wise

All in all, Wise's task was not simple. While the AJCong was waging an open and dauntless battle against Nazism, the AJC and B'nai Brith were attempting to play down the dangers. *'The B'nai Brith Messenger'* that appeared after the Nazi rise to power in January, 1933 stated that

> in at least one respect Hitler's rise to power should be welcomed. We must realize, after all, that Hitler IN power is not as dangerous as Hitler OUT of power. In his new role he will be compelled to measure his words and deeds to a great extent.[12]

It was difficult for the AJC and B'nai Brith, representatives of German-American Jewry that leaned towards assimilation, to accept the fact that the emancipation of the Jews in Germany was a failure. Accepting that proposition meant challenging their own belief that in our times Jews were capable of attaining equality and security in the lands of their dispersion. As these organizations were composed mainly of Jews of German descent still attached to German culture, and who maintained family ties in Germany, they found it difficult to absorb the fact that Germany had changed. Perhaps that was the reason that they were unable to perceive the Nazi menace. Irresponsible acts, they believed, might only destabilize the position of German Jewry even further and endanger their wealth. They also feared that if they went too far, their own status and wealth in the U.S. might be put in jeopardy.[13] Even after they realized that Hitler was actually doing all that he had vowed to do, they still reckoned that as long as they avoided a public uproar the situation would not deteriorate. They also believed that pressure by world Jewry would be used by Nazi propagandists as proof of the existence of an international Jewish conspiracy. They therefore concluded that "we[...] consider that such forms of agitation as boycotts, parades, mass meetings and other similar demonstrations as futile, they serve only as an ineffectual channel for the release of emotions."[14]

The issue that finally brought the conflict between the various Jewish organizations to a head was the organization of an economic boycott of Germany. The Nazis proclaimed a one-day national boycott of Jewish stores in Germany on April 1, and threatened that if the attacks upon Germany by world Jewry did not cease, they would undertake even more drastic action. However the initiators of the boycott in the U.S. did not buckle under the Nazi threat, and in May a group of activists, at whose head stood the well-known lawyer Samuel Untermeyer, declared an economic boycott of Germany.[15] Wise was not opposed to the boycott, but he saw it only as an ultimate weapon. However, the situation of the Jews in Germany continued to worsen, and Wise did not see any results from his endeavor to move the Administration to take some sort of action to aid the Jews of Germany. Therefore, at the end of the summer, under pressure by the rank and file, the AJCong joined the boycott movement. From the moment that they joined in the boycott, the 'Congress' people became the leading factor in that struggle until the boycott was abandoned in 1939 with the outbreak of the war.

The ambition of the American Jewish Congress to lead in a struggle against Nazism was great, but their ability to carry it out did not stand in any proportion to their aspirations. They suffered, all those years from a chronic lack of funds, poor organization, and too small a staff to handle the many projects that they attempted to implement. More than once it happened that these shortages led one of their component organizations, or members, to threaten to resign as a result of frustration or despair.[16] The archives of the AJCong are full of documents from which we learn of failed schemes to organize fund-raising campaigns for specific projects. In 1933, for example, it was decided to establish an emergency fund of $2,000,000 to deal with the new threat posed by the Nazi regime. The campaign, however, succeeded in raising no more than $100,000.[17] The same story repeated itself throughout the years of the war. Wise was aware of the poor state of his organization and once complained that "the moment anyone [in the AJCong office] shows any promise of being significant or effective, he is doomed to extinction or exclusion".[18] The boycott, as all its other ventures, suffered from those same shortcomings.

How can one evaluate the significance of the economic boycott of Germany? If its purpose was to overthrow the Nazi regime, it obviously did not achieve its goal. Edwin Black, in his book 'The Transfer Agreement', claimed that the boycott was capable of actually bringing down the Nazi regime, and that only the 'Transfer Agreement' which the Zionist movement signed with Germany, prevented its collapse.[19] The 'Transfer Agreement' permitted German Jews intending to emigrate to Palestine to transfer their wealth to the

(Zionist) Anglo-Palestine Bank, which in turn would buy German products and sell them in Palestine. Upon settling in Palestine the immigrant would be reimbursed by the Bank. Black's contention, which is accompanied by a bitter indictment of the Zionist movement, is highly implausible. His claim, in effect, is compatible with the then-existing belief regarding the enormous power of the Jews. However, as we shall see, the Jews stood before their new predicament almost entirely powerless.

In effect, the economic boycott of Germany would not have led to the collapse of the Nazi regime because Hitler did not base his economic policies on exports. On the contrary, Nazi economic policies were founded on the principle of developing an autarchic economy (which they defined as "orientation upon the internal market") and Hitler preferred to strive for autarchy rather than attempt to increase German exports.[20] Even when the Germans sought to increase their exports, they deliberately sought markets in South East Europe and in Latin America, and an economic boycott by American Jewry could not have effected German penetration of those areas.[21] The economic boycott by American Jews could restrain the Germans, to some degree, but was incapable of changing Nazi policies towards the Jews. It certainly could not have lead to the overthrow of the Nazi regime.

There were some within the American Jewish Congress who also believed that the boycott could bring about a collapse of the Nazi regime, but Stephen Wise was not among them. He did maintain, however, that the boycott was capable of placing a brake on German persecution of the Jews. Indeed, it did succeed temporarily in moderating the Nazi attacks on the Jews. Hitler needed to establish himself in power, and Germany urgently needed to revive its hard hit economy. The Germans were therefore extremely sensitive to world opinion, and they were concerned about the state of their international trade. Even Goebbels admitted that the boycott acted as a curb on their anti-Jewish activities. He explained to the Nazi leadership that "It might be asked why the Administration undertakes nothing more against the Jews. It can't for policy reasons, since further boycotts, further foreign exchange difficulties and other troubles are thereby threatened."[22]

Wise saw the boycott not only as a means of putting economic pressure on Germany, but also as a way to alert the general public to the dangers of Nazism and of the need to combat it. In the climate of isolationism prevailing in the U.S., this was an extremely important objective. For many Jews the boycott was a way of releasing pent up emotions, and provided them with a feeling that at least they were doing something. Their self pride would not allow them to trade with a country that so blatantly was persecuting Jews.

The rift between the Jewish organizations not only was not bridged, but rather was further widened with the ascension of Hitler to power. At a time when grave decisions lay in the balance, each side accused the other that its ill-advised actions could bring tragedy to the Jews. The organizations did attempt to establish a modicum of cooperation once the Nazis took power. In 1933 they set up a consultative body, but the mass meeting held at Madison Square Garden created a serious crisis in the first month of its existence. The final rift between the organizations, which lasted for five years, came when the American Jewish Congress officially joined the boycott in the summer of 1933.

Wise was not prepared to sacrifice his response to the Nazi threat on the altar of unity. Thus the AJCong declared its willingness to cooperate with other Jewish organizations, but that "It can't surrender its convictions and it will not forego action in the interest of so-called unity."[23] Neither did the American Jewish Committee see unity as the need of the hour. Morris Waldman, its influential secretary, recommended the AJC not to be tempted to unite just because of the crisis. He held that the gulf between their differing outlooks was too profound to minimalize, and that the Jewish community was in no need of what he termed *gleichschaultung*.[24]

From the very first days of the Nazi rule the Jews of Germany began to feel the harsh situation that arose and many were searching for a place of refuge anywhere in the world. 37,000 Jews emigrated from Germany in 1933 and until the outbreak of the Second World War, 404,809 Jews succeeded in fleeing Germany, (including Austria, and Czechoslovakia after they too fell under German occupation).[25] Even then, there remained in those countries at the end of 1939 some half million Jews who still sought a way to escape from Nazi rule.[26]

Precisely, on this cardinal point of making visas available for German Jews nearly all the Jewish organizations were of one mind. They were all resolved not to raise the question of increasing immigration quotas as a public issue. Opening the gates of the United States to Jewish refugees would have alleviated their distress more than any demonstrations were capable of doing, and even more than an economic boycott. Had they succeeded in moving this issue forward, even a little, they might have been able to save tens of thousands of more Jews. Even if they had been able just to exploit the full quotas provided for Germany and Austria (of which only 48.2% were utilized from 1933-1940) then 113,000 additional refugees from those two countries could have entered the U.S. before the war began.[27]

Perhaps American Jewry was unable to grasp the fact that the Jews of Germany, a community that had existed for nearly 2000 years, was being uprooted in the cruelest of manners. It appears that Brandeis saw what the future held in store, and quickly realized what need be done. As early as 1933, he firmly told Wise that "I would have the Jews out of Germany. They have been treated with the deepest disrespect. I urge that Germany shall be free of Jews. Let Germany share the fate of Spain."[28]

In addition to the already existing quotas, in each year of the 1930's resolutions were introduced in Congress to further limit immigration, or to actually discontinue it entirely. In 1931 a bill was introduced in Congress aimed at curtailing immigration by 90%. The legislation passed in the House, and according to observers at that time, would have passed in the Senate had it not recessed before the bill came to a vote.[29] In 1939, at the end of that same decade, a number of similar bills were debated in Congress, the most ominous a packet of laws introduced by Sen. Robert Reynolds (D-N.C.). These called for totally suspending immigration for ten years, or, at least, until unemployment in the U.S. dropped to under the ten million mark.[30] Between the bill proposed in 1931, and those proposed by Reynolds in 1939, many other similar bills were submitted which would have either limited, or banned, immigration.[31] Proposals were even moved in Congress to expel all foreigners from the U.S.[32]

The fear raised by restrictionists that America would be flooded with refugees had no basis in reality. During those years more people actually left the U.S. than entered. During the years 1933-37 174,067 people immigrated to the U.S, while at the same time 221,239 left the country – a negative balance of migration of 47,172 during those five years.[33] The restrictionist views expressed in Congress were merely a reflection of the opinions of the electorate, a fact that was substantiated in all the public opinion polls taken during those years. A Fortune magazine survey in July, 1938 showed that 67.4% of those polled were of the opinion that "in present conditions" they were opposed to absorbing any additional refugees in the U.S.[34] While the condition of European Jewry went from bad to worse during those years, the opposition of the American public to absorbing refugees only intensified. In a poll taken in November 1938, during the very days following the 'Kristallnacht' pogrom, 71% stated that they opposed absorbing "a larger number of Jewish exiles from Germany", and 8% had no opinion on the matter.[35]

There were a number of reasons for this attitude: a) Nativism – a wave of xenophobia that had swept the U.S. after World War I. b) The economic crisis, that brought unemployment, poverty and suffering in its wake. c) The growth of antisemitism, as has already been noted. These were the same potent forces that had brought about the immigration laws in the 1920's, and the stringent immigration policies in the 1930's. Thus, in the fiscal year 1934 (i.e. from July, 1933 to June, 1934) only 3,744 refugees from Germany (including non-Jews) were able to find a haven in the U.S.[36] In this atmosphere the representatives of the Jewish organizations were loath to raise the demand for opening the gates of America to the refugees. There was a fear that such a demand would achieve just the opposite result, i.e., cancellation of the existing quotas and the total curtailment of immigration. The Jewish leaders also feared that a public campaign on their part to increase immigration would also increase the antisemitism which was already rampant in the streets.[37] Many people feared that the refugees, if they came, would take away jobs from Americans at a time of high unemployment.

Despite the stand of the organizations, two Jewish Congressmen, Samuel Dickstein (D-N.Y.) and Emanuel Celler (D-N.Y.) ventured to introduce legislation that would have mitigated the immigration restrictions that prevented Jewish refugees from entering the U.S. Yet it was actually delegations of the Jewish organizations themselves that convinced these Congressmen to retract their proposals. In March, 1933 Dickstein proposed a bill that would have permitted the full utilization of existing quotas set aside for Germany. As a result he received a letter from the immigration specialist of the American Jewish Committee, Max Kohler, asserting that America was already suffering from unemployment and that "You create a situation where it will be charged that America's Jews want to sacrifice America's obvious and essential interests on behalf of their German coreligionists." Kohler added that "The Jews of America are unable to take care of their own destitute [...] without bringing needy newcomers over."[38]

Though the Jewish organizations shrank from raising the immigration question publicly, they did, nonetheless, strive to advance the matter through the use of quiet diplomacy. They were aware of the fact that American Consuls in Europe were raising many barriers for the Jews attempting to emigrate to the U.S., and that State Department officials were also creating difficulties for potential immigrants. The Consuls acted according to instructions laid down by President Hoover in September, 1930. Hoover determined at that time, that as a result of the economic crisis in America and the resulting unemployment, U.S. Consuls should interpret strictly the clause in the 1917 immigration act that prevented any person who was 'Likely to become a Public Charge' (LPC) from entering the U.S.[39] Anybody who wanted to emigrate to the U.S. had to prove, beyond any doubt, that he had the necessary means to maintain himself. During the first year of the Roosevelt Administration the State Department continued to apply this policy rigidly.[40]

Congressman Emmanuel Celler

Having no other avenue of recourse, the Jewish leaders turned to Roosevelt and to others in his Administration, requesting, that at least within the framework of the existing laws, they facilitate the issuance of immigration visas. It appears that this pressure did succeed to a small degree. At the end of 1933 the State Department drafted a number of regulations that reduced, in some measure, the impediments facing the refugees.[41] At the end of 1935, Roosevelt himself intervened, for the first time, and instructed the Consuls to take into consideration the special needs of the refugees.[42] He did this in response to an appeal by Herbert Lehman and Felix Warburg, part of the old-time leadership of the German-Jewish community who were connected to the AJC. In December, 1936, at the intervention of the President, the U.S. State Department sent new instructions to its Consuls abroad, ordering them to be more lenient in interpreting the LPC clause. As a result, the number of Jews permitted to enter the U.S. grew constantly. In 1937, 11,536 German refugees were permitted to enter, three times as many as were granted visas in 1934.[43] Yet even those numbers were in no proportion to the growing need.

With the Nazi ascent to power, the Jews of Germany began feeling the realities of racial antisemitism, though there were also periods of respite. When the pogroms against the Jews abated somewhat in 1933, there were some Jews in Germany who contended that the worst was now past and that the situation would stabilize itself in the future.[44] The Nuremberg Laws in 1935, disbarring Jews from German citizenship and attendant rights, put that belief to the lie. The Berlin Olympics brought the Jews a temporary reprieve, but in 1937 the Nazis returned, once again, to their campaign against the Jews. In 1938, the condition of world Jewry took a turn for the worse. The Germans went over to physical attacks against the Jews of Germany, while at the same time the condition of the Jews in the rest of Europe also deteriorated.

America, in general, maintained its silence during those years, and Roosevelt, as well, was mute concerning what was happening to the Jews of Germany. Not a single Jewish organization openly protested the President's silence, not even the American Jewish Congress. The Jews of America did not want to attack a President whom they perceived to be a loyal friend, and who, in those years, was extremely popular among the American public. Franklin D. Roosevelt achieved an overwhelming victory in the presidential elections of 1936. In the climate of antisemitism that was intensifying in the U.S. the Jewish leadership also feared attacking the President, which would have been perceived as placing the interests of world Jewry above those of their own country.

CHAPTER 3
Closing the Gates

(a) America and the Refugee Problem
"A time for Jews to lie low"
(FDR to his Jewish assistant David Niles)

In March 1938 the German Army crossed the Austrian border and annexed that country to the Third Reich. What the Nazis had wreaked upon the Jews of Germany during five preceding years, they now inflicted upon the Jews of Austria in a very few days. The Gestapo spread terror amongst the Jews of Vienna and took upon itself to handle 'emigration' matters. From then, and until the outbreak of the Second World War, 125,000 Jews left Austria, nearly two-thirds of those living there.[1] Now, together with those fleeing Germany, the "refugee problem" reached serious proportions.

The news of what was happening to the Jews of Austria outraged the citizens of the U.S., and the American press gave vent to the public anger.[2] On March 25, 1938, less than two weeks after the 'Anschluss', President Roosevelt held a press conference, and for the first time since entering the White House, he publicly referred to the tribulations of European Jewry. He informed the reporters that from then on he would allow the full quotas of both Germany and Austria to enter the United States. At that same press conference, Secretary of State Cordell Hull called for the convening of an international conference to deal with the problem of 'political refugees.'[3] Both the Evian Conference, which was a result of this initiative, as well as the Bermuda Conference held in 1943, were called to deal with the problem of 'political refugees'. Everything possible was done to prevent giving the impression that, heaven forbid, the U.S. was aiding Jews.

What had moved the President to break his silence regarding the Jews of Germany – to intervene, as was not his custom, in the internal affairs of another country; and to initiate an international conference on the problem of the refugees? Certainly the sufferings of the Jews touched Roosevelt, and he sought a way to alleviate their sufferings. But Roosevelt's decision to speak out was primarily a result of the forceful response of the American public to what was happening to Austrian Jewry. An historian, Deborah Lipstadt, believes that Roosevelt took that step to demonstrate America's disapproval of the Nazi actions, but also to "move American public opinion away from isolationism."[4] However, we may assume that Roosevelt also understood that if the refugee problem continued to increase, the pressures upon him to do something to ease their lot would also grow. The gesture taken by the President won him a number of 'points' among American Jews and liberal world opinion, while at the same time not antagonizing the American public.

Americans were perhaps shocked by the Nazi acts, yet they became even more determined to prevent America from being flooded by refugees. Roosevelt did not intend to open the gates of his country to more refugees than he had promised on March 25th. In his own words, Roosevelt explained that an international conference would not be able to solve the refugee problem, and that most refugees "won't find a haven of refuge, either here or elsewhere."[5] So, if the Jews of Europe now drew the compassion of the American people, nothing in this sympathy could bring about any real aid, beyond the quotas circumscribed by American law.

At the same time that Roosevelt resolved to call an international conference he also decided to set up a committee to advise him on refugee matters – the President's Advisory Committee on Political Refugees (PACPR). The committee, comprising representatives of Jewish organizations, Christian Churches and representatives of the State Department, met for the first time at the White House on May 16th. However, after meeting briefly with the committee and fleetingly exchanging views with them, the President no longer took any real interest in the workings of this committee that he had set up supposedly to advise him. Whenever refugee matters came up, the recommendations of the PACPR did not win the ear of the President to the same degree as did the views of the State Department, which in general were hostile to the plight of the refugees.

After the short, polite meeting with the President, the committee received a briefing from Assistant Secretary of State George Messerschmidt as to the position of the U.S. government in preparation for the forthcoming international conference, which was set to convene at Evian, France. In his briefing Messerschmidt (considered the State Department official most friendly to the Jews) clearly stated that though the U.S. was the initiator of the conference that was intended to solve the refugee problem there should be no illusions that America itself was prepared to contribute to that solution. Among the State Department directives prepared for the U.S. delegation to Evian were: there was to be no changes in the U.S. immigration laws, nor in the immigration policies; the U.S. will not contribute funds to the refugees nor to any plans for their resettlement; and any solution will be a long-range one and therefore there is no need to expedite matters. If that were not enough, Messerschmidt made it clear that the U.S. would not agree to expand the mandate of the conference to include the problem of Polish or Romanian Jewry, who were also under growing pressure to leave their respective countries. The U.S. was also opposed to raising the issue of Palestine as a potential haven, since "Any attempts to interject the Palestine and Zionist problems [...] would probably lead to the early disruption of the Conference"[6] (i.e. the British delegation would walk out).

The Evian Conference convened in July 1938. Though it may have been anticipated that the Conference would not achieve much toward solving the refugee problem, no one could foresee that it would, in effect, achieve opposite results. At Evian the governments of the world indeed grasped the immensity of the refugee problem, and as a result, a number of countries, which previously had no quotas on immigration hastened to enact them.[7] The American delegate to the Evian Conference, Myron Taylor, warned the State Department that if the U.S. itself did not provide an example, then other governments would claim that they too were not obligated to act.[8] However, the American Administration felt that the U.S. had already contributed generously to solving the refugee problem. All the other participating countries in the Conference quickly grasped that the very same country that had initiated the conference was reluctant to absorb more refugees, and therefore they too balked at making a commitment. Thus, the Conference was doomed to failure.

The Nazi attacks on the Jews of Germany on November 9th, outraged all of America. No longer were the Germans merely discriminating against the Jews, or of curtailing their rights. On 'Kristallnacht' the murderous nature of Nazi antisemitism was revealed. This time they were no longer able to dismiss the reports of journalists as lies, rumors, or imaginary atrocity tales as the official German spokesmen had always insisted.[9] Church leaders and politicians, editorial boards and radio stations around the country all joined in condemning Germany, and in expressing their horror at the atrocities.[10] Roosevelt hesitated for a few days before reacting, perhaps to ascertain whether the American public would support his actions. Finally, on November, 18th he called a press conference in which he sharply condemned the German acts, and announced that he was recalling the U.S. Ambassador from Germany.[11]

Destroyed Ohel Ya'aqov Synagogue after Kristallnacht

American hostility towards Germany was intensifying, but so too was its compassion for the victims of Nazism. But this sympathetic atmosphere was in direct contrast to the willingness of Americans to do something to ease the lot of German Jews. After 'Kristallnacht' the Germans arrested 30,000 Jewish males, mostly heads of families, and informed them that they could be released from the concentration camps on condition that they leave the country. Now almost all the Jews were prepared to fulfill the German demands, but the question still remained: Where to? The U.S., for one, was not prepared to offer them refuge. A public opinion poll taken by Fortune magazine in March, 1939 showed that 83% of Americans were opposed to allowing more refugees to enter the U.S.[12] A different poll taken after the 'Kristallnacht' pogrom showed that 67% of Americans were in favor of totally barring immigration.[13] Even the small stream of refugees entering the U.S. was now in danger of being blocked. The Nazis, perceiving the reluctance of other countries to absorb Jews, ridiculed what they saw as a hypocritical world. "It is a shameful example to observe today how the entire democratic world dissolves in tears of pity but then [...] closes its heart to the poor, tortured people", Hitler gloated.[14]

Hitler's cynical words were not far from the truth. Congressman Martin Dies (D.-Texas) called upon his fellow countrymen not to pay attention to the tears of "sobbing sentimentalists and internationalists" and declared that "we must permanently close, bar and lock the gates of our country to new immigrant waves, and then throw the key away."[15] But there were also others in Congress who attempted to restore to the U.S. its proud tradition as a place of refuge for the persecuted. After the 'Anschluss', Dickstein and Celler introduced legislation in Congress whose purpose was to make full use of the unused immigration quotas for the benefit of the refugees from Europe (For the years 1933-43 there remained nearly a million and a quarter of such unused visas[16]). But even then delegations of Jewish organizations appealed to the two Congressmen to desist from the legislation for fear of making the situation even worse. Each organization presented its own reasons for opposing the bill. The spokesman for the AJC stated that bringing Jewish refugees to the U.S. "is helping to intensify the Jewish problem here."[17] And in a letter to Justice Frankfurter, Rabbi Wise labeled Celler's proposed bill as "very bad", for it would propel the entire country to oppose Roosevelt's initiative for an international conference.[18]

After 'Kristallnacht' Senator Robert Wagner (D-N.Y.) and Rep. Edith Rogers (D-Cal.) proposed legislation that would permit bringing 20,000 refugee children to the U.S. in the next two years "until the termination of the emergency."[19] Even the idea of bringing in children on a temporary basis met strong opposition both on Capitol Hill and among the general public. There were some who claimed that the bill was intended to help only Jews,[20] while others voiced their fear that at the end of the period of emergency the children would not want to return to Europe. There were some who suspected that the children would eventually also bring their parents to the United States. Sen. Reynolds expressed his concern that the children were none other than German spies.[21] Even so staid an individual as Sen. Robert Taft raised the bizarre reason that scattering families was worse than the situation then facing the children.[22]

The Jewish organizations feared raising their voices in favor of the Wagner-Rogers initiative and were satisfied to work only behind the scenes. The Administration also did not say a word in favor of the legislation despite the fact that Sen. Wagner was one of Roosevelt's most ardent supporters. The Wagner-Rogers bill to bring Jewish children to the U.S. did not pass in Congress, but a year later, when the war broke out in Europe, 10,000 British children were brought to the U.S. "on a temporary basis and for the period of the emergency". For British children facing the horrors of the 'Blitz' a spot was found in the U.S. – for Jewish children facing the Nazi terror there was no place of refuge.

The President himself took a number of steps that were the only expression of American aid to the refugees. Roosevelt instructed the State Department to permit 15,000 refugees who were in the U.S. on temporary visas to remain there.[23] At least these fifteen thousand were saved from the fate of the others, such as the passengers on the St. Louis, who despite having fled Germany, were unable to find a place of refuge and were forced to return to Europe. (In May 1939 more than 900 German refugees sailed for Cuba on the German liner 'St. Louis'. After the ship was forced to leave Havana harbor, efforts were made to convince the American authorities to allow them to enter the U.S. The efforts did not succeed, and they were forced to return to Europe).[24]

The St. Louis in Havana Harbor

The measures that were taken by Roosevelt to ease the lot of the refugees were only a meager contribution of the U.S. in comparison to the immensity of the problem. The discrimination and the persecution of the Jews during the preceding five years; the attacks on the property and persons of the Jews in the 'Kristallnacht' pogrom; the tens of thousands of Jews incarcerated in concentration camps and tortured there; all these pointed to one conclusion – that the Jews of Germany had to leave that country as long as it was still possible.

In November 1938, 160,000 people in Germany were awaiting entry visas to the U.S.[25] Even this was not the full picture, because a considerable number of refugees were still stranded in 'transit countries' throughout Europe on a temporary basis, awaiting visas that would allow them to find a permanent refuge in the U.S.[26] However, even those limited steps taken by Roosevelt were carried out against the counsel of most of his advisors, even the Jewish ones, and certainly against the wishes of the restrictionists in Congress. In Autumn, 1938 Samuel Rosenman, a member of the AJC and a close advisor of Roosevelt, presented the President with a memorandum in which he stated that all attempts to change the immigration laws of the U.S. would only arouse the ire of Congress and put off the possibility of any other solution. In addition, Rosenman also raised the specter of antisemitism as a justified reason to avoid absorbing Jewish refugees.[27]

If Roosevelt and the Jewish organizations reached the conclusion that it was preferable that the U.S. not raise its immigration quotas, they were both of the opinion that the solution should be sought, mainly, in the resettlement of the refugees in underdeveloped countries. Such a step, they believed, could alleviate the lot of the refugees, while at the same time avoiding a conflict between the Jews and the general American public or between the President and Congress. This proposal had the additional advantage, that in those countries, generally, there was no need to take into account the feelings of the public.

During these years Roosevelt toyed with many ideas of possible places of settlement for the Jews. He spoke of British Guiana and of the establishment of a 'United States of Africa' similar to the United States of America that had been settled by immigrants from Europe.[28] At one stage Roosevelt even approached Mussolini to permit the settlement of Jews in Ethiopia.[29] An American agency was set up to find areas of settlement for the refugees. It checked out 666 different places.[30] The American government was prepared to consider any locale, just not the U.S. There were also proposals to settle Jews in various U.S. territories, such as Alaska, or the Virgin Islands, and these received the support of the Cabinet member responsible for the Territories, the liberal Secretary of Interior Harold Ickes.[31] However, the State Department was totally opposed to these ideas and saw them only as attempts to circumvent U.S. immigration laws. Roosevelt also decided that the proposals were too problematic and removed them from the agenda. All the various ideas for the resettlement of the refugees never materialized. The only serious attempt to carry out one of the schemes, the plan to settle Jews in Sosua (the Dominican Republic) encompassed only a small number of Jewish refugees, was very expensive, and in the end it too failed.[32]

Nor did all the Jews favor these resettlement schemes. The Jewish Labor Committee (JLC – a federation of trade-unions in which there were a large concentration of Jews.) still believed in the right of all Jews to live as equals in their present places of residence, or, on the contrary, their right to emigrate to any country that they desired, including the United States.[33] The Zionists found it difficult to accept the fact that Jews would settle anywhere else than in Palestine. Only when the British 'White Paper' (which decreed that only 75,000 Jews could enter Palestine over the next five years, and afterwards the gates would be closed entirely to Jewish immigration) was published in 1939, and the situation in Europe deteriorated while the number of refugees kept increasing, did many Zionists comprehend, that without forfeiting the right of Jews to settle in Palestine, there was a need to find other immediate, temporary solutions, as well.[34] Rabbi Wise's reactions to the various resettlement proposals that were raised are typical of the ambivalence of many other Zionist leaders regarding any alternative to Eretz Yisrael. Alaska and British Guiana did not seem appropriate to him.[35] The Dominican Republic, he complained, was a Fascist country.[36] How could one think of settling Jews in Tanganyika, he queried, when that country might yet be returned to Germany?[37]

Ever since Evian, the 'Intergovernmental Committee on Refugees' (IGCR) that was established there had been given the task of finding a solution to the refugee problem. The veiled intent had been to take pressure off the U.S. to ease immigration, and the demand off Britain to open the gates of Palestine. Therefore, the IGCR tried to convince other countries, mainly in Latin America, to admit more refugees. The Intergovernmental Committee achieved some minor results. After 'Kristallnacht' the Latin American countries increased the number of refugees they absorbed. However it was a fleeting achievement, and after a short time the number of refugees admitted to Latin America declined once more.[38]

In Autumn of 1938 the Secretary General of the Intergovernmental Committee, the American George Rublee, attempted to open talks with the German authorities in order to work out an orderly exodus of Jews from their country.[39] The first contact was made in October, though nothing came of it until a month after 'Kristallnacht' when Hjalmar Schacht, the 'financial wizard' of Germany, approached Rublee with a comprehensive program for the emigration of Germany's Jews. Germany was motivated, on the one hand, by a desire to change the harsh impression that 'Kristallnacht' had made on the world. On the other hand, they wanted to rid themselves of the Jews; confiscate their wealth; and obtain foreign currency. The Jewish organizations that met to discuss the Schacht plan viewed it as nothing more than "blackmail and international kidnapping", and completely rejected it.[40] In the meantime Schacht was dismissed from his position, and Helmut Wohlthat, a senior official in the Economics Ministry, was appointed to replace him in the negotiations. Wohlthat's proposals were less abrasive than those of his predecessors, and Rublee and Wohlthat got down to talk serious business.

Despite the fact that the negotiations pertained to the Jews of Germany, and that it was also clear that world Jewry would have to finance its implementation, no Jewish representation was invited to take part in the discussions. Even after an agreement was reached between Rublee and the Germans, many segments of organized Jewry continued to oppose it. The more assimilated elements of American Jewry feared that the establishment of an international Jewish body to carry out the agreement would only be used to prove the existence of an 'International Jewry'.[41] Many Zionists, such as Rabbi Abba Hillel Silver who headed the United Palestine Appeal (UPA), were concerned that money for the resettlement of Jews in far-flung corners of the world would be at the expense of donations needed to build up Eretz Yisrael.[42] Others opposed the plan because they saw it as approval for the confiscation of Jewish wealth, and that it would only lead the Nazis to further attempts at blackmail.[43] But above all else, there was a real concern that the plan might actually aid Germany economically and perhaps politically.[44]

This opposition of many American Jews threatened to bring the Rublee-Wohlthat plan to nought. Roosevelt, who was unable to grasp the reasons for the opposition of American Jews, put all his political weight behind the scheme. In May, 1939 he gathered a number of Jewish leaders in his White House office and after applying heavy pressure brought them to support the plan.[45] In order to carry out the agreed upon plan a 'Coordinating Foundation' was established in July, 1939 under the Chairmanship of Samuel Rosenman, whose purpose was to raise one hundred million dollars in the coming five years.[46] Even this vast amount of money would have been unable to more than dent the refugee problem. According to the estimates of experts, the resettlement of a single family would cost $10,000, and therefore the Coordinating Foundation could not possibly have settled more than ten thousand families, even if it did succeed in raising that enormous sum.

Whatever may have been the value of Roosevelt's initiatives to resettle the Jews of Germany it is important to note the changed situation in those critical two years before the war. In the first five years of the Nazi regime it was the Jewish organizations, or at least some of them, which had raised an outcry against the Nazi acts. They were the ones who had organized rallies and marches and launched the economic boycott of Germany. During those years the President had remained silent; the press had treated the atrocity stories with great skepticism; and the American Congress did not concern itself with the fate of German Jewry, but precisely in those years when the Nazi attacks on the Jews intensified and the warnings became clearer, the voice of American Jewry fell silent. Now it was Roosevelt who called for an international conference, recalled his Ambassador from Germany and took a number of measures to enable more refugees to enter the U.S. Not the Jewish organizations, but a few Congressmen such as Celler, Dickstein, Wagner and Rogers were now those who initiated legislation whose purpose was the rescue of Jews. The American press and leading Churchmen reacted angrily to the barbarism of 'Kristallnacht'. But Rabbi Stephen Wise, who was like a roaring lion in 1933, maintained silence after the 'Kristallnacht' pogrom. More than that, he made certain that the Jewish community would not react. Neither the Zionist press nor the Orthodox press reacted to the pogrom with more than a whimper.

The only demonstration organized to protest the attacks on the Jews was a rally held at Manhattan Garden on November 21, under the auspices of the 'Jewish People's Committee', a Communist front organization. Perhaps the reason for their demonstrating was the sharp condemnation of 'Kristallnacht' which had appeared in Pravda. Despite the fact that the rally was organized by a clearly left-wing group, it succeeded in drawing 20,000 people (a sign of the influence of the 'left' on the Jewish public at that time), and even received the official endorsement of a number of Senators and Governors.[47] The lack of response of U.S. Jewry brought the (non-Jewish) Secretary of Interior Ickes to pour out his feelings to Justice Brandeis about the cowardice on the part of the rich Jews of America [...] I would like to get two or three hundred of them together in a room and tell them that they couldn't hope to save their money by meekly accepting whatever humiliations others chose to impose upon them.[48]

Why did the Jewish community not respond at a time when the condition of Germany's Jews was constantly growing harsher? For some of the Jewish organizations, their silence was both traditional and ideological, as we have noted. The American Jewish Congress explained its lack of response as due to the fact that it believed it preferable that the American public should be the one to react. In a declaration that was read on November 18th at a meeting of the General Jewish Council (GJC – set up in 1938 as yet another attempt to coordinate stands between the four major Jewish defense organizations: B'nai Brith; AJC; AJCong and JLC). the AJCong explained the reasons for its silence. "Non-Jewish opinion has been sufficiently outraged to demand action against the Nazis and succor for the victims thereof. For the first time [...] the President of the U.S. has spoken out directly in condemnation of Nazism.[49] If we compare the words of this declaration written in 1938 with those of Wise five years earlier, when Hitler first reached power in Germany, we can easily see the major reversal that occurred in the stands of Wise and his colleagues.

1933	1938
How can we ask our Christian friends to raise their voices in protest against the wrongs suffered by Jews if we remain silent.[50]	Christian Churches and leaders should take this initiative in publicly demanding justice for the Jews.
You have to choose between virtual silence-and silence is acquiescence – or support this tremendous protest.[51]	Utmost restraint should be exercised by the Jews, public protest meetings by Jews would not help the situation.
No matter what the Hitlerites now do, it will not be more than the overt commission of acts that would have been covertly performed protest or no protest.[52]	The Jews should not by any act of theirs give Hitler the slightest peg on which to have a new pogrom.[53]

What brought about this reversal in Wise's tactics, and that of his organization, precisely on the eve of the most crucial trial in the history of the Jewish people? Rafael Medoff, in his book *'The Deafening Silence'* claims that the reason is simple and clear-cut: "In short, Wise had been "co-opted".[54] Medoff's brash verdict is too simplistic and one-sided, and does not take into consideration the complicated situation which then existed. Nor does it take Wise's own words into account.

It is true that after a number of years in which Wise was shunned by Roosevelt because of his attacks during the time that he was Governor of New York,[55] the relations between them were reestablished in 1936. In time these ties strengthened and eventually Wise became a keen supporter of Roosevelt, referring to him in his letters to the President as 'Skipper' or 'Boss'. On Wise's part the change in his attitude towards Roosevelt came about for two main reasons: a) Already during Roosevelt's first days in office (the famed 'Hundred Days' of the New Deal) Wise learned to value Roosevelt's bold leadership, and during the 1930's Wise certainly identified completely with the policies of Roosevelt's New Deal. b) Wise understood, that as a Jewish leader who had to maintain relations with the Administration, nothing of value, neither for himself nor for his mission, could come out of remaining on bad terms with the President. Adverse relations with the President would prevent him (as did occur) from placing before the President the appeals of American Jewry. He hoped that good relations with the President, and his loyalty to the Administration, would stand him in good stead when he approached the highest office in the land with requests to deal with Jewish problems.

It is also true that Wise's devotion to Roosevelt prevented him from placing additional obstacles in the path of the President, specifically at a time when Roosevelt was endeavoring, contrary to the prevailing isolationist mood, to bring America into the struggle against Nazi aggression. Wise totally supported Roosevelt's internationalist foreign policy. He saw it as part of the battle against Nazism, and therefore as a component in the struggle to guarantee the future of European Jewry. It is also true that the AJCong attempted to modify its stands to comply with its new partners in the General Jewish Council, and also because it felt that during a period of crisis for the Jewish people, it did not want to rupture Jewish unity, as had occurred in 1933.

I believe that the main reason for the change in Wise's tactics was his assessment that the world situation had changed, and especially that of the Jews. In light of the new conditions, Wise believed that there was also a need to change Jewish tactics. Germany had grown powerful and aggressive, while the U.S. had dug deeper into its isolationist stance. On the other hand, in the U.S., as in the rest of the world, antisemitism was surging and American Jewry was now anxious about its own security. Wise felt that the Americans were not even concerned with the problems of their own Jewish population, let alone with the difficulties of the Jews of Europe. He understood that it is impossible to carry on an open and courageous battle without a sympathetic audience to whom they could turn. He feared that any Jewish attempt to publicly raise the question of the sufferings of European Jews would only increase antisemitism at home, while at the same time not help the Jews of Europe, at all.

Medoff himself writes that in Wise's private letters he explained his stand as due to a fear of "the real rising tide of anti-Semitism."[56] It does not appear that Medoff himself believes that the then-existing antisemitism was reason enough to prevent Wise, or the Jewish organizations, from acting. We cannot deny the fact the organizations did take the rising tide of antisemitism in America into account. At that same meeting of the GJC in which the organizations defined their stand regarding a Jewish response to the pogroms in Germany, the other points that appeared on the agenda were: the tensions between the Italian and Jewish communities in the U.S.; Father Coughlin's antisemitic campaign; a report by James Waterman Wise on different approaches to how best to confront antisemitism; as well as other matters that related to the same subject.[57] Therefore, it is not startling that at that same meeting the American Jewish Congress declared that "Utmost restraint should be exercised by Jews" in response to what was happening in Germany, and that "public protest meetings by Jews would not help the situation."[58]

For a number of years antisemitism had been a weighty factor restraining the actions of the Jews in the U.S. However by 1938, antisemitism became a real brake, because American Jews were concerned, first and foremost, for their own safety and status. No longer was it only a matter of prejudices, or discriminating against the Jews. At the end of that decade, and on the backdrop of what was happening to the Jews of Europe, antisemitism in the U.S. began to take on a form that appeared to threaten the very future of the Jews in America. In those years a number of groups sprung up that both verbally and physically abused the Jews. These were groups, such as the organization of the pro-Nazi Protestant Minister Gerald Winrod; the 'Black Legions' in Michigan; and the Fascist 'Silver Shirts' which blamed the "international Jewish conspiracy" as responsible "for all ills of society, the depression, Communism, and the spread of immorality."[59] These bodies, and similar ones, numbered their members in the tens of thousands.[60] Millions tuned in weekly to the antisemitic sermons of Father Coughlin. On February 21st, 1939, barely three months after 'Kristallnacht', 22,000 members of the pro-Nazi 'German-American Bund' rallied in a mass demonstration at Madison Square Garden, in the heart of New York City.[61]

German American Bund NY • Oct 30, 1939

It is therefore not surprising that the Jews of America no longer were concerned only for the safety of their brethren in Europe. Now they were anxious about their own security. Non-Jewish friends were also confounded by the spectacle of antisemitism, and they recommended Jewish leaders to be cautious. President Roosevelt advised his Jewish assistant, David Niles, about "the necessity for the time of Jews lying low[...] [because] of the appalling growth of antisemitism in America."[62] Aside from their anxiety over rising antisemitism, the Jews of America were also concerned, together with all Americans, with the dire economic situation. At the end of 1937 the economic crisis once again took a turn for the worse, unemployment grew, suffering increased, and people worried above all about their own economic survival.[63]

The year 1938 marked a change in the response of the American Jewish community to what was happening to the Jews of Europe. At a time when the condition of European Jews was deteriorating, the public struggle of American Jews was also weakening. The Jews were completely involved with anxieties over their own future, and they also feared to respond. Even more so, they believed that their struggle, their public outcry, would only harm and not help the Jews of Europe. Therefore they placed all their hopes on President Roosevelt, and believed that "their good friend in the White House" would take care of Jewish matters.

Indeed, in 1938 Roosevelt did not disappoint them in his initiatives, his words and his deeds. About two months after 'Kristallnacht' Roosevelt appointed Felix Frankfurter, a Jew, to the Supreme Court, contrary to the public attitude opposing this step. Many saw this as a declaration of the President's support for Jews during their desperate times.[64] Roosevelt also circumvented Congress and took a number of steps that led to the full utilization of the immigration quotas from Germany for the first time. The reluctance of American Jews to carry out an open public struggle, and their reliance on the President to defend Jewish interests, became a pattern of conduct typical for them during the years of the Holocaust, even if they occasionally digressed from this general policy.

(b) "No time [...] to be soft-hearted"
     (Breckinridge Long in referring to the refugee problem)

In the two years preceding America's entry into the war, the Jewish defense organizations maintained their policy of avoiding public protest and public demands to open the gates of the U.S. to the refugees. This course continued despite the fact that after Germany's conquest of Europe it was clear that the Jews of Europe were in dire need of aid from their brethren in America. It was no longer only German, Austrian and Czech Jews – now nearly all of Europe's Jews were in danger.

The publication of the British 'White Paper' in March, 1939 aroused the ire of American Jewry and opened a new channel of struggle to aid the Jews of Europe. It was simpler for the Jews of America to claim that Palestine, the ancient homeland of the Jews, was close to the centers of Eastern European Jewry, and therefore, in time of war, when transportation was dangerous, it was a logical choice to serve as a haven for those fleeing for their lives. Such a demand also avoided a confrontation with the 'restrictionists' in the U.S. Thus, the slogan 'Open the Gates of Palestine' became a rallying cry for many Jews in the United States.

Even in this controversy the American Jewish leadership hesitated to apply its full pressure. The reason for their hesitation was that after the conquest of Western Europe by Germany, Britain remained alone as the last barrier before the German threat to dominate the entire world. In this situation the Jewish leaders questioned whether it was appropriate to aggressively attack the British. That same dilemma also faced the leadership of the 'Yishuv' (the Jewish community in Palestine) and there, too, they decided in favor of supporting Britain in its war against Nazism. David Ben-Gurion declared that "We must support the [British] Army as though there did not exist the White Paper, and we must stand up against the White Paper as though there wasn't a war going on."[65] Aside from the small group in the Lechi underground (the so-called 'Stern Gang'), the entire Yishuv joined in aiding Britain. Could they have acted otherwise?

The vacillation of the Jewish community in America as to how to fight against the British White Paper, began even before the British came under the German 'Blitz'. Already in July 1939, before the war had commenced, when the 'Poalei-Zion' (Labor-Zionist) group demanded to organize a mass demonstration against Britain, the American Jewish and Zionist establishment rejected their demand. In a letter to Justice Brandeis, Wise explained his position as due to feel[ing] so deeply that any demonstration now against the British would merely furnish material to the isolationists; in other words give comfort to the enemies of FDR. This is the last thing in the world that I want to do – the last thing in the world that we have a right to do![66]

The considerations which determined the stand of the Jews were a desire not to burden the President, whom the Jews saw as a barrier against the forces of the right, and the view that the effort to have America adopt an internationalist foreign policy was a part of their struggle against Nazism. However, that same concern as to "what will the gentiles say", paradoxically, also tended to have the Jewish organizations avoid openly supporting Britain. They feared it would be said that America was scampering to help Britain only because of the Jews. At the beginning of hostilities in September, 1939 Wise wrote to Maurice Perlzweig, one of the leaders of the World Jewish Congress (WJC – established in 1936, with the expectations that it would be the representative of World Jewry) in England, explaining that

Those of us who feel as deeply pro-British as I do, must be trebly careful, because if too much be said in favor of the Democracies, the President will find it still more difficult to get from Congress the legislation which he desires [...] Jews must be trebly careful lest they seem to be guilty of war-mongering, with which we are being charged.[67]

Above all, Jews felt they had to take into account how their neighbors in America would react!

When England entered the war at the beginning of September 1939, it barred entry to Palestine for all Jewish refugees from countries occupied by the Nazis not holding valid immigration certificates. It also was made clear that Britain would not hesitate to use force to prevent Jews from entering Palestine. Despite the tragedies that befell the 'illegal' immigrants on the 'Tiger Hill' (two of whose passengers were the first victims of British soldiers in World War II when the ship arrived in Palestine on September 2nd, 1939)[68] and the 'Patria' (a British transport ship about to deport illegal immigrants, which was sunk by a bomb in November 1940, and many Jews on board were drowned), the Jewish community in the U.S. did not protest against these British acts, so as not to hinder the President's efforts to convince Congress to proffer aid to Britain in its war against Germany.[69] When the illegal immigrant ship, the 'San Salvador', sunk in December, 1940, a British Foreign Office official said: "There could have been no more opportune disaster from the point of view of stopping this traffic."[70] The sinking of the ship was also the last straw for the American Zionists. David Ben-Gurion, who was in the U.S. at the time, appeared before the Zionist organizations and demanded that they join the battle against the White Paper, and the struggle for the establishment of a state as a solution for the Jews of Europe after the war.

The 'San Salvador' incident was a turning point for American Jews, whose leadership then began an open fight against the White Paper.[71] However, when the 'illegal immigrant' ship 'Struma' was torpedoed in February, 1942 with nearly 800 Jewish refugees on board fleeing from Nazi persecution, the Zionist movement did not succeed in drawing more than 2500 Jews to a protest rally, causing bitter disappointment.[72] Finally, a Zionist convention held at the Biltmore Hotel in May, 1942 decided, for the first time, to support the demand for the establishment of a Jewish State at war's end.

The Jewish organizations in the U.S., and especially the Zionist movement, did their utmost to persuade Britain to open the gates of Palestine to the stream of Jewish refugees trying to flee Europe. Attempts were also made to prevail upon the U.S. to grant entry visas, even if only to a small number of refugees. Roosevelt's steps in 1938 did ease the restrictions on immigration for a short period, but in 1940 the situation deteriorated once again. In 1939 the German quota was filled to 119.7%, in 1940 to 95.%, and then in 1941 to only 47.7%.[73]

One of the factors for the stiffening of the American stance regarding the refugees stemmed from the hysterical fear that the country would be flooded with spies, saboteurs and 'fifth columnists'. That same hysteria, whipped up beyond reality, was also the main reason, two years later, for the incarceration of the Japanese population living on the West Coast. It may appear ironical today, but it was the Jewish organizations that were among the leading causes of that hysteria, by their constant harping on the dangers from Fascist organizations in the U.S. This fear of spies led to transferring the Immigration Bureau from the Labor to the Justice Department, and many new obstacles were placed in the path of the refugees.[74]

The decision to grant visas was in the hands of the State Department. From 1940, and until the beginning of 1944, the divisions responsible for refugee matters and for granting immigration visas were all under the supervision of Assistant Secretary of State Breckinridge Long, a man who showed little favor to aliens in general and to Jews in particular. Long was one of the circle of appeasers in the State Department. While serving as Ambassador to Italy he had lauded Mussolini and Fascism,[75] and in 1936 he proposed granting Germany equality in rearmament and permitting it to regain control of its former African colonies.[76] After the German conquest of Norway and Denmark, Long opposed an American condemnation of the German aggression claiming that the Danes had not opposed the German invasion, and that it was the English who were the first to violate the neutrality of Norway.[77]

Assistant Secretary of State Breckinridge Long

Nor was Long affected by the sufferings of the victims of Nazism, and he viewed the administration officials – "who for sentiment or for sympathy" opposed the restrictions that Long had placed on immigration – as 'soft-hearted.'[78] As to the unfortunates on the refugee boats who plied the sea lanes from country to country while none opened their gates to them, he perceived them as "victims of greed of their fellows – not of the German or the U.S. policy."[79]

Long was a descendant of an old, and esteemed, American family, and never hid his nativist feelings. He was irate at Wise for his attempts to bring refugees to the U.S. The refugee advocates, he wrote in his diary "each and all believe that every person, everywhere, has the right to come to the U.S. I believe nobody, anywhere, has a right to enter the U.S. unless the U.S. desires."[80] The fact that Long was closely associated with Roosevelt permitted him to present his case to the President more readily than could the rescue advocates. In the two years before America entered the war, he was able to win the backing of the President for most of his policies.[81] He held in his hands many powers and much influence which he did not hesitate to use to prevent immigration to the U.S. He explained to his colleagues at the State Department that "we can delay and effectively stop for a temporary period of indefinite length the number of immigrants into the United States. We could do this by simply advising our Consuls to put every obstacle in the way."[82]

When in 1940 the proposal was again raised to allow a number of refugees to find a haven in the Virgin Islands, the idea gained the support of both Secretary Ickes and of the Governor of the Islands.[83] Long was quick in convincing the President to oppose the plan, and he also turned to the Navy's Chief of Intelligence, Admiral Kirk, to declare the Islands a closed security zone in order to prevent the entry of refugees.[84] To even further hamper the entry of immigrants, the State Department prepared an application form nearly five feet long, printed on both sides, which the potential immigrant had to fill in. Long was also conspicuous in his extreme concern to prevent spies among the applicants from infiltrating the U.S. He accused "the communists, extreme radicals, professional Jewish agitators, refugee enthusiasts" that they all hated him and that they wanted "to get control of these places in Government – to control foreign policy and to admit Fifth Columnists."[85]

Actually, he was not too concerned about the opposition of the Communists, the radicals or the Jews, all of whom he felt he could handle. His main fight was with the 'refugee enthusiasts' who were members of the President's Advisory Committee. At one point he boasted that he had succeeded in closing the list of rabbis and labor leaders "and it remains for the President's Committee to be curbed in its acts so that the laws can again operate in their normal course."[86] It was true that the PACPR was waging a delaying battle against the harsh decrees of Long. Two Jewish representatives sat on that committee, Rabbi Stephen Wise and Paul Baerwald, President of the Joint Distribution Committee (JDC – the prime Jewish relief organization), yet it was primarily the chairman, James McDonald, who led the fight against Long. McDonald had served as the League of Nations' High Commissioner for Refugees, but in 1936 he resigned his post in protest over the lack of action in attempting to solve the problem of the refugees from Germany. It was the task of the committee to prepare for the State Department a list of individuals to whom they proposed granting immigration visas. The recommendations of the committee did not obligate any party, and therefore the State Department acted upon the proposals as it wished. In August, 1940, the PACPR presented the State Department with 567 names that the committee believed urgently needed to be removed from Europe before they fell into the hands of the Nazis. Three months after the request was presented, and under constant pressure by the committee, only 200 of the requests had been granted, and only a few of them had actually received visas.[87]

Both the PACPR and the Jewish organizations did not dare to stand up and openly fight against the hysterical charge that the security of the U.S. demanded emergency measures and that there was need for a rigorous examination of the refugees, despite the fact that even the Department of Justice supported the stand of the PACPR[88] And when, two years later, that same supposed security demanded the internment of Japanese-Americans, then too there were few courageous souls, including the liberal press, who protested the injustice.

The Jewish organizations did not wage a public battle for the Jews of Europe during those two years. American Jews were not called upon to raise their voices in aid of their persecuted brothers in Europe. They contented themselves that they were supporting the internationalist policies of Roosevelt.

The President's goal at that time was to send aid to the British who were battling Germany, while a stubborn group of isolationists hounded that policy at every step. Rabbi Wise saw support for Roosevelt, and his policies, as the primary need. In a letter to Professor Otto Nathan he declared that "Cruel as it might seem... [Roosevelt's] re-election is much more important for everything that is worthwhile and counts than the admission of a few people, however imminent their peril."[89]

(c) Attempts to Provide Relief

The war in Europe placed the leaders of the Boycott Committee in a difficult predicament. It was clear to them that with Britain's imposition of a naval blockade on Germany at the start of hostilities, there was no longer a need to maintain the apparatus of the boycott. Thus in September 1939, a joint committee consisting of representatives of the American Jewish Congress and the Jewish Labor Committee closed the boycott offices.[90]

During the First World War Britain had established a naval blockade of Germany that succeeded in seriously hindering its war capability. With that experience, Britain repeated the same tactic in the Second World War. By that act, however, it also prevented the possibility of sending relief to Europe.

James Nicholson of the American Red Cross (ARC) reported to Nachum Goldmann of the WJC:

> It is the intention of the Allies to strangle Germany economically as soon as possible. This involved making it clear to the Germans that the conquest of Poland would bring them no profit but rather a burden, namely the feeding of Poland [...] anything that would lighten the burden of the Germans [...] would not be permitted. [91]

The British and the American governments held firmly to this position throughout nearly all the years of the war, though it quickly became clear that Germany did not intend to take upon itself the "burden" of "feeding Poland", and certainly not of its Jews. The opposite was the case. The Germans carried out a deliberate policy of starving the Jewish population of Poland. Already, in the first few months of the war Nicholson reported that "it was known that they [the Jews] had been excluded from the distribution of available food supplies."[92]

With the establishment of the blockade all possibilities of sending material and financial aid to the Jews of Europe were now halted. The Jewish organizations were on the horns of a dilemma. To circumvent the blockade (if that was at all possible) meant sabotaging the war efforts of Britain and clashing with both the British and the American governments – but to hold back on relief, meant abandoning the Jews of Europe to their bitter fate. For a period of time the Jewish organizations were accessories to the decision of the blockade authorities which forbade sending relief to the Jews of Europe, despite their deteriorating situation. The most far-reaching attitude was that of the boycott committee (and most specifically of Joseph Tennenbaum), who a year and a half after the invasion of Poland still demanded that no food parcels be sent to the Jews of Poland, claiming that such action was harmful to Britain, and also that it enhanced the German treasury with American money. Tennenbaum declared that the boycott committee "will undertake the necessary measures to stop such undesirable practices."[93] Despite the strict decision of Britain to prevent sending relief supplies to the Jews of Europe, it was mainly the Jews of America who were most generous in mustering aid for Britain itself. It was reported that 25% [!] of relief contributions to Britain were donated by American Jews.[94]

At first, the American Jewish organizations responded to the outbreak of the war with attempts to provide relief to the Jews of conquered Europe and to Jewish refugees who had succeeded in escaping the Nazi net and were living in dire need of help. This was carried out by several Jewish organizations, but the two major groups that dealt with rescue and relief were the World & American Jewish Congress and the Joint Distribution Committee. The 'Congress movement' did the main political work of approaching the government to obtain support for relief activities and effected the major breakthroughs in obtaining U.S. government support. It also attempted to induce international relief organizations to assist European Jewry and set up, as well, a relief organization in Geneva, RELICO, which had at its disposal only meager sums of money. However, by pioneering efforts, it succeeded in sending parcels of food to Poland, and to aid the Jews of France.

Joint, with its well-organized relief apparatus, its devoted and capable representatives overseas and its comparatively large financial resources, carried out the main relief activities in Europe and in centers of Jewish refugees who had fled from Nazi occupied Europe. Joint's aid consisted, mainly, in transferring funds to their various branch offices around the world to provide relief for Jews in need. The activities of the various branches, most specifically the one in Warsaw, contributed greatly to alleviating the difficult plight of the Jews in the first years of the war.[95]Joint avoided doing anything to endanger the position of American Jewry or of its own legal status. They also identified with the 'shtadlan' (the 'Court Jews' in Medieval Europe) approach of the American Jewish Committee. However, the realities in the field were often very different from what they envisaged.[96] Though the central core of officers at Joint were Jews belonging to the German-Jewish elite, the professionals had gained a great deal of influence during the past years. Joint's representatives in the various countries of Europe had also acquired a large degree of independence in executing policies during the war years and worked according to their own judgment. More than once they acted contrary to the stated policies of the main office in New York.

The leaders of Joint defined their organization as a philanthropic body that deals only with the disbursement of relief to needy Jews overseas. Therefore, they believed, their organization should not have any political dealings, fearing that it may prove injurious to their work. Yet how can one draw a thin line between the struggle to obtain permission to disburse relief, in effect a political struggle, and the actual relief activity? The people at Joint were aware of this discrepancy, and knowingly often crossed that line. That stance was also a convenient alibi for them not to cooperate with the World Jewish Congress. They claimed that the WJC was a political organization and therefore they could not deal with it.

Animosity existed between Joint and the WJC, and each side openly aired its disparaging views of the other. Each saw the other as the embodiment of everything wrong in the Jewish world. Joint persistently opposed cooperating with the WJC. "I object to the name [WJC], even to their breathing, to everything", declared a member of Joint's Executive.[97] On the other hand, the members of the WJC who were deeply rooted in their Judaism, saw the people at Joint as symbols of the 'Yahudim', a designation for wealthy, assimilated German Jews. "I don't want the Joint Distribution Committee" complained Joseph Tennenbaum at the World Jewish Congress, "They don't speak our language, I mean the language of our hearts."[98]

The ideological controversies were only an external expression of the conflicts that arose over the attempt of the WJC to break the monopoly of Joint in the field of providing aid. The Joint did everything possible to maintain its exclusive control of relief. The money was in their hands, and they rejected all proposals to cooperate with the WJC, and attempted to prevent them from stepping into the field of providing relief to European Jews. In the years 1939-45 the Joint raised more than $73,000,000 to finance its operations. The budget of the WJC for rescue operations in the years 1942-43, amounted to only $120,000.[99] This rivalry between two major Jewish organizations hampered attempts at providing aid, and assisted the government's efforts to avoid allowing aid to the Jews of Europe.

The leadership of the World Jewish Congress wanted to create a relief organization based upon a national outlook that would not have to take account of the feelings of the Jewish community in the U.S., but would primarily consider the needs of world Jewry. Power struggles also influenced the WJC to enter the field of relief. Rabbi Wise saw this struggle not only as a contest over who would provide relief, but as an opportunity to break the 'Uptown Jews' control over Jewish life in America. Many in the WJC saw relief activities as a necessary precondition for their organization to achieve status as representatives of world Jewry. Tartakower believed that "to give up relief work today, when relief and rehabilitation are becoming central to Jewish life, is suicidal."[100] This view was not held by all members of the WJC. The famed Jewish demographer, Jacob Lestchinsky, opposed that concept claiming, that in that field "other great organizations" (i.e. Joint) are active.[101] Leon Kubowitzki asserted that the WJC should focus on political action in which it had gained experience and not on relief since it did not have the necessary funds.[102] Opposed to them, Goldmann saw relief work as a goal not to be relinquished.[103] Aryeh Tartakower, who headed the WJC's Relief Department, supported Goldmann: "even small amounts could be effective if they are given at the right time."[104] The views of Dr. Goldmann (one of the founders of the WJC, and head of its Administrative Committee) generally prevailed. The World Jewish Congress genuinely wanted to provide relief but it was impossible to do so only with declarations and good will. The United Jewish Appeal (UJA) agreement of 1939 that aimed at unifying Jewish fund-raising efforts in the U.S., precluded a separate WJC campaign. Money raised by the UJA was divided between the United Palestine Appeal, Joint and the National Refugee Service that dealt with the absorption of Jewish refugees in the U.S.[105] The amount that the WJC could raise in Latin America countries and Canada were too meager to be effective in the field of relief.

The mass executions of Jews at Babi Yar and the gas chambers of Auschwitz symbolize the Holocaust today, but the first weapon used in the Nazi mass extermination of European Jewry was starvation. Raul Hilberg estimates that 20% of Polish Jewry died of malnutrition and disease in the ghettos of Poland in the course of the 'Final Solution.'[106] News of the abominable situation of Polish Jewry began reaching Jewish leaders early in the war. Many of them, like Dr. Jacob Robinson of the WJC, continued to believe well into 1943 that starvation and disease were the prime causes of death among European Jewry.[107]

German Chancellor Adenauer with Nahum Goldmann

Despite the British naval blockade of German-occupied Europe, the Jewish organizations nonetheless hoped they would be permitted to provide a measure of relief for the Jews. In November 1939, Dr. Goldmann spoke with James Nicholson on the possibility of sending aid. Nicholson told him that the German authorities had agreed to allow the American Red Cross to forward $250,000 for aid in Poland. He had previously told Goldmann that he hoped eventually to send $25 million.[108] Money forwarded by the Jewish organizations to the Red Cross would not be used solely for Jewish relief, he said, but would be distributed among the entire Polish population. The Jewish community would receive only its proportional share of relief materiel. This agreement, whereby the Jewish community would receive only 17% of the relief distributed in Poland, was actually discriminating against the Jewish population whose suffering from hunger and disease was much more intense. Even the Polish authorities admitted that "the problem was only one of obtaining food for the SEMITIC population."[109]

In December, Goldmann again met with Nicholson who informed him that the German Red Cross, who Nicholson believed could be trusted, was prepared to distribute relief in Poland to Jews and non-Jews alike. Nicholson maintained that at the moment only clothing and sanitary supplies could be shipped but if that went well, eventually food could also be sent. He also reported that Red Cross officials had discussed the question of relief with the Blockade Authority and had "met with much sympathy", and he thought there would not be many problems.[110] The ARC and the 'Commission for Polish Relief" did send food and medicines to Poland until they were forced to stop in 1941. Joint in New York provided considerable sums for these two relief organizations to cover their activities in Poland.[111]

Joint's funds played an important role in keeping Polish Jewry alive in the first two years of the war, though already mass starvation and epidemics were rapidly wiping out much of Polish Jewry. During the 17 months, between January 1941 and May 1942, there were 65,999 deaths in the Warsaw Ghetto alone,[112] which was approximately one sixth of the population of what was the largest ghetto in Europe. Joint allocated $3,090,684 for aid to Poland during the years 1939-41, but that does not indicate the actual amount spent by them in Poland during those years. [113] Their representatives in Poland often raised funds on their own by borrowing from wealthy local Jews with the promise that they would be reimbursed by the New York office after the war.[114] This method was opposed by Joint's executive, which forbade its Polish representatives to continue this practice.[115] The dispute became mostly irrelevant however after the Nazis appropriated all Jewish wealth in Poland. In the spring of 1940, Joint developed an alternative arrangement whereby potential Jewish emigrants from Germany, Austria and Bohemia (until October, 1941 the Jews of these areas were permitted to emigrate from the Reich) transferred their money to the local Jewish community and were later reimbursed. A part of these funds were transferred to Poland to maintain Joint's operations there. This arrangement lasted as long as Jews were permitted to emigrate from Germany.[116]

Aside from the transfer of relief funds to Poland, a number of Jewish organizations aided the Jews by dispatching parcels of food to Poland. Though some of these packages were confiscated by the German authorities, at first a large number did reach their destinations. Throughout 1940, RELICO, with funds from the World Jewish Congress, sent parcels to the Polish ghettos (they claimed to have sent 100,000 parcels in this period[117]) as did the Vaad Hahatzala (the Rescue Committee set up by the ultra-orthodox Agudas Israel which attempted to rescue the Rabbis, and Yeshiva students of Europe) which sent two to four thousand parcels a month.[118] The Jewish Labor Committee did not send parcels but transferred funds to the Bund in Poland via underground channels to help their members survive.[119] Joint's representatives in Europe organized some relatively small food shipments to the Jews of the GeneralGouvernment, most notably one that was intended to arrive in Poland in time for Passover in 1940.[120] In December 1940, despite the opposition of their European representatives, and the views of the more liberal minority, Joint decided to terminate food shipments to Poland.[121]

In the spring of 1941 the British Blockade Authority categorically demanded that the Jewish organizations stop sending food to the occupied territories. The British authorities were supported by the American government who, in the ABC plan decided on by the Chiefs of Staff of the two countries in March 1941, had listed the blockade as the first of three primary measures to be taken against Germany.[122] The British Embassy in Washington pressured the American Jewish organizations to cease sending parcels to Poland, claiming they were not reaching the people for whom they were intended. Even if the parcels do arrive, the British asserted, the food allotments of the receiving parties are reduced, and therefore no meaningful help is achieved.[123] The Jewish organizations were accused by the U.S. government of being 'blockade-runners', and they were warned by the naval blockade authorities that their relief activities were illegal and absolutely forbidden.[124]

The Jewish organizations were left no other choice but to abide by the blockade if they intended to continue to exist. Rabbi Wise acceded to the British demands explaining to the 'Congress movement' that "it is madness on our part to continue the money transfer or food transfer to Poland. We are risking everything for the veriest trifle[!]... there is only one important thing, and that is not only that Britain wins, but that we stand with Britain."[125] In May, 1941, Wise ordered the American Jewish Congress to stop sending parcels to Poland and he demanded the same of the World Jewish Congress in Geneva.[126] RELICO, nevertheless, discretely continued sending 1500 parcels of food to Poland every week.[127]

When the WJC became aware that not all nations conquered by Germany had stopped sending relief to their citizens, there were people like Aryeh Tartakower, who felt a sense of guilt for abandoning their brethren and demanded the renewal of the shipments. Louis Segal, of the Labor Zionists, claimed that "Letting the Jews starve will help Hitler, not hinder him. That is his objective."[128] At a meeting of the Administrative Committee of the WJC convened in October, 1941 to discuss relief, Nachum Goldmann declared that

> Neither Dr. Wise or I can remain on the executive of any organization that may be blacklisted by the British government. No matter how many packages that we sent it would not repair the damage which might be caused by such action.[129]

Most members of Joint's Executive also favored abiding by the regulations of the naval blockade.[130] That same April, Paul Baerwald informed the Secretary of State that the Joint did not intend to send any material relief, and that

"It has been our consistent viewpoint that we should not attempt to do anything that might [...] embarrass or impair the effectiveness of the British government in the conduct of the present war."[131]

The heads of Joint refused to undertake measures not within the compass of the law, or not desired by the Administration. They did, nonetheless, find ways to continue sending financial aid to the Jews of Poland that did not breach the blockade regulations.[132]

Only the ultra-Orthodox Vaad Hahatzalah continued for a while to violate the blockade. It sent parcels to Rabbis and Yeshiva students who found themselves in particularly dire straits because they lacked any skills to provide for themselves. The Vaad was pressured not to send parcels to Poland, not only by the British authorities and the State Department, but also by Jewish organizations in the U.S. Their attempts to continue providing aid created a clash with the Joint. The people at Joint grasped that the Vaad's method was first to act and then ask Joint to cover the expenditures. That occurred in 1940 when the Vaad attempted to rescue the Rabbis,[133] and again when they expanded their activities in 1944 and borrowed a million dollars from Joint to cover their deficit.[134] The 'Joint Boycott Council' picketed the N.Y. offices of the Vaad demanding an end to, what it called "the food package racket."[135] In August 1941 the Vaad Hahatzalah declared that it would abide by the blockade and act according to "the wishes of the British authorities in Washington."[136]

Were the British contentions true, that the parcels were not received by the addressees, and if they were, then the food allotments of those families were consequently reduced? Could the dispatch of food parcels and medication to the ghettos of Poland have, in any serious way, stemmed the mass starvation of the Jews there? Certainly the parcels that arrived in Poland were a blessing for the families that received them. However if we consider the whole picture, with two million Jews of the GeneralGouvernement facing dreadful starvation, the number of parcels arriving every week were no more than a meager palliative. Would the Nazi authorities have permitted a more substantial shipment of food? The answer, most probably, is no. The historian, Christopher Browning, relates that in January 1942, the German Red Cross transmitted to Gestapo chief Heinrich Müller a request made by RELICO to permit the shipment of foodstuffs to the Jews of the Lodz ghetto. Müller stated unequivocally, that "the planned Final Solution for the European Jewish question, known to you, does not permit that food shipments be made from abroad to Jews in Germany and the General Gouvernement."[137]

As late as the summer of 1942, the German authorities were apparently still allowing a relatively limited number of parcels to reach their destinations. The Holocaust historian, Yisrael Gutman claims that between September 1941 and June 1942 (he does not have statistics for November and December 1941) a total of 315,384 parcels arrived in the Warsaw ghetto, of which the Nazis confiscated 22,627, which was 7.17% of the total sent. Only in July of 1942, on the eve of the mass deportations from Warsaw, confiscations rose significantly – 22.6% of the parcels were seized by the German authorities.[138]

A number of other sources indicate that Gutman's facts are indeed correct and that, in this period, most parcels were not confiscated. In December 1941, Aryeh Tartakower, head of the Relief Department of the WJCong, received a letter from Natan Schwalb in Geneva, concerning the possibilities of sending parcels to Poland. Schwalb, the emissary to Hechalutz (the Zionist Pioneer movement) in Europe, stated that he had been sending both parcels and money to "Chaverim" (comrades) in the Warsaw Ghetto that reached their destinations both "easily and speedily." He urged the WJC "to send more packages now for who knows if we will be able to send them in the future."[139]

The British claim that Polish Jews receiving food parcels from abroad consequently had their food allocations reduced, appears to be pure conjecture. We have no information to prove their contention. Had the Jewish organizations been permitted to send food parcels to Poland, most would probably have reached their destinations, at least until the mass deportations began in the spring of 1942.

The Jewish organizations, while seemingly acceding to the demands of the Blockade Authorities, attempted to circumvent their regulations by devious means. The WJC, being an international organization, was able to channel funds to its local branches in Latin American countries who subsequently forwarded them to Switzerland. There RELICO continued shipping parcels of food to Poland via the WJC representative in Portugal, though on a very limited scale.[140]

In January 1942, Aryeh Tartakower was summoned to the offices of the British government in N.Y. City and was told that the British suspected the WJC of being 'blockade-runners' and was under investigation.[141] At a joint meeting of high-ranking representatives of the U.S. State and Treasury Departments, with the British Ministry of Economic Warfare, in March 1942, Secretary Hull noted that the British were complaining that money from the U.S. was reaching neutral countries in Europe via Latin America, and that these funds were being used to send food parcels to Poland. Treasury official, John Pehle, who a year later became a strong advocate of rescue and relief, declared that such transactions were strictly prohibited by Executive Order # 8389, and that he would personally see to it that such practices would cease.[142]

Until the summer of 1942 the Jews of America knew very little about the immensity of the destruction that had overtaken the Jews of Europe. But in light of the little that was known: such as the internment of the Jews in ghettos; the deliberate starvation of the Jewish population; the physical attacks and dire suffering of the Jews of Europe, it is difficult for us today to understand how they continued their daily routine without rising up to demand aid for these suffering people. In the first two years of the war, between 1939-41, when the U.S. was not yet a partner to the conflict, and its citizens were not yet burdened with concern for their own soldiers or for the war effort, American Jewry complied, in effect, with barring the gates of America to the refugees; they did not press to be permitted to send relief supplies; nor did they demonstrate against the tragedies that befell the illegal immigrant ships. Despite the grave crisis that descended on the Jews of the world and despite the fact that America (and most specifically the Jews) were already emerging from the economic depression, the monetary contributions of American Jews to Jewish causes actually declined during those years.[143]

CHAPTER 4
America Goes to War

(a) "This is a Jewish war"

August 11, 1941 – on a warship moored in the North Atlantic, President Roosevelt and Prime Minister Churchill signed a document known as the Atlantic Charter. The Charter annunciated the principles of the two leading democracies at a time when it appeared that totalitarian aggression would sweep the world. It guaranteed freedom of speech, freedom of religion, freedom from fear and freedom from want for all people. The Charter also provided for the disarmament of aggressors and called for the principle of self-determination to be applied to all peoples and nations.[1] On the very next day, August 12, the U.S. House of Representatives, by only a single vote, passed a law extending the year-old peace time draft. It was between these two poles, the one – a commitment to democratic ideals and the other – a hesitancy to take up arms in their defense, that a divided America was finally forced into the war by the Japanese attack on Pearl Harbor.

America of the 1930's, across all political barriers from Left and through Right, was firmly determined not to become involved again in what many believed to be "nothing more than another chapter in the bloody volume of European power politics."[2] The Nye Commission's investigation of U.S. involvement in World War I had left Americans convinced that it had not been "to save the world for democracy", nor even to protect genuine American interests, that the U.S. had entered that war. The Senate inquiry claimed that it was the machinations of the arms industry and of the bankers that led America to diverge from its century old policy of not involving itself in European conflicts.[3]

Americans were resolved never to be 'taken in' again. Besides, in the wake of the 'Great Depression', there were enough domestic problems needing to be solved which demanded the mobilization of the entire country. While Germany rearmed and threatened its neighbors, the U.S. Congress, expressing the popular will, had passed a series of Neutrality Acts, whose purpose was to guarantee that neither politicians nor financiers would ever again entangle

America in the morass of European wars. Anti-war sentiment in the U.S. ran so deep that in 1938 a proposed amendment to the Constitution that would have required holding a national referendum (!) in order to declare war, failed to pass in Congress by only a slim margin.[4]

The Neutrality Acts shackled the President's hands in his attempts to deal with Germany's aggression. When, in 1937, he called for the 'quarantine' of aggressors, there was a strong outcry in America against involving the U.S. in European politics. Astute politician that he was, Roosevelt learnt the lesson of his 'Quarantine Speech' – not to move too fast, nor too far, ahead of the public, but only gradually to bring America to the goals he sought. If he wanted to lead, Roosevelt could not permit himself to take steps that the country, as yet, was not ready to countenance.

In the following years Americans became increasingly revolted by the actions of the Nazi regime and concerned with German aggression. However when war broke out in Europe, the U.S. public still, almost totally, rejected the idea of joining the Allies in their struggle. A public opinion poll taken in September 1939 showed that only 2.5 % favored American intervention on the side of the Allies, while 29.9% wanted the U.S. to have nothing whatsoever to do with any of the warring countries. Between these extremes of interventionism and isolationism, most Americans favored providing aid to the Allies, short of entering the war.[5]

The isolationist camp was composed of the most diverse elements in American life – Communists and Fascists, leading businessmen and labor leaders, Irish-Catholics in the Eastern cities and small Protestant farmers in the Mid-West. Though as yet only a minority, the isolationists became very vocal and active during the following two years. Organizing themselves in the 'America First Committee' they attacked all of Roosevelt's attempts to aid Britain, fearing that such steps could only lead America to war. For the most part the isolationists were not pacifists. Many of them were fervent anti-Communists who believed that it was not Germany, but the Soviet Union, that should be constrained. Even more significant, many of the isolationists favored America taking a firm stand against Japanese aggression. The 'America Firsters' were adverse only to the U.S. becoming involved in a European war against Germany. Many of the isolationists were people of the same stripe as the 'appeasers' in Europe. Even after Germany's conquest of Europe they still believed in the possibility of achieving a 'modus vivendi' with Germany that "could maintain peace and civilization throughout the world as far into the future as we can see."[6]

Despite the vociferous, and often vicious, opposition by the isolationists, Roosevelt's policy of slowly bringing America to a commitment in support of the Allies paid off. People who favored an internationalist foreign policy also began to organize in order to better confront the isolationist camp. In May, 1940 an organization called 'The Committee to Defend America by Aiding the Allies' was established. Headed by the well-known Republican editor, William Allen White, the committee carried the brunt of the public campaign to arouse the American public to the Nazi danger. By effective use of the media, they succeeded in mobilizing broad support in favor of the President's foreign policy.[7] Working step by step, and cleverly using presidential powers to avoid a conflict with Congress, Roosevelt succeeded in extending massive aid to Britain and in converting America into an 'Arsenal for Democracy'.

Most Americans began to fall in behind Roosevelt's lead. A May 1941 poll revealed that 64% felt that it was more important to support Britain in its struggle than to keep America out of the war.[8] The historian, Robert Dallek, believes that Roosevelt's "appreciation that effective action abroad required a reliable consensus at home and his use of dramatic events overseas to win national backing from a divided country [...] were among the great Presidential achievements of the century."[9] Thus Roosevelt succeeded in bringing America to support a world struggle to contain totalitarian aggression.

Though it appeared that America was slowly edging towards war – and most Americans suspected that such was the case – the law proposed by the President in 1940 to establish compulsory military service was strongly opposed by a broad cross section despite the fact that the U.S. Army, at that time, numbered only three divisions.[10] It was, however, only the surprise attack by the Japanese that finally led to America's involvement in the war. It is not surprising then that most Americans wanted, above all, to avenge the bitter blow dealt to their pride at Pearl Harbor and in the subsequent defeats throughout the Pacific. Racial undertones were not lacking in this attitude. Americans viewed the Japanese as a somewhat backward, inferior race. To suffer defeats at the hands of the Japanese was certainly a trauma for most Americans. The cry went up across the country for a 'Pacific First' policy. A February 1942 survey showed that while 62% wanted to focus the war on defeating Japan, only 25% favored concentrating American efforts against Germany.[11] Once again, the Jews of America stood outside the majority consensus in their obvious desire for a 'Europe First' policy.

Concentrating first on the defeat of Germany was not only the wish of American Jewry, it was also the policy adopted by Roosevelt, who saw it as the most effective path to achieve military victory. The President was supported in this view by most of his senior military officers. That plan had been decided upon at joint American-British staff conversations in February 1941. The 'ABC' plan adopted at those meetings stipulated that if the U.S. and Britain were to be drawn into a war simultaneously against both Germany and Japan, the Atlantic Theater of Operations was to be the prime area of military engagement and most of the Allied forces would be concentrated there. As to the Pacific Theater of Operations, the plan called for sustaining only a war of attrition against Japan until the final defeat of Germany had been accomplished.[12]

Despite the atmosphere that had been engendered by the attack on Pearl Harbor, that principle was reiterated by the American Chief of Staff, Gen. George Marshall and Admiral Harold Stark, at the Arcadia Conference in December, 1941. Marshall informed his British counterparts that "our view remains that Germany is still the prime enemy and her defeat is the key to victory. Once Germany is defeated, the collapse of Italy and the defeat of Japan must follow."[13] For obvious reasons that position was not openly expressed in the declaration that was issued at the end of the conference. As he had done previously, the President, now strengthened as war-time Commander-In-Chief, went his own way and carried out his 'Europe First' policy, hoping that the public would eventually embrace his views.

But Americans were slow in grasping the meaning of the war, or what was required of them to win that war. Most Americans believed, at first, that with America's entry into the conflict on the side of the Allies, the battle would be over in a year or two.[14] Unlike the other major participants in the war, the civilian population of America never experienced the hardships of the war. Aside from a few panicky moments at the start of hostilities, the danger generally remained remote, and the U.S. fought the war on foreign soil. As Morton Blum described the situation "Only the United States[...] was fighting the war on imagination alone."[15]

After Pearl Harbor few Americans any longer questioned the necessity to fight the Axis powers, yet as late as 1944 most Americans did not perceive the war as a struggle between democracy and dictatorship, between civilized values and the brutal rule of naked force. America had been attacked, and there was a need for the country to defend itself. Beyond that basic fact, there was little comprehension of the ideological meaning of the conflict. A confidential poll taken in 1942 showed that a majority of Americans declared that "they had no clear idea what the war was all about."[16] The historian, James MacGregor Burns concluded that "Americans were interested not in form but in manpower, resources, logistics; not in moral victories, but in victory."[17]

Roosevelt often spoke in terms of lofty ideals, and stated that the 'Four Freedoms' were part of America's war aims, yet discrimination continued within the U.S. itself. Throughout the entire war Black-Americans served in segregated units, and the U.S. Army, with the blessings of the American Red Cross, even separated the blood plasma of Blacks and Whites.[18] While President Roosevelt proclaimed at a press conference in March 1944, that "The United Nations are fighting to make a world... in which all persons regardless of race, color, or creed may live in peace, honor, and dignity,"[19] nevertheless in September of that same year the State Legislature of South Carolina declared that "We are fighting [the war] to preserve white supremacy."[20]

Throughout most of 1942 the news from the warfronts was disastrous for Americans. The Japanese had turned much of the Pacific Ocean into a Japanese lake. The Germans and Italians had achieved the same in the Mediterranean. Continental Europe, from the Atlantic Ocean to the very outskirts of Moscow was almost totally under German control. It was therefore understandable that the war news, and the war effort, completely consumed the interests of Americans and their leaders. Some ten million young Americans had been inducted into the Armed Forces and the primary concern of their families was that the war end quickly, with the least possible loss of lives of 'their boys'.

Not having to face bombardment, nor knowing what it meant to live under Axis domination, it was the petty inconveniences of war – rationing, transportation problems, long work hours – that weighed most heavily on Americans. Though isolationism had been shattered by the realities of the war, the President still found it difficult to impress upon America the international obligations it would have to assume in the post-war world. The trauma of the depression years still affected America. In a public opinion poll in late 1942, most Americans expressed a greater concern for domestic affairs than for international issues. By a margin of more than two to one, Americans stated that they would oppose post-war aid to devastated Europe if that would affect their own standard of living – and most believed that such would be the case.[21] In a democracy, such as the United States, these problems quickly became the concern also of the elected officials as well.

Early in the war Roosevelt had decided that he would attempt to bring about a total and rapid victory, and this determination guided his actions more than any other consideration. To achieve this aim Roosevelt was prepared to postpone many of his cherished domestic programs – nor did he balk at curbing certain civil liberties.[22] The President was prepared to push aside any matters he felt would interfere with attaining this goal. He even confided in the Secretary of Treasury Morgenthau that he "would be perfectly willing to mislead and tell untruth if it will win the war."[23] Roosevelt was ready to sacrifice many of his declared principles if he felt that such acts could expedite an early victory. After the invasion of North Africa, Roosevelt negotiated with the French Fascists, even giving the Vichyites civilian control over the French colonies. He did this despite the protests of both Jews and liberals over the continuing Vichyite discrimination against North African Jewry. The following year Roosevelt was ready to bargain with the Italian Fascists in order to obtain the surrender of Italy. The same was true concerning Roosevelt's principle of self-determination for peoples. Though at first he did attempt to prod Churchill to meet Indian demands for independence, he did not pursue the matter once he felt that it might strain Anglo-American relations and hinder the war effort.[24]

One principle that Roosevelt refused to abandon in his striving for a speedy victory, despite the protest of some that it would only prolong the war, was his decision (and it was mainly his[25]) to demand unconditional surrender by Germany and Japan as the basis for terminating the war. As is often the case, Roosevelt, too, was fighting the battles of the previous war, and he was determined not to allow Germany to claim once again that it had not been defeated on the battlefield, but only 'stabbed in its back' by Jews and Socialists. Roosevelt's insistence on the unconditional surrender of Germany was also the result of the President's determination to maintain the unity of the 'Big Three' that he had forged, and not to allow distrust over the possibilities of a separate peace to damage America's relations with the Soviet Union.

As understandable as was the American public's desire to achieve a speedy victory, and as commendable as was the President's total dedication to that goal, it is valid to ask whether 'a speedy victory' should have been the only measure by which to judge wartime policy? World War II was a war waged against a totalitarian aggressor, the scope of whose carnage was unprecedented in human history, and basic principles of civilization and human values were at stake in this conflict. Was it enough to win the war, while compromising these principles and values? Expediency is often a factor in war time or in peacetime as well. The question to ask in judging those acts of expediency should be – what harm was done, what advantages achieved?

Roosevelt's expedient behavior in dealing with the Vichyites, Marshal Peyrouton and Admiral Darlan, in North Africa is a case in point. True, for those who had opposed the Vichy regime in North Africa the hurt was great, and many (mainly Jews) continued to suffer even after the liberation. But these Vichy officials were replaced within the year, and in the total context of the war, the damage was slight. That, however, was not the case regarding European Jewry during the Holocaust. The six million Jews who were exterminated while America pursued its goal of a speedy victory, can never be returned to life. The centers of Jewish life that disappeared will not return. While America sped to its victory, European Jewry was pushed to its doom.

The American public showed no sign of interest in the fate of European Jewry, and many Americans barely tolerated the Jews in their midst. Therefore the American Administration was wary to come to the aid of the Jews of Europe for fear of antagonizing voters. Antisemitism in America had a profound influence on the way American Jews responded to what was happening to the Jews of Europe, even after America's entry into the war. As a result of antisemitism, American Jews weighed their every step, fearing that they might intensify the native antisemitism that was increasing in any case.

What real danger did antisemitism hold for American Jews at that time? Was the threat perceived by American Jews and their organizations really justified? In retrospect, more than seventy years after the period we are discussing, it may seem that their fears were groundless. True, the threat of antisemitism did hang over American Jewry during the war, yet it began to wane almost immediately after. Nonetheless, during that period we can easily understand the anxiety that gripped American Jews. On the background of events in Europe, and of what was happening to the Jews there, the expressions of antisemitism in the U.S. were a danger signal. Jews saw a forewarning in the public opinion polls, such as one in carried out in 1944 that showed that 44% of Americans polled said they would either support or sympathize with a campaign against the Jews after the war.[26]

Today, when the status of American Jews is safe and secure, as it never before had been in the history of Diaspora Jewry, it is difficult to grasp the fears that concerned American Jews during World War II. Then, there prevailed an ugly climate of antisemitism, and on the backdrop of such an atmosphere it required no small degree of courage for American Jewry to act on behalf of the Jews of Europe. As they perceived it then, they had to choose whether their obligations to their persecuted brethren in Europe preceded their own desire to 'be accepted' in American society, and to assure their own safety. Most American Jews were prepared to help their kinsmen, although cautiously, because they feared to arouse the wrath of their fellow Americans. Only few acted without fear of the consequences. After the war, when the extent of the Holocaust became known, Lewis Strauss, a leading member of the American Jewish Committee wrote: "I might have done so much more than I did. I risked only what I thought I could afford."[27]

Many among those who insisted upon rescue efforts in the U.S. during the Holocaust were refugees only recently arrived in the U.S., such as Nachum Goldmann, Leon (Arieh) Kubowitzki, Arieh Tartakower of the World Jewish Congress; Rabbi Kalmanovits of the Vaad Hahatzala; Jacob Pat of the Jewish Labor Committee; and members of the Irgun delegation in the U.S. Temporary visitors to the U.S., such as Leib Jaffe and Rabbi Meir Berlin, may also be included in this category. These people not only acted, but insisted that American Jewry respond as well. They constantly pressured the Jewish organizations to work for rescue.[28] What characterized these individuals, despite the fact that each came from a very different background, was that they were not concerned to 'be accepted' in American society, and several did not intend to remain in the U.S. after the war.

When George Backer, the director of the Jewish Telegraphic Agency (JTA), proposed to the American delegation at the Bermuda Conference (see Chapter IXb) methods for rescuing European Jewry, the influential Senator Lucas warned him that "someday this will be a serious issue in this country if we aren't careful. Especially if the American people feel that you're [...] endangering the lives of **our** boys (my emphasis-A.H.)."[29] The insinuation was very clear. Even close associates of the President warned him of dire consequences if the public thought him to be too friendly to the Jews. Harold Ickes (who unquestionably was a friend of the Jews) believed that Roosevelt had made a grave mistake when he appointed a Jew, Samuel Rosenman, to his innermost circle of advisers.[30] At one point Ickes advised the President to instruct Secretary of Treasury Henry Morgenthau Jr. (who was Jewish), that he drop his plans for a speaking tour, because antisemitism had penetrated deeply into American society. "The President agreed with me", he recorded.[31]

Even if some proposed measure was capable of furthering the war effort, the Cabinet hesitated to adopt it if it was connected with Jews. This was the case in November, 1942 when the Cabinet met to discuss the manpower shortage. The Attorney-General, Francis Biddle, proposed that refugees from Germany be permitted to work (among them were 2500 doctors). The entire Cabinet agreed that "the matter will have to be carefully handled on account of the feeling in the House, both antisemitic and anti-refugee".[32] For those same reasons the President decided to drop the proposal.

Roosevelt was sensitive to the accusation that he was being controlled by Jews,[33] and was therefore careful to avoid any steps that might arouse a controversy at time of war. He was aware that the American public was critical of his appointment of so many Jews to high positions. Despite this ugly atmosphere, Roosevelt maintained his loyalty to his Jewish assistants. He did not abandon them, and he even added Sidney Hillman, from the CIO, to his senior circle of advisors. Though Roosevelt remained loyal to American Jews he was, nevertheless, not prepared to tackle the prevalent antisemitic biases that were a stumbling block on the path to rescue European Jews. He also clearly avoided any steps that would reinforce the fairly prevalent view that the U.S. was, purportedly, fighting the war solely for the benefit of the Jews.

This situation was a barrier to all attempts at rescue. American Jews feared to intensify the animosity against them and the Administration did not want to distance itself from the public. Attacks on Jews became rifer, and in November, 1943 there were riots against Jews in Boston and outbursts of vandalism against Jewish stores in New York City. Swastikas appeared on the walls of Jewish institutions.[34] According to the historian Morton Blum who examined the public mood during the war, "The Jews appeared a stronger emotional symbol of the enemy than did the Germans."[35]

It may have been assumed that when the U.S. joined in the conflict, antisemitism would begin to wane in America. The results, however, were exactly the reverse despite the government's attempts to unify the nation, and the fact that America was now fighting Nazi totalitarianism whose principle victims were the Jews. The tensions, frustrations, confusion and shortage of goods that the war brought in its wake only served to increase antisemitism in America. Antisemites now accused the Jews of shirking the draft, avoiding combat, and claimed that Jews were unpatriotic.[36] At one point the Director of Selective Services, Gen. Lewis Hershey, was forced publicly to refute these allegations.[37] Jews were also accused of profiteering from the sufferings of others by black market dealings in rationed goods. When the bitter debate broke out over opening a 'Second Front', the Jews once more were the subject of antisemitic accusations. Opening up a 'Second Front' meant the loss of countless soldiers, and to many Americans it seemed that the Jews wanted to drag the U.S. into a greater involvement that would lead to the death of more American boys.[38]

CHAPTER 5

The Final Solution: What Did They Know

(a) A failure to believe the unbelievable

"No one [...] can possibly understand"
(Jewish underground leader in Poland – November, 1942)

Why was there no outcry in America to stay the hands of the Nazis when they were murdering millions of Jews? Why, until late in the war, did the American government abstain from any attempts to aid the victims of Hitler's terror? Why do we constantly hear many Americans who lived through that period claim: "I had no idea, I barely knew"? Were the Germans really successful in preventing news of their massacres from reaching the outside world?

Anyone who has examined the American press during the Holocaust years is well aware that most of the facts of what had befallen European Jewry were available. True, the Germans did attempt to cover up their acts of horror and prevent news of the killings from leaking out. The death camp guards were all sworn not to reveal what was taking place within the camps.[1] The Nazis also used euphemisms and ruses to confuse, and to conceal their real intentions. In July 1943, for example, Martin Bormann, head of the Party Chancellery, ordered, in the Fuhrer's name, that

> in the future at times of public discussion of the Jewish problem, it is forbidden to mention the 'Final Solution' of the Jewish problem; it is permitted to say, that the Jews were all mobilized for work necessary for our goals.[2]

These methods of the Germans certainly succeeded in deceiving both journalists and political leaders for a long time.

Today Auschwitz stands as the symbol of Nazi mass killings, and there are few adults in the West not aware of the meaning of the place, or who do not know what occurred there, yet as late as March 1944, Arieh Kubowitzki, (head of the WJC Rescue Department and at that time one of the people most knowledgeable about the fate of European Jewry) wrote the WJC representative in Europe, "One report speaks of Auschwitz as an extermination camp. Is this information reliable?"[3] In the daily bulletin of the Jewish Telegraphic Agency from August 25, 1944 (barely 2 months before the killings ceased at Auschwitz), there appears an item stating that "65,000 [!] victims were murdered in Oswiecim in a period of two and a half years."[4] In the end, however, all the German attempts to prevent news of the killings from seeping out were unable to keep the information from reaching the West. Even in a totalitarian regime, and at time of war, it was impossible for six million people to disappear from the face of the earth without anyone aware of what was happening.

What prevented people from understanding what was happening to the Jews in Europe, therefore, was not the lack of information. The problem was to search it out, give it credence, internalize its meaning and understand what really was transpiring in Europe. Deborah Lipstadt's study, *Beyond Belief*, gives an excellent picture of the role of the American press at that time. According to Lipstadt, the press 'buried' the news of the massacre of the Jews on the inner pages of the newspapers; made the items appear to be of no importance; and created doubts as to the veracity of the reports. This coverage of the events of the Holocaust failed to present the readers with a true picture of the extent of the killings, and thus prevented an awareness of the Holocaust from developing among the American public. By such reporting, she claims, the press helped shape the response (or lack of response) of the American public "to this watershed event in human history."[5]

Throughout the entire period of the Holocaust (until the death camps were liberated, when it was plain for all to see) the American press often disregarded stories of the massacres. What they did carry generally appeared as small items on the back pages, and was often treated with a great deal of skepticism. Frequently, the papers denied the very stories that they themselves published. It is no wonder, therefore, that the general public was either unaware, or else was led to believe that the tales of massacre of millions of people were either of no credence or, for some reason, were unimportant. A Gallup poll taken in January 1943 (more than a month after Rabbi Wise's press conference at which he revealed the German plans for liquidating European Jewry, and only a few weeks after the Allied governments publicly declared Germany's "intention to exterminate the Jewish people in Europe?"[6]) revealed that less than half of those polled believed that two million Jews had perished in Europe.[7] The true number then was closer to three million, but that was not yet known in the West.

What were the sources of information available to the press and public, and why were they given so little credence? Firstly, until the very end of 1942, there were still a considerable number of people who returned to the West in exchanges of nationals – returning newspapermen and representatives of various organizations. Many of these people had experienced the Nazi brutalities at first-hand; others had seen or had heard what was occurring. American correspondents who had been interned in Germany at the start of the war were returned in the spring of 1942, and they immediately began to publish articles and books on what they had seen and heard in Europe. They already had information about what was happening to the Jews of the Soviet Union and the Baltic nations. They described the actions of what they called 'cleanup squads' (the 'Einsatzgruppen') in the extermination of Jews. They wrote that at least 200,000 Jews had already been killed in these actions.[8] Another important witness was Bertrand Jacobsen, Joint's representative in Hungary, who returned to the U.S. in March, 1942. He told of 240,000 Jews who were murdered in the Ukraine alone, and brought the tales of one eye-witness who spoke of Jews being buried in shallow graves, and graphically described how "the field was heaving like a sea."[9]

A second source of information were reports emanating from the Jews of occupied Europe. This information was either smuggled out by the undergrounds, or arrived in apparently innocent letters that contained coded messages concerning the fate of the Jews. The most famous of these were the Bund report sent to the West in May 1942, via the Polish underground,[10] and the detailed account of the Polish courier Jan Karski in November, 1942 in which he disclosed the situation of the Jews in Poland as described to him by Jewish leaders in the Warsaw Ghetto, and what he himself had seen.[11] Typical of the letters was one received in September, 1942 by the Sternbuch family, representatives of the Vaad Hahatzalah in Switzerland. That letter revealed the ongoing deportation of the Jews of Warsaw. Code names were used, such as "the family achenu" ['brothers' in Hebrew] was invited by "Herr Jaeger" [the Germans] to visit in the kever"['grave' in Hebrew].[12]

A third source of information, though generally not directly available to the press, were anti-Nazi Germans, who, repelled by the acts committed in their country's name, attempted to alert the world to the fate of the Jews. Such was Eduard Schulte who relayed information about the 'Final Solution', the basis for the Riegner cable (see part b), and the S.S. officer Kurt Gerstein who passed on details of the extermination camps to Sweden and to the Vatican and attempted to sound the alarm as to what was happening to European Jewry.[13]

There was also information available from the neutral countries that still maintained diplomatic relations with both sides of the conflict. On July 4, 1942 an item appeared in the *New York Times* whose source was a Swedish journalist just returned from a tour of Poland and the Ukraine. He recounted a rumor about a massacre of 40,000 Jews in Zhitomir, and reports that 100,000 Jews in the Baltic states had been killed in the last months of 1941.[14] In September, 1942 a report appeared in the New York Yiddish daily *Der Morgen Journal,* based on information from a Swedish businessman who had visited Poland. He had been told that half the Jews of the Warsaw, Lodz, Cracow, and Lwow ghettos, were no longer alive.[15]

There were also reports which emanated from the Governments-in-Exile and, after 'Operation Barbarossa' began, also from the Soviet government. These governments maintained some degree of contact with their occupied territories and were fairly well informed on events in their countries. At a press conference held on June 29, 1942, Ernst Frischer, a member of the exiled Czechoslovakian National Council, told of the high mortality rate of Jews as a result of starvation and disease, and stated that those whom the Germans do not succeed in exterminating by these methods, they do "by slaughter committed against Polish Jews and Jews from other countries deported to Poland."[16] On November 24, 1942 the Polish government-in-exile reported about a plan by Himmler that "under the guise of resettlement in the east, a mass murder of the Jewish population is being carried out", and that a quarter of a million Jews had already been murdered that year.[17] Despite the ban of the S.S. on reporting news of the killing process, it was possible, nonetheless, to glean some material from the German press and radio, and the German media often reported news of the deportations of the Jews, as well as the oft-repeated statements of Nazi aims to make Europe 'Judenrein' (cleared of Jews).[18]

There could and should have been, an additional and especially important source of information: the various international bodies, such as the International Red Cross and the Vatican, who had representatives and contacts in all the countries of Europe. They, however, were generally averse to making their information known.[19] To this last group we should add government agencies such as the State Department or the Office of War Information, whose very purpose was to gather and disseminate such information, but who ignored the Holocaust. We shall return to them later.

Why did the press treat these many sources with mistrust despite, as we know today, that most of the information was accurate? Reports from the Soviet Union and Communist sources were treated then, much as they are today, with great skepticism. The Soviets were known to create news to serve their purposes – in this case, to convince the U.S. to provide material aid to the Soviet Union, and to open a Second Front in the West. This skeptical attitude was true not only of the American press, but also of the Jewish organizations. The official organ of the American Jewish Congress, *Congress Weekly*, responding to the Soviet Foreign Minister Molotov's report in January, 1942 of Nazi pogroms and atrocities in the Ukraine (including a description of the massacre of Jews at Babi Yar), warned its readers about believing "news which is given out by so-called 'free' movements or governments."[20]

Information coming from the occupied peoples was also suspected by the American public as being exaggerated and intended mainly to garner American sympathy and support. This was especially true of news emanating from Jewish sources. The Jewish organizations were well aware of this situation and it seriously impaired their attempts to publicize news of the Holocaust. They knew that if Jewish organizations issued reports of the killings, few in America would care, and most would not believe.[21] Therefore they occasionally had non-Jewish groups place ads in newspapers to carry news of the Holocaust, which were paid for by the Jewish organizations. Thus a group of liberal Americans of

German descent placed an ad in the papers in December 1942, condemning the massacre of the Jews. The AJCong had to pay for the ad out of its own, very limited, resources.[22] The Jewish organizations concluded that if they wanted information published in the press, they first must pass it on to government agencies to have it corroborated – however, the gentlemen at Foggy Bottom refused to do so.

Another factor that prevented the press from presenting proper coverage to news of the Holocaust was their bad experience with the 'atrocity tales' of World War One. Like the politicians and the generals, the press, too, was still fighting the battles of the previous war. Then they had given full coverage to Allied stories of the 'Rape of Belgian Nuns', and of other purported German atrocities, which later were proved to be false. The journalists felt their integrity was at stake, as well as the prestige of their papers. They were resolved this time not to be 'taken in' by Allied propaganda.[23] Both the OWI and the British Ministry of Information were reluctant to disseminate news of Nazi atrocities towards the Jews, for they thought that the public would believe the stories to be exaggerated, and thereby the agencies would lose credibility.[24]

Another reason for the difficulty in proving the veracity of the information was the difficulty of obtaining 'neutral' and 'reliable' first hand witnesses. Reliable, generally meant to the newspapers, someone whom they knew, whom they trusted, who was not biased. Therefore, condemnation of the Nazis atrocities by Christian leaders was more apt to be believed than those made by Jewish leaders.[25] This was true not only of the general press, but of the Jewish press as well. Marie Syrkin, an editor of the respected Labor-Zionist magazine *Jewish Frontier*, described how on receiving the Bund report with information of the murder of 700,000 Jews, the staff could not believe the story and therefore buried it in the back pages.[26] One may speculate, had the report come from what the editors of *Jewish Frontier* may have considered a more reliable source, such as 'Hechalutz' (a Labor-Zionist movement), whether it, too, would have been concealed in such a manner.

Stories of the brutal treatment of the Jews, at first, blended with other news of German brutality towards all the conquered peoples, all of whom were suffering under the German heel. Not many were able to grasp the 'special treatment' being meted out to the Jews, nor grasp the uniqueness of their fate. Few understood the central role that the destruction of the Jews played in the Nazi war aims. Not even the vast numbers mentioned were enough to cause alarm. Throughout 1942 headlines reported tens of thousands of British soldiers surrendering at Tobruk, and hundreds of thousands of Russians falling prisoners on the Eastern Front (eventually more than three million Soviet POWs died in captivity[27]). The public became accustomed to hearing about tragedies of mass proportions, and the large numbers no longer impressed them.

Perhaps it was the immense numbers themselves that worked against belief. The numbers were not only unbelievable, they were incomprehensible as well. It appears that the fate of a single individual, with a face and a name, is more easily grasped than that of a nameless multitude. Paradoxically, the larger the number of victims, the less possible it was to identify with their fate. How can one explain the story of a "Lovesick Woman Kills Self" on page one of so respectable a newspaper as the *New York Times*, and a report on page 10 of the same issue, that two million Jews have already been killed in Europe.[28]

In Palestine we find similar manifestations in the Jewish press. A June 24, 1942 issue of *Davar* carried a large front-page story of three Palestinian Jews dying of typhoid fever, while on the inner page there appeared a four line item of 60,000 Jews reported killed in Vilna.[29] *Ha'Aretz*, of the same date, carries a front page article entitled "A Call to Citizens – To Fight Against Rumor Mongerers", while that same story about the Jews of Vilna, and other stories about the fate of European Jewry, were 'buried' on the inner pages.[30] Secretary Ickes was aware of that truism when he told Rabbi Wise "I suspect that if the atrocities were only ten percent of what they are, we would be much more horrified and people generally would cry out."[31] Perhaps this can be explained by the fact that what interests people most are issues familiar to them and occurring in their close surroundings. The discerning Democratic politician, Tip O'Neill, once coined the phrase: "All politics is local."[32] What happens in the immediate vicinity is what concerns the average American citizen, more than what happens on the national level, and certainly more than what is occurring overseas.

A particular burden of blame for the failure to cover the Holocaust must be borne by the so-called 'Jewish-controlled press', and in particular The *N.Y. Times*. For a century the *Times* has been the leading newspaper of the United States, providing guidelines for what is newsworthy, especially on national and international matters. Its masthead, "All the news that's fit to print", is taken seriously by the editors and by other papers. If The *N.Y. Times*, a 'Jewish paper', with a large Jewish readership, felt that news of the purported atrocities was not "fit to print", then certainly there was no place for it in the *Des Moines Register*. However, it appears that precisely because the Times had been accused of being too Jewish, that its owners had deliberately avoided pushing Jewish issues to the front.[33] The same may be said of another prestigious American paper, The *Washington Post* whose publisher, an assimilated Jew – Eugene Meyer, opposed America becoming involved in attempts to rescue European Jewry.[34]

Then, too, news of the war, of the fate of their nation, of their sons and neighbors, was the prime concern of most Americans. Their first year at war brought only news of continuing catastrophes on all fronts. That riveted their attention to the warfront, as did later the turnabouts that came at El-Alemein, Stalingrad and the battle of Midway. An American journalist caught the national mood when he asked, "Is there room in bewildered minds, obsessed by personal problems, to ponder about the fate of remote individuals?"[35]

Free from the horrors of the war front, which was distant, Americans allowed themselves the 'luxury' of being concerned with what, on the backdrop of the cataclysmic struggle then being waged, one can only describe as the minor displacements and discomforts of the war, such as gas-rationing and 'Meatless Tuesdays'. These were the issues that touched them personally, unlike the fate of some alien people whom many Americans increasingly disliked. If, as a pre-war poll had shown, more than half of Americans believed the persecution of the Jews in Germany to be partly, or entirely, their own fault,[36] why should they now be concerned? Even as the first news of the Holocaust was being received, there were still some 17% of Americans who believed that the Jews were only getting what they deserved when Hitler deprived them of their, supposedly, enormous power in Germany.[37] The journalists and editors attempted to present their reading public with issues of interest to them. If the battles of the war and the problems at home were what interested the American public, then that was what the papers offered their readers. Very few papers felt that it was their role to develop an issue that the public showed no interest in, nor the government encouraged them to tackle.

The problem, common to all who confronted the Holocaust in those years, was not only to know the facts, but to understand and believe them. The various reports were adding up to a single picture – an attempt by the Germans to eradicate an entire people, and to do so in the most brutal and bizarre fashion. There was no precedent in history for such action. The twentieth century mind, with faith in a world constantly progressing from the barbaric to the civilized, certainly could not believe that in their own age, and in a country steeped in culture and civilization, such barbarity could really occur. The inability to grasp this formed a veritable barrier to believing, not only for journalists, but also for statesmen and public, for Jew and non-Jew, both in and outside of Europe. When two Jews from Czestochowa escaped from the Treblinka death camp and made their way back to the ghetto, their neighbors refused to believe their stories about the fate that awaited them.[38] A Jewish underground leader in Warsaw warned the Polish courier Jan Karski, who was to bring news of the massacres to the West: "No one in the outside world can possibly understand. You don't understand. Even I don't understand."[39]

William Casey (later head of the CIA), chief of the OSS intelligence in Europe, wrote many years later that

> We knew in a general way that the Jews were being persecuted... and that brutality and murder took place in these camps. But few if any comprehended the appalling magnitude of it. It wasn't sufficiently real to stand out from the general brutality and slaughter which is war.[40]

Deborah Lipstadt contends that this inability to comprehend was "the most formidable obstacle to the spreading and acceptance of news of the Final Solution."[41] One can understand this inability to comprehend preventing most journalists from giving credence to these, so-called, 'atrocity tales' in the early period of the war, and the decision of their editors to 'bury' those stories. However, it is difficult to imagine why, when the information piled up and was corroborated by various sources, these journalists did not see that there was no longer any purpose in playing down these accounts. Nor did the newspapers question them much longer. By 1943, certainly by 1944, the media dealt with the stories of the Holocaust as trustworthy news – trustworthy, yes, but not yet newsworthy. Until the very end of the war, until General Eisenhower's well known visit to the Ohrsdurf camp, they continued to bury reports of the liquidation of the Jews as short items on the back pages of their papers.

The failure to properly cover the Holocaust was not the failing only of the printed media. The national radio networks hardly mentioned the massacres of the Jews, and Rabbi Wise's press conference in November 1942, where he spoke of two million Jews murdered by the Nazis, was not reported by any radio network.[42] What is even more significant, is the film industry which played an important role in arousing public sentiment to fight the Axis. Hollywood never dealt, more than tangentially, with the fate of the Jews. Many films pictured the brutal Nazi oppression of the conquered peoples, and a film, "Hangmen Also Die", was produced in the wake of the Lidice massacre.[43] However, nothing was done to portray the suffering of the Jews. The Nazi's prime victim as portrayed in films was the resistance fighter, not the Jew. Yet Hollywood was constantly accused of being under the control of Jews. Certainly the Selznicks, Goldwyns and Mayers did nothing to create public awareness of the Holocaust despite the repeated requests of the American Jewish Congress to produce a film on the subject.[44]

The media in a free society has great power in determining what news is deemed important, and whether or not to bring it to the attention of the public. Whether the decisions not to emphasize the stories of the extermination of the Jews were the personal reasons of the publishers, editors and journalists themselves, or were made because it was felt that they were of no major interest to the public, is of no consequence. Throughout the Holocaust the media failed to fulfill its task of creating an informed and aware public, and therefore shares a blame, which it has never attempted to confront, of being one of the factors that prevented the United States from developing a rescue effort to save European Jews from the fate awaiting them.

The media was not alone negligent in its failure to present the public with news of the Final Solution. Many governmental departments and agencies were equally responsible for the failure to alert the public to the fate of the Jews. The State Department, as we shall see, not only did not make information in their possession available to the press and public, they consistently attempted to prevent such information from reaching the advocates of rescue. Whenever Rabbi Wise, or other Jewish leaders, announced news of the murders, the State Department refused to corroborate their stories, thereby laying them open to doubt.

The Office of War Information, whose prime purpose was the dissemination of news and 'propagandizing' the Allied war effort, was also accused by the Jewish leaders who dealt with them, of being part of "a conspiracy of silence."[45] The Deputy Director of the OWI, Arthur Sweetser, ordered one of his subordinates to play down the stories of the massacre of the Jews claiming it would be "confus[ing] and misleading if it appears to be simply affecting the Jewish people."[46]

Nor, for a long time, did the President utter anything that might have led Americans to become aware of the destruction of the Jews, or to believe that such news should be of importance to them. Roosevelt was one of the most public opinion conscious presidents in American history. He generally held twice-weekly press conferences, and his famed 'Fireside Chats' were listened to by the entire nation. Yet until late 1943 he never publicly mentioned news of the Final Solution, nor did he express his concern for the fate of European Jewry.[47] Only on November 5, 1943 did the President first address himself at a press conference to the question of the destruction of European Jewry, and even then only indirectly.[48]

(b) The News Filters Out

"An end to silence"
(A *Congress Weekly* editorial -June 26, 1942)

On April 24, 1942, Chaim Weizmann, the President of the World Zionist Organization, met with the Emergency Committee for Zionist Affairs (ECZA) to discuss problems facing world Jewry. Dr. Weizmann reported to the Zionist leadership that perhaps as many as two to five hundred thousand Jews might perish in the war.[49] Two years earlier, however, Nachum Goldmann had already predicted that one to two million Jews would die, in Poland alone.[50] In addressing the War Emergency Conference of the WJC in May, 1942, Rabbi Wise chided the delegates: "Too much is being said in this day about Jewish survival [...] as though nothing more than mere survival might be hoped for [...] There are questions that are treasonable not only to answer in the negative but even to posit."[51] Three months earlier Dr. Jacob Robinson who was responsible for research at the World Jewish Congress, and who should have been most knowledgeable about the fate of European Jews, advised his organization to stress the economic extermination of the Jews "since the Jews have no monopoly on atrocities aimed at them."[52]

The first news about the massacre of the Jews did not arrive in the West until the late spring of 1942. There had been occasional reports of pogroms against Jews in Poland but the main concern appeared to be the privations caused by starvation and disease. In November 1941 Rabbi Wise's magazine, *Opinion,* reported that the death rate in the Warsaw Ghetto was fifteen times the pre-war average. Yet the editorial gave no hope of alleviating the situation since "protest will not avail for there is no public opinion to which to appeal, outside of the democratic world, which have no standing in totalitarian eyes."[53]

The actual killing-process started only with the mass exterminations by the *Einsatzgruppen* after the invasion of the Soviet Union in June 1941, and news of those killings began to reach the West at the beginning of 1942. One of the first indications of the fate of the Jews came in a statement handed to the American Ambassador in Moscow by the Soviet Foreign Minister, Molotov. It was printed in Pravda on January 7, 1942, and subsequently was reported by the press agencies[54] However, Molotov's story of tens of thousands being massacred in the Ukraine, "most of them Jews", was dismissed as Soviet propaganda.

Throughout the spring, small news items arrived about the fate of Eastern European Jews. They comprised a story of mass extermination. In March 1942, the testimony of Bertrand Jacobsen was published. Jacobsen, as a representative of a Jewish organization, may not have been considered an 'objective' source by the general public, yet his account should have made some impression upon the Jewish organizations. However, Jacobsen's testimony was not first-hand evidence but stories he had heard from Hungarian soldiers. Doubts still lingered as to its credibility.

One of the first sources of information was from a group of American reporters who were stranded in Germany at the outbreak of the war, and were later exchanged for German nationals living in the U.S. On May 18th, the *New York Times* printed an article by Glen Stadler (UPI) who returned to America in a prisoner exchange. Stadler wrote that in the Baltic countries "the killing of the Jews has become an open hunt". He estimated that 100,000 Jews had already been slaughtered in the Baltic countries and an additional 200,000 in Western Russia.[55] In June, the newspapers printed a story from an eye-witness that told of 60,000 Jews massacred in the city of Vilna.[56] However, these stories were very brief and unauthenticated, and therefore most of the public were still reluctant to believe them, or unable to accept the full import of the news.

David Ben Gurion, who was in the U.S. at that time, was one of the first major Jewish figures to have understood that the Jews of Europe were facing oblivion. In a speech delivered to the Labor Zionists at the end of May, Ben Gurion spoke of the Nazi's subjugation of the peoples of Europe, whom, he contended, Hitler intended to keep as slaves. "However", he claimed, "it is his [Hitler's] clear intention, which he is carrying out as far as he can, to destroy physically the Jewish race throughout the world."[57] Ben Gurion told the conference that it was the responsibility of American Jews to attempt to aid the Jews of Europe, even though he questioned whether they could actually be saved. He attacked the timidity of American Jewry, and in words reminiscent of Justice Brandeis (Brandeis had told a group of Jewish leaders that "The American is essentially a manly being and admires nothing more than courage. We must fight and fight."[58]) he told them "it isn't an American ideal to be timid when one is insulted", and that in this respect they should behave as Americans.[59]

The first information concerning the mass killings that made an impact on Jewish leaders, though not on all, was the Bund report that reached the West in June 1942.[60] This had been sent to London by the underground of the Jewish-Socialist Bund which had been a very strong force in pre-war Poland. The Bund was represented on the exiled Polish National Council in London, providing it contact to occupied Poland. The report, which was limited to news about the Jews of Poland, spoke of 700,000 Jews in Poland who had already been murdered, noting that the killings had begun with the outbreak of the Russo-German War. It detailed by communities the extent of the massacres (Lwow – 30,000; Vilna – 50,000 etc.) which it saw as proof of "Hitler's prophecy that he will wipe out all Polish Jews."[61]

The two Jewish members of the Polish National Council – Shmuel Zygelboim (a Bundist) and Ignacy Schwarzbart (a Zionist) – persisted in bringing the news of the killings to the attention of both the media and the British government. The BBC immediately broadcast the report and somewhat later the British Minister of Information, Brendan Bracken (a close confidant of Churchill), participated in a press conference in which he too spoke of 700,000 Jews having been murdered. The Roman Catholic Prelate of England, Cardinal Hinsley, also took to the air to speak out against the atrocities perpetrated on the Jews of Europe.

At the end of June the British Section of the WJC held a press conference where they declared that more than a million European Jews had already been murdered. This information was procured both from the 'Bund Report', and from its own sources.[62] The British Section pressured their compatriots in New York to respond forcibly to the news.[63] In June, Dr. Goldmann also received a cable from Yitzchak Greenbaum, head of the Rescue Committee in Palestine, with additional information urging him to have America threaten "to treat Germans under their domination" much as the Germans treat the Jews.[64]

Whether due to the information borne by the Bund report, or whether in response to the call of Jewish leaders in Britain and Palestine, by the end of June the American Jewish Congress began to press American Jewry to respond to the unfolding disaster of their European brothers. A series of editorials appearing at the end of June in *Congress Weekly* called for "An End to Silence,"[65]and "America Must Speak Out."[66] Finally, in an editorial "Why Has American Jewry Been Silent?", the AJCong called for a mass demonstration in Madison Square Garden.[67] They decided to hold a rally on the day before Tisha B'Av for the dual purpose of "expressing sorrow over the fate of our fellow-Jews", and to petition the Allies that the Yishuv (endangered by Rommel's advances in North Africa) "not be sacrificed and be permitted to defend themselves in their land."[68] Branches of the American Jewish Congress in ten other cities were asked to organize similar rallies, and other Jewish organizations were asked to share in their co-sponsorship. The Jewish Labor Committee, B'nai Brith and the Zionist Emergency Committee supported the demonstration, though the latter did so with grave misgivings. It was not that the Zionists were opposed to demonstrating, but their funds were so meager that after contributing their share to the cost of the rally, ECZA was left with only $385.[69] At Joint, Paul Baerwald questioned demonstrating solely on the basis of Jewish persecution[70] and the American Jewish Committee decided not to sponsor the rally because one of its purposes was a call for the creation of a Jewish Army. For the first time, however, they did send a message of support.[71]

At the State Department information began arriving from Foreign Service officers stationed in neutral countries of Europe telling of mass deportations of Jews from the West, and of mass killings of Jews in the East. Ironically, it was the FBI, responsible only for internal security, which provided the State Department with news of intensified deportations from Germany and the Protectorate.[72] In July, the U.S. Minister to Sweden, Herschel Johnson, sent the State Department information from what he believed were well-informed and reliable sources, accurately describing the methods of mass murder used by the S.S., and reported that 284,000 Jews had been deliberately killed in the Soviet Union alone.[73] The State Department did not release any of this information to the American public, nor did it inform the various Jewish organizations. On the contrary, it tried to prevent the news from becoming a public issue, in the United States or elsewhere.

On July 24, Wallace Murray, a senior political adviser at State, told the Under-Secretary of State Sumner Welles, that Rabbi Wise and Dr. Goldmann should be informed that

> in our view mass meetings throughout the world, protests and appeals for the protection of a particular racial group would not contribute to the general united war effort, even though that group had itself been singled out for persecution by the Axis.[74]

Though the State Department could not prevent demonstrations in the U.S., it did hold up messages sent by the World Jewish Congress Executive in New York to Jewish communities around the world urging them to organize demonstrations of protest.[75] Nor did the State Department show any initiative in organizing any form of diplomatic protest. When the Secretary of State was informed of a Brazilian initiative to have the nations of the world appeal to the Pope to publicly condemn Nazi atrocities (without even mentioning the Jews), Secretary Hull instructed his Minister to join the protest only if the Brazilian government persisted in the appeal.[76]

The Tisha B'Av rallies succeeded in attracting tens of thousands of Jews. The organizers rejoiced at the message sent by President Roosevelt promising that

> The American people [...] will hold the perpetrators of these crimes to strict accountability in a day of reckoning... [In conclusion he expressed] the confident hope that the Atlantic Charter and the just world order to be made possible by the triumph of the United Nations will bring the Jews and oppressed peoples in all lands the Four Freedoms. [77]

This was understood to be a statement of support for the creation of a Jewish State in a post-war settlement. However if the rallies were intended to publicize the murder of the Jews and to move the U.S. government to rescue action, they were a dismal failure. It is not even certain that the organizers made clear to the general American public precisely why they were demonstrating. Harold Ickes, who was invited to address the rally declined to speak. He confided in his diary that he understood the rally held on Tisha B'Av to be nothing more than a memorial to mark the anniversary of "The fall of the Temple in Jerusalem, whatever that may mean."[78]

Neither the general, nor most of the Jewish public were aware, as yet, of the tragedy overtaking the Jews of Europe. Even Peter Bergson (Hillel Kook), who later became totally involved in the attempt to rescue Jews, claims that it was not until some months later, at the end of November, that he realized what was happening. The news that the Germans had begun to carry out Hitler's threat, that war would bring "the destruction of the Jewish race in Europe," was still beyond the grasp of people who had been raised with Jewish moral values and in the American liberal tradition. Many more months had to pass, and more evidence disclosed, before American Jewry (no less the general public) understood the significance of this information. And even then, there were still many who continued to doubt the veracity of the reports. Nor did the rallies raise any cry for any specific government action to stop the killings. For the organizations to accomplish this, they needed more time. They had not only to understand what was happening to European Jewry, but they had also to realize that some action could still be taken to rescue Jews.

There had been some emotional calls to respond to the killings, such as the one by Greenbaum, calling for American retaliation in kind against Germans who were in the hands of the Allies,[79] yet it wasn't always clear who was actually to be punished for the acts of the Nazis. If the intention had been to retaliate against Americans of German ancestry, it was absurd to even entertain such an idea. If retaliation was meant for German aliens living in Allied countries, certainly a large percentage of them were themselves anti-Nazi refugees. Nor would the democracies consider punishing innocent civilians, especially since they feared retaliation in kind against Allied Prisoners of War or Civilian Internees held by Germany. State Department officials expressed their opposition "to further publicizing the President's promise to make the Nazis stand trial... This seems a little unreal."[80]

Aryeh Kubowitzki was among the first to grasp what was happening in Europe, and was the most active in demanding formulation of a policy to stop the massacres and deportations. At his insistence, the WJC established a policy committee at the beginning of August whose purpose was to formulate concrete plans for rescue to be presented by them to the American government. Yet despite the rallies in July, an awareness of the tragedy had not yet fully developed, even among the Jewish leadership. At the end of August, two weeks after the policy committee had been created, Kubowitzki complained that time was passing and nothing had been done.[81]

In August, Kubowitzki, who consistently expressed his concern that news of the killings was not reaching anyone outside the readers of the Yiddish press, appealed to the American Jewish Congress that the *Congress Weekly* devote at least six pages of each issue to news of European Jewry. "The least we could do for our hard-tried people" he pleaded, "is to tell what we know, tell the truth". "Perhaps", he hoped, "it may overcome the lack of reaction of the Jewish public and of American public opinion."[82] On August 28 the editors of *Congress Weekly* replied: To devote so much space to news from European Jewry would change the character of their journal, they argued, and would appeal only to a limited readership.[83]

However, that same afternoon, just before the Sabbath, Rabbi Wise received a cable from Sidney Silverman M.P. in London, which brought a final reversal in the understanding and the attitude of Jewish organizations as to the fate of European Jewry.

(c) The worst is confirmed

"I am unable to sleep"
(Rabbi Wise in a letter to a friend – September, 1942)

On August 1, Dr. Gerhart Riegner, the World Jewish Congress representative in Geneva received information from what he believed to be an impeccable source to the effect that the "Führer's Headquarters" had decided upon a plan, to be implemented that coming fall, aimed at destroying by poison gas all of European Jewry. Though Riegner had been sending news of the condition of European Jewry to his New York headquarters since 1940 and had been pressing hard for its dissemination, he nevertheless mulled over this latest information for a week before passing it on. Even Riegner, probably one of the best-informed individuals in non-occupied Europe regarding the fate of the Jews, found the news difficult to believe and uncertain how it would be received. On August 8, Riegner met with the American Vice-Consul in Geneva, Howard Elting Jr., and reported his information to him. He requested that it be forwarded both to the State Department and to Rabbi Wise, and that an attempt be made to verify it. The carefully worded cable concluded with Riegner's own doubts: "The information [is] transmitted with reservation as exactitude cannot be ascertained."[84]

Dr. Gerhart Reigner

Elting was probably the most sympathetic of the many State Department officers through whose hands the Riegner cable passed. Though Elting, too, found the story difficult to believe, he, nonetheless, sent it to his superiors in Bern recommending that it be forwarded to the State Department along with his stated belief that Riegner was "a serious and balanced individual and would not bring the report if not the truth."[85] The U.S. Minister in Bern, Leland Harrison, forwarded it to the State Department with an accompanying disclaimer that the Legation had "no information that would tend to confirm this report [...] The report has earmarks of war rumor inspired by fear and what is understood to be the actually miserable conditions of these refugees."[86]

The same State Department officials who had already been attempting to prevent leakage of news of the massacres, decided not to deliver the cable to Dr. Wise. Elbridge Durbrow, of the Division of European Affairs, reasoned that "it does not appear advisable [to pass on the cable] in view of the Legation's comments, the fantastic nature of the allegation" and, what probably concerned him most, "the impossibility of our being of any assistance if such action were taken."[87] As far as State was concerned, it was decided that Rabbi Wise was not to be informed of the news that had arrived concerning the Nazi plans. However, at the same time that Riegner had approached the American Consul, he had also requested the British Consulate to cable Sidney Silverman, Chairman of the British Section of the World Jewish Congress. Both Riegner cables were identical, except for an additional note asking Silverman "To inform and consult New York."[88] The British Foreign Office also debated how to handle the news but ended up deciding to forward the cable to Silverman, who after all, was an important Member of Parliament. Silverman immediately wired a copy to Dr. Wise.

Rabbi Wise received the cable on August 28, a late Friday afternoon. The Rabbi was about to leave town, but conferred first with his senior associates who advised him to bring the news immediately to the attention of the State Department. They reasoned that if it were true, the only possibility of aiding the Jews in Europe could solely be with the assistance of the State Department and so they must be brought into the picture.[89]

It has generally been assumed that news of the Riegner cable was shared at first only with a few leaders of the WJC, and ten days later among an equally small circle of heads of other Jewish organizations. That, however, was not the case. It appears, rather, that a fairly large number of Jewish leaders knew of the cable, and nearly all concurred in the actions taken. I have found that on the morning of August 31, the Office Committee of the American Jewish Congress assembled, without Dr. Wise, to discuss the cable and what actions should to be taken. That afternoon, both the Office Committee and the Central Committee of the Labor-Zionist 'Farband' also deliberated their response.[90] If the entire AJCong and Farband leaderships knew of the cable by the 31st, one may conjecture whether other Jewish leaders, or the many other affiliates of the American Jewish Congress, were also informed and also deliberated the matter.

The response of the American Jewish Congress, and of the Farband, to the Riegner cable was similar to that of Rabbi Wise and his associates. Firstly, none who received the news questioned its veracity until doubts were implanted by the State Department. Kubowitzki said that the cable was not really news, for it should have been apparent all along that the purpose of the deportations had been to ship the Jews to the East "where it would be easier to destroy [them]."[91] Secondly, all were of the opinion that the news should not be made public by the Jewish organizations. They reasoned that if the Jews were the source of information, it would make no impression on the general American public. Therefore, it was concluded, Sumner Welles (considered the State Department official most sympathetic to the Jews) and Elmer Davis, who headed the OWI, should be informed immediately, and it was hoped that they would officially release the news.

The minutes of the Farband indicate the differences of opinion that existed as to what actions, if any, should be taken, and what proposals should be forwarded to the U.S. government. Kubowitzki told the Farband leadership that he had proposed to the WJC that they demand military action to stop the killings, but had received no support for his proposal. David Wertheim, the Executive Secretary of the Labor Zionists, responded "Perhaps we should declare war against Germany? Aside from leading the war and winning it, there is no other help". The Farband Treasurer, A. Kalman Levin, suggested that a mass demonstration of 500,000 Jews would make the proper impression. But Isaac Hamlin, head of the Histadrut campaign, thought that "we can do little alone", and Professor Feiman, President of the Farband, believed that "demonstrations today are a difficult matter, because America is at war." The Chairman concluded that there were no concrete proposals, aside from organizing a conference of Jewish and non-Jewish leaders to discuss the matter.[92]

Such was the tone of discussion concerning the first news of the 'Final Solution' at the Farband, which was one of the most outspoken advocates of public action and of rescue. Only three months earlier Ben Gurion had urged the Labor Zionists not to be timid, and told them that they "are responsible for what is happening [...] to that wretched nation, people called Jews."[93] It is apparent that even in such an activist organization the leadership was at a loss to decide what steps to take to aid Jews whom the people at Farband certainly perceived as their 'brethren' in Europe. They felt that all the cards were held by the Germans, and to them it was impossible to turn to alleviate the condition of the Jews. Those were among the darkest days of a cruel and bitter war, with the Allied forces still retreating on all the fronts and the U.S. mobilizing for the war effort. The Farband leadership understood that to demonstrate in the streets in those days with particularistic demands, would be seen as harming the war effort. It would be interpreted as a personal attack on President Roosevelt, to whom all turned in the hope that he would lead the Allies to victory over Nazism.

After conferring with the leadership of his movement, Wise did not go to Washington but on September 2, he sent a copy of the Riegner cable to Welles, naively believing that the State Department had no prior knowledge of the report. Wise wrote Welles that Riegner was a reliable individual and asked that the American Minister in Bern meet Riegner to substantiate his story. Dr. Wise also, rather hesitatingly, suggested that Welles inform the President.[94]

Welles promptly phoned Wise without informing him that the Riegner cable had been in the State Department for three weeks. He told Wise that it was the Department's understanding that the Jews were being deported to work for the German war effort.[95] Welles promised that State would attempt to verify Riegner's information, but most significantly, he requested Wise not to circulate the news until they established its veracity.[96] Rabbi Wise acceded to the request, and together with the leaders of the other Jewish organizations, did not inform the American public of the plans for the 'Final Solution' until the end of November. It is rather surprising that with so many people already in the know, Rabbi Wise could 'sit on the lid' and prevent the Riegner cable from becoming general knowledge for nearly three months.

In the meantime more information was beginning to arrive concerning the fate of European Jewry. On the same day that Welles spoke to Wise requesting his silence, a cable was received by the Agudas Israel in New York from Isaac Sternbuch, an Orthodox Jew living in Switzerland. Through a friend, Julius Kuhl, an assistant in the Polish Legation in Switzerland, the Sternbuchs had maintained underground contact with Poland. Kuhl also permitted the Sternbuchs the use of the Polish diplomatic pouch, as in this instance, to transmit messages to the United States, circumventing the heavy hand of the American censor. Sternbuch reported that he had received information from Poland that some 100,000 Jews, from Warsaw alone, had already been deported and killed and their bodies were being used to produce fertilizer and soap.[97]

Jacob Rosenheim, President of the World Agudas Israel cabled this to President Roosevelt and conferred with other Agudas leaders and with James MacDonald, Chairman of the PACPR. MacDonald forwarded a copy of the

Sternbuch message to Eleanor Roosevelt, with the hope that she would pass it on to the President.[98] Agudas Israel also called a meeting of representatives of the major Jewish organizations to discuss the Sternbuch cable. Rabbi Wise used the opportunity to inform the other organizations of the information that he had received from Riegner.[99] Neither at that meeting, nor at a second one two days later, were they able to decide upon any plan of action. Wise, however, did inform the other Jewish organizations of Welles' request to maintain silence until the news had been corroborated. Despite the misgivings of Jacob Pat (Executive Secretary of the JLC), it was agreed to accede to Welles' request and to postpone any action until Wise was able to meet with Welles after an extended Labor Day vacation.[100]

Today all criticism is directed at Wise, as though he alone had agreed to keep secret the horrifying news. The 'blame' for the action, or inaction, of American Jews in response to the cable has been placed squarely upon the shoulders of Stephen Wise by people such as Elie Wiesel.[101] Some even claim that Wise did not inform the other Jewish leaders about the cable until after the war.[102] True, Wise did promise Welles that he would not divulge the contents of the cable until they were verified by the State Department. However his promise was not binding on the other Jewish leaders, nor on Silverman in England, nor on the PACPR members who also knew of the cable. There were dozens of others who were aware of the cable and of its contents. Why did they all maintain silence?

The President of Czechoslovakia, Eduard Benes, when approached with news of the Riegner cable, informed the World Jewish Congress that he believed the story false, and he, too, suggested that they not publicize the matter until he checked it out.[103] Benes was considered a close friend of the Jews and very knowledgeable about what was transpiring in occupied Europe, and his recommendations carried much weight with the Jewish leaders. The feeling of most Jewish leaders was that they had no choice but to acquiesce to Welles' request. Failure to heed Welles might only antagonize their only friend in the State Department and lead the government to deny them all sources of information from Europe. Besides, if the information was true, action to aid the Jews of Europe could only be carried out with the support of the government. It would therefore be counterproductive to offend the Administration, they reasoned, without first heeding Welles' request. Wise was correct in assessing that without Welles their contact with Europe would be cut off.[104]

The Jewish leaders also believed that if the Jewish groups publicized the news of the mass killings, and of the seemingly implausible plan to destroy European Jewry, the general public would not believe them. America would not have accepted atrocity stories vaguely reminiscent of similar discredited tales from the First World War. Consequently, they would be unable to arouse the public to demand government intercession and rescue action. We must remember, as well, that Riegner himself had reservations as to the veracity of his information – and he also noted that the plan had not yet been put into operation. The American Jewish leadership, distanced by thousands of miles from the scene, and told by authorities that Jews were 'only' being deported to slave labor, were not really certain that Riegner's report was credible. They certainly hoped that the news would prove false.

Wise anguished over the news he had received from Riegner, and wrote a friend of his inability "to sleep since that earlier cable came to me."[105] His promise to Welles prevented him both from speaking out and from taking any public action. The only pursuit that now remained open to Wise and to the other Jewish leaders, was to alert their few friends in Washington to the tragedy and hope that they in turn might prod the President to take some steps to alleviate the Jewish suffering. During those two and half months, Rabbi Wise constantly returned to Washington and met among others, with Vice President Wallace, Assistant Secretary of State Dean Acheson, Secretary Ickes, and most consistently with Sumner Welles. His meeting with Secretary of Treasury Henry Morgenthau Jr., though not particularly important at that moment, eventually had a profound effect on the development of an American rescue effort some eighteen months later.

Wise did not ask to see Roosevelt, though he did ask Welles, Morgenthau and Justice Frankfurter to consider approaching the President with the news. Wise apparently hesitated to 'burden' the President in those dark hours of the war and doubted whether the President would be able "to avert the horror."[106] In truth, those fall months of 1942 found the Allies in great despair. Rommel stood at the gates of the Suez Canal; Von Paulus was in Stalingrad and other German armies had reached the foothills of the Caucasus. The possibility seemed real that the German forces might join up and conquer the entire Middle East, or that, possibly, the Japanese might break through in India and link up with their Axis partners. Nor did the President feel that the nation was united behind him. Roosevelt faced a difficult Congressional election, and the political bickering was becoming more strident. Robert Sherwood, who was close to the President, said of those months that "In the battle of Washington [...] this was the lowest point of the war."[107]

Having been told by Welles, Benes, and the Polish Ambassador,[108] and later by Roosevelt via Frankfurter, that the deported Jews were only being used for forced labor, Wise asked Samuel Caevert, a non-Jewish member of the PACPR who was leaving on a mission to Geneva, to ask Riegner for a clear confirmation "whether deportation means extermination?" Riegner cabled a one word reply – "Yes."[109]

More information and details of the massacres kept coming in from Europe, yet the Jewish organizations maintained their sworn silence. At the end of September the World Jewish Congress and the Zionist Emergency Committee each received copies of a report sent by Richard Lichtheim, the Jewish Agency representative in Switzerland, further detailing news of the massacres: in Warsaw – 100,000 deported and dead, 100,000 dead from starvation; Vilna – only 10,000 remain of a pre-war population of 65,000; and similar tales in other communities throughout Europe. At the Zionist Emergency Committee meeting, a note was appended to the report stating that "we believe the report to be true and quite in line with Hitler's announcement that at the end of the war there will be no Jews in Continental Europe."[110]

Yet the burgeoning information did not succeed in quelling the doubts of some. A number of Jewish leaders feared that if the horror tales of Riegner and Lichtheim were published and later proved to be false, the American public would never again believe any of their claims of Jewish suffering. Maurice Perlzweig, head of the Political Department of the WJC, warned his colleagues that "we ought to be more careful not to be led astray [...] if we want to convince others we must be sure that we have evidence of some value." In conclusion he appealed to them "Can't we do anything to regulate the circulation of such documents as this?"[111]

But pressure was also building up to break the silence, to let America know what was happening to the Jews of Europe, and to mobilize forces for rescue. Joseph Held of the JLC told Wise of his dissatisfaction with Welles' request for silence.[112] After reading Lichtheim's report, Kubowitzki wrote to the WJC Executive "I think we have no right to keep secret any longer the information we have. I believe that our prolonged silence risks becoming complicity."[113] And from Switzerland Lichtheim wrote to the Zionist leadership criticizing the Jewish organizations of America and England for not "inform[ing] the public, the press and the leading statesmen of what was happening to the Jews of Europe."[114] Wise knew that by keeping "the thing out of the press up to this time, [I am] thus accepting great responsibility if the threat should be executed."[115]

Though all further corroborating news received by the WJC was also passed on to the State Department by Rabbi Wise and Dr. Goldmann,[116] yet in the atmosphere prevalent at that time it would not have mattered how many more similar reports would come from Riegner, Lichtheim or other Jewish sources. The only verification of the stories that might possibly have been accepted by the American public would have been those coming from the State Department. On September 3, Sumner Welles promised Rabbi Wise that the State Department would attempt to verify Riegner's report without delay, and on the basis of that promise Wise had agreed to maintain silence. However it was not until three weeks later that Welles made his first request to American representatives in Europe to ascertain the fate of Europe's Jews. This request was not made in response to the Riegner cable, but to the Lichtheim report that Wise had just sent to Welles. On September 23, Welles sent a copy of the Lichtheim report to the President's special envoy to the Vatican, Myron Taylor, and asked him to "ascertain whether the Vatican has any information which would tend to confirm the reports." If the reports were confirmed, Taylor was asked to discuss with the Pope "any suggestions as to the practical manner in which the civilized forces of public opinion could be utilized in order to prevent a continuation of barbarities."[117]

Nearly two weeks later, Welles wired the State Department representatives in Bern that "Jewish Congress leaders" had been receiving information concerning the slaughter of Jews, and of a deliberate German policy for their complete extermination. Welles wrote that Wise had told him that both

Riegner and Lichtheim had "factual evidence" which they could not send by cable or mail for fear of interception. He requested that Foreign Service officers meet with them and cable him any factual evidence that they might submit.[118]However, there was no general request by the State Department to all its overseas representatives to forward any information they have about the fate of the Jews, nor were they requested to seek such information. Nor does it appear to have been any such request made to the Office of Strategic Services (OSS), the wartime intelligence agency whose prime responsibility was obtaining information concerning Occupied-Europe.

It is not surprising that the State Department did not energetically pursue verification of the Riegner report, though more was expected of Sumner Welles, a liberal and a humanitarian, who was considered sympathetic to the Jewish cause. However, Welles was practically alone among senior State Department officialdom in his concern for the Jews. When the Riegner cable arrived in August some in the State Department not only opposed delivering the message to Dr. Wise, but had also proposed informing the Legation in Bern to suppress any further news of atrocities emanating from Jewish sources. A cable had been drawn up by the European Division directing Harrison and his colleagues to "refrain from accepting information of this kind for possible transmission to third parties."[119] This cable was not sent then, though a similar one was dispatched a half year later (see Chapter XIIa). The same individuals at State had also squelched a cable sent by the British Section of the World Jewish Congress in which they had urged their American counterparts to publicize the Riegner report, to mobilize moral support, and to appeal for action by the Allies to save the Jews of Europe.[120]

The first verifications of Riegner's cables to reach the State Department were two unsolicited reports, one sent by Paul Squire, the U.S. Consul in Geneva, and the other by Harrison from Bern. In late September Dr. Riegner had met with Squire and submitted two memos concerning the fate of Europe's Jews. The first came from Riegner himself, in which he apprised Squire that his source of information was a Swiss Professor, though it had originated from an anti-Nazi officer in the OKW (Military High Command) who was described as "reliable and having close relations with military and industrial circles in Germany". Riegner also reported that trains from Western Europe arriving in

Poland contained only corpses and that the Jews were being killed by injections of air and their bodies used to manufacture soap, glue and lubricants. Today we know that this information was incorrect, though there are still many who believe these stories. The second memo contained copies of two letters that the Sternbuchs had received from Poland. The letters revealed, in coded messages, news of the fate of the Jews in Warsaw.[121]

Harrison's report of September 23rd, also contained information provided him by the Polish Government-in-Exile which described the Jews of Poland being shipped to the East in "lots of five to ten thousand."[122] Two weeks later Harrison informed State that numerous reports "indicate beyond a doubt that Jews are being systematically evacuated from Western European countries to Poland and Russia and from Polish cities to the East to fate unknown."[123] Obviously, neither Squire nor Harrison felt these reports were of urgent interest to the Department, for both were sent to Washington by slow diplomatic post. They arrived only in late October, and Welles did not see them until mid-November.[124]

From the Vatican, Harold Tittman, the American Chargé d'Affaires, cabled the State Department on October 10, notifying it that the Pope had told him that he had heard "of severe measurements taken against non-Aryans" but that "he was unable, as yet, to verify these reports."[125] A full report, detailing the massacres, was dispatched by the Vatican on November 23, but this was also sent by slow mail and only reached the State Department in mid-January. The report described the general German atrocities:

> Mass execution of Jews continues. At Warsaw, Lwow, Wilno, Lublin (etc) – the numbers of Jews killed is numbered by the tens of thousands (each) without mentioning all the others. They are killed by poison gas in chambers especially prepared for the purpose and by machine gun fire [...] Convoys of Jews being led to their death are seen everywhere.

The report spoke of the killing being near-at-hand, and that beggars and old people will then be exterminated "to reduce the number of persons to be fed."[126]

On October 20th, Myron Taylor met with Rabbi Wise, his son James, and Dr. Goldmann. The meeting was held with the express knowledge of the President and the Secretary of State.[127] Taylor told them of his impressions of the situation as he had seen it during his recent trip to Europe. In his report of this meeting, which he sent to Roosevelt and Hull, Taylor unequivocally stated that he had informed the Jewish representatives "That the atrocities in France, Poland and Yugoslavia are confirmed as generally reported". He also told Rabbi Wise that he had left documents with the President "which bear upon the subject."[128] We do not know what these documents were and how Roosevelt responded to them, but most unclear is why Sumner Welles did not accept Taylor's report as corroboration of the atrocities and waited an additional month before confirming the news. Nor is it understandable why Wise and Goldmann did not view Taylor's account as verification of the Riegner cable and had not pressed Welles to release them from their pledge of silence. Certainly Taylor was highly knowledgeable and a more senior Government representative than any of the Foreign Service officers in Switzerland. He was also known to be close to the President. For some unexplainable reason, both Wise and Welles did not react to Taylor's firm confirmation of the killings.

In Europe Jews were being gassed, but in Bern, Harrison was still moving at a leisurely pace. In response to Welles request of October 5, he met with Riegner and Lichtheim more than two weeks later, on the 22nd. The Jewish representatives provided Harrison with additional new information, including first hand reports acquired from newly arrived Jewish refugees in Switzerland. Most importantly, at Harrison's insistence, they revealed that Professor Carl Burckhardt, the Vice-President of the International Committee of the Red Cross, had knowledge of a German plan to liquidate European Jewry. They also handed him a sealed envelope containing the name of the German industrialist, Eduard Schulte, the high-placed source of Riegner's cable, who had been promised that his identity would never be revealed.[129] Riegner and Lichtheim also submitted an Aide-Memoire stating that four million Jews were "on the verge of complete annihilation". It implored that:

a) Action be considered to "alleviate [...] the present most desperate situation";

b) "Public denunciations of the perpetrators of these crimes should be broadcast";

c) "All facts concerning the persecution of the Jews be placed on record[...] and that a special machinery should be created in close cooperation with Jewish bodies to investigate the position"; and, most concretely,

d) "Urgent measures should be taken to save the one million 300,000 Jews living in the semi-independent states of Hungary, Italy, Rumania, Bulgaria and Vichy-France."[130]

Harrison and his staff checked out the new information and on November 23rd sent a cable to the State Department which was, at last, seen by Welles as official a verification of the annihilation of the Jews as could possibly be obtained. On November 24th, Welles wired Dr. Wise summoning him to Washington at once. Wise arrived that same day and was informed by the Under-Secretary that the government now had information "which confirm and justify your deepest fears."[131]Welles also submitted to him a copy of the Riegner-Lichtheim Aide-Memoire, and freed Dr. Wise from his pledge of silence so steadfastly maintained. That evening Wise called a hurried press conference in Washington in which he reported that sources, confirmed by the State Department, had revealed that two million Jews, half of all of those under Nazi occupation, had been killed in a Nazi "extermination campaign."[132] For most Jewish leaders it was now apparent that that their greatest fears had been proven true and that the Germans had already embarked on a campaign to liquidate all the remaining Jews in Europe. The way now lay open for Jewish organizations in America to mobilize public and governmental support in an effort to thwart Hitler's plans.

CHAPTER 6
Breaking the Conspiracy of Silence

(a) Meeting the President
"The mills of the gods grind slowly"
(President Roosevelt at meeting with Jewish leaders–
December, 1942)

Although it was Rabbi Wise's press conference that caught the public eye, the news of the plan to exterminate European Jewry had already begun to emerge. In October the JTA carried the Riegner story in its daily bulletin.[1] In November the editors of *Jewish Frontier* (who previously had buried the Bund report on a back page), issued a special, black-bordered edition devoted entirely to the Jewish tragedy. Perhaps it was Kubowitzki, a Labor-Zionist, who had leaked the information accumulated at World Jewish Congress headquarters, hoping by that act to break "the conspiracy of silence" with which he differed. The magazine proclaimed that "In occupied territories of Europe, a policy is now being put into effect whose avowed object is the extermination of a whole people."[2]

However it was Rabbi Wise's claim that the information he had presented at his press conference had been confirmed by the State Department, which made his revelations appear trustworthy, and was therefore picked up by the press. Most American newspapers carried news of Wise's press conference, though once again, the most prestigious dailies – The *N.Y. Times, Washington Post, L.A. Times* and *Christian Science Monitor* – placed the news on the inner pages making the story appear as neither overly important, nor very certain. Despite Wise's attempt to have the information appear to have come from the State Department, most newspapers, in headlining the story, made it clear that Dr. Wise was the source of the claim that two million Jews had already been murdered.[3] In the short article, which appeared on page 10 of the *New York Times* it explicitly stated that the State Department was not the source of the information.[4]

The State Department officials who all along had been opposed to disseminating news of the Holocaust, were riled at Wise's implications that they had confirmed his information, and they pressured him in the future he desist from so implying.[5] They also probably made it clear to reporters checking out the story, that they had no hand in corroborating the information. The lack of clear-cut confirmation by the government led some to believe that America was again being asked to swallow wild atrocity tales. The liberal Protestant weekly, *Christian Century*, characterized the story as "unpleasantly reminiscent of the 'cadaver factory' lie", which was one of the propaganda myths of the First World War. It questioned whether "any good purpose is served by the publication of such charges."[6] Nor was the *Christian Century* alone in this reaction. Max Gottschalk, head of HICEM (the Jewish immigration society), also accused Rabbi Wise of lending himself to "atrocity propaganda".[7]

Though the pledge to maintain silence had prevented Jewish organizations from carrying out acts of public protest, they had been meeting on an irregular and informal basis ever since they first met to discuss the Sternbuch and Riegner cables on September 6th. Although verification had not as yet arrived, a small group representing some of the major organizations met on November 5th at the initiative of the 'Congress movement'. Dr. Goldmann proposed a three-point plan of action which, despite minor differences among the participants, was accepted in whole.[8] The plan called for:

> a) A meeting of Jewish leaders with President Roosevelt, at which a memorandum would be presented to the President describing the plight of European Jewry. There were to be no specific requests for action, nor was the President expected to respond immediately. All that was asked of Roosevelt was that he issue a statement condemning the atrocities in general, "but emphasizing the Jewish end." This seemed to them the most they could achieve. Goldmann told the meeting that he and Wise had already approached Welles, and that he had agreed to take up the matter with the President.

b) That a memo condemning the atrocities be sent to Roosevelt by the heads of the three major religions in America. The President's response should be made to these groups. This had been suggested to Goldmann and Wise by David Niles, a Jew who was an adviser at the White House.

c) That a conference of "important Americans" be convened to deal with the horrors confronting European Jewry. They hoped that "Such a conference would result in the flow of publicity material on all fronts, and would create a nucleus of a permanent committee to carry forward the necessary work in connection with the continued oppression".

It was obvious that those at the meeting had no faith neither in Jewish pleading, nor Jewish pressure, achieving any result. It was necessary to organize non-Jewish Americans to press for action. Libby Schultz of the American Jewish Congress, who coordinated the activities, reported that invitations to such a conference had already been sent, and several leading personages had responded to the call. Why this form of action was never further developed by the well-connected organizations who attended the meeting is not clear. Perhaps they thought the time was not yet ripe for such a summons. However, eight months later the outsiders in the 'Bergson Group' used this same method most successfully, both to publicize the facts of the Holocaust and to form a core of prominent individuals to pressure the government for rescue.

The meeting adjourned with a decision to constitute a permanent planning committee consisting of one representative each from the American Jewish Congress, American Jewish Committee, Jewish Labor Committee, B'nai Brith and Agudas Israel. On November 11th, Rabbi Wise sent invitations to the five groups. The AJC replied that they already belonged to the General Jewish Council, but agreed to send a representative to that specific meeting. Wise responded, that if that were the case, then the committee would only be a temporary one and would disband after meeting with the President.[9]

The first meeting, of what later came to be the Joint Emergency Committee, was held on November 25th, the day after Wise's Washington press conference. Whether this meeting had been previously scheduled for that date, or came only as a result of the news conference is not clear. The meeting was attended by the four major Jewish defense organizations, and by both Agudas Israel and the Synagogue Council of America, an umbrella organization of the three main religious streams of American Jewry. Though Dr. Goldmann attended, the World Jewish Congress was not formally considered part of the new body, which was to be composed only of American Jewish organizations.

Plans were presented which were further worked out by a sub-committee that met on November 30th.[10] Two major actions were decided upon – one, a meeting of the committee with the President, and the other a 'Day of Mourning' on December 2nd, the day after Chanukah, to be held in Jewish communities throughout the United States. They decided that at the meeting with Roosevelt only a short statement would be read. A detailed document summarizing all the information they had regarding the massacres of the Jews would then be left with the President. No proposals for concrete action were offered. It was hoped only that the President would make a statement condemning the atrocities as he had done after the Nazi massacre at Lidice. Though the number of Jews massacred were many thousand-fold larger than those murdered at Lidice, news of atrocities against the Jews never captured the imagination of the American press and public as did the slaughter at Lidice.[11] In June, 1942, in reprisal for the assassination of Reinhardt Heydrich (Chief of the SD – Security Police), 190 men from the Czech town of Lidice were murdered, and the entire town razed.

The second major action, a 'Day of Mourning', was to be held concurrently with Jewish communities in 29 countries throughout the world. The memorial event was first intended to center around religious services in Synagogues. It grew in scope when Jacob Pat (JLC) reported that David Dubinsky, a leading Jewish trade-union leader, had obtained support from trade union locals representing a half million workers to carry out a ten minute work stoppage on the 'Day of Mourning'. This mass work stoppage was the only impressive outcome of all the committee's plans. They had spoken of obtaining radio coverage, but only two minor New York stations had agreed to present programs on the subject. Wise had sent telegrams to 550 American newspapers requesting editorial responses to the atrocities, but at first only few complied. Previously proposed plans to contact the OWI, and to request leading non-Jewish personalities to speak out against the atrocities, had not been pursued. Despite the major effort of the Jewish organizations to bring the news of the killings to the attention of the public, the 'Day of Mourning' did not receive much coverage in the American press.[12]

Though the plans for meeting the President were already set in motion in early November, it was only on December 2nd that Rabbi Wise wrote the President and formally requested the meeting. In his letter, Wise described the news of the atrocities that had been received. To underline his loyalty to the Administration, anticipating that the President would respond in kind, Rabbi Wise boasted of his success "in keeping these [the Riegner and Lichtheim reports] out of the press" as requested.[13]

On December 8th representatives of the Jewish community met with the President for half an hour. The delegation did not include Agudas Israel, as Roosevelt's secretary, 'Pa' Watson, had requested that only five representatives attend the meeting. Rabbi Wise read a statement which asked Roosevelt "to raise your voice – in behalf of the Jews of Europe" and "to warn the Nazis that they will be held to strict accountability for their crimes". Aside from a further appeal to establish an American commission "to receive and examine all evidence of Nazi barbarities", no other proposals were made.[14]

The written memorandum submitted to the President was a resume of all the information the Jewish organizations had gathered in the last few months. It offered no proposals for action, but alluded to the one response they sought from the President. The memorandum stated that

> The grinding process of slow, but nonetheless inexorable, extermination has never abated. Nevertheless, the Nazi regime has sometimes retreated in the face of energetic and clear-

cut warnings on the part of President Roosevelt and Prime Minister Churchill.

The Jewish leaders as yet had no tangible rescue proposals other than warnings to the Germany. However it is surprising that the one concrete scheme cited by the delegation, the possibility of military reprisal as a deterrent to Nazi atrocities, was only mentioned in the negative. The delegation appears to have been appealing to the President to rule out such methods as bombing since "they have almost invariably resulted in a new burst of mass murders of Jews."[15]

Roosevelt, as usual, monopolized most of the conversation. He attempted to charm his Jewish listeners by telling them that he had appointed Herbert Lehman (a Jew) as his administrator for relief, because he (FDR) was a sadist. He said that he wanted to have the pleasure of going to Germany after the war and "see Junkers beg Lehman for bread." Roosevelt also told the delegation that he was aware of the facts, which is not surprising since Taylor had reported them to the President more than a month before. The President tried to explain his difficulties in handling the situation as due to having to deal with a madman (Hitler). Roosevelt hedged on making a strong condemnation of the German war crimes as "it is not in the best interest of the Allied cause to make it appear that the entire German people are murderers." He did, however, agree to issue a statement as requested.[16]

The statement that followed the conference was not issued by the President himself, but was written and released by the members of the delegation. It reiterated Roosevelt's declaration on the accountability of the criminals and his warning that "The mills of the Gods grind slowly, but they grind exceedingly small." The release also declared that the President had promised "to take every possible step [to stop the killings] [...] and save those who may still be saved,"[17] notwithstanding that Roosevelt himself had never made such a statement.

Though any activities concerning the President were usually considered newsworthy by the American press, his meeting with the Jewish delegation received the usual treatment reserved for news of the Holocaust, and was barely reported on the inner pages of the dailies.[18] How little an impression the meeting made on the press, and therefore on the general American public, can be judged from a report by Dorothy Thompson. Ms. Thompson, a well-known, liberal journalist of German descent, had been asked by the WJC to meet with American journalists in an effort to mobilize their support in publicizing news of the fate of European Jewry. In reporting on her meeting, Thompson revealed that "These newspapermen never heard about the Jewish delegation that met with the President."[19] If news of the meeting with the President had eluded the attention of newsmen who sat at the very center of information, how could the general public possibly be expected to know?

Meanwhile more news confirming the Final Solution had been reaching the press, the State Department and America's Allies, and pressure was slowly building up for some formal condemnation of the Nazi atrocities. On December 9th, the State Department received an aide-memoire from the Polish Foreign Minister Raczynski, in which he explicitly defined the Nazi "aims at total extermination of the Jewish population of Poland". Raczynski chronicled the development of the Nazi campaign against Polish Jewry. He recounted the use of gas for killing at Chelmno and described the liquidation of the Warsaw Ghetto where, he stated, only 40,000 ration cards were distributed in October (i.e. only that number of Jews were still alive in a ghetto which once contained nearly 500,000 Jews). Raczynski claimed that Himmler had ordered the extermination of 50% of Polish Jews by the end of 1942.[20] The essence of this report had appeared in a press release from the Polish Government-in-Exile on the same day that Wise held his press conference in Washington. What was new and of particular importance in Raczynski's report was his request for a formal United Nations condemnation of the mass murders. The British Government, under heavy pressure from the British public, from the churches and even from Parliament, was the first to respond. Their first draft of a proposed declaration condemning the atrocities was received with caution by the State Department.

The State Department's 'expert' on Jewish affairs, Robert Reams was totally opposed to issuing such a declaration. He cautioned his superiors that it would be taken as a confirmation of the reports on the massacre of the Jews. Consequently, he feared, "The way will be open for further pressure from interested groups for action which might affect the war effort." As for Reams, the only solution for "all the unhappy people of Europe" was to win the war. Declarations, he claimed, could do no good "and may in effect induce harsher measures towards the Jewish population of Europe."[21]Reams also tried to convince the British to drop their proposal for a declaration. He warned the First Secretary at the British Embassy that issuing such a declaration would expose all the governments of the United Nations "to pressure [...] to do something more specific to aid."[22] The State Department's only contribution to the British draft was the deletion of a few unambiguous words, thereby hedging, somewhat, on official confirmation of the news.

The United Nations declaration, signed by eleven countries, was released on December 17th. It clearly stated that the German authorities "are now carrying into effect Hitler's oft repeated intention to exterminate the Jewish people in Europe." The Allies once again condemned Nazi atrocities and vowed "to ensure that those responsible for these crimes shall not escape retribution." But the declaration contained no word of hope for those condemned to death, something to suggest that the Allies were considering ways to alleviate their suffering. The Allies only stated their resolve (which in any case was known) "to overthrow the barbarous Hitlerite tyranny."[23]The only value of the declaration lay in its clear statement that there existed a German plan to exterminate, specifically, the Jews, and in the proclaimed determination of the Allies to prosecute the guilty at war's end. This time the source of information on the massacres was not a pronouncement by the Jewish organizations, but an official declaration made by eleven Allied nations. It is not surprising, therefore, that this news received better coverage in the press than had earlier reports. It even made page one of the *N.Y. Times*, the first time that it afforded news of the massacres such coverage.[24] But in the rush of war, and of other matters that engrossed the public, even this report quickly vanished and made no lasting impression.

While this flurry of activity was occurring during the first half of December, it was still not clear how American Jewry would organize to deal with the situation. Nor was it evident what action the Jewish organizations would take. The initiative in obtaining the news of the Holocaust; in presenting it to the Administration; in organizing the 'Day of Mourning' and in obtaining the meeting with the President, had been handled mostly by the World and American Jewish Congresses. The Temporary Committee had been set up with the express assurance of Rabbi Wise that it would disperse after presenting its case to President Roosevelt. The American Jewish Committee had made its commitment to join the committee contingent on it being only a temporary body.

The American Jewish Congress leadership may have also preferred such an arrangement. The other three defense organizations had been working together in the framework of the General Jewish Council, which the American Jewish Congress had left the previous year in a bitter quarrel over funding. Both sides still carried deep scars and only grudgingly had agreed to cooperate on the meeting with the President. Furthermore, the AJCong leaders were constantly aware that cooperation with the AJC meant toning down their activities, and limiting their actions to those that fitted into the quiet diplomacy favored by the Committee. Though no formal decisions had been taken as yet by the AJCong regarding specific plans of action, they were, nevertheless, contemplating a campaign to mobilize public support and create public pressure for Allied intervention to ease the lot of European Jewry. They believed that the AJC would not countenance such actions.

The American Jewish Congress had received a joint cable on November 10th sent by the Jewish Agency Executive and the Vaad Leumi (the Jewish National Committee) in Palestine informing them of the massacres of Jews and urging them to arouse the world conscience to protest the killings.[25] The cable was sent in response to the Lichtheim report, which had been received by the Jewish Agency Executive a few days earlier. The report by the Zionist representative in Switzerland had taken nearly a month to arrive in Palestine[26] Two days later the Governing Council of the AJCong met to discuss plans for action. In addition to the previous decisions taken by the Executive they decided: a) to look into the possibility of sending relief parcels to the Jews in the ghettos; b) to find havens for the refugees (the Virgin Islands were again to be explored); c) to increase the number of Jewish children from France who would be permitted to enter the U.S. A discussion ensued whether to link the Jewish sufferings with those of other conquered peoples in Europe. Louis Segal, of the Labor Zionists, warned of the danger of such an approach. Irving Miller, however, informed the Governing Council that Dr. Wise, upon the suggestion of Sumner Welles, "had finally consented [...] to link the Jewish problem with that of other civilian populations." The Council concurred in the actions already taken by Dr. Wise, though in the end, the massacres were presented to the President as a specifically Jewish issue.[27]

At the end of November, American Zionist leaders began receiving urgent calls for action from Palestine. Knowledge of the actual fate of European Jewry had reached the Yishuv in Palestine, by chance, at exactly the same time as Wise's press conference in Washington. In mid-November a group of Palestinian Jewish nationals, who had been trapped in Poland since the outbreak of the war, returned home as part of a civilian exchange between Britain and Germany. These Jews, who had personally witnessed the 'Final Solution' in action, were interviewed over the next few days by leaders of the Jewish Agency. Initially these leaders reacted the same way as others when first confronted with the startling information about the mass liquidation of the Jews: 'It couldn't be, it wasn't possible'. But after a week they reported to the public the crux of the testimonies they had gathered, excluding only information whose veracity they questioned. This report appeared in the Palestinian press on November 23rd, the day before Rabbi Wise's press conference, and it stirred the Yishuv to call for rescue action.[28]

However the Jewish Agency Executive felt that the possibility of their influencing the Allies to act was very limited. It therefore appealed to the Jewish communities of the world, particularly to the large and supposedly influential Jewish community of America, to induce their governments to rescue. Henrietta Szold, head of the Jewish Agency's Youth Aliyah, cabled the Hadassah Women's Organization, stressing that hundreds of thousands of Jewish children had been massacred. She urged them to take the lead in "the formation of a women's world organization under the presidency of Eleanor Roosevelt with the object of removing endangered children from Nazi occupied territory."[29] The Zionist Emergency Committee, as well, received cables from Jerusalem urging it to initiate rescue action. The WJC and Joint were both asked to send representatives to the neutral countries of Europe to establish contact with the Jews in the occupied countries.

The appeal from Palestine was discussed at a special meeting of the Zionist Emergency Committee held two days before the meeting with the President. It was decided to set up a special joint sub-committee together with the American Jewish Congress to work out a plan within 48 hours and to determine which organizations, both Jewish and non-Jewish, would be asked to join in the campaign – the Zionists were well aware that both they and the AJCong had neither the apparatus nor the funds to carry out so massive a program of public relations on their own.[30] It was also decided that it would be wrong to emphasize the Zionist solution, but they should concentrate on finding ways of stopping the Nazi policy of destruction. They concluded that only when Jews were saved "and public opinion aroused, the committee should in due course suggest Zionism as the ultimate remedy."[31]

Meyer Weisgal, Chaim Weizmann's close associate, was designated to recommend a course of action for the Zionist movement. In a proposal submitted to the Zionist leadership, Weisgal recommended that the Zionist movement concentrate on explaining the reasons for the particular fate of the Jews, i.e. their anomalous situation as a nation without a homeland. Weisgal pessimistically assessed that American Jewry "can't do much practically for the Jews under Hitler". He did believe that if the Jews were given a homeland after the war it would guarantee, at least, that such tragedies would not recur. Weisgal proposed to the Zionist movement "not [to] give up concrete Zionist proposals for the tears and sympathy of America, for it won't guarantee the future of the Jewish people." He declared that if the campaign for rescue did not include Zionist objectives, because certain Jewish organizations (such as AJC and the JLC) would not participate on that basis, then the rescue effort should be left to the endeavors of the American Jewish Congress. The Zionist movement, as such, should not be involved. Weisgal expressed his certainty that AJCong would handle the job well.[32]

The American Jewish Congress, meeting in separate session, also decided that the initiative for rescue and relief activities should be left jurisdictionally in their hands.[33] They would ask other organizations and individuals to join in their efforts, but they ruled out the possibility of joint action with the Zionist Emergency Council. Rabbi Wise, who a week earlier had stated that rescue "was a Zionist matter as well as of general Jewish concern", did not oppose the decision. What with Weisgal's recommendation and the AJCong decision, the

Zionist Emergency Council readily reversed its previous decision and now concurred in the division of efforts. The AJCong would assume the initiatives for rescue, while the Zionist Emergency Council would carry out the struggle for the creation of a Jewish State.[34]

The only Zionist group opposing the decision was Hadassah. Ten days after the Zionist Emergency Council decision, Hadassah asked the Zionist movements to reconsider its decision, claiming that the Jewish Agency directives had "placed responsibility on all Zionists to act as such" in attempting to rescue European Jewry. The Zionist Emergency Council decided that in light of the American Jewish Congress position there was no point in reversing its stand.[35]

Though on the one hand, the Hadassah women strenuously favored acquiescing in the Jewish Agency request for a Zionist initiative in rescue efforts, on the other hand they rejected the request to organize an international women's organization for the rescue of children. In December, Hadassah discussed the proposal with other Jewish, and non-Jewish, women's organization. In January they reached the conclusion that "the plan was unfeasible."[36]Hadassah cabled Henrietta Szold that they believed that "such over all organizations can be useful for channeling public opinion, but are useless for fund-raising and intensive practical action."[37] It is not clear why Hadassah felt that even if such an organization succeeded 'only' in mobilizing American public opinion that was not reason enough to form such a group. Perhaps they too were despondent at the general lack of public response to news of the massacres, and believed that nothing would come of their efforts. Yet had such an organization been established, headed by the President's wife (there was a reasonable possibility that she would have agreed), it could have done much to bring the news of the fate of the Jews to the attention of the American public.

The American Jewish Congress had taken upon itself to be the vanguard in the effort to rescue European Jewry, and throughout December it considered bold initiatives to activate public and governmental support for rescue efforts, though the actual form of these efforts was not as yet clear. The arguments which arose every time rescue was discussed – whether first to mobilize the Jewish or the non-Jewish public – was now resolved by a decision to work in both directions simultaneously. There were proposals for a mass procession in New York City of hundreds of thousands of Jews, with Jewish shops closed; Jewish students leaving school to participate in the march; work in factories with high concentrations of Jews to be halted. Secondly, a massive public relations campaign was envisaged with paid ads. Professional, ethnic and religious groups were to be activated, as well as local politicians, to condemn the horrors and to demand rescue. The third avenue of endeavors was to concentrate in Washington, where attempts would be made to have the U.S. Congress pass a resolution condemning the atrocities. They would also try to get the OWI to disseminate the information both in America and in Europe and to bring the government to act for rescue.

Not much, however, evolved from this burst of enthusiasm. The proposed procession was never held, though a rally at Madison Square Garden was organized three months later. Only one ad signed by a number of leading liberal German-Americans appeared. In December, the Federal Council of Churches of Christ decided to express its concern for the fate of the Jews by organizing a 'Day of Compassion' in its tens of thousands of affiliated congregations. This did not take place, however, until May 1943, and it appears to have made a very meager impression upon the public.[38] The same fate met attempts to secure Congressional action. On March 9, 1943, the Senate passed a resolution and a week later, on March 18, so did the House of Representatives. The resolution once again condemned Nazi atrocities and promised that the guilty would be brought to justice. However, all attempts to add to the motion a call for government action to save Europe's Jews failed,[39] nor did the resolution succeed in either publicizing news of the Holocaust or in moving the public to demand rescue.

(b) "Our friend in the White House"

By the end of 1942 it was quite clear that European Jewry was being destroyed. In light of such a threat, how then did American Jewry and its leadership not protest forcefully and attempt to place the issue of Jewish suffering in Europe on the agenda of the Administration? Why did they not "proclaim hunger strikes to the end", or "organize daily and weekly marches to the White House", as Elie Wiesel demands today?[40] Why did they not press for opening the gates of America for those who succeeded in escaping from the inferno, as Rafael Medoff implies they should have done.[41] Why of all the plans proposed in the various committees the only ones that appear to have been implemented were the 'Day of Mourning', whose effect was minimal, and the half-hour meeting with the President, that did not succeed in forwarding rescue efforts even one iota? Why, asks Medoff, was the American Jewish leadership afraid to attack the President and his Administration for their callousness when an entire people were being exterminated? On the contrary, American Jewry placed all its trust in Roosevelt, their 'friend in the White House', hoping that he would do everything possible to save Jews. Is Medoff correct in claiming that "as the long, dark night of Nazi horror descended upon Europe's Jews, the leaders of the American Jewish community seemed to be turning a deaf ear to the anguished cries of their brethren?"[42]

Some of the proposed plans were indeed carried out. However, the effect of all these activities was negligible and unavailing, and we tend today to forget that such steps were actually taken. The meager response of the shapers of public opinion in the United States, and of the political, moral and intellectual leadership to the pleas of the Jewish organizations had a profound effect on the Jewish leaders. They were led to believe that it was not possible to seek compassion from the leadership of American society. If their pleas to the media and to leading Americans did not bring results, what then, they reasoned, could they expect from an appeal to the general American public. The Jewish leadership concluded that militant action, insistent demands and attacks against the nation's leaders would only exacerbate antisemitism, and not provide any help to the Jews of Europe. This assessment was a weighty factor that curbed the activities of the Jewish organizations. This appeared constantly in their protocols and is seen in personal letters of Jews active at that time. Occasionally, they even made their apprehensions public. The Bulletin of the Council of Jewish Federations (December 1, 1944) stated: "a feeling of perplexity was felt in certain circles from the aggressive tone in the ads (of the CJA) which might create antisemitic responses."[43]

There were a few Jewish leaders who did not flinch, and who insisted that the Jewish community protest, without regard to antisemitism. However, generally speaking, these were not American citizens, and were closer in their mentality to the Jews of Eastern Europe than to the Jewish community in the U.S. Illustrative of this attitude was Jacob Pat of the Jewish Labor Committee. Pat was the only one who reacted angrily when Rabbi Wise reported that Sumner Welles had requested that they maintain silence about the Riegner cable. He hurled in the face of the other Jewish leaders that "If Polish Jews will be annihilated, I don't care what is going to happen to the Jews here and to you, and to *your government!*"[44] (my italics-A.H.). Medoff describes the reaction of Bergson to the warning of Senator Lucas that criticism by the Jews of the government's stand on rescue may only increase antisemitism: "Bergson was not impressed [by the warning]."[45] But the American Jewish leaders were certainly moved by this warning, and as leaders of the Jewish community in the U.S., it is not surprising that they responded in such a manner.

Wyman believes that antisemitism was only a minor factor in limiting the efforts and responses of American Jewry. In his opinion, despite antisemitism "Many thousands of Jews were publicly vocal on a variety of controversial issues."[46] However, there is a vast difference in being an American Jew involved in the internal politics of his country, or one demanding that the U.S. act for the Jews of Europe. This is especially true when many Americans feared that this would affect the running of the war, and would cost many additional lives of their soldier boys.

As we have seen, this sensitivity to taking a public stand on controversial issues was already apparent in the two years prior to America's entry into the war. In those years Jewish leaders were cautious not to appear too publicly on such issues as American aid to Britain, for fear of jeopardizing the results. They also were apprehensive lest their support would promote native antisemitism. How much Jews shrunk from expressing unpopular views in public can be seen in the 'Anglo-Saxon' names that Jewish Communist leaders adopted for themselves (e.g., John Gates – née Israel Regenstreif, or James Allen – née Solomon Auerbach[47]), so that they could work among the American public without suspicion. Not only Communist leaders changed their names. Nearly all Jewish actors in Hollywood or on Broadway (and they were many), had to change their names as well (e.g.: Paul Muni – née Munio Weisfish, Edward G. Robinson – née Edward Goldberg) to be accepted by the public and so further their careers.

Medoff is correct in claiming that until March 1943 the Jewish organizations refused to publicly demand the opening of the gates of America, and when they did, it was "minimalistic" and "still inadequate in relation to the European crisis."[48] Medoff, however, does not explain the reasons for this stand: fear of antisemitism, and the suspicion that such a demand would only strengthen the claim that America was fighting the war for the Jews. Above all, they feared that a demand for the entry of Jews into the U.S. would not pass in Congress, and would only create the opposite reaction, i.e. barring the gates hermetically to the Jewish refugees. This feeling was based on the realities of the U.S. during those years. Friends in Congress and in the Administration warned the Jewish organizations not to raise the question of immigration because of "the prevalence of antisemitic feelings in Congress."[49]

The deportations from Vichy France to Auschwitz that began in July 1942, shocked the American public. They were more shocked by the deportation of tens of thousands of French Jews than by the expulsion of millions of Jews in Eastern Europe.[50] Congressman Celler proposed a bill calling for the U.S. to provide a haven for any person in France who can prove that he is a candidate for deportation or imprisonment by the Nazi authorities or the Vichy government. The Congressional committee that was to handle this legislation did not even deal with the proposal, and thus it was dropped from the agenda.[51] In November, the President asked Congress to pass a bill that would grant him, for the duration of the war, freer action in matters of customs, visas and immigration. His intent was to provide a response to the special conditions created by the war, which required neither routine, nor bureaucratic, handling. Not for a moment did Roosevelt think of using these powers to permit Jewish refugees to enter the country. However his opponents believed that was his intention. *Newsweek* magazine wrote that "The ugly truth is that anti-Semitism was a definite factor in the bitter opposition to the President's request for power to suspend immigration laws for the duration."[52]

The opponents of immigration foiled this bill, proposed by the President himself, by preventing the House from debating the issue until Congress recessed in December.[53] On the other hand, there were still hundreds of proposals in Congress during the war which called for a total halt to immigration, or to limiting the quotas to a bare minimum,[54] this despite the fact that during the war years only 10% of those quotas were filled.[55] In a discussion held with the Speaker of the House, Sam Rayburn, and Vice-President Wallace, Roosevelt raised the possibility of easing immigration restrictions. Rayburn made it perfectly clear that such a proposal would meet stiff opposition in Congress. FDR immediately dropped the idea.[56]

In the fall of 1942 the Administration made an unusual gesture to absorb Jewish refugees. When the Vichy government began to deport Jewish adults and thousands of Jewish children were torn from their parents, Eleanor Roosevelt and the PACPR appealed to the State Department to allow 5000 Jewish children from France to enter the U.S. This time the State Department acquiesced, though only for 1000 youngsters.[57] Not only did Roosevelt support this plea, he agreed to allow all 5000 to enter. He placed only one condition for his agreement – that no publicity be given the decision.[58] Roosevelt did not place this reservation out of modesty – that certainly was not his style. As a clever politician who knew the public mood, he feared angry reactions from Congress and the electorate and did not value the 'points' that he would gain by his action from Jewish or liberal circles.

Though Roosevelt always gave the impression of being fearless, in reality, according to his biographer MacGregor Burns, "He seemed unduly sensitive to both Congressional and public opinion."[59] Roosevelt was correct in his assessment of the political situation. In the Congressional elections held a month later, the forces which opposed his liberal policies were strengthened. During the next two years, the U.S. Congress was controlled by a right-wing coalition composed of Republicans and conservative Democrats from the South.

But even the Congress that yet sat in 1942 was not outstanding in its concern for the suffering of oppressed minorities. On November 23rd, a day before Wise's press conference at which he announced the news of the Holocaust, the U.S. Senate re-endorsed the Poll Tax Law. The purpose of that law, common in the South, was to prevent Black citizens from carrying out their constitutional right to vote in elections.[60] If the U.S. Senate acted thus towards a large minority of citizens, then serving in the Armed Forces in the hundreds of thousands, what could American Jews expect if they came before Congress to plead for aid to people who were not even American citizens? And all this was at a time when the U.S. itself was caught up in a bitter war.

Like all other Americans, the thoughts of the Jewish leaders were burdened with considerations of the war, which until the end of 1942 leaned towards the Axis powers. From the slogan tossed to them by the Administration, that the best way to save the Jews of Europe was by a speedy victory, American Jewry understood that in the dire straits of the Allies, they must, first and foremost, guarantee victory over the Axis powers. As long as Germany held the upper hand, the Jewish leaders were not even certain that real possibilities existed to aid the Jews of Europe.

In the course of 1942, nearly all of the many requests concerning European Jewry made to the various governmental offices, to the Allies, and to the international organizations, came up against barriers of callousness and bureaucratic delays. The truth was that the Jewish representatives had no ready answer to those officials who claimed that it was impossible to aid Jews in Occupied-Europe because the German authorities prevented them from doing so. When James Wise met the representative of the Red Cross in Washington he concluded that there was only the slightest possibility of convincing either the Red Cross, or the Germans, to recognize the Jews as Civilian Internees.[61]

The 'Bergson Boys', until December 1942 had not dealt with attempts to rescue the Jews of Europe. Therefore, they had not experienced the difficulties involved in moving the various agencies to act for rescue. As a result the group entered the arena with fresh forces, at a period when the war began to tilt toward the side of the Allies and the government and public were more prepared to listen to requests for aid. The 'Bergson Boys' held one other advantage in their struggle for rescue action, their young and dynamic leadership.

Wyman includes among the failings of the American Jewish community during the Holocaust, the lack of a young and resourceful leadership.[62] He quotes an article from the Jewish press in 1944 that claimed that the American Jewish leadership at that time was nearly identical with that of ten years earlier. The reasons were probably connected with events in the American Jewish community during the Thirties, when all energy was focused on economic survival during the depression. Few found time to involve themselves in organizations. The 'universalistic' outlook, as previously mentioned, also attracted many young Jews, especially those concerned with the social issues. But above all, we must remember that during the war years, most young Jews who may have been an initiating force in the community were serving in the Armed Forces. Those not drafted were involved, each in their own way, in the war effort. The youngest member among the American Jewish Congress activists during the war was James Wise, the Rabbi's son, who then was already in his forties. In contrast, the 'Bergson Boys' were all young men, who until 1943 were exempt from the draft because they were not U.S. citizens, nor did they volunteer for service.

Medoff claims that one of the major factors that limited the Jewish response to events in Europe was that "the American Jewish Congress was not willing as yet to challenge Roosevelt."[63] He is quite right in this assertion, but does not explain the crucial factors that shaped their conduct. Unquestionably, one of the most important causes for the decision not to embark on a strong public campaign for the Jews of Europe was their fervent desire to avoid attacking the President. There were three major reasons for this: a) They did not want to criticize the President, nor weaken him, neither in the war against Germany nor in his struggle against the forces of the Right. b) They were afraid of turning him against themselves. c) In their hearts they still hoped (and some believed) that Roosevelt would take the necessary steps to ease the agony of European Jews.

As mentioned, Wiesel accused the Jewish leadership of having been "taken in by Roosevelt's personality", as though that was the sole reason for their support of the President. Critics claim that Roosevelt captivated American Jewry with his charm, soothed them with his words, and bought their silence with a few empty gestures and therefore they were so entranced by him. This simplistic criticism voiced by Roosevelt's critics concerning the loyalty of American Jews to the President shows that they are unable to grasp the real reasons for this 'blind' admiration for the President.

Undoubtedly, Roosevelt's charm influenced the Jewish leaders, much as it influenced many others and beguiled them. Years later many affirmed these features of Roosevelt's personality. Dr. Israel Goldstein, who participated in the meeting with the President in December 1942, pictures Roosevelt as a man who "had a deep understanding of human nature and how to play up its weaknesses."[64] Even a sharp politician like Emanuel Celler who sat in Congress for 30 years, testified that he himself fell prey to Roosevelt's traps, and that

> Whenever I visited Roosevelt on official business, I found a man adroit, voluble, assured and smiling. I was never quite sure he was interested in the purpose of my visit; we spent so little time on it. Mostly he talked [...] and when I left, I found that he had committed himself to no point of view[...]At the end of each visit I realized that I had been hypnotized.[65]

However, there were more serious grounds for the devotion of American Jews to Roosevelt. One reason for their support was the feeling Roosevelt gave them of being equals in American society. The Twenties were a period in which pressures were exerted on ethnic minorities to adjust to the majority Anglo-Saxon (WASP) society that dominated the country.[66] One of the more important changes in American society brought about by the Roosevelt Administration was raising the status of ethnic and religious minorities in the U.S. and imbuing them with the sense that they were full partners in American society. This wasn't 'cultural pluralism' as yet, but Roosevelt's approach to social equality blazed the trail to the pluralistic concept that later was accepted. According to the historian, William Leuchtenberg, "Under the New Deal, new groups took their place in the sun. It was not merely that they received benefits they had not had before but that they were 'recognized' as having a place in the commonwealth."[67]

There were also concrete expressions to this sense of equality felt by the Jews, which were not simply other aspects of Roosevelt's 'policy of gestures'. Roosevelt appointed many Jews to important posts and the number of Jews in his close circle of friends and advisors was conspicuous. These included Secretary of Treasury Henry Morgenthau Jr.; Governor Herbert Lehman; Professor Felix Frankfurter, who until his appointment to the Supreme Court served as Roosevelt's main 'talent scout'; Samuel Rosenman, his chief speech writer and political advisor; Ben Cohen; David Lillienthal; Bernard Baruch; David Niles; Sidney Hillman and many others. Jews not only stood out in leading positions in the Administration. Young Jews, university graduates who could not find employment because of the depression or as a result of discrimination, filled many middle-level positions open to young talents in the 'alphabet' agencies created by the New Deal.

One might presume that this was simply good politics and the reason for Roosevelt's appointment of Jews. He received almost total support from the Jewish electorate, particularly in New York which was especially important because of the large number of New York State ballots in the electoral college. However, was 'cornering' the Jewish vote worthwhile to Roosevelt considering the hostility that he engendered as a result of his friendly attitude towards Jews? Jews were then only 3.6% of the American population. The many posts Jews held in the government led to Roosevelt's Administration being labeled the 'Jew Deal'. During all those years public opinion polls showed that 41 to 58% of the American public believed that Jews had too much power in the U.S.[68] As many as 24% of those polled expressed their belief that the Jews constituted a menace to the U.S.[69] Those voters were not pleased with the prominent role that Roosevelt assigned Jews in his Administration.

Roosevelt paid a high price politically for his appointment of so many Jews. In every election campaign he was attacked as being a captive of the Jews. In the 1944 presidential campaign the slogan "Clear it with Sidney" [Sidney Hillman] was widely used, and was meant to infer that so long as Roosevelt was in power, it was the Jews who would really be running the country. Despite all this, Roosevelt never disavowed his Jewish assistants. During all those years Roosevelt remained loyal to America's Jews as American citizens. It is therefore not surprising that American Jews maintained their loyalty to Roosevelt. Roosevelt had no need to worry that he would lose the Jewish vote, for in the political situation at that time it did not appear to the Jews that they had any other alternative but to support Roosevelt.

The fidelity of the Jews to Roosevelt was due not only to his positive attitude towards them. American Jews identified almost totally with the policies of the New Deal. The two main components of Roosevelt's policies – his liberal, social policies as a solution for the internal problems of the U.S., and his 'internationalist' approach in foreign policy – were completely in keeping with the political outlook of America's Jews. The fact that these policies created many enemies for Roosevelt only furthered Jewish support for the President, and their desire to 'close ranks' behind him.

Roosevelt's liberalism expressed itself in his belief that the duty of government is to concern itself with the welfare of its citizens. These beliefs are also rooted in Jewish ethno-religious values.[70] In addition, not only in the U.S., and not only at that time, Jews viewed liberalism as the main guarantor of their civil liberties and as a bar to antisemitism.[71] This conviction of American Jewry has remained intact until this very day despite the socio-economic changes in the American Jewish community in the past generation.[72] The 'internationalist' approach to foreign policy also fitted the world outlook of American Jews who, more than any other ethnic group, favored American intervention in world affairs.[73] The very import of internationalist policies meant stopping the expansion of Nazism that threatened Jewish existence in Europe.

At a time when antisemitism was constantly gaining strength, the Jews could not help but believe that Roosevelt, who displayed signs of favor to the Jews, would prove to be a barrier to the antisemitism which was destroying the Jews of Europe. This patron-client relationship suited the mentality of Eastern European Jews newly arrived in America. Helen Fein describes the psychological mechanism that affected the Jews as "the human need to balance positive and negative sentiments in relations so that they are symmetrical, leading to the truism 'my enemies enemy must be my friend.'"[74]

The enemies of the Jews in the U.S., and in the world at that time – Father Coughlin, Gerald Winrod, or Adolph Hitler – were also filled with blind hatred of Roosevelt and of all he stood for. If the enemies of the Jews reacted thus to Roosevelt, it is not surprising that the Jews banded around the President to strengthen his hand. Another truism also sustained Jewish support for Roosevelt – "A friend of my friends is my friend." If the political 'idols' of American Jewry, people such as Gov. Lehman, Sen. Robert Wagner, and New York Mayor Fiorello LaGuardia, were ardent supporters of Roosevelt, then the Jews, too, joined them in their support. Even if Roosevelt did not fulfill all of the expectations of the Jews could they have expected more from any one else? The answer of nearly all the Jewish leaders, as well as that of Jewish masses, was decisively – no!

It is impossible to conceive that at time of war, and especially in 1942 when the Allies were still losing battles, that American Jews could even consider openly confronting the President, the esteemed leader of all the forces fighting Nazi barbarianism. The American Jewish leadership was especially sensitive to what was happening around them and they clearly saw limits to the tolerance of the gentile world towards the Jews. They feared that attacking the President meant overstepping those limits. In addition, there is grave doubt whether a call for such an attack by Jewish leaders could have brought a response from the Jewish masses. Henry Feingold claims that the Jewish leaders could not use the Jewish vote as a threat because Roosevelt did not need the leaders to obtain the Jewish vote. Feingold claims that quite the opposite was the case. The Jewish leaders needed Roosevelt to assure their own position among American Jews.[75] If it is possible to label anyone as the leader of American Jews at that time, it was not Rabbi Wise, nor Rabbi Silver, nor Judge Proskauer, nor Monsky nor Pat. It was, on the contrary, the gentile President of the United States, Franklin Delano Roosevelt, who was acclaimed by the Jewish masses and accorded a special place of honor in Jewish history.

Could the Jewish leadership have acted otherwise than to rely on the President? Those were times of war and if they wanted to achieve any success whatsoever in saving European Jews, they could only do so by means of the U.S. government. The world outside the U.S. was so totally closed to them so that even a simple letter overseas had to pass the censor, who often rejected urgent letters sent by the Jewish organizations. To send money or food to Europe it was necessary to obtain special government licenses. Until the end of 1942, all attempts made to obtain even the smallest relief for the Jews of Europe ran into a stone wall. What then would happen if they sought a policy of large-scale rescue and relief? In such matters only the President could decide, and the Jewish leaders feared that if they attacked him, then that avenue of help would also be closed to them.

Rabbi Wise considered issuing a statement declaring that there was no hope that the United States would do anything to rescue European Jewry.[76] During the ten years since the Nazis rose to power in Germany, Wise had frequently spoken of his plans to attack Roosevelt for his lack of concern for the fate of European Jewry, but always drew back at the last moment. Whether due to a lack of courage; or out of loyalty to the President; or as a decision that 'discretion is the better part of valor', Wise once again remained silent and did not attack the Administration. Neither the President, nor his Administration, believed that it could either aid or rescue Jews without hampering the war effort. The bureaucrats at the State Department and in other government agencies were not even prepared to seriously examine the various rescue and relief proposals and to determine if anything at all could be done without gravely affecting the war effort. New initiatives to rescue Jews would only 'rock the boat' and for most of those concerned, saving Jews was not one of their personal priorities, therefore at a time of great pressures it was not their concern.

From the President down to senior officials in government and in the military command, the attitude of most was that little could be done to alleviate the suffering of the Jews. Their only hope lay in a speedy United Nations victory, they claimed. Many Jewish leaders, as well, did not see any other possibility. Just as time was needed to understand and absorb news of the massacre of European Jews, time and additional information were needed to develop practical plans for rescue.

Only those close to the arena of events and who had established contact with the Jewish undergrounds in the occupied countries, were able to begin to understand that it was still possible to rescue at least some of the remaining Jews. In the beginning of 1943 they began to send plans for action to the Jewish organizations in Palestine and in the U.S. Menachem Bader, a Jewish Agency rescue emissary in Constantinople, wrote that

> They did not know in Palestine, nor did they believe, that it was still possible to help [...] much as previously the mind could not grasp that they were murdering Jews, so now the mind could not grasp that there are nooks and crannies and ways to help.[77]

Only in the following two months did the Jewish leaders in the U.S. begin to learn about those nooks and crannies, and attempt to convince their government to try to penetrate through them. Many Jewish leaders also began asking, what good would an Allied victory be for the Jews of Europe once they were all annihilated?

CHAPTER 7

Confronting the Blockade Authority & The International Red Cross

a) "Who are we to ask a government to justify its policies?"
(Marc Peters, of the International Red Cross, in response to
a WJC request to pressure the Germans to permit aid to the Jews of Europe)

At the beginning of 1942 the Jewish organizations changed their position on the subject of sending food to the Jewish population of Poland and began pressing government agencies to let them send foodstuffs and medication to the ghettos. This reversal was the result of a growing awareness by the Jewish leadership of the vast extent of starvation among the Jews in Poland resulting in an unbelievable death rate;[1] as well as the revelation that during the winter of 1941-42 massive shipments of wheat had been sent by the Allies to the starving population of Greece, notwithstanding the regulations of the Blockade Authority.[2]

Greece, which before the German conquest had imported most of its wheat, was cut off from food supplies by the German invasion in May 1941 and faced a grave threat of mass starvation. The Greek government-in-exile and the Greek community in the United States pressured the Allied governments to permit food shipments to Greece. The British government, which viewed Greece as part of the British 'sphere of influence', acquiesced and arranged for the shipments to appear as a Swedish initiative. The problem of finding ships, which always seemed to be a major obstacle when rescue of Jews was under discussion, was easily dealt with when the Swedes provided ships to carry 15,000 tons of wheat from Canada to Greece.[3] Ironically, one shipment of food for starving Greece, was sent from the port of Haifa.[4]

Less than three months after the Axis conquest of Greece, Wallace Murray, who headed the Near East Division in the State Department, proposed that the U.S. government should also sanction the Greek request. In a memo to his colleagues Murray explained the reasons for his stand. He claimed that the food situation in Greece was the worst in Europe and that it was impracticable for

Greece to obtain wheat from neighboring Turkey. What Murray considered "most important of all" were the political considerations: to demonstrate to Turkey (whom the Allies wished to win over to their side) that the U.S. does not abandon its allies.[5] As to funding the food shipments, Breckinridge Long was of the opinion that feeding the Greeks was an obligation of the British and that they alone should cover the costs, if not the President's Emergency Fund could be used to defray the expenses. [6] By the end of 1942, the U.S. had sent seven million dollars worth of foodstuffs to Greece and the British a few million dollars more.[7]

The Jewish organizations, aware that Polish Jewry faced no less a danger of extinction through starvation than did the Greeks, felt discriminated against. They tried to use the precedent of Allied aid to Greece as a wedge to obtain similar permission to help the starving Jews of Poland. In April 1942, at the initiative of Adolph Held, Chairman of the JLC, the General Jewish Council together with the American Jewish Congress asked Joint to approach the State Department for permission to ship food to Jews in Poland on the same basis as was done for the Greeks.[8] Joseph Hyman, vice-chairman of Joint, informed the GJC that his organization thought the issue should not be treated as a solely Jewish problem, but as a broad humanitarian issue in conjunction with non-Jewish relief agencies.

In the discussion at Joint, James Rosenberg stated:

> ... that there being in Poland more non-Jewish than Jewish suffering, and since any help brought into Poland may be construed as helping in an enemy country, we ought to do this, even in inquiry, only if the Quakers and the Federation of Christian Churches join[...] As a purely Jewish thing[...] it is dangerous at this time with the war psychosis.

Bernard Kahn went even further in opposing the proposal, declaring that "I see no reason for the Joint Distribution Committee to take any action at all in the feeding of Poles or Jewish Poles. We could feed our Allies in China – 480 million of them."[9] It is obvious that there were still many in Joint, the major

Jewish relief organization, who at this date were as yet unaware of the distinct tragedy that was the fate of European Jewry.

Joint's apprehensions to approaching the State Department for permission to ship food to Poland were also practical. Hyman said that he doubted that the Greek precedent was analogous to that of Polish Jewry. "Militarily and politically, it is not analogous."[10] Though it was difficult then for the Jewish organizations to accept this fact, and today there are those who point to the Allied agreement to feed the Greeks as an example of what a sovereign nation was capable of achieving,[11] Hyman was basically correct in his evaluation. The Greek situation was not the same as the situation of the Jews of Poland. In permitting food shipments to be sent to Greece, the German and Italian occupation authorities had agreed to a neutral commission which would oversee the distribution of food and guarantee that the shipments would not be confiscated by the Germans for their own use.[12] The Germans however would not agree to food shipments to Polish Jewry, and without such a guarantee Britain and the U.S. would never have consented to an arrangement.

When the World Jewish Congress first discussed the issue in March 1942, Kubowitzki indicated that the Greeks "got food through an intensive publicity campaign [headed by Spyros Skouras President of RKO Studios]", and concluded "so should we do it."[13] Though most of the effort to get the U.S. to allow food shipments to Polish Jewry was made by lobbying the various government agencies, the American Jewish Congress did organize a public meeting in Town Hall in New York City in June, 1942 which demanded that relief be sent to Polish Jewry.[14] Calls for feeding the Jews of Europe were also incorporated in all of the rescue proposals sent by the Jewish organizations to the U.S. government in the following months.

Upon the insistence of Joint, both the General Jewish Council and the American Jewish Congress agreed to present the American government with a joint proposal to send food supplies in conjunction with the non-sectarian relief organizations. Deliberations between the numerous organizations dragged on and the memorandum to be presented to the government was only finalized in November 1942.[15] In the meantime the World Jewish Congress submitted other diverse relief proposals to various government agencies.

On September 29, 1942, Nachum Goldmann and James Waterman Wise succeeded in getting Assistant Secretary of State Dean Acheson to join them in an approach to Breckinridge Long to permit food shipments to the Warsaw Ghetto and other cities in Poland. To their surprise Long, though rejecting the idea of mass shipments, did agree to allow the WJC to send food parcels from Portugal to the ghettos of Poland to the sum of $12,000 a month. This would be done on a trial basis for three or four months, during which time it would be determined if the parcels were actually received by the Jews. If so, Long said, the arrangement would be continued. Long made the agreement conditional on the WJC not giving the arrangement any publicity, nor would he agree to any public fund raising for that purpose.[16] Long did not want to open the U.S. government to additional pressure from other ethnic minorities to demand separate relief programs.

What had brought about such a sudden change in the attitude of the State Department? Only a few months earlier, Breckinridge Long had opposed sending "any quantities of food" to Europe, arguing that it was clearly against U.S. policy.[17] As late as September 1942, there were still officials who opposed any food shipments to Europe claiming that such a move "would mean opening Pandora's box."[18] J. Kealey, of the State Department's Special Division, admitted that though the situation of the Jews was "appalling", "sending relief would do violence to our general relief policy, if this particular group was singled out from all other needy groups in the area."[19] At the Treasury Department, Randolph Paul also recommended to Morgenthau, that they deny a request by Joint to send relief, because it was U.S. "policy to make feeding of civilians incumbent upon the enemy."[20]

The change in policy came about firstly, because it had become apparent to the State Department that while the U.S. had been abiding by the regulations of the blockade, the British government had begun to permit shipments of food and medication to various countries of Occupied Europe. At the beginning of October, State informed Treasury that they were aware of the fact that the British "for some time have been allowing the shipment of food parcels from Portugal into occupied Europe." According to State, relief shipments totaling four tons each were being shipped monthly to Belgium, the Netherlands, France,

Luxemburg and Poland. This was in addition to the previously agreed upon shipments of wheat to Greece, and medications to Yugoslavia. The Belgians were also allowed to ship £250,000 worth of bulk food each month from Portugal. Breckinridge Long made it clear to Treasury that the "State Department has decided solely on political grounds that the American policy should parallel the British policy." State's reasoning was practical and had nothing to do with humanitarian principles. The feeling was that "if the British relief policy is more liberal than ours, it might give them a preferred position with such countries [in the post-war period]."[21] Long wrote that he "did not want that policy [of preventing food shipments][...] to serve as a basis of antagonism towards us after the war."[22]

Secondly, the proposed shipment of parcels to Europe was no more than a meager gesture to placate the rescue advocates. In no way could it seriously affect the food situation in the ghettos of Poland. As Long himself stated in his diary, "The decision was taken on purely political grounds. The amount of food involved is infinitesimal."[23]

Thirdly, it appears that the change in U.S. policy on food shipments to Occupied Europe was actually made by the President himself. On August 26, 1942, David Morris, a friend of the President, had written Roosevelt requesting permission to send relief supplies to Belgium. Roosevelt's reply (which is undated, but was initialed by Long on September 29, i.e. the same day that Long proposed to Goldmann the possibility of sending food parcels) stated: "I have asked the Secretary of State to consider the feasibility of adopting a policy of token shipments of food for the purpose of enheartening the people oppressed by cruel occupation of the Nazi Army."[24] It appears, then, that Goldmann's visit was propitious for it came on the very day that the American government had finalized its new policy of permitting limited shipments of food parcels to Europe.

The WJC now had a permit to send food parcels to Poland, but it did not have the funds for even so limited an aid project. Therefore, it turned to Joint and asked it to finance the shipments.[25] Joint was furious that the WJC had approached the State Department on its own, for it had been previously agreed that the approach would be made on a non-sectarian basis. Joint claimed that as a result, an opportunity had been missed to get American agreement to a plan of mass feeding, and not just a palliative of sending a limited number of parcels. Besides, it was obvious that the credit for securing the agreement would now accrue to the WJC who, Joint believed, had acted behind their backs.[26] This would help establish the WJC in Jewish relief work, which they believed was the sole province of Joint.

Joint decided to approach the State Department to recommend to the Treasury that the proposed food license be granted to them, as the major Jewish relief organization. Once again, the inability of the various Jewish organizations to coordinate their activities presented the American government with the sad picture of a fractured and squabbling American Jewish community. Morgenthau notified the State Department that he did not want to be the one to decide which of the two Jewish organizations should receive the license. Long told Pehle that he should make the decision.[27] A delegation of Joint and the GJC met with Long on December 2, and requested that the license be granted to Joint, as it was an American organization, while the World Jewish Congress was not. Long agreed to recommend granting them the license.[28] On December 8 (the same day that the Jewish delegation met with the President), Dr. Goldmann and James Wise also met with Long to try to convince him that the WJC be granted an additional license. They contended that they were an international organization, most of whose funds came from South America, and therefore they should be permitted to send relief in the name of Latin American Jewry.[29]

The license to ship food from Portugal to Poland was granted Joint on December 11, 1942.[30] But as with all other relief and rescue measures attempted at that time, the shipment bogged down because of an inability to overcome bureaucratic obstacles on the one hand, and because of German opposition on the other. The original Treasury license had permitted only the collective shipment of supplies to the Jewish communities in Poland. In March, 1943 Joint was informed by the government that collective shipments were ruled out. Joint then asked that the original license be amended so that they could send a trial shipment to individual Jews in Poland, and only in April were they granted the adjusted license.[31] The first parcels were sent that month, more than a half year after Long had first told Goldmann that the U.S. government would permit limited shipments to Polish Jewry.

By then, however, sending parcels to individual Jews in Poland had become anachronistic. The previous year the Germans had begun the mass deportations of Polish Jewry to labor camps and extermination centers and by spring of 1943 it was nearing completion. In October 1943, Joint received reports that of the first shipment of 12,559 parcels sent in April, 76 had been received and signed for by the addressees; 849 had been received by the Judenrat; 549 parcels had been returned; 4000 had been confiscated; and 7000 were unaccounted for.[32] Of more than 12,000 parcels, only slightly more than 7% were known to have reached their destination.

The Jewish organizations were despondent over the results. In September 1943, they debated whether to apply to the government to renew their license. Nachum Goldmann expressed his opinion that due to the poor results, he did not believe the State Department would agree.[33] For quite a while Maurice Perlzweig had been pointing out the paradox inherent in the Jewish organizations' demand to permit shipment of food to the starving Jews. Perlzweig asserted, that on the one hand the Jewish organizations were claiming that there existed a deliberate German policy to starve the Jews of Europe. On the other hand, they were claiming that Hitler would allow food shipments to reach those starving Jews.[34] Presenting both such diametrically opposed views would be disbelieved.

The attempt to send food parcels had shown that Perlzweig was basically correct, and that the possibility of feeding European Jewry was primarily in the hands of the Germans who did not permit any serious aid to reach their victims. In April 1943, the Geneva office of the WJC reported to New York that "As far as Poland and other European areas under German occupation[...] the relief scheme submitted by us and the International Red Cross was rejected definitely by the German officials." [35]

It was true that permitting food shipments to reach European Jews was basically decided upon by the German authorities, yet this did not absolve the U.S. government from the fact that it did not even attempt to develop any relief measures. Until the fall of 1942, U.S. policy was to maintain strict adherence to the blockade of Europe. Even afterwards, it granted only token gestures. The problem was not only one of government policy it was also a question of the attitude of government officials. Until the creation of the War Refugee Board (WRB) in January, 1944, the reaction of most officials to requests to stave off the starvation of European Jews was one of a lack of concern; an unwillingness to cooperate; and responding to requests with slow, bureaucratic handling as though the issue could be dealt with at leisure. A few examples can demonstrate the attitude of most Administration officials throughout those years.

In April, 1943, in reply to a WJC initiative on the possibility of the Red Cross sending food parcels to the Jews of Occupied-Europe, L. Osborne (Chief of the Division of Special Relief Problems) wrote to James Wise that "the department can not properly offer its facilities for this purpose, and must therefore leave it to you to arrange further information as to the manner in which parcels may be sent."[36] That month the German authorities agreed to allow the Red Cross to send collective food shipments to the Jews in Theresienstadt.[37] As these collective shipments would be handled by the Red Cross and were agreed upon by the Germans, there was now a reasonable guarantee that they might actually reach their destination. The Allies could at least have assented to a trial shipment to ascertain if the Nazis would keep to their pledge. By the summer of 1943 hundreds of thousands of German soldiers had fallen into Allied captivity, and German cities were being bombed daily. The German government itself was now in dire need of assistance from the Red Cross and wanted to maintain good relations with the organization. Yet nearly one year later the WJC was still requesting the U.S. government to "reconsider [the] formalistic attitude adopted by the American and British authorities" which prevented the shipment of collective parcels, even though the Theresienstadt plan was of a very limited scope.[38]

We shall see in the following chapter that the American delegation to the Bermuda Conference joined the British delegation in preventing relief even being discussed at the Conference. The State Department instructions to the American delegation did not mention opposing food shipments because it had been decided to maintain the blockade. The memo stated that demands for sending food to Europe must be considered in the light of American civilian and military needs "which have necessitated the institution of a food rationing system in the United States,"[39] though the total extent of American 'suffering' due to the lack of food supplies was limited to a 'Meatless Tuesday' and a slight sugar shortage.

The Blockade Authorities also prevented the shipment of foodstuffs to neutral countries, which were necessary in order to enable them to absorb Jews. In the fall of 1943 attempts were made to convince the Swiss government to allow more refugees to enter their country. Such an approach required guaranteeing the Swiss that they would be supplied with additional food supplies to support those refugees. Both the American and the British authorities refused to agree to such an arrangement, though such shipments would not have reached the Germans, nor would it have "freed them from their obligation to feed their conquered peoples." The talks consequently broke down.[40]

Perhaps the account of a WJC initiative to send tea to the Warsaw Ghetto is indicative of the attitude of American government officials toward aiding the famished Jews of Poland. On July 20, 1942 Aryeh Tartakower (WJC) and Abraham Fertig (AJCong) met with J.C. Foulis of the Board of Economic Warfare and requested permission to send two tons of tea to the Jews incarcerated in the Warsaw Ghetto.[41] Their intention was not that the tea would be used by the Jews in the ghetto. The Jews, they claimed, could exchange the tea on the black market for more vital food since tea was hard to find in wartime Poland, and was therefore in great demand. Tartakower claimed that the two tons of tea could stave off starvation of 4000 families for a few months.[42]

The reasoning behind the request was to see if the shipment would be allowed to reach its destination. If so, then attempts would be made to broaden the scope of the shipments. If the tea was confiscated by the German authorities, the amount was so insignificant that it would be difficult for anyone to claim that two tons of tea could, in any profound measure, "bring aid and comfort to the enemy". Foulis immediately raised the standard objections – that the Germans might confiscate the tea; if they did not, it would be deducted from Jewish rations (tea was certainly not part of their rations). In addition, he pointed out that it would be difficult to obtain so large a quantity of tea and it would be hard to find space to ship the tea (two tons!) to Portugal.[43]

Two months later in response to a WJC inquiry, Foulis informed them that he was checking out the matter with the Red Cross. During the following year, numerous letters were sent to the many government agencies that dealt with the subject. Leading Jewish functionaries, such as Rabbi Wise and Dr. Goldmann, raised the issue with important government officials. The Board of Economic Warfare was approached and so was the Red Cross. The Vice President and the State Department were asked to help, and so was the Treasury Department. The Commerce Department was approached, for it was a subject of trade; and the Department of Agriculture had to give its approval for it was a matter of food. The British Embassy and the British Ministry of Economic Warfare were also asked to agree. In the archives of the World Jewish Congress one can find dozens of letters dealing with the request, as well as many memos of meetings on the subject with government officials. A year later the British still had no reply. On June 25, 1943, two months after the Warsaw Ghetto had been destroyed, Tartakower once again asked the British if they had an answer to the proposal but none was forthcoming.[44] The quantity of food at issue was minor but perhaps one can conclude from the petty quantity involved – a minori ad majus – that if such a minor request was rejected by the government, what then was the fate of attempts for large-scale efforts to send food.

Even if the Blockade Authorities had permitted shipments of food to the Jews in Occupied-Europe, they would never have granted their consent without a fairly firm guarantee that such shipments would reach their destination and not be confiscated by the Germans. The only organization that could possibly oversee such shipments, and assure their delivery, was the International Committee of the Red Cross (ICRC) with headquarters in Switzerland. The expressed purpose of the Red Cross was to

> act as a benevolent intermediary between governments, peoples and nationalities for the purpose of itself carrying out or making it possible for others to carry out the humanitarian task of relieving sufferings arising out of war, sickness or disaster.[45]

The Geneva Convention of 1929, to which the Germans were signatories, however provided only for the ICRC to care for Prisoners of War in the event of hostilities. There had been a plan, the Tokyo Project, which envisaged broadening the scope of the Red Cross to guarantee legal protection for

'Civilian Internees', and grant them the right to receive parcels. It had been intended to ratify this treaty at an International Conference to be held in 1940, but the outbreak of war in 1939 scuttled the plans.[46] Nonetheless, most warring nations abided by the proposed rules. However, the Germans declined to view the Jews of Europe, neither those incarcerated in the ghettos, nor those in the concentration camps, as 'Civilian Internees'.[47] The ICRC refused to force the issue with the German authorities.[48]

In August 1942, the WJC approached the Red Cross to obtain 'Civilian Internee' status for the Jews of Poland. Marc Peters, the ICRC representative in Washington informed them that to procure 'Civilian Internee' status, a person must "be actually interned in camps, what is so far not the case for the Jews of Poland". He, therefore, held out little hope of convincing either the ICRC Executive, or the Germans, to regard Polish Jewry as 'Civilian Internees'.[49] As news of the deportations began reaching the Jewish organizations in the West, Kubowitzki wrote the Red Cross, that

> If some doubt has existed concerning the status of Polish Jews living in Polish ghettos, there can be[...]no doubt that Jews that have been deported from other countries to ghettos in German occupied Eastern Europe have to be considered as Civilian Internees.[50]

It must be remembered that aside from the Jews of Germany, Austria and Slovakia, all other deported Jews were Allied nationals. Kubowitzki knew that only by achieving such status might the deported Jews be allowed to receive food parcels, and the Red Cross be permitted to oversee conditions in the concentration camps. As this was dependent on the good will of the German authorities, the WJC decided, in February 1943, to attempt to negotiate with them through the offices of the ICRC.[51]

Two months later Kubowitzki complained to Rabbi Wise that "The attitude of the International Red Cross, as far as the Jewish plight in Europe is concerned, has been a disgrace." He accused the ICRC that not only did they achieve no results but also that "All our demands for an inquiry [...] did not even receive an answer."[52] The war situation had clearly altered, he claimed, and Germany itself was now in need of Red Cross assistance. Therefore, he asserted, the ICRC was capable of bringing pressure to bear upon Germany to allow them to aid the Jews in their territories.[53] In May, Tartakower appealed to Peters for Red Cross intervention to send food to the interned Jews in order to slow down the killing process. In July, Peter passed on to Tartakower the reply of the ICRC in Geneva. They stated that the German authorities had refused to allow the Red Cross to visit the camps and therefore they were unable to fulfill the Blockade Authority's requirement to supervise the distribution of food.[54]

Towards the end of 1943, aware that there was no hope that the Allies would allow negotiations with the Germans to release the Jews, nor permit sending foodstuffs to them without proper supervision, Kubowitzki reached the conclusion that the WJC should concentrate its efforts on achieving 'Civilian Internee' status for interned Jews. He felt that obtaining this status held the best hope for saving the remaining Jews, and that because of their own worsening situation, the Germans might acquiesce to such a demand if proper pressure were brought to bear on them.[55] However, none of the bodies capable of bringing pressure to bear on Germany were ready to do more than appeal to them.

Norman Davis, Chairman of the American Red Cross, expressed his government's fear that any attempt to achieve Civilian Internee status for the Jews of Europe might jeopardize the suitable arrangements that had been worked out with Germany, and that "The inclusion of any other groups [...] under protection of treaty [...] [might] jeopardize the smooth operations protecting Prisoners-of-War."[56] America's concern was first and foremost for its own soldiers and civilians, and it was not prepared to endanger them in order to alleviate the plight of the Jews interned in camps. In December, Marc Peters answered Kubowitzki's's demands for pressuring the Germans to recognize the interned Jews as 'Civilian Internees'. He wrote:

> When a war breaks out the Committee can [...] only offer its
> services to the Belligerent countries [...] To bear pressure upon a
> Belligerent government which does not observe the Convention
> dictates, would, indeed, be tantamount to threatening the

withdrawal of the Committee's help and relief [...] This the ICRC can not do [...] Our first duty is to the individuals regardless of the policies of their particular government.[57]

Kubowitzki refused to accept this formalistic approach advanced by the ICRC, nor its unwillingness to intervene. In a meeting with Peter, in January 1944, Kubowitzki demanded that the Red Cross: a) Ask Germany to justify its distinction between Jews and non-Jews in defining Civilian Internee status. b) State publicly that it views segregated and interned Jews as Civilian Internees to whom the benefits of the Red Cross Convention apply, and that the ICRC is prepared to proffer them assistance. Peter did not accept Kubowitzki's demands. He claimed: "Who are we to ask a government to justify its policies?" He did agree, nonetheless, to pass on Kubowitzki's request to his headquarters in Geneva.[58]

In a post-war evaluation of its activities, the ICRC concluded that "Stirring up a scandal over the Jewish problem would have endangered everyone, without saving a single Jew."[59] It was against this policy of the Red Cross that the Jewish organizations, and especially the World Jewish Congress, attempted to struggle. Only in October, 1944 did the Red Cross finally demand that all aliens in German-Occupied Europe be granted Civilian Internee status.[60] The war was approaching its finale. The Germans were now in dire need of Red Cross assistance, and the Red Cross was no longer hesitant about making demands upon the German authorities. In the latter half of 1944 the ICRC began to abandon its previous refusal to intervene actively to rescue Jews, and became involved in saving Hungarian Jewry. In the last five months of the war, under the new leadership of Professor Karl Burckhardt, the ICRC took an increasingly active role in attempting to save what were now only the remnants of European Jewry.

❖ ❖ ❖

December 31, 1942, had been set as the final date for 'Operation Reinhardt', the S.S. plan to make Poland 'Judenrein'.[61] Throughout all of 1942, trains had sped to the six 'killing centers' in Poland, carrying daily tens of thousands of Jews to their death. News of the mass killings had been filtering to the West since the spring though the American government made no effort to obtain details of the stories that had emerged. On the contrary, it deliberately attempted to prevent such news in general from reaching Americans, and more specifically, tried to keep the Jewish organizations from learning of the fate of their Jewish brothers. The State Department officials rightfully assessed that if the full story were known, pressure would mount for the government to thwart such atrocities.

In 1942, unwavering in their view that rescue would only come through speedy victory, neither the State Department officials, nor anyone else in the government, including the President, were prepared to do anything for rescue. At most, the American government was prepared to condemn the atrocities, though not always to acknowledge their specific Jewish nature. It was also prepared to promise (though hesitatingly) that the perpetrators would stand before the bar of justice at war's end. Words of comfort and consolation had been spoken, but they were what Rabbi Abba Hillel Silver sarcastically called "New Year greetings from the President."[62]

CHAPTER 8
Rallying the Public Protest

(a) The Madison Square Garden Rally
"America must act now!"
(Call for rally in Madison Square Garden)

By the beginning of 1943 there were signs that the tides of war had begun to favor the Allies. Rommel's flaunted Afrika Korps was in full flight before Montgomery's Eighth Army and Eisenhower had invaded and secured most of French North Africa. Twenty-two German Divisions under Von Paulus were cut off at Stalingrad and on the verge of surrender. In the Pacific, the U.S. Navy won a number of naval victories, and the Army and Marines were taking the offensive against the Japanese. The despondency that had characterized America's mood in 1942 was now replaced with a feeling that the war could be won quickly. The State Department began concentrating on American plans for the post-war period.

However, Hitler's determined and often baffling behavior in the face of defeat bode ill for the remaining Jews of Europe. He turned down Von Paulus' request to retreat from the banks of the Volga, nor did he permit Rommel to withdraw his crack Afrika Korps to Europe. In wild temper tantrums, he bullied his military command to obey his most illogical orders and fired any officers who dared not obey. The Nazis were determined to maintain their conquest of Europe no matter what the cost. They were equally determined to rid the world of its Jews, once and for all.

In December the American Jewish leadership had appealed to their government to condemn Hitler's plans for the annihilation of the Jews. They began planning to mobilize American public opinion to call upon their government to rescue Jews wherever possible, but they soon realized that there were not many who were marching along beside them. An editorial in the *Congress Weekly* recalled the public outcry in America after the pogroms of Kristallnacht, and bemoaned the fact "that the murder of two million and the doom of other millions have affected the conscience of the world much less than the events of four years ago". The editorial clearly stated for the first time that words of comfort and promises of retribution were no longer sufficient, and "what was needed now – is rescue!" The pace and magnitude of the killings brought home to the American Jewish Congress leadership the reality that "rescue through speedy victory" would not save the Jews of Europe. They called upon the world leaders to make rescue of Jews a part of the United Nations' war aims. "This is a separate and distinct battlefield which so far has been ignored by the Allies", they wrote.[1] But in the winter of 1942-43 neither the military, nor the political leadership in America, were prone to see it that way.

The status imposed on German-Jewish refugees in the United States can be seen as an indication of the American government's attitude towards European Jewry at that time. After America entered the war, all resident aliens from Japan, Italy and Germany were classified as 'enemy aliens'. Astonishingly, this also included the victims of Nazism who had fled to the United States to escape persecution. Before the Congressional elections in 1942, Roosevelt, in a bid to win the Italian-American vote, had removed Italian aliens from this category. But for the German Jews who had been denationalized by Nazi racial policies, the blot and the restrictions as 'aliens' still remained.

At the end of January 1943, Morris Waldman, of the American Jewish Committee, appealed to Sumner Welles to utilize the opportunity of the tenth anniversary of Hitler's appointment as Reich Chancellor, to remove German Jews from classification as 'enemy aliens'. Fawningly, Waldman admitted that in the past the decision had been "wise, just and politic", but he questioned "If there is no doubt about the loyalty of the Italians in our midst, can there be any doubt about the loyalty of the Jews from Germany?"[2] Quite obviously doubts still remained, for Secretary Hull informed Welles that the matter was under the jurisdiction of the Justice Department and of the President and that "they want to consider it further."[3]

In the House of Representatives, Emanuel Celler reproached America for its lack of response to the massacre of Jews. He compared the forceful response America had made to the bombing of Rotterdam, and to the razing of Lidice, with American indifference to the murder of two million Jews. There had not [been] a word of rebuke or disgust of shame or warning. Hardly a word from the Christian churches [...] Not an adequate word from molders of public opinion in the press and on the radio. Not a word from intellectuals, those guardians of civilization. That silence, sinister in its implications, has now lengthened into weeks.[4]

Celler's impassioned speech did not rouse his colleagues to emulate his call, nor did it move them to demand action to save the remnant of European Jewry.

However, more than the lack of government action or lack of response from the American public, the poor response of the American Jewish community was what most disturbed the Jewish leadership. They could not comprehend how, after receiving news of the Holocaust, Jews could continue life in their 'business as usual' manner. *The Reconstructionist* magazine wrote of "a paralysis" that had seized American Jewry. The journal accused part of American Jewry as being "wholly indifferent to the tragic plight of our European brethren, either because of plain ignorance of the facts, or out of fear of raising an undo clamor about what erroneously seems to them to be a specifically Jewish tragedy". As for the rest of American Jews – "stricken dumb by grief [they] seem to have accepted resignedly the fate of European Jewry."[5]

But the sharpest attack against the lethargy of American Jewry's response to the Final Solution came from Chaim Greenberg. Though he was the editor of the Labor Zionist monthly *Jewish Frontier,* he chose to use the Yiddish magazine of his movement, *Der Yiddisher Kampfer,* as the vehicle for his bitter attack upon America Jews. Greenberg probably did not want to wash the 'dirty linen' of the Jewish community in public. Recalling the 'Day of Mourning', Greenberg bitingly called for a day of fasting and prayer to be held for American Jews. Their "misfortune [...] consists of a kind of epidemic inability to suffer or feel compassion [...] a horny shell seems to have formed over the soul of American Jewry to protect and defend it against pain and pity". He accused the American Jewish community of having "fallen lower than perhaps any other time in recent times" for not carrying out "its elementary duty towards the millions of Jews in Europe".

The American Jewish community, he reproached, "all five million of us, with all our organizations and communities and leaders [are] politically and morally bankrupt."[6]

Even the AJCong, of which he was a member, was not spared Greenberg's wrath. He attacked its bumbling and charged that "when the Angel of Death uses airplanes, the American Jewish Congress employs an ox-cart express." The main thrust of his article was a plea to the manifold Jewish organizations to put aside their quarrels for "when the axe of the executioner hangs over neck[...] What differences of opinion can there exist on such rescue work?"[7] On this latter point Greenberg was mistaken, for basic differences of opinion still existed among the Jewish organizations, both as to what actions to demand and even more important, how to demand them.

In January 1943, Leib Joffe (head of the Zionist Colonization Fund), who was in the U.S. at the time, met with Judge Proskauer, the newly-elected President of the American Jewish Committee, to discuss methods of inducing the U.S. government to act for rescue. Proskauer informed Joffe that he was opposed to organizing a mass movement to demand rescue, for "It is liable to cause Anti-Semitism."[8] Indeed, during those same critical months in the winter of 1942-43, when Jewish organizations were discussing the nature of their response to news of the Holocaust, much of their meetings were also devoted to dealing with the upsurge of antisemitism in America.

When the United States entered the war after the attack on Pearl Harbor one would have expected that the antisemitism, prevalent before the war, would abate. The results were the opposite. Public opinion polls conducted during the war showed that as many as 48% of Americans said they would either support or sympathize with a campaign against the Jews after the war.[9] On the backdrop of what was happening to the Jews of Europe those words, 'a campaign against the Jews', took on a sinister meaning and certainly were a cause for deep concern among American Jewry. Young Jews who had been drafted into the Armed Services were for the first time facing physical antisemitism, barely experienced in their sheltered lives in the urban 'ghettos' in which they had grown up. Some Jewish organizations feared making too vocal a demand for rescue of Jews and giving credence to the antisemitic, and Nazi, claim, that America was fighting the war for the Jews. [10]

In January, the American Jewish Committee held its annual conference and devoted much of its time to discussing post-war solutions to the problem of Europe's Jews, but not a single word was said in its resolutions concerning the ongoing extermination of those very Jews. Even after Rabbi Wise's revelations at his November press conference, a blind spot still remained as to the fate of Europe's Jewry. The conference spoke of "The overseas problem affecting Jews are still in many ways those that existed before the outbreak of the war [!]" and decided that the solution to those problems would be "deferred until the end of the war."[11]

Despite the news that all of Europe's Jews had been marked for destruction, the AJC still talked of restoring Jewish rights in Europe, and that some Jews would want to emigrate after the war. Assuming that both the U.S. and Palestine would be closed to Jewish immigrants, George Medalie, Chairman of the Overseas Committee, proposed pressuring Latin American countries to absorb Jewish immigrants in order "to further the development of countries with potential and hitherto unexploited wealth."[12] The vast amount of time devoted to post-war planning was indicative of the new mood that gripped America after the Allied victories at El-Alemein and Stalingrad and the U.S. invasion of North Africa. The feeling that there would be an early victory removed the urgency to press for rescue.

The 'blind spot' that led the AJC to believe that the problems of European Jewry were still mainly "those that existed before the outbreak of the war" was limited not only to them. The news that had accumulated concerning the fate of the Jews in Europe had not penetrated the consciousness of most Americans. They were not able, as yet, to grasp that all of European Jewry was facing total annihilation. A public opinion poll in January 1943 showed that the majority did not believe news of the massacres. Less than half of those polled believed that two million Jews had been killed. The others replied that these stories were only rumors or they had no opinion on the subject.[13] Today we have many testimonies by Holocaust survivors that tell of the reluctance of Jews in the ghettos to believe the reports by other Jews who escaped from the extermination camps and told of the killings in the gas chambers.[14] These reports came from neighbors, people they had known for years. Is it surprising, then, that many in the U.S., thousands of miles away from the atrocities, still refused to believe? Perhaps a human defense mechanism was at work here – to deny situations that people could not cope with.

Maybe the Jewish leadership had not been forceful in making their point. But they, too, shared the same inability to fully comprehend the news that reached them. How else can one explain the reaction of the Jewish leadership to a British rescue proposal in March 1943? When they were informed of the possibility that 5,000 Bulgarian Jews would be permitted to emigrate to Palestine, they told the British Foreign Minister, Anthony Eden, that the certificates should be given to Jewish adults for, as they said, it was 'obvious' that children would not be sent to Eastern Europe,[15] despite the fact that they had previously warned the government that "there exists a deliberate plan to destroy all the Jews in Europe."

The lack of response by the Jewish masses bore most heavily upon the 'Congress movement' which in December had been the prime mover in organizing Jewish action. Nachum Goldmann repeatedly spoke of the apathy of both the American public and the Jewish masses concerning the fate of European Jewry.[16] The planning committee of the AJCong dropped the proposals for a procession in New York City and for a march on Washington. With a war going on, and antisemitism on the rise, even the most activist Jewish organizations feared that such demonstrations would be labeled unpatriotic, and that American Jews would be accused of disloyalty to their country.

But such concerns did not prevent American workers from calling long and bitter strikes. In the midst of the war, when production was the key to a speedy victory, not a week passed in 1943 without a labor crisis.[17] Charges that the miners, factory workers and railroad men were sabotaging the war effort did not deter them from striking for better wages. Perhaps that ability to act despite the war was the difference between workers who felt they belonged in America, and Jews who still felt insecure and eagerly sought to be accepted as loyal citizens.

The mobilization of public opinion in the U.S. and catalyzing the Jewish masses to act was not the concern of the World Jewish Congress. In the division of labor within the 'Congress movement', that work had been left to the American Jewish Congress, which was an American organization and could speak for American Jewry. The WJC concentrated on developing and presenting programs of rescue to the proper American authorities, and to the Washington representatives of the various international organizations and of the Allied nations. However, the 'Congress movement' lacked a suitable organizational set-up to deal with the authorities. In a period in which crisis followed upon crisis, it was no longer sufficient for Rabbi Wise or Dr. Goldmann to make an occasional trip to Washington to meet with leading government officials and to lobby for rescue action. Matters had to be attended to on a daily basis if they hoped for any success.

During December, Maurice Perlzweig was dispatched to Washington to handle problems there for the duration of the emergency. But Perlzweig's expertise lay in dealing with the British government and the other Allied nations. As a foreign citizen of no particular standing he was in no position to deal with officials of the U.S. government, nor did Perlzweig remain in Washington long enough to develop the necessary contacts. In February, James Waterman Wise was sent to Washington to represent the WJC Political Department. Though the Wise name was respected in Washington and afforded access to many government offices, James Wise had neither the experience nor the stature to deal adequately with what should have been the major endeavor of world Jewry at that time. Once the WJC realized that its main efforts required concentrating on prodding the American government, the Allies and the international organizations to act for rescue, they should have transferred their main office to Washington. Only in Washington could acts of rescue and of relief be decided upon.

Action to mobilize the Jewish masses had to be concentrated in New York; political action demanded strong representation in Washington. Both the Bergson group, and the Zionist Emergency Committee when reconstituted under Rabbi Silver, realized that fact and much of their successes can be attributed to their development of a strong lobby in Washington. The Bergson group responded easily to the need for they were young and dedicated bachelors who could easily go from Chicago to Philadelphia to Washington as needed. It was more difficult to uproot the older family men at the core of the World Jewish Congress activities.

In January, Nachum Goldmann reported to the WJC Administrative Committee that their principal demands in Washington were: a) That the United Nations officially approach Germany to allow Jews to leave Nazi occupied Europe. b) That places of refuge be set aside for those refugees who are able to escape. c) That arrangements be made for shipping food to the Jews of Europe.[18] He also stressed that special emphasis be placed on developing schemes to save children in particular. A confidential bulletin issued by the AJCong Emergency Planning Committee elaborated on this work. It related that an "influential government" (not specified) had undertaken to secure permission for Jews to leave German-occupied territories; that representatives of the WJC had begun negotiations with the neutral countries of Spain, Portugal, Sweden and Turkey to provide havens for Jews; that the British Section of the WJC was similarly negotiating with the British government for the entry of Jews into Britain and her colonies. The most that they were asking from the United States was permission for Jews to enter U.S. possessions, like Alaska and the Virgin Islands. No one had even considered approaching the Administration or Congress, to allow Jews into the U.S.

While the AJC, as Proskauer stated, still opposed using public protest as a means to induce the government to act for rescue, the ACong remained convinced that mass demonstrations could place Jewish demands on the public agenda and even move the government to act. Though they had rejected the idea of a march on Washington, the AJCong intended to organize a mass demonstration at Madison Square Garden. In the past such demonstrations had proved effective in arousing the faithful while not antagonizing government officials who looked askance at Jewish protest. The demonstration was preceded by several smaller rallies by various Jewish organizations, the most impressive a rally organized by Jewish Communists at 'Carnegie Hall' at the end of December, 1942.[19]

The mass meeting had originally been set for January 7,[20] was postponed to February 2,[21] and then put off again. Hillel Kook (Peter Bergson) claims that the American Jewish Congress never meant to carry out the rally. Wise's decision to hold a demonstration in the Garden on March 1, he asserts, was intended only to upstage the Bergson group's plan for a pageant on the

Holocaust the following week.[22] The March date for the rally had been decided in January,[23] though Kook knew of the decision only in mid-February and therefore believed that the specific date had been set to spoil the Bergson group's pageant. Kook had other complaints against Rabbi Wise which today he admits were erroneous. He told the author that for many years he believed Wise had deliberately chosen to remain silent over the Riegner cable even though the State Department had permitted him to release the information. Kook based his belief on what Adolph Berle, an Assistant Secretary of State had told him. Today he knows that Berle had lied to him.[24]

Though the date for the Madison Square Garden rally had already been set, it appears that it was another cable from Riegner and Lichtheim that impelled the AJCong to finalize preparations for the rally. The message once again confirmed the killings and disclosed tales of "6,000 Jews killed in one place in Poland daily". It included reports from Berlin and Prague that by March no Jews would be left there. The cable also related the death of nearly half of the 130,000 Romanian Jews who had been deported to Transnistria, and the slow death of the remainder by starvation.[25] The cable had been detained by the State Department for two weeks before it was dispatched to Wise. Durbrow recommended that the Department, in forwarding the cable, should tell Wise in no uncertain terms, that he had misinformed the public when he stated that the Department had verified the previous Riegner cable.[26]

But the State Department decided to do even better than this. Some of the senior officials in the Department drew up a message to the American Legation at Bern, similar to the one they had intended to send after receiving the first Riegner cable in August, 1942. This time they obtained Welles' signature, apparently without his knowledge. The cable (#482) instructed the Berne Legation "not [to] accept reports submitted to it to be transmitted to private persons in the United States". The reason they offered for the directive was that "Such private messages circumvent neutral countries censorship" and as a result, "those neutrals might possibly curtail official U.S. government mail."[27] As the State Department cable referred specifically to the recent Riegner-Lichtheim message (cable # 354), the real intent was clear to the American representatives in Switzerland. The Legation in Bern continued forwarding other private and business messages through their diplomatic pouch for the remainder of the war.[28]

The plans for the Garden rally received important support when the two major trade union organizations, the American Federation of Labor (AFL) and the Congress of Industrial Organizations (CIO) agreed to co-sponsor the rally. The Free World Association, a liberal group of emigrés to which the American Jewish Congress, for some reason, attributed much significance, also agreed to co-sponsor the rally. The only church group that lent its support was the marginally small Church Peace Union. On the other hand, many Jewish organizations agreed to co-sponsor the rally, the only major exception being the American Jewish Committee, and even it sent a telegram of endorsement to be read at the rally.[29]

An editorial in *Congress Weekly* calling for the rally, chided the American government and the public for "not uttering their righteous indignation and demanding some form of immediate action." But it reserved its main condemnation for "the most frightening aspect of the situation"--the "spell of general lethargy" that had fallen on American Jewry. It harshly accused the American Jewish community of "having [been] given over primarily to material cares," and that "it has not yet discovered its soul". It questioned whether, as a community, American Jewry was "sufficiently mature to assume the obligations placed upon us."[30]

The full-page ad in the *N.Y. Times* calling for the demonstration was no less eye-catching than those of the Bergson Group. It showed a returned envelope from a Jew in Warsaw and bore the stamp of the German authorities –"Died in the course of liquidation of the Jewish problem". In bold type the ad demanded that "America must act now!" It warned that "Hitler thought up Total War, he now has thought up Total Murder". The main proposal made in the ad was a call to provide sanctuaries for the remaining Jews, especially those in the Balkans.[31]

The Madison Square Garden demonstration was the most impressive of the many Jewish rallies held during the twelve years of Nazi power. It probably was also the most effective though it did not succeed in moving the American government to change significantly its attitude toward rescuing the Jews of Europe. The rally filled the Garden to its 22,000 capacity and some 50,000 people listened in the streets to the speeches broadcast outside.[32] Professor Chaim Weizmann spoke to the masses about the verdict of the future which would never understand "the apathy of the civilized world in the face of the immense, systematic carnage of human beings". He rebuked the Allied governments that "expressions of sympathy, without accompanying attempts to launch acts of rescue, become a hollow mockery in the ears of the dying." All speakers stressed the fact that threats of retribution "or heart-felt expressions of sympathy" were no longer an answer "in the face of immense, systematic carnage of human beings.[33] The entire tone of the gathering was one for a call to immediate action.

Aside from an impressive array of speakers and messages sent by prominent personalities, the demonstration adopted an eleven point program that had been prepared by the American Jewish Congress Special Planning Committee which was a summary of the intensive planning carried out since the previous December when arrangements were initiated to meet the President. This program was the basis for all future requests by the Jewish organizations for action. The appeal was addressed to President Roosevelt and to the U.S. government, and through them to the United Nations and to the neutral countries. The preamble spoke of registering "our solemn and public protest against the continuing failure to act, against the strange indifference of the United Nations to the fate of five million human beings."[34]

The most far-reaching resolution was an appeal to have neutral agencies and governments approach Germany and her satellites to "secure their agreement to the release of their Jewish victims and to consent to their emigration to such havens of refuge as will be provided." The following five points dealt with proposals for creating places of refuge for those Jews who might be permitted to leave Nazi occupied territories, or for those who might succeed in fleeing on their own. These included: a) Immediate steps by the UN to find and establish havens of refuge "in allied or neutral states." b) A call to the United States to change its immigration procedures and enable the Jewish refugees to make full use of the existing immigration quotas. c) A request to Great Britain to accept a reasonable number of victims. d) Urging Latin American countries to remove procedures which hinder immigration and to allow an agreed number of refugees to enter their countries on a temporary basis. e) An appeal to Britain to put aside "prewar political considerations" and permit Jews to enter "Palestine – the Jewish Homeland."

Point seven called on the Allies to guarantee financial assistance to neutral countries to cover the cost of feeding and maintaining Jewish refugees and for an Allied guarantee that the refugees will be evacuated at the end of the war (they deliberately did not speak of repatriation). The next item called for feeding Jewish victims "who are doomed to linger under Nazi oppression." Point nine called for the United Nations to assume financial responsibility for proposed acts of rescue. The next resolution was for the establishment of an intergovernmental agency "to which authority and power should be given to implement the [rescue] program." The last point called on the United Nations to implement finally their previously declared intention to create a War Crimes Commission. The resolution ended with a call "In the name of humanity – for the sake of that cause which the armies of democracy have risen to defend [...] that effective action be taken without delay."[35]

The March 1st rally and the resolutions there adopted, were the high point in the efforts by the organized American Jewish community to bring about effective action to rescue European Jewry. The resolutions contained nearly all the major rescue proposals, including many that the Jewish organizations until then had never dared to request. They contained a call for negotiations with Germany, a proposal which the Jewish leaders knew the Allied governments opposed, though they themselves did negotiate with Germany on civilian and prisoners-of-war exchanges. The resolutions also called for opening up the U.S. to immigration, a request which American Jewry had always feared to propose. The appeal to allow food to be shipped to the starving Jews no longer spoke of palliatives of food parcels to be sent on a limited basis (as was already agreed upon), but rather called for mass feeding of Europe's Jews. The call to the United Nations to assume financial obligations for rescue and relief was also a departure from previous policy, which always sought to finance rescue solely through funds raised by the Jewish community.

The decision to propose the creation of an intergovernmental agency for rescue and relief, and not a specifically American agency as was later requested, seemed the most logical choice at that time. The American Jewish Congress obviously did not envisage the resurrection of the impotent and near-defunct Inter-Governmental Committee on Refugees. It believed that an international agency, properly staffed, funded and empowered with sufficient authority, would mobilize the efforts of all the Allied nations in a combined attempt to rescue Jews. It hoped that in such a joint agency, countries that appeared as stronger advocates of rescue, such as the Polish Government-in-Exile, might prevail upon the U.S. government to expand its rescue work. The resolutions relegated to last place the demand for retribution. What had once been the major demand no longer sufficed. The need, it was realized, was first and foremost to save as many Jews as still was possible.

The resolutions adopted at the rally were broad and inclusive but Medoff described them as "inadequate."[36] Rather, he commends the six-point program developed by the rabbinical students of the Conservative movement. [37] The student's proposals were basically similar to those adopted at the Garden but were much less encompassing. The fact that the student's proposals included a call for the establishment of a Jewish army such as the 'Bergson Boys' demanded, perhaps was the reason they won Medoff's approval.

The rally, described as the largest gathering of its kind ever held in the United States, [38] drew large and favorable coverage in the press and strong editorial comment. Many papers reversed their previous stands which had depicted the United Nations as unable to rescue Jews and had emphasized that salvation would come only through a speedy victory. After the rally, a number of influential publications, led by The New York Times, called for the Allies not "to spare any efforts that will save lives", and for the American government "to set a good example" by revising "the chilly formalism of its immigration regulations."[39] The editorial also summoned the United Nations to work along the lines of the proposals adopted at the rally.

The American Jewish Congress was very pleased with the outcome of the rally and its positive effect on American public opinion. A formidable rescue plan had been developed and presented in an impressive manner, supported by all the major Jewish organizations. They believed the administration would react accordingly. The resolutions were immediately sent to the President, to various leaders in the government and Congress, and to the media. The ads in newspapers before the rally, the press coverage of the rally itself and the many rallies held a few weeks later throughout the country, did much to publicize the Nazi plan to exterminate the Jews of Europe. It may also be assumed that the rally influenced Congress to accede to the request of the Jewish organizations and, after months of dallying, to finally pass a resolution condemning the Nazi crimes "especially the mass murder of Jewish men, women and children."[40] This resolution was adopted a week after the Madison Square Garden rally.

The effect of the rally even penetrated official Washington. Cordell Hull, who had never shown any interest in the tragic fate of European Jewry, wrote President Roosevelt that the rally, and similar ones held in its wake, were an indication of the "intense and widespread feeling on this subject" among Jews and others, and proposed that the U.S. government respond in some manner to the demand for rescue. [41] The preparations for the rally and the rally itself, contributed to the decision of the Jewish organizations to establish the 'Joint Emergency Committee for European Jewish Affairs' (JEC), an umbrella organization which succeeded in coalescing the entire organized American community (except the 'Bergson Boys') into a united Jewish front to demand the rescue of the Jews of Europe.

Secretary of State Hull with President Roosevelt

But all these rallies did not move the American government to act for rescue, as can be seen in the stand of the American delegation to the Bermuda Conference just a month and a half later. What else could the Jewish community have done to induce its government to act? Perhaps they should have made a sustained effort at lobbying Congress. But the Jewish leaders did not believe neither in the ability, nor the desire of Congress to contribute to rescue. Even the attempt of several Congressmen to add a clause to the resolution condemning Nazi atrocities that would have called for the rescue of Jews, was unable to pass in Congress. The Jewish leadership avoided an open confrontation with the administration and preferred to place their faith in the President, hoping that he would act.

The politicians who had spoken at the Garden rally and had called for immediate rescue of Jews included some very influential people, such as Gov. Thomas Dewey of New York, Sen. Robert Wagner, and Mayor Fiorello LaGuardia. Yet, aside from calling for the rescue of Jews, they did not exploit their connections to influence the Administration so that words become deeds. Nothing had changed within the administration. Breckinridge Long and his cohorts in the State Department were still the ones who, in reality, determined the rescue policy of the U.S.

The following week, Madison Square Garden was the scene of another impressive assemblage of Jews who came to view a pageant on the Holocaust organized by the Bergson group. Since Rabbi Wise's press conference in November the 'Bergson Boys' had become increasingly involved in mobilizing American public opinion to move the American government to "Save Jews Now!", as their giant ads proclaimed.

(b) The Bergson Boys

"Action Not Pity!"

(slogan of a CJA ad that appeared in the *New York Times*, 2/2/43)

The activities of the group that came to be known as the 'Bergson Boys' is receiving much praise today from many historians and journalists who have written about American Jewry and the Holocaust. However, at the time of their activities the 'Bergson Boys' were almost totally ostracized by the leadership of the American Jewish community, and were constantly harassed by the U.S. government. That small group, composed mostly of Palestinians, arrived in the U.S. at the beginning of the war as a delegation of the Irgun Zvai Leumi (the Zionist Revisionist underground) in Palestine to organize political and financial aid for the Irgun underground. In December 1942, it began to involve itself in the struggle for the rescue of European Jewry and added a new dynamism to the lethargic American Jewish community which had responded so falteringly to news of the Holocaust. Ironically, it was precisely this group, so violently opposed by Rabbi Wise, which carried out the very policy that Wise had once vigorously propounded – to publicly and boldly demand Jewish rights.

The group is generally called the 'Bergson Boys' both for the alias assumed by their leader Hillel Kook (Peter Bergson), and because they had formed so many different front organizations at that time that it is otherwise difficult to identify them. The chronicle of the 'Bergson Boys' during those years reads like an American success story. The group, which generally numbered only five or six members, all penniless aliens lacking any status in the American Jewish community, succeeded within a relatively short time to form organizations that obtained the support of 27 Senators, 75 Representatives, and scores of Governors, Mayors and leading personalities in the fields of arts and the media.[42]

They first functioned as The American Friends of Jewish Palestine and attempted to garner support for the Irgun underground, without much success. They soon changed direction and began working to create an independent Jewish Army within the framework of the Allied forces. This army was to be composed of 'Stateless and Palestinian Jews', though they also spoke of organizing 100,000 American volunteers.[43] Throughout most of 1941 they stubbornly propagated the idea of a Jewish Army.

On the eve of the Japanese attack on Pearl Harbor Bergson formally organized the 'Committee for a Jewish Army' (CJA), whose platform was a demand to grant the Jews, the principal victims of Nazism, the right to fight under their own banner in the struggle to defeat Germany, and in the defense of Palestine. They also proposed using Jewish units in retaliatory acts against Germany in an effort to dissuade the Nazis from harming the Jews of Europe.

The CJA proposed establishing Jewish 'suicide squads' who, in reprisal for every 10,000 Jews killed, would bomb "Nazi cities until 10,000 Nazis were killed."[44] The Irgun delegation's outlook was a political one, and they viewed a Jewish army as a tactic to achieve world recognition for the Jews as a nation and as a tool to achieve a Jewish State at the Peace Conference, which they assumed would be convened at the end of the war.[45]

The Bergson Boys were fortunate that among the first contacts they made upon arrival in the U.S. were some talented public relations people and gifted popular writers who were of immense help to them. Lacking a broad base in the American Jewish community, they turned to the mass media to present their message. They believed that in a democratic society, such as the United States, public opinion plays an important role and if properly mobilized it could move the government to action. "We believe in the overwhelming power of public opinion, as the greatest, if not the only power in a democracy,"[46] they wrote. They also concluded that since U.S. Jewry comprised less than 4% of the population, they would have to turn to the general American public to achieve results. Therefore they organized their various committees on a non-sectarian basis, including both Jews and non-Jews. The chairman of the CJA was Senator Edwin Johnson, an anti-Roosevelt Democrat from Colorado.[47] Their principal supporters in Congress, such as Senators E. Johnson, Guy Gillette (Iowa), Elbert Thomas (Utah), came from states with small concentrations of Jews. It is, therefore, difficult to assert that the actions of these politicians were attributable to a concern for "the Jewish vote."

Forming a Jewish army was not a new idea. The Zionist leaders, Ben-Gurion, Shertok and Weizmann, had also negotiated with the British on the same proposal, though they envisaged a Jewish force fighting under its own banner within the framework of the British Army. The Committee for a Jewish Army, on the other hand, demanded an independent Jewish army "with status similar to that of Poland, Czechoslovakia or of the Free French armies."[48] The negotiations between the Zionist Movement and the British came very near to achieving success in the Fall of 1941,[49] though this was unknown to the general public.

In 1941, American Zionists who favored the right of Jews in Palestine to defend themselves were nevertheless hesitant about enlisting American volunteers for a Jewish army fearing they would be accused of dragging the

U.S. into the war. They were also afraid that this would interfere with the President's attempts to aid Britain which, until the summer of 1941, stood alone against the Nazi 'Blitz'. Thus, the Zionist movement vacillated and its ambiguous message left many Zionists uncertain where their movement stood on the issue.[50] In contrast, the CJA's message was clear and forceful, even if some of their ideas had no basis in reality. They claimed, for example, that it was possible to mobilize at least 150,000 Palestinian Jews into a Jewish Army – a quarter of Palestine's Jewish population at that time.[51]

The determined struggle, and the clear statements, of the CJA drew a favorable response from many sections of American Jewry. This was particularly true in the Jewish communities outside New York where the national Jewish organizations were less able to assert pressure over local chapters to prevent contact with them. The CJA had begun winning over by default many rank and file Zionists who previously had evinced no leanings toward the Revisionists. The Zionist leadership consequently began to show concern. Emanuel Neumann, a Zionist leader closely associated with the militant wing of Rabbi Abba Hillel Silver, warned the Zionist organizations that if they themselves would not take the lead in the struggle for a Jewish army then "they shouldn't seek for any scapegoats and explanations."[52]

From the time the Bergson Boys had formed the Committee for a Jewish Army, some Zionists favored reaching an agreement of cooperation between the two groups. A few of these voices came from people, like Neumann, who tended towards the activism of the Irgun underground. But there were others, like Meyer Weisgal and Dr. Goldmann who, though far removed from Revisionism, believed it preferable to bring Bergson into the establishment so as to neutralize his influence.[53] As they saw it, the Bergson Boys inside the Zionist camp were less dangerous than the Bergson Boys outside.

In 1942 negotiations were held between these two bodies to see if an accord could be worked out. The Zionist movement demanded that the CJA accept the authority of the Zionist bodies as the price for its entry into the Zionist Emergency Committee.[54] Bergson saw in these demands a Zionist tactic to completely control his group, and insisted that the agreement be based on parity between the two bodies.[55] The Bergsonites also claimed that the CJA was not a Zionist organization, nor even a Jewish one, and therefore it could not accede to the authority of the Zionist movement.[56] From the discussions held in the CJA and from its internal correspondence, it appears that the Irgun delegation itself was not thrilled with the idea of joining the Zionists but had only agreed to the move under pressure of some of its American members.[57]

The Zionists carried out their negotiations with the Committee for a Jewish Army in such a manner that the latter could respond only in the negative. The mainstream Zionist organizations distrusted the Bergson Boys. They viewed them as representatives of the breakaway Irgun underground that had rejected the authority of the Jewish Agency Executive and which had resorted to violence against Palestinian Arabs. The American Zionist movement feared that the CJA would continue to act, in what they viewed as the irresponsible manner of the Irgun in Palestine.

Rabbi Wise and others in the Zionist movement, viewed the Irgun as a pro-fascist group, which at times had flirted with the idea of making a deal with fascist states. Truly, some members had seriously considered such ideas. In 1939 William Ziff, an early and staunch supporter of Bergson, had expressed his view on the possibility of forging "an actual Jewish alliance against [the British] with their present enemies, even though at the present moment these enemies are anti-Jewish."[58] For the strongly anti-fascist Wise these individuals were personae non gratae. But what Wise, and other Zionist leaders, did not realize was that Bergson, separated by the war from close contact with the Irgun underground (which at that time was under weak leadership and unable to assert its authority) had begun developing an independent position of his own in the United States.

However, it was David Ben-Gurion, in the U.S. at that time, who was most responsible for vetoing the agreement between the Zionists and the CJA. He met with Peter Bergson and demanded that both the Bergson Boys and the Irgun undergound, of which Bergson was a leading member, acquiesce to the authority of the Jewish Agency Executive as a pre-condition for acceptance into the Zionist Emergency Committee. When Ben Gurion realized that Bergson would not agree, he opposed any compromise with the CJA and his decision was approved.[59] Years later, Bergson (Kook) admitted that he also hesitated to join the Zionist Emergency Committee, fearing his organization would be co-opted by the Zionist movement.[60]

After the United States entered the war and began drafting all available young men, enrolling American volunteers in a Jewish Army became irrelevant. After Rommel's defeat at El-Alemein, defending Palestine also became less urgent. In the late fall of 1942, the CJA faced the predicament of losing the momentum it had gained in the past year. The Committee became revitalized in November 1942, when it learned from Rabbi Wise's press conference of the Nazi plans to exterminate the Jews of Europe. Bergson maintains that he immediately grasped the sense of this information and the next evening convened the CJA Executive and demanded that they put all else aside and work for the rescue of the Jews, the most burning issue at that moment.[61]

Does Bergson's statement today, that he was prepared to defer his efforts to create a Jewish army and a Jewish State for the urgent issue of rescue, truly reflect his views at that time? Is it conceivable that so staunch a disciple of Vladimir Jabotinsky (leader of the Revisionists – the ultra-nationalist wing of Zionism) would act in such a manner? There is no doubt, from reading Bergson's letters from that period and from the views he expressed at committee meetings, that for a period of time he did hold such views. In a letter Bergson wrote in 1944 to the head of the CJA in England, Jeremy ('Yirmie') Halperin, he confessed "I consistently prevented any possible action that did not directly and immediately affect the rescue of European Jewry."[62] And in a letter he sent to the Zionist Emergency Committee he explained:

> I have a decidedly secondary interest in establishing a Jewish Palestinian Army and whether there is established a Zionist homeland to the exclusion of other methods of saving those people [European Jews] from destruction.[63]

However, Bergson did not immediately harness his group solely to rescue matters as he claimed later. For Bergson, as for many others, the appalling truth did not immediately penetrate his consciousness. Even after the decision in November, to concentrate on rescue, the CJA circulars hardly even dealt with the situation of European Jewry. For many months they wrote exclusively about forming a Jewish army, and the CJA continued to struggle for the creation of such an army.[64] For the first two months after the decision to undertake rescue, they still saw a Jewish army as the main instrument for rescue.[65] Thus they did not visibly deviate from their previous approach.

Today some claim that the Bergson Boys were the first to make an appeal for rescue and only later, they were joined by the Jewish establishment.[66] But that was not the case. As we have seen, the 'Congress movement' publicly protested long before the CJA made its first call. We should recall the Madison Square Garden rally organized by the American Jewish Congress in July 1942, and the 'Day of Mourning' sponsored by the Jewish establishment that was held in December. Apart from these two major events, the Jewish organizations organized other meetings of smaller scope, throughout 1942. These demonstrations are generally not mentioned in the literature about that period. An example is the Town Hall rally in May 1942 that demanded shipments of relief for the Jews of Europe.[67] It is true that these demonstrations did not generally call for acts of rescue. Their purpose, in the main, was to protest the murder of Jews in Europe and to demand that Germany be warned to desist from its policies against the Jews.

Requests by the American Jewish Congress to the Allies not only to warn the Nazis, but also to develop and carry out a rescue policy, emerged in December, 1942. In an editorial in the *Congress Weekly* of December 18th, they stated that warnings to the Nazis are no longer a solace because "words have lost their efficacy [...] Unless extraordinary measures are taken Hitler will carry through his plan of extermination to the fullest."[68] A week later *Congress Weekly* again called for "practical steps [...] not only thoughts of apprehending the guilty persons [...] but also means of rescue[...] the United Nations might make use of all their resources to find havens for those who might be saved."[69] The 'Congress movement' devoted itself to developing rescue proposals in the hope that it could persuade the U.S. government and the international organizations to implement them. More important, during this entire period the Joint, the World Jewish Congress, the Jewish Labor Committee and the Vaad Hahatzalah were not only appealing for help, but were also carrying out actual rescue and relief activities.

On December 7, 1942 (a day before the meeting of Jewish leaders with the President) the CJA issued a full-page appeal in the *N.Y. Times* calling on the public for its support.[70] The ad, written by Pierre Van Paasen, a renowned non-Jewish journalist and author, was called "A Proclamation on the Moral Rights of Stateless and Palestinian Jews" and it served as the ideological platform of the organization.[71] It forcefully presented the fate of the Jews as the primary, and principle, victims of Nazism and declared that it was no longer possible merely to sympathize with their sufferings. In this ad the CJA did not, as yet, place rescue as its major priority nor did it present any concrete proposals. The ad was basically a political manifesto.

In light of the distressing situation of the Jews of Europe, the ad raised two major demands:

a) We recognize the right of these Jews to return to their place among the free peoples of the earth [...] [and] take up life as a free people". This meant recognition of the right of Jews for an independent state.

b) [T]he right [...] to fight as fellow-partners in this war, i.e. a demand for a Jewish army.

The appeal, simple and dramatic in its plea to save Jews, made its impact both on Jews and non-Jews alike. Many important personalities signed the manifesto and large amounts of money rolled into the coffers of the CJA. These funds were not used for actual rescue, in which the CJA was not involved, but were poured back into wider public relations. The more the CJA publicized its call for rescue, the more funds it acquired.

In February the CJA appeared in another vivid ad calling for "Action Not Pity."[72] This ad explained in detail the need to form a Jewish Army which the Bergsonites still saw as the primary response to the need for rescue. In smaller print, however, the ad also proposed, for the first time, that "an inter-governmental committee of military experts be appointed to find ways of stopping the slaughter." A week later the CJA produced a most eye-catching, though controversial ad, which declared "For Sale To Humanity 70,000 Jews Guaranteed Human Beings at $50 Apiece."[73] The ad, written by the journalist-playwright, Ben Hecht, was a response to a *N.Y. Times* article a few days earlier which had reported a Rumanian offer to release the Jews of Transnistria for the sum of 20,000 Lei per person. By this time, the CJA had reversed its position and stated that now their principal goal was a United Nations inter-governmental committee that would seek means for rescue.

These dramatic ads, and others placed during the following few months, did much to publicize the tragedy that had overtaken European Jewry, and the need for the Allies and Jews to act quickly if any Jews were to survive. But these ads also antagonized the Jewish establishment which felt that ads proclaiming that Jewish lives could be saved for a mere $50, were simply a fraud. All the more so since the Jewish leaders knew the CJA was not actually carrying out any rescue work.

In January Bergson decided on an even more effective method of dramatizing the tragedy of Europe's Jews. Ben Hecht, who previously had little contact with Judaism, wrote a pageant entitled "We Shall Never Die!" which it was decided to present at the Garden on March 8. Billy Rose, a famous Broadway producer, produced the pageant. Moss Hart directed the performance and Kurt Weill, himself a refugee from Germany, composed the score. The cast included famous actors of stage and screen. The pageant went off as planned and concluded with an impressive chorus of twenty Rabbis who intoned prayers for the dead Jews of Europe.

CJA ads urging people to attend the pageant again placed emphasis on making it "a decisive turning point in the campaign for a Jewish Army."[74] Despite the obstructionism of the Jewish establishment, the pageant drew 40,000 people to the two performances at the Garden. People were turned away for lack of space. The show was repeated in a half dozen other cities, and its performance in Washington, D.C. attracted many prominent American political figures, including Cabinet Ministers, Supreme Court Justices and the President's wife, Eleanor. The CJA had planned to repeat the presentation in many other American cities but the Jewish establishment, concerned over the recognition won by the Bergsonites, did all in its power to prevent such performances, and in many instances succeeded.[75]

When it became apparent that both the American Jewish Congress and the Committee for a Jewish Army would be holding rescue rallies at the Garden within a week of each other, Bergson arranged for Hecht to convene representatives of Jewish organizations to persuade the AJCong to cancel its rally. At the meeting in the Hotel Algonquin, attended by representatives of 33 Jewish organizations, Hecht presented the plans of his pageant. He proposed that the Jewish organizations support the pageant (not financially), and that all profits be shared among the sponsoring organizations.[76] The Jewish organizations rejected Hecht's offer, hoping that by ostracizing the Bergson group they would prevent it from establishing itself in the American Jewish community. Besides which, the Jewish organizations perceived a need to hold a public rally of their own at which they could present the public, and the Administration, with a program for rescue, and imbue it with the stamp of mass support.

The articles that had begun to appear in the Jewish press; the ads in the American papers; the Madison Square Garden rally; and the "We Shall Never Die!" pageant, had all created the beginning of a climate of protest in the American Jewish community and a call for "Rescue Now!" This new-found militancy did not escape the notice of government officials who now realized that some action must be taken to mollify the American Jewish community. Barely two days after the rally at the Garden, the State Department released to the press a message they had sent to Britain on February 25th, proposing a joint Anglo-American conference to be held in Ottawa, to explore the possibility of rescue.[77] This release made it appear that the U.S. government had provided the initiative for advancing rescue action. This was not the case. The diplomatic exchanges between the State Department and the Foreign Office had been initiated the previous December by the British and had been totally concealed from the Jewish organizations. The initiative finally led to the only Allied attempt to deal with the fate of European Jewry – the Bermuda Refugee Conference in April, 1943.

CHAPTER 9
The Struggle for Action

a) Joint Emergency Committee for European Jewish Affairs
"I have no right to sit in an ivy tower"
(Judge Proskauer explaining why he agreed to join the Joint
Emergency Committee)

On January 20, 1943, the Foreign Office sent the State Department an Aide-Memoire concerning "Refugees from Nazi-Occupied Territory". The career officers at Whitehall, however, were no more concerned with the fate of European Jewry than were their colleagues at Foggy Bottom. On the contrary, their Aide-Memoire revealed what really worried them: the possibility that the Axis states "may change over from the policy of extermination to one of extrusion", and embarrass the Allies "by flooding them with alien immigrants." Introducing "an excessive number of Jews" into Britain, they feared, might intensify antisemitism.[1] In addition the British stated that the problem should not be dealt with as solely a Jewish problem, for there were also many non-Jewish refugees.

The British note enumerated their many past contributions in helping to solve the refugee problem and asserted that despite the many difficulties, which stood in the way of aiding the refugees, Britain favored making some further contribution to the cause. The British suggested that if the two major Allied powers would accept a limited number of refugees, then it would be possible to call an Allied conference and to approach other governments to make similar contributions to the refugee problem. The British note spoke only about 'refugees', i.e. people who had already escaped from Nazi-occupied territories and had reached some temporary haven.

The British initiative, as seen in the notes sent by their Foreign Office was a result of strong public pressure exerted on the British government to save European Jewry. Ever since the first news of the massacre of Jews arrived in England the previous spring, the British section of the World Jewish Congress and the British Board of Deputies (an umbrella organization representing British Jewry) had been active and vocal in urging their government to find methods to ease the suffering of European Jewry. They succeeded in mobilizing political and church leaders to support their demands. The strong public outcry against the atrocities was significant because in Britain it came from non-Jewish leaders. These personalities demanded that the Allies take action to prevent further killings. On December 17, 1942 a moving ceremony was held in the House of Parliament. The Allied 'Declaration of War Crimes' was read, and the House stood in silence as a demonstration of sympathy with the suffering Jews.

In the following months, Parliamentary and Church leaders were relentless in pushing their demands for effective and immediate action. The leading archbishops of the Anglican Church (who were also members of the House of Lords), the Catholic prelate and other prominent clerics, met with members of the British Cabinet to induce them to initiate immediate rescue activities for the Jews.[2] Perhaps the proximity and the lobbying of the various Governments-in-Exile who had taken up refuge in Britain, and especially that of the Polish Government which at that time was a vocal advocate of relief, also influenced the British Foreign Office. The Polish government had initiated the call for the Allied declaration. The main victims of Nazism were Polish-Jewish citizens, but a large numbers of Polish non-Jews were victims of Nazism, as well. It was "the first time that an Allied government had undertaken to act as a spokesman for Jews under Nazi rule."[3]

The British Aide-Memoire was given to Breckinridge Long for an American reply, and he, in turn, requested his subordinates to make "a careful, liberal and thorough study of the whole subject."[4] Why Long used the adjective 'liberal' is surprising, for in all of his years in the State Department, Long never showed any signs of adopting a 'liberal' approach to the problems of Jewish refugees. The adjective missing from Long's request to his subordinates was 'expeditious'. Perhaps his request for a "careful and thorough study" was a signal to deliberately drag out the matter. It was apparent that Long was upset with the British initiative which he saw as "a plain effort to embarrass us by dumping the international aspects of that question on our lap."[5]

When a month had passed and there still was no American response, the Foreign Office informed the U.S. Embassy in London that they could not put off for more than a week some reply in Parliament. The British proposed issuing a call for a United Nations conference on the refugee problem to be held in London.[6] On February 22, Long drafted a reply, but there was nothing in it of his request for 'a liberal and generous' consideration of the refugee problem. Though Long wrote of America's readiness to allow refugees who qualify to enter the U.S. within the framework of the immigration quotas, he nonetheless emphasized that there was practically no shipping available for transport. Most ships, he claimed, were needed to transfer Axis Prisoners-of-War to the U.S. Nor, stated Long, could the U.S. press Latin American countries to open their doors to Jewish refugees for that would entail America assuming responsibility for them, a commitment the U.S. was not prepared to undertake.

The only solution that seemed viable to Long was for the neutral countries to accept refugees and to have the U.S. and Great Britain guarantee the neutrals that the refugees would be repatriated at the end of the war. Long suggested that Hull inform the Foreign Office that the U.S. did not favor calling an international conference, but preferred only consulting with the United Nations to the end that any efforts of the enemy to confuse the United Nations or to spread chaos by the extrusion of indigent and homeless persons may be defeated and not permitted to interfere with the successful prosecution of the war.[7] It was quite apparent that Long, like his British counterparts, was more concerned that Germany would actually agree to the departure of Jews, than he was troubled by the fate that had overtaken them.

Cordell Hull sent his reply to Britain on February 25th, detailing as the British had done, America's many past contributions to solving the refugee problem. He stated that the Intergovernmental Committee on Refugees, created at the Evian Conference, was best suited to deal with "further efforts" for the refugees – "not confined to any particular race or faith." He defined this as an attempt to find havens as near as possible to the places where they were. To prepare the IGCR once again to assume responsibility for refugee work, the State Department proposed that the U.S. and Great Britain hold "exploratory" talks in Ottawa.[8]

The unilateral publication on March 3rd of the American reply made in response to the Madison Square Garden rally angered the British officials. They protested to the State Department and then released to the press details of their own efforts to solve the problem. Nonetheless, the British agreed to the American counterproposal to hold an Anglo-American conference in Ottawa. The Canadians, however, who had not been informed of the proposal beforehand, objected to convening the conference in Ottawa, they feared that a refugee conference held in Canada would embarrass them.[9] (During the entire period of the Holocaust the Canadians had barred their gates to refugees, even more effectively than had the U.S.[10]). It was finally decided to hold the conference at Bermuda, a convenient location, for wartime travel restrictions would prevent delegations of Jews from reaching the island and lobbying for rescue.

The Jewish organizations had in the meantime met in a new attempt to achieve unity in order to deal with the crisis facing European Jewry. In the preceding months the World & American Jewish Congresses had been the main initiators of rescue plans. They had organized the various demonstrations and rallies throughout the U.S. The Temporary Committee set up to arrange the meeting with the President in December had dispersed on December 14th as Rabbi Wise had promised. What led Wise to make another effort at Jewish unity in March is not clear. One of his considerations was the imperative need for the American Jewish community to rally all its resources to impress on their government the need for rescue efforts. However, it was not always clear to the 'Congress movement' that unity in the Jewish community would, of necessity, enhance the struggle for government action. In the past they had feared that "unity may lead to unending, paralyzing discussions in the joint committees."[11] What the Congress movement feared most of all was that unified action might mean pandering to the quiet diplomacy favored by the American Jewish Committee, which would lead to no public action at all. Nachum Goldmann averred that "I am not for unity [...] It is better that one body approach the government with demands than that all bodies maintain silence."[12]

However the decision to achieve united action was not in the hands of the World Jewish Congress, but in those of the American Jewish Congress, and they decided to support the effort. Wise may have thought that in uniting the Jewish organizations he and his movement, which had been in the forefront of rescue efforts, would achieve their long sought hegemony of the Jewish community.

Wise called a meeting of the leading Jewish organizations that met on March 15th, and decided on the name, 'The Joint Emergency Committee for European Jewish Affairs' (JEC). It was composed of the American Jewish Congress,

American Jewish Committee, Jewish Labor Committee, B'nai Brith, Synagogue Council of America, Union of Orthodox Rabbis, American Emergency Committee for Zionist Affairs, and Agudas Israel The groups decided to invite the Joint Distribution Committee and the United Palestine Appeal also to join, or at least to send observers to committee meetings. The Zionists wanted to include Hadassah, claiming that their rescue work in Youth Aliyah entitled them to be represented. The JEC decided not to increase its membership, and suggested that a Hadassah member be one of the Zionist representatives (probably the real reason was that including Hadassah would have disturbed the balance between Zionists and non-Zionists on the committee). It was also decided to reject the request of the Committee for a Jewish Army to join the committee. Five co-chairman were appointed but no real organizational apparatus was ever created.

Why was no organizational machinery ever set up despite the constant prodding by the Jewish Labor Committee to do so? Perhaps it was due to lack of funds, or because of Wise's indifferent attitude to organizational matters. Perhaps it was because after the Bermuda Conference the JEC lost a sense of purpose and therefore saw no need for an infrastructure. We have no proof to suggest the reasoning of Wise or Proskauer. On the other hand, we do have a memorandum by Libby Schultz which states her opposition to setting up a formal organizational structure for fear that the American Jewish Committee would exploit the JEC thereby undermining the American Jewish Conference which was to convene that summer.[13]

If it appears surprising that Wise was willing to cooperate with the American Jewish Committee, we should also ask why Proskauer reversed his previous objections and joined the Joint Emergency Committee on a permanent basis. Proskauer was criticized for this by some members of his organization. His replies to his critics clarify his motives. In answer to the objection of Rabbi Gerstenfeld, Proskauer explained that

> There is a very terrible crisis created by the Jewish atrocities and [...] I have no right to sit in an ivy tower and refuse to collaborate with other organizations addressing themselves to solutions of this problem because we differ with them on other ideologies.[14]

Proskauer explained to another critic that their presence would enable them to modify the more activist elements on the JEC, "fellows like Lipsky and Nachum Goldmann."[15] The American Jewish Committee did have a restraining effect on JEC policies. Proskauer must also have realized that failure to join the JEC and to become involved in rescue efforts would estrange the Committee from the Jewish community and make it, in effect, irrelevant to Jewish life.

Even after the establishment of the JEC many in the American Jewish Congress were still opposed to cooperating with the AJC. Libby Schultz, who had coordinated the Emergency Planning Committee, warned that the AJC had not changed and that once it became entrenched it would hamper the rescue effort. An opportunity had been lost, she said, to isolate the American Jewish Committee and cut it down to its proper size.[16] Not only did Proskauer join with the other Jewish organizations, but in a complete turn about called upon AJC members to endorse and cooperate in the dozens of rallies organized by the JEC throughout the U.S.[17] For a number of months Proskauer and Wise worked fairly congenially until the American Jewish Committee left the American Jewish Conference, and became active in an anti-Zionist campaign.

The JEC was established as an umbrella committee consisting only of American Jewish organizations. This was done to exclude the World Jewish Congress, for neither the AJC nor Joint would have agreed to join any committee on which the WJC was represented. In preliminary talks with the other Jewish organizations the American Jewish Congress had stated, sine qua non, that "Any cooperation [...] to be taken by us with other agencies would have to be on the basis of simultaneous cooperation with the World Jewish Congress."[18] However, in the end they acquiesced to the exclusion of the World Jewish Congress.

When it appeared, at first, that the JEC might become the major vehicle for approaching the American government on rescue proposals, there was concern at the World Jewish Congress that rescue efforts would now be solely in the hands of American and British Jewry and that "non-English speaking Jews will be left out." Maurice Perlzweig warned that such a situation "will have serious repercussions [for the WJC] at the time of the Peace Conference."[19] However, through efforts of Wise, the World Jewish Congress leadership was able to make its views felt in the JEC. That was so evident that Joseph Hyman,

Vice-Chairman of Joint, recommended not joining the JEC because "Nachum Goldmann's influence is growing there" and creating dissension "which might lead to a split."[20] Nevertheless, the Joint did send observers to the Committee.

One of the first acts of the JEC was to send a delegation composed of Rabbi Wise and Judge Proskauer to meet with Anthony Eden, the British Foreign Minister who was in Washington for consultations with the American government. They presented him with proposals for rescue. Though they had been forewarned by Myron Taylor that Eden would not be receptive to their demands, nonetheless the meeting with Eden left the Jewish organizations despondent regarding the possibility of achieving their ends. Eden's attitude gave the Jewish leaders a premonition of what to expect at the forthcoming Bermuda Conference.

The main item in the memorandum presented to Eden was a request for the United Nations to appeal publicly to Hitler to allow Jews to leave Occupied-Europe. Eden responded that the proposal was "fantastically impossible", and suggested that the main emphasis should be on taking the refugees out of Portugal (where they had already found safety). A second request – that England assist in evacuating the Jews of Bulgaria – led Eden to remark: "Turkey does not want any more of your people" and that any such attempt would require Britain to increase its staff in Turkey, a very difficult matter. The other major proposal made to Eden – that the United Nations ship food to the starving Jews of Europe – "seemed to make no impression on him."[21]

Rabbi Wise's report of the meeting with Eden was a serious blow to the JEC. The minutes of the meeting describe the heavy pall that descended and that people "felt there was little use in continuing agitating for a demand on the United Nations."[22] However they decided to press ahead with plans for demonstrations in major cities of America. It was also decided that Rabbi Wise, who was considered to be a friend of the President, meet with him to gain his support in persuading the British to act (as though the British were the only barrier to action). They also determined to ask Jewish members of Congress to meet with the President (an unprecedented step, for there never before been a Jewish Congressional lobby) to urge him to obtain United Nations action.[23]

Immediately after the Garden rally Wise had written to the President presenting him with the resolutions and asking him to act on those proposals. The reply to Wise's letter was drawn up by Long who suggested that some one else sign for the Roosevelt because he "would like to keep the President out of this difficulty as far as possible."[24] After the JEC meeting, Wise wrote the President, once again asking to meet with him to discuss rescue proposals before the commencement of the Bermuda Conference. The reply was sent on April 14th, the day before the American delegation left for Bermuda. Secretary of State Hull informed Wise that there was no point for such a meeting since the delegation was already leaving the next day. He suggested that Wise forward him a copy of the proposals and the State Department would consider them.[25] The proposed meeting between Wise and President Roosevelt did not take place for another three months, though when it did occur it was to be of utmost consequence to the rescue cause.

On April 10th, the JEC heard a report from Congressman Celler on the meeting held by the Jewish members of Congress with the President, and to decide on a course of action for the forthcoming Bermuda Conference. Celler related that the main request of the delegation from the President was an appeal to him to simplify immigration procedures for the admission of refugees into the U.S. Roosevelt handled that request readily, and immediately arranged for a meeting of the Jewish Congressmen with Breckinridge Long and the government's Visa Review Committee. There it was decided to pass the matter on to a Steering Committee, which in turn appointed a sub-committee to draft recommendations. That bureaucratic entanglement was the only concrete 'result' of the long sought after meeting with the President. Roosevelt had also told the Congressmen that "perhaps" he would again issue visitor's visas to refugees, as he had done after 'Kristallnacht'. It is astounding that the Congressional delegation neglected this excellent opportunity personally to present the President with the full rescue program that had been drawn up by the Jewish organizations at Madison Square Garden, and to urge its acceptance. The only other request by the delegation – a plea to permit a Jewish delegation to appear before the Bermuda conference – was rejected by the President.[26]

Despite the disheartening report by Celler, the Committee discussed whether to persist in pressing the government to allow some Jewish experts to appear before the conference. Many felt that even if the government did allow a Jewish delegation to appear at Bermuda, it would serve only to cover up the vacuity of the conference. There already was a strong feeling that the expressed intentions of the Bermuda Conference – that it would be only of "an exploratory nature" and would deal with only a limited part of the problem – doomed it to prove itself a fiasco, much as the Evian Conference had been five years before. The inclusion in the American delegation of the Jewish Congressman Sol Bloom, Chairman of the House Foreign Affairs Committee, was seen as an attempt by the State Department to cover up any failure of the Conference to achieve concrete results. Bloom was considered by the Jewish organizations as a willing lackey of the State Department, who would not antagonize the Administration by pressing Jewish demands, even though the fate of European Jewry hung in the balance. The JEC, nevertheless, decided to meet with Bloom to acquaint him with their demands. Though at the time they were not aware of it, Bloom did make a short-lived attempt to advance some Jewish demands, particularly to put forth the point urged by Proskauer: to demand Allied negotiations with Germany and her satellites for the release of Jews. In the end his courage failed and he retreated under pressure of the other delegates.

Congressman Sol Bloom

At the April 10th meeting, the JEC finalized its proposed rescue program to be submitted to the Bermuda Refugee Conference on April 14th. The proposals followed the 11 point program that had been adopted at the Garden rally. The only major differences were the inclusion of a twelfth point, suggested by Joseph Schwartz, Joint's dynamic representative in Europe, and the omission of a reference to Palestine as "the Jewish homeland", at the insistence of the American Jewish Committee.[27] Schwartz, experienced in the field of rescue, had proposed adding a request for special passports, similar to the 'Nansen Passports' of the League of Nations, for the thousands of stateless Jews stranded in neutral countries.[28]

The preamble to the program emphasized that though all the conquered peoples were suffering from Nazi oppression "the Jews are the only people who have been singled out and marked for total extermination by Nazi Germany." It also stated that previous condemnations and threats of retribution had not "arrested the mounting tragedy", and that there was a growing public demand (as expressed at the Madison Square Garden rally) for the government to rescue as many victims as possible.[29]

In a separate memorandum to the State Department on the eve of the Bermuda Conference, the JEC made clear to the American government "the anguish of the Jewish community of this country over the failure of the United Nations to act until now to rescue the Jews of Europe". "Six months have elapsed", they charged "and no action has been taken."[30] Once again they asked that a delegation of the Jewish organizations be received at Bermuda. They knew the reply would be negative, but they did not want to give the State Department the opportunity of claiming that the Jews had never even asked to attend. The reply came from Breckinridge Long, who declared that their concerns were groundless as the U.S. was sending a competent delegation and there would be ample press coverage.[31]

Actually the State Department had encountered great difficulties in putting together the American delegation. The Jewish groups had hoped and been led to believe, that Myron Taylor, a strong advocate of rescue, would head the American delegation, as he had at the Evian Conference. But Taylor declined, supposedly because of his prior obligations to the post-war planning of the American government, but most probably because he felt that, once again nothing would result from the conference.[32] President Roosevelt, who had taken a minimal interest in the planning of the conference, proposed that Supreme Court Justice Owen Roberts head the delegation, but the Justice claimed that he couldn't free himself from the Court calendar until June. Roosevelt regretted that Roberts would not be able to head the delegation for "the State Department evidently decided (under British pressure) that the meeting should be held at once instead of waiting to June."[33] Roosevelt himself, quite obviously, saw no urgency to call the conference at once.

After further searching for a delegation chairman, it was finally decided, barely one week before the conference began, to appoint Harold Dodds, the President of Princeton University, to head the delegation. The other two members of the delegation were Representative Sol Bloom and Senator Scott Lucas. The delegation did not include a single strong advocate of rescue, but did include a few 'experts', such as Robert Reams, the State Department's 'Refugee expert' and Robert Alexander of the Visa Division, both of whom had in the past proved themselves adept in building barriers to rescue proposals. The British delegation, headed by the Parliamentary Under-Secretary for Foreign Affairs Richard Law, was composed of members of higher rank than their American equivalents.

A "strictly confidential" memorandum prepared by State regarding topics to be included on the agenda of the conference indicated some of their concerns as to what might transpire at Bermuda. As opposed to the JEC's call to the American government to recognize that it was only the Jews who were singled out for total extermination, the memorandum warned the delegation not to take steps "exclusively in behalf of the Jews" (deleted in the final copy) for it "would be vulnerable to criticism by or on behalf of other unfortunate peoples". It warned that the Germans were claiming that America was interested only in the fate of the Jews, and therefore "the conferees [...] should endeavor to avoid any possible implication which might be of assistance to the Nazi-Fascist propagandists."[34]

Bringing Jewish refugees to the Western Hemisphere was ruled out because it would require naval convoys. The memorandum did not state that such convoys were not feasible militarily, but only that Congress and the American public were not prepared to accept such action. In a section deleted in the final form, the Department raised the specter of native antisemitism as a reason for not bringing refugees, even within the framework of the quotas. The memorandum demanded not placing the American government in a position where it could be "accused of an attempt to fill with European refugees the places of our men and women in the armed services of the U.S. who have been sent to Europe to lay down their lives." Such action, they warned, "might well cause profound and serious repercussions."

The delegation was reminded that all past attempts to aid the refugees, such as the Wagner-Rogers Resolution, had been defeated in Congress.[35] The Near East Division of the Department also opposed placing Palestine on the agenda of the conference as a possible refuge for Jews. They claimed that such an act "would create serious risks of disaffection, perhaps accompanied by outbreaks in the Arab and Moslem world", and thereby impede the progress of the war.[36] The one positive element in the memoranda, was an intimation that the government might possibly allocate funds for rescue if other nations did so as well.

Though the Jewish organizations were unaware of the directives prepared for the American delegation, they already knew enough about the planning of the Bermuda Conference – the choice of the site, the decision to hold only "exploratory talks", the composition of the delegation – not to expect any positive results. Some in the JEC, such as Nachum Goldmann and Henry Montor, had proposed exerting public pressure on the government through mass demonstrations and lobbying Congressmen and government officials. But all those proposals had been rejected by the committee.[37]

This did not prevent Long from confiding to his diary that "one Jewish faction under the leadership of Rabbi Stephen Wise has been so assiduous in pushing their particular cause [...] that they are apt to produce a reaction against their interest [...] It might easily be a detriment to our war effort".[38]

On the eve of the Bermuda conference the chairman of the Committee for a Jewish Army, Sen. Edwin Johnson, proposed a resolution in the Senate that called on the delegations to act for immediate rescue of the Jews of Europe. The proposal died in committee and never reached the floor of the Senate.[39] There was no longer anything for the Jewish organizations to do but to wait and hope for the Conference to act.

(b) The Bermuda Conference and its Aftermath

"A sordid chapter in Jewish history"
(Rabbi Wise, describing the outcome of the Bermuda Conference)

The delegates to the Bermuda Conference did not waste time making clear that their intentions were not to embark upon any major attempt at rescue of European Jewry condemned to extermination, but, at best, to present a few palliatives that might placate the demands of rescue advocates. As host of the conference, the head of the British delegation, Richard Law, presided at the first session on April 20th, and in his opening remarks immediately ruled out the possibility of three major rescue proposals:

a) Negotiating with Hitler over the release of Jews;

b) Exchanging Nazi prisoners-of-war or German civilian internees, for refugees;

c) Sending food through the blockade to feed the peoples of Europe.[40]

Law candidly announced that it "was the hope in England" that if it were decided to approach the Nazis for the release of Jews, that Germany would answer with "a blank negative". He explained the British position as due to fear that the Germans might infiltrate agents among the refugees. What worried Britain even more was its apprehension that Hitler might say "Alright, take a million or two million", and there would be no shipping available.[41]

This fear that the Nazis might acquiesce to an Allied demand to release the Jews had been expressed several times in the past by British officials. No less a person than Anthony Eden had voiced the view three weeks earlier at a meeting with Roosevelt, Hull and Welles. When Hull raised the possibility of evacuating Bulgarian Jewry threatened with deportation, Eden replied:

> If we do that, then the Jews of the world will be wanting us to make similar offers in Poland and Germany. Hitler might take us up on any such offer and there simply are not enough ships and means of transportation in the world to handle them.[42]

However, what really bothered the British government was the possibility, that if Jews were released from Europe, Britain would be pressured to allow them to enter Palestine. This in turn, would bring Britain into conflict with the Moslem world, a situation which they wanted to avoid at all costs.

All the delegates concurred with Law, except Congressman Bloom. For a few bold moments, Bloom proposed that the Allies agree at least to negotiate with Germany, and to see what could be done. Proskauer had written to Bloom before the Conference explaining that the request for negotiations was the most important point in the JEC program, and prevailed upon him to press that issue at the conference.[43] Bloom's attempt to urge such negotiations led to a dispute among the delegates. They tried to explain the impracticality of opening negotiations with Germany, let alone having them release Jews. One delegate warned, that if the Allies accepted the refugees "it would be relieving Hitler of an obligation to take care of these useless people" [!].[44] Both Dodds and Reams made it clear to Bloom that his views were contrary to those of the American government, which opposed "negotiating on any terms with Nazi Germany." Under the pressure of his fellow-delegates, Bloom backed down.[45]

The delegates went on to deal with the two other far-reaching proposals. The possibility for a prisoner-of-war or a civilian exchange for refugees was ruled out without much discussion. Still remaining was the question of sending food to the starving Jews. The first delegate to address this question was Sol Bloom who, perhaps because he wanted to recoup his position after irritating his fellow-delegates on the first issue, announced that he was "generally against sending food."[46] Dodds immediately stated that sending food was altogether outside the terms of reference of the conference, and there was no place to make any recommendations.

After disposing of the three principal proposals in short shrift, the delegates devoted the rest of the morning to discussing problems of shipping with Julian

Foster, State's expert on the subject. Foster emphasized that all Allied shipping was tied up with bringing troops and materiel to Europe and returning wounded soldiers and Axis POW's to America on the homeward voyage. According to him, the only shipping available to the refugees were a few neutral ships. It was decided to investigate the possibility of obtaining their use for transporting refugees.[47]

The lack of shipping was the excuse consistently used to explain why the U.S. was unable to bring refugees to America during the war. In his book, *The Abandonment of the Jews,* David Wyman convincingly shows that there were enough ships of neutral countries (especially Spain and Portugal) to transport the refugees. Army transport and cargo ships often returned from Europe without any cargo, and at times even found difficulty furnishing ballast for the return voyage.[48] During the war years there were tens of thousands of Yugoslav, Polish and other non-Jewish refugees transported to various places in Africa and the Western Hemisphere. Shipping was always available for them.[49]

Many of the following sessions were devoted to the problem of transferring refugees interned in Spain, to other countries. Of the 21,000 refugees in Spain, 14,000 were French nationals and were therefore entitled to enter French North Africa. It was estimated that of the remaining 7000 refugees, some 3000 were of military age and thus candidates for the Allied armies. Thus, there was no need to worry about them either. The lingering problem, to which the delegations devoted much time, was what to do with the remaining 4000 refugees in Spain. The object of the plan was that if Spain were to be relieved of those refugees that were there at the moment, it might allow others to enter in their place. This offered some hope for Jews in Western Europe who might on their own smuggle themselves across the Pyrenees to safety. The obvious place for transfer, at least temporarily, was French North Africa, most of which had already been liberated.

Once again Bloom raised the most objections to the proposal. He rejected the idea, he said, because: a) Fighting was still going on in North Africa and the U.S. military was opposed to increasing difficulties in a war zone by bringing over refugees. b) The local Arab population opposed bringing Jews to North Africa. c) He feared the strong disapproval from Administration critics if Jews were to be placed in camps by the Allies. When Law realized that even so minimal a scheme was about to be dropped, he pleaded that the conference must come up with some proposal for immediate action, for which there was great public pressure in Britain.[50]

In the discussion as to the specific contributions Britain and the U.S. would make to accept refugees, the American delegation explicitly declared that it was impossible to change the American quotas. Both Congressmen stated that any such attempt would lead Congress to further reduce the present quotas for refugees permitted to enter the U.S. However the quotas were not the only factor limiting America's acceptance of refugees. Although the quotas allowed the annual entry of tens of thousands of immigrants, the delegation stated that the U.S. would accept only 1,000-1,500 refugees, if shipping was available.[51] The British stated that they would accept a similar amount and had already offered to allow 29,000 refugees, mostly children, to enter Palestine using the remaining certificates allocated by the 'White Paper'.

A number of sessions were devoted to setting up machinery to deal with the refugee problem. The American delegation proposed reviving the defunct Intergovernmental Refugee Committee (IGRC), which last had met in September 1939. They claimed there was no need for a new agency when one already existed, even though all knew it had done nothing over the years. At first the British opposed resurrecting the IGCR, but they yielded to American demands.[52] The only problems raised on this issue were some technical questions such as how to handle Argentina, a member of the IGCR Executive but who now had pro-Axis leanings. There also was the problem that the original mandate of the IGCR permitted it to deal only with refugees from Germany. It was proposed to allow the IGCR to expand its activities to include all European refugees. On the other hand, the new mandate contained an express condition barring negotiations with Germany (the original mandate expressly called for negotiations with Germany).[53] They also discussed the need for an effective organizational framework and for capable people to operate the committee. Its financing should be, it was determined, primarily by the private organizations with the Allied nations also contributing.

On April 25, the American delegation met in separate session to review its position on various proposals made at the Conference. At that meeting, late in the conference, the only serious attempt was made to deal with the problem of the massacre of European Jewry, though to no avail. George Backer, editor of the Jewish Telegraphic Agency and President of ORT, who been invited to the session, valiantly attempted to counter the half truths and lame excuses presented at the discussion. When Dodds declared that if shipping were available there would be no obstacle to America admitting refugees from Spain, Backer informed the delegates that at that very moment there were 45 Jewish refugee children in Barcelona who had qualified for admission to the U.S., but had not been taken out of Spain despite available shipping.[54] Nor, he continued, had there ever been a shipping problem. "Shipping", he claimed, "is available to private sources."[55]

Backer attacked the 'security hysteria' which effectively had cut off immigration to the U.S. He compared this to the attitude of the British who were in "a more dangerous position", yet security considerations did not drive them "to a point where they are 100% exclusive."[56] When Reams claimed that many Nazi agents had been found among the refugees, Backer, better informed on refugee problems than the official American delegates, countered that, in fact, only one such agent had been discovered during those years.[57] When the delegates tried to convince Backer using their standard line that Hitler would only agree to release the refugees in order to undermine the Allied war effort, Backer shot back that if that were so Hitler wouldn't have waited for the Allies to request the release of the Jews but would have forced them out on his own.

In the evening session Backer attempted to push forward the 12-point program drawn up by the JEC. (The delegates, for some reason, referred to the proposals as emanating solely from the WJC). Backer contended that the main problem was that of the Jews of Eastern Europe, and that would not be altered by the contemplated removal of a few thousand refugees from Spain. Instead, he proposed negotiating with Germany's satellites, such as Rumania and Bulgaria, where sizable Jewish populations still remained. Riegner and Lichtheim had been stressing for months that the best hope for rescue lay in approaching Germany's satellites who, since Stalingrad, were seeking ways to disengage themselves from the war. Backer declared that at least 125,000 people must be taken out of Eastern Europe if the conference were to claim that it had yielded any results. He said that he would not ask the Allies to request the release of all Jews, and he expressed his own feelings that their fate had already been sealed. He appealed, however, as "an act of moral force", that the Allies attempt to save the children who "are helpless and can harm no one."[58]

Senator Lucas carried the brunt of the attack on Backer and attempted to have him drop his proposals. The Senator asked Backer, what would happen if Hitler took them up on the overture and offered 100,000 Jews to the United Nations. "If you take care of 100,000", he contended, "you would have to stop this man's war". Backer, at no loss for words, retorted that "If 100,000 Germans would offer to surrender we would find some way to get them out."[59] Finally, Lucas raised the specter of antisemitism in America to convince Backer to abandon his proposals. He warned that the mass meetings and the twelve point program, which was "expecting the impossible", were detrimental to American Jewry. He cautioned that

> sooner or later this is going to become a serious issue in our own country if we are not awfully careful, especially when this thing gets to the point that American people believe that when you attempt to take out 100,000 or 200,000 or more and stop military effort – and that will be done – and prolong the war thereby endangering the lives of 100,000 of our own boys, you will have a pretty serious problem on your hands.[60]

Nonetheless, Backer still tried to get the delegations to approach Germany's satellites to allow 125,000 children to leave and for the Allied countries to find havens for them. He promised that no Jewish organization would propose any rescue efforts that might endanger the life of a single American soldier. Lucas continued warning Backer that he was taking "upon [his] hands the blood of American boys". Sol Bloom brought an end to the argument by summing up his feelings about the Bermuda Conference. The delegates, he proclaimed, "were going back feeling a great deal better than when they came here". He expressed his feeling that the committee had "done a job", and promised Backer that he, too, would be satisfied when "he reads the report."[61]

The report of the Bermuda Conference, however, was not made public at its close for fear that publication would lead to public outcries in the U.S. and Britain that the conference had been only a sham. The Conference delegates had readily obeyed the limitations their respective governments had imposed on the proceedings. The first point in the Summary of Recommendations of the conference – sent only to the two governments – was to reiterate the Anglo-American stand that "no approach be made to Hitler for the release of potential refugees in Germany or German-occupied territory". The second point called upon the two powers to consult immediately about obtaining neutral shipping to transport the refugees. This, however, was barely dealt with after the conference. Third, that the British consider admitting refugees into British-held Cyrenaica. This proposal was not intended for Jewish refugees, but rather for Greeks and had been proposed to demonstrate to the public that the conference had been called to deal with the problem of refugees from all nations and not solely with the 'Jewish problem.' The following points dealt with the transfer of between 4,000-5,000 Jewish refugees from Spain to North Africa. This proposal incurred difficulties with the State Department and the U.S. Militarye. The Conference also proposed examining the possibility that some of the refugees in Spain be allowed to enter the U.S., Palestine, Jamaica, Britain and Madagascar. Another recommendation made was that the Allies issue a joint statement, declaring that the refugees would be repatriated at the end of hostilities. This was intended to allay fears of those neutral countries, which had accepted refugees and were concerned that they would remain after the war. The remaining points dealt with proposals to establish and fund the Intergovernmental Committee on Refugees and a number of proposals that were referred for consideration to the IGCR, when it would begin to function.[62]

Knowing that practically nothing had been accomplished, the delegates issued only a short press statement at the close of the conference. A few weeks later they released a preliminary report which attempted to hide from the public the fact that the conference had done nothing to further rescue. None of the JEC's meaningful rescue proposals had even been discussed, except briefly, and even then only in the negative. None of the concrete rescue possibilities had even been touched upon. Pleading 'security reasons', and that publication of the conference's work "would be of aid or comfort to our enemies or might adversely affect the refugees", the report stated that it could not divulge details of all the decisions at Bermuda. To reassure those who feared that too much had been done for the 'refugees' (there was no mention of Jews), the communiqué stated that the Conference had acted upon two basic premises: a) That their recommendations not interfere with war operations. b) That the proposals could be carried out under conditions of war.[63]

The opening of the Bermuda Conference was announced in articles appearing on the front pages of many newspapers. Thereafter they scarcely covered the proceedings or the outcome of the conference. Once again the American press failed to make an issue of the need to rescue European Jewry, nor did the American public demonstrate any particular interest in the subject. Emanuel Celler later wrote about the American attitude: "There were few who had followed the proceedings of the Evian Conference[...] [but] there were fewer who followed the proceedings of the Bermuda Conference."[64]

Had the British and American governments intended the Bermuda Conference to be a public relations coup and to present themselves in a humanitarian light, attempting to solve the problem of civilian suffering in Europe, they obviously did not succeed. Their unwillingness to tackle the vital problem of rescue was so apparent that not only Jewish organizations, but also the press, saw that nothing of consequence would result from the conference. One of the reporters, wrote that it was "floundering in its own futility", while the attitude of the delegates was one "of doleful defeatism."[65] A number of newspapers expressed their disappointment that the Bermuda Conference had produced no results.[66]

While the conference was in progress, Breckinridge Long remained in Washington providing answers to the occasional questions posed by Dodds, and relied upon the American delegation to keep to his instructions and not deviate from the policies that had been laid down by the State Department. On the opening day, Long confided to his diary his distress with Rabbi Wise and the rescue advocates who had "been pushing their particular cause", and worried "that their acts may lend color to the charges of Hitler that we are fighting this war on the account of and at the instigation and direction of our Jewish citizens."[67] But as far as Long was concerned, the Bermuda Conference had achieved exactly what he had hoped – defusing the pressure of the rescue advocates. Two months after its conclusion, he was able to summarize "The refugee question has calmed down. The refugee groups have temporarily withdrawn from the assertion of pressure" even though, he admitted, "The recommendations of the Bermuda Conference have not been carried forward."[68]

However, the State Department's most invective attack on the advocates of rescue came from Robert Alexander, who had been attached to the American delegation. In a confidential memorandum to Long a week after the conference, Alexander likened the rescue slogans of the Jewish organizations to those of the Nazis, and implied that Hitler was behind the Jewish efforts to pressure the American government to act for rescue [!]. Alexander claimed that the rescue advocates had no real plan, only "a mere slogan first proclaimed by Hitler – 'Action Not Pity'". He mistakenly attributed this slogan of the Bergsonites to the World Jewish Congress. Alexander enumerated the dangers embodied in this slogan, and said that the purpose of this slogan was to take "the burden and the curse off Hitler". He asserted that

> It is not difficult once the facts are known to see who is really behind the pressure groups. However, we must not permit Hitler to get away with it[...]we may prevent Hitler from using the refugees once more to break through our defenses and prolong the war.[69]

On May 7, Secretary Hull sent President Roosevelt a summary of the recommendations made at Bermuda and asked for directives as to how the U.S. should deal with them. He divided the proposals into two categories: those that required immediate action by the American and British governments; and those to be handled later by the IGCR when it began functioning. Of immediate urgency was for the U.S. to defray half the cost of evacuating 5,000 Bulgarian Jews to Palestine (no comment by the President). The second proposal envisaged moving 20,000 refugees from Spain to North Africa so more refugees could enter the country. During the Bermuda Conference the American Chiefs of Staff had opposed this proposal claiming that North Africa was still a theater of war, and that bringing refugees there would interfere with the war effort. They were primarily concerned with arousing Arab hostility by bringing in Jews. However, Hull reported to Roosevelt that General Eisenhower, who commanded the American troops in North Africa, and General Giraud, who was appointed the French commander of North Africa, had agreed to first bring 14,000 French refugees from Spain, and only then to allow the others to enter. Roosevelt wrote Hull that he agreed to the proposal, but that the refugees should be allowed to enter only on a temporary basis. He also "raise[d] the question of sending large numbers of Jews there. That would be extremely unwise." [70]

The outcome of this plan to move refugees from Spain to North Africa, the one concrete plan that the American government had taken upon itself at Bermuda, was a farce. A year after the Conference not a single stateless refugee had been sent from Spain to North Africa, and in June 1944 there were only somewhat more than 600 Jews in the refugee camp in Morocco. [71] Yet Hull had written that this plan would "save as many [refugees] as quickly as possible". Nor did the scheme to send refugees to Cyrenaica materialize.

The other recommendations of the Bermuda Conference concerned the work of IGCR. Hull reiterated to the President, Myron Taylor's view that if America and Britain did not lead the way by making actual commitments of their own, nothing would be accomplished. As to financing rescue operations, Roosevelt wrote Hull that the U.S. should not "give unlimited promises", but occasionally should share the cost in specific cases.

As to allowing refugees to enter the U.S., Hull warned of the danger in changing, or circumventing, U.S. immigration quotas. Hull pointed out that both Congress and the public favored a drastic curtailment of immigration to America "when our own citizens are going abroad to lay down their lives". Roosevelt expressed his agreement that there should be no revision of the immigration laws, nor should refugees be admitted on a temporary basis. [72] No mention was made of exploiting the existing quotas to the maximum, an act which would have permitted tens of thousands of refugees to enter the U.S. each year. Chaim Weizmann was correct when he wrote in a memorandum to the Bermuda Conference that "the world is divided into countries in which Jews cannot live, and countries which they must not enter." [73]

There still remained the problem of an American delegate to the IGCR, the body that was supposed to develop and execute rescue proposals. Myron Taylor was again the obvious choice, but he did not want to become involved in an organization which he believed would achieve nothing. Roosevelt urged Taylor to accept, promising that "You need not devote your personal time and energy to attend meetings. You could designate an alternate."[74] Quite obviously, Roosevelt himself did not attach great importance to the proposed rescue agency. Only in August did Taylor choose Patrick Malin as the U.S. Vice-Director of the IGCR, and Herbert Pell as Taylor's alternate on the Executive.

The Intergovernmental Committee on Refugees held its first meeting in August 1943, but over the following few months devoted its efforts to the sole task of setting up its organizational structure before beginning to act. Even after many months spent in restructuring itself, the IGCR continued to operate at a leisurely pace. It never envisaged itself performing any major rescue operations. Herbert Emerson, the British director of the IGCR, conceived the main role of the committee as playing "a big part in the post war problems."[75] Nor did the British or American governments concern themselves with the IGCR once they had gone through the motions of creating that agency, quite obviously, for the purpose of muting the demands of rescue advocates. The two million dollars that each government had promised to the Committee for the first year, did not materialize until 1944.[76]

In the end, the Bermuda Conference produced no more results than had the Evian Conference. Even Richard Law, head of the British delegation to the Bermuda Conference, admitted many years later that "we had said the results of the Conference were confidential, but in fact there were no results I could recall."[77]

The Jewish organizations, who even before the Bermuda Conference convened, were aware that nothing would be achieved, were quick to respond. Publicly they declared their indignation at what Rabbi Israel Goldstein, President of the Synagogue Council of America, termed "a mockery", privately they expressed their despondency over any hope of rescuing the still surviving Jews of Europe. Rabbi Wise called the conference "a fiasco" and a "sordid chapter in Jewish history", but saved his main barbs for Sol Bloom who had said that as a Jew, he was satisfied with results of the Bermuda Conference. Wise claimed that Bloom had been put on the American delegation "in order as a Jew he might serve as a defense of whatever policies of inaction or reaction Bermuda might choose to adopt."[78] The paucity of results from the Conference and the absence of protests from the public to this lack of action, led Chaim Weizmann to divulge to American Zionists that "He did not think England or America [were] morally capable of doing anything."[79]

In the days immediately preceding the Bermuda Conference there had been those in the Jewish organizations who had wanted to organize demonstrations to press the Conference to act. After the Conference there were few who any longer believed that public pressure could achieve any results. Even so strong a rescue advocate as Kubowitzki felt that the public was apathetic, and that "Roosevelt was very much antagonized by the many mass demonstrations."[80] Goldmann, who previously had advocated a strong public response, concluded, after the failure of the Bermuda Conference, that mass demonstrations had been unsuccessful. In the wake of Bermuda he felt that the few sources of manpower and funds available to the Jewish organizations would be better used in a struggle against the White Paper.[81]

So despondent were they over the outcome of the Bermuda Conference that the JEC did not even respond to its failures until almost a month after its conclusion. Only on May 21, did Herman Shulman present the committee with a draft of a letter to be sent to the State Department accusing it of an "unwillingness to act" to rescue Jews, and charging that the negative policy of the United Nations regarding the extermination of European Jews "is an incentive to their destruction". Following the lines of Goldmann's proposals at the Zionist Emergency Committee, Shulman called for concentrating on sending the Jews of Europe to Palestine "the only permanent and immediately available refuge for Jews."[82] Proskauer strongly rejected the tone of the letter, refusing to acquiesce to an attack on the Administration that "will stir up bad blood". He also warned that if the wording of the proposal on Palestine remained, he would resign from the Emergency Committee.[83]

The JEC letter that was finally sent to the State Department merely expressed their "deep disappointment" that the Bermuda Conference had decided to implement only "in a small degree" the 12-point program that they had submitted. In their new appeal they now proposed only that: 1) The Allies attempt to negotiate with the satellite nations; 2) Havens be established in the neutral countries, United Nations territories and Palestine (Palestine as the "only permanent and immediately available refuge for Jews" was dropped); 3) Returning troop ships be used to transport refugees; 4) Britain and the U.S. ease their visa regulations, and the U.S. accept refugees within the quota. They implored, once again, that the proposed War Crimes Commission be established. For the first time the JEC, well aware that the IGCR would accomplish nothing, proposed the establishment of an American agency for rescue.[84]

The new proposals dropped the previous requests for negotiations with Germany; feeding the starving Jews of Europe; settling refugees in Latin America; and financing rescue operations by the Allies. The last point was dropped because the Jewish organizations decided to limit their requests, and to finance rescue operations themselves. Joint informed the State Department that it would support, within its limits, "any projects which our government may develop and undertake looking to rescue or relief of distressed Jews in Axis-occupied territory,"[85] and the World Jewish Congress launched another major attempt at raising funds for rescue.

In a memorandum by Long on the JEC requests, he confided to his colleagues that the State Department had intercepted letters sent by the WJC in New York to their offices in London. From the intercepts Long had concluded that the WJC (which the State Department viewed as the chief culprit among rescue advocates) was not going to press for most of the rescue program but intended to emphasize creation of the War Crimes Commission. Long proposed that the State Department establish the commission, so that this act, no more than a symbolic one, would diminish the demands for rescue.[86]

❖ ❖ ❖

The Joint Emergency Committee had functioned for only a few weeks preceding the Bermuda Conference, but its activities were impressive. In this period it had presented the 12- Point Program as a joint statement of the entire organized American Jewish community. It had lobbied all its contacts in Washington to advance the rescue proposals and it had organized rallies in cities throughout the U.S. After Bermuda, realizing that all its efforts had been in vain and despairing of any hope of influencing the government, the JEC in actuality ceased to exist. It continued to meet occasionally until it was replaced by the Rescue Committee created that summer at the American Jewish Conference. When criticized by the Jewish Labor Committee for its dearth of activity, Proskauer responded that the Emergency Committee "is inactive because there isn't a single thing I can think of that it can do, and to keep threshing around is harmful and not helpful."[87]

Goldmann also explained to Shertok that "All our efforts have been unsuccessful" and that all their suggestions "were categorically turned down". He felt that there was no point any longer in organizing mass meetings "in view of the determined policy of the British and American governments". The only proposal Goldmann felt was still worthwhile pursuing was the creation of a War Crimes Commission, hoping that it would warn the murderers and possibly have a deterrent effect.[88]

Yet not everything was at a standstill. Joint's representatives in Europe were still pushing relief efforts as best they could, and the WJC continued to press their programs on governmental agencies and international organizations. The Jewish Labor Committee and the Vaad Hahatzalah were still continuing their secret relief activities. At the time that Goldmann and Wise were expressing their despair, they were about to become participants in some of the first major breakthroughs in the barriers that surrounded the rescue efforts. These were the harbingers of a changing attitude of the American government toward saving what were now only the remnants of European Jewry.

❖ ❖ ❖

By the second half of 1943 the war had swung decisively to the side of the United Nations. On all fronts the offensives were now those of the Allies. The Axis Powers were on the defensive and were drawing deeper into their dwindling resources of manpower and supplies. In July, American and British troops began their first invasion of Europe, landing in Sicily, and Mussolini was deposed by the King. Two months later, Allied forces stormed the Italian mainland causing the surrender of the Italian government. This was not, as yet, the cross channel invasion that Stalin had demanded, but at the Quebec Conference in August, the United States and Britain resolved to open a second front in the spring of 1944.

The vast majority of Jews who had fallen into Germany's hands were dead by the summer of 1943 – some hundreds of thousands had perished from hunger and disease; a million and a half had been executed by the Einsatzgruppen; and a similar number gassed in the death chambers of Treblinka, Majdanek and other extermination camps. On the same day that the delegates arrived for the start of the Bermuda Conference, the remnants of Warsaw's Jewry began their desperate revolt. By May practically nothing remained of the half million Jews who had been incarcerated in the Warsaw Ghetto – only a few thousand lingered in hiding. In July, Riegner and Lichtheim wrote the State Department protesting reports in the American press that four million Jews yet remained under Axis rule. They claimed that only one and half to two million Jews were still alive, and that four million had already perished.[89]

Yet for those Jews who still survived, and they were mainly those living in Germany's satellites, some new developments were occurring which offered hope of outliving the Nazi demise. These satellites had suffered heavy losses on the Eastern Front They feared invasion and bombardment and were aware that the Allies were now winning the war. They began to seek methods of extricating themselves from the conflict and hoped that better treatment of their Jews would stand in their favor at war's end.

Since the fall of 1942, both Lichtheim and Riegner had been attempting to convince the Zionist Movement and the World Jewish Congress that the most practicable chances for rescue lay in the Allies approaching the satellites with offers that a humanitarian attitude toward the Jews would be taken into consideration in peace negotiations. Though this ran counter to Roosevelt's declaration to accept nothing less than the unconditional surrender of the Axis countries, he himself had already modified this demand by his willingness to negotiate a separate peace with the King and the Fascist government of Italy.

The changing war situation also affected the attitudes of some in the Administration. They were now willing to depart from their previous position of not permitting any rescue or relief activities, which they felt might hamper the war effort. The senior officials at the Treasury Department, who until then had been adamant in their opposition to the transfer of funds to Jews in enemy-occupied territories, now proposed reversing the Department's stand. They cited the changed war situation and the fact that the relatively small sums of money "would have little chance of significantly benefitting the enemy."[90] The President, too, was now prepared to make a significant departure from his previous position and though he did not initiate any rescue activities, he was amenable when approached to approve some far-reaching rescue proposals.

The changing tide of the war following the Nazi defeats at Stalingrad and El Alamein, caused the American government to launch intensive planning for the post-war period, a matter of vital concern to Roosevelt who wanted to avoid the failure of Wilson and the Versailles Conference after World War I. That same atmosphere, which looked to an early conclusion of the war, also spurred the Jewish organizations to begin making their post-war plans. None was as persistent in planning and in activity as the Zionist movement which saw the need and the opportunity, to solve the age-old Jewish problem by creating a Jewish state in the wake of the war.

CHAPTER 10
Zionism and Rescue

(a) "Tears and Sympathy"
*"We shouldn't give up concrete Zionist proposals for the tears
and sympathy of America, for it won't guarantee the future
of the Jewish people."* (Meyer Weisgal to the AJCong, 12/42)

Did the attempt to rescue European Jewry fall within the realm of the Zionist
Movement, or was its task only to work for the rebuilding of Palestine and the
establishment of a Jewish State? Did there exist, at all, a dichotomy between
Zionist goals and rescue efforts? The first question was at times deliberated by
the Zionist leadership, and the matter was finally decided in December, 1942.
At that time it was determined, at the request of American Jewish Congress,
that rescue activities be handled by them, in cooperation with other Jewish
groups and that the Zionist Movement was to abstain from such activities. It
was not difficult for the Zionist Movement to acquiesce, for it was an integral
part of the 'Congress movement' and the leadership of both organizations
overlapped to a great degree. Rabbi Wise was, at that time, the central figure
both in the Zionist Emergency Committee and in the American Jewish
Congress. The meaning of that decision was no more than the clear division
of labor between these two sister organizations. A similar question had arisen
in the 1930's when plans were made for creating the WJC. Some Zionist
leaders questioned the need for an additional world-wide Jewish organization.
Goldmann saw it as complementing the activities of the Zionist Movement.
"There must be two separate Jewish organizations – one for Palestine and
another to fight for Jewish rights", he asserted.[1] Thus the Zionist Movement
in America, as such, did not deal with rescue activities despite the request of
the Jewish Agency Executive in Jerusalem that the Zionist Movement should
become involved in rescue work.

The second question, whether there existed any contradiction between
Zionist goals and the rescue of European Jewry, is much more complicated.
At times, during the Holocaust, this question, which steps American Zionists

should take to aid the Jews of Europe was often discussed. It should be noted that, in general, the Zionists saw no contradiction between Zionist aims and rescue. On the contrary, as the condition of European Jewry deteriorated, the Zionists became more and more convinced of the validity of their prognosis – that without a sovereign state of their own there was no foundation for the continued existence of the Jewish people. Nonetheless, many times American Zionists had to choose between paths of action in which the Zionist goals and rescue attempts seemed to contradict each other. Should American Zionists have supported the 'Transfer Agreement' in the 1930's, which meant maintaining commercial relations with Germany, or should they have imposed a total boycott of German products? Should Zionists have demanded that Jewish funds be used solely for creating a Jewish homeland in Palestine, or did the needs of the hour to save lives require them to support and finance attempts to settle Jews in scattered corners of the world?

Shabbtai Bet-Zvi, in a scathing indictment of the Zionist Movement, accused both the movement, and the leadership of the 'Yishuv', of adhering to a distorted view of the tasks of Zionism perceiving them as limited only to developing and settling Eretz Yisrael. According to Bet-Zvi, it was that very same 'Palestinocentric' ideology that led the Zionist Movement to abandon Diaspora Jewry during the Holocaust.[2]

Bet-Zvi not withstanding, it is difficult to find a uniform approach to the question of rescue among all the Zionist leaders in America at that time, nor even a consistent approach by each of them separately. Their stand varied according to changing circumstances. There were Zionist leaders such as Rabbi Abba Hillel Silver who did not deal at all with rescue matters but only fought to achieve a sovereign state for the Jews that would survive the war. And there were Zionist leaders, like Rabbi Wise, and they were the majority, who attempted to achieve both goals.

The Zionist Movement which had been on the periphery of American Jewish life between the two World Wars, strengthened its position toward the end of the Thirties. During the Holocaust, Zionism captured a pre-eminent place among American Jewry as can be seen in the elections to the American Jewish Conference in 1943, in which the Zionists won an overwhelming majority.[3] The

Zionist Organization of America, a mainstream Zionist organization, grew from a few thousand members in the early 1930's, to 50,000 members in 1942 and to 250,000 members by 1948. The membership of all the Zionist organizations in the United States totaled nearly one million by the time the State of Israel was established.[4] The Zionist message that proclaimed that the Jews of Europe can no longer exist in the countries where they lived, and that the world was obligated to grant the survivors of the Holocaust a safe and sovereign state of their own, was well understood by the mass of American Jews who, until then, had been remote from Zionism.[5] By the end of World War II, 80% of American Jewry said they favored the creation of a Jewish State while only 10% were opposed.[6]

The struggle against the British 'White Paper' and the efforts to open the gates of Palestine to the refugees struck a responsive chord among American Jewry. During the 1930's, when European Jewry was seeking asylum, Palestine had proven itself the main haven for Jewish refugees before the British imposed limitations on Jewish immigration in the wake of the Arab revolt in 1936. In the years 1933-37, only about 35,000 Jews managed to enter the United States, while 42,000 refugees from Germany alone found a haven in Palestine during that period.[7] In the four years preceding the British decision to limit immigration, 161,000 Jews had been absorbed in Palestine.[8]

In the attempts to rescue Jews during the Holocaust, Palestine, located so near to the centers of Jewish populations in Eastern Europe, appeared to be the logical refuge for endangered Jews. The struggle for the abrogation of the White Paper, in essence a struggle against Britain, was easier for American Jews to embrace than to battle against their own Administration and an unfriendly American public. By demonstrating against Britain, American Jews were able to clear their consciences of not having done enough for their brethren in Europe by refraining to demand a relaxation of immigration restrictions in the U.S. The Zionist leadership understood this to be the reason for the change of attitude of American Jews to the Zionist struggle. Moshe Shertok (later Sharett) reported to the Jewish Agency that

> There is a collusion between the Jews and the American public
> opinion and the American government [...] the Jews won't raise

the question of opening the gates of America to the refugees, and as a reward the American government will aid us on the Palestinian issue.[9]

Since the eve of the Second World War the various Zionist Movements had united in the American Emergency Committee for Zionist Affairs (ECZA), under the chairmanship of Rabbi Wise. Wise may have been the spiritual leader of the American Jewish Congress and of the Zionist Movement, but he was unable to provide effective organizational leadership. Perhaps the many tasks that he took upon himself: Vice-President of the Zionist Organization of America; Chairman of the Zionist Emergency Committee; President of the World Jewish Congress; President of the American Jewish Congress; President of a Rabbinical Seminary; Rabbi of a large congregation; editor of a magazine, to mention just some – prevented him from devoting the necessary time to the task of rescue.

The Zionist Emergency Committee was constantly bogged down in fruitless discussions on such issues as determining their attitude to the 'Ichud' group in Palestine (a group of Jewish intellectuals who favored the creation of a bi-national state of Jews and Arabs), an issue which they debated endlessly in the critical months following the arrival of Riegner's cable informing them of the Final Solution.[10] Even more than the 'Congress movement', ECZA suffered from insufficient funds for its activities. In January 1943, Emanuel Neumann, who had been a key figure in running ECZA, resigned, frustrated by the inability of the committee to function. In the critical period following the Biltmore resolution, which called for the creation of a Jewish State in Palestine, the American Zionist Movement was wrought with dissension, poorly organized and unable to exploit fully the changing attitude of American Jewry to Zionism. Yet despite that, it achieved impressive results in winning many supporters to Zionism, both among Jews and non-Jews.

Only after Rabbi Abba Hillel Silver was named co-chairman of the committee, and after a bitter conflict with Rabbi Wise, did the Zionist Emergency Committee acquire a new impetus. The name was changed to the American Zionist Emergency Committee (AZEC) and with a new, more dynamic and militant leadership, it led American Jews in the struggle for the creation of the State of Israel. It organized local chapters, and improved its organization on the national level. Under Rabbi Silver, money was raised for new initiatives and the annual budget of $100,000 was increased to $510,000 for the first 15 months of Silver's leadership[11]– enabling him to open a Washington office, lobby Congress and expand the activities of the Zionist Movement.

As we have seen, there were many Zionist leaders, such as Rabbi Wise and Dr. Goldmann, who worked simultaneously both for rescue of European Jewry and for Zionist goals. How did they divide their time and their energies to achieve these different aims? Did one have preference over the other? The answer is not clear. The attitude of the Zionist leadership to rescue attempts varied according to their degree of knowledge of what was happening to European Jewry. It was also affected by what they believed they could achieve to aid and rescue their fellow Jews facing annihilation. It is a matter of wonder how Stephen Wise, a man of seventy and ill, was able to find so much spiritual and physical strength to work so intensively during those years.

Dr. Goldmann was keenly aware of the difficulty of concentrating the limited Zionist resources to achieve either one or the other goal. After the failure of the Bermuda Conference, Goldmann despaired of moving the Allies to rescue efforts and proposed concentrating on Zionist aims.[12] But others in the Zionist Movement – members of Hadassah, Mizrachi (Religious Zionists), and the Labor Zionists – opposed Goldmann's thinking.[13] He too changed his stand when he perceived that there again existed possibilities of rescue.

The main opposition to the Zionist Movement was the American Jewish Committee, which held to the emancipatory view that Jews should integrate into the lands in which they lived. It viewed Judaism only as a religion, not as a peoplehood. It was at odds with the Zionist movement that dreamt of creating a Jewish state, and with the World Jewish Congress that believed that Jews, no matter where dispersed, were still one people. The AJC feared that if Jews were to be recognized as belonging to one nation, then their own position as loyal Americans would be brought into question. "What is the American Jewish Committee?" one of its members asked rhetorically. His answer was that "We are first and last American citizens, and don't recognize special interests of Jews or divided loyalty."[14]

Ben-Gurion, who was then in the United States, attempted to reach an agreement with the American Jewish Committee. He felt that it was essential for the Zionists to achieve an understanding with them in view of their good connections in the Administration, and because they were the conduit to wealthy American Jews whose financial aid would be needed in the establishment of a Jewish State. Also, there were members of the AJC on the 'Broad Executive' of the Jewish Agency, which was officially recognized by world governments. It was presumed that it would be present at the Peace Conference when war ended. If the American Jewish Committee broke up the Jewish Agency, Zionist leaders feared that the Zionist representation at the Peace Conference could be endangered.

After the Biltmore Conference Ben-Gurion began negotiations with the AJC. In June 1942 he reported to the Zionist leadership that it was possible to reach an agreement with the Committee on a joint statement on Palestine. However the AJC demanded, as a precondition "the dissolution [of the World Jewish Congress] or so great a change in its name and acts that it can no longer be an embodiment of the theory of diaspora nationalism."[15] Ben Gurion thought that if it were possible to reach an agreement with the AJC on the future of Palestine, something could be worked out with the World Jewish Congress. Rabbi Wise, however, asserted that such an act would be a betrayal of the Jewish people, and that it was not within the province of the Zionist Movement to discuss the fate of the WJC. For American Zionists, to whom Zionism had never meant themselves settling in Eretz Israel, the concept of Galut (Diaspora) nationalism as embodied in the WJC, was very meaningful, and therefore they opposed relinquishing the organization.

In December 1942, the Kirsten Committee, set up by the American Jewish Committee to negotiate with the Zionists, proposed "an agreement that the national conception of Jewish life was to be renounced by all organizations, but that the principle of ultimate self-government in Palestine by Jews residing in that country was to be endorsed."[16] Though the proposal contained a rejection of basic Zionist ideology, it did accept the idea of a Jewish State, and coupled with the opposition of the AJC to the 'White Paper', it met the immediate goals of the Zionist Movement. There was, however, much opposition in the AJC to the Kirsten proposal and that body decided first to consult with the State Department before finalizing its stand.[17]

The election of Judge Proskauer as President of the American Jewish Committee in January 1943, placed that organization squarely in the camp of the anti-Zionists. From a non-Zionist body, they became, under the leadership of Proskauer, a militantly anti-Zionist force. This bitter conflict, between a group small but influential and the mass Zionist movement, became a stumbling block in the path of Jewish unity. Both camps contended bitterly for the leadership of the American Jewish community. In April 1942, Proskauer had written Morris Waldman that there was a wave of anti-Zionist feeling growing in the U.S. which has "got to have an expression", and clearly saw himself as its spokesman. He believed that the creation of a Jewish state would be "a Jewish catastrophe."[18] Upon election, he wasted neither words nor time in making it clear to the State Department that he intended to fight both the Zionists and the 'Congress movement'.[19] In January 1943 the Zionists made their first major move to create a broad consensus of American Jewry in support of the establishment of a Jewish state. Henry Monsky, the dynamic President of B'nai Brith, who had brought about his organization to support Zionist principles, called for a meeting of all major Jewish organizations. Monsky's invitation set as the goals for the meeting: the consideration of steps towards reaching an agreement among American Jewry regarding the post-war status of the Jews of Europe, and the building up of a Jewish Palestine.[20] Monsky was probably encouraged by the Zionist leaders to call the meeting. They believed that Monsky's status would deter organizations from rejecting his call.[21] Most Jewish organizations responded to his summons and met in Pittsburgh at the end of January. However, both the Jewish Labor Committee and the American Jewish Committee, fearing that the meeting was intended to pressure them into supporting a Zionist platform, did not attend.

The Pittsburgh meeting decided to convene a conference of representatives of the American Jewish community, who were to be chosen in democratically held elections. Though Wise's revelations two months earlier had made rescue an urgent issue, it was almost not touched upon at the Pittsburgh meeting. Only belatedly was a resolution adopted that expressed solidarity with the suffering Jews of Europe, and which called on the United Nations "to save those who can yet be saved."[22] The sole purpose of the proposed 'American Jewish Assembly', to be convened that summer, was to develop a program for the post-war problems of world Jewry including the future of Palestine, and to elect a delegation whose task would be to carry out this program. At that point there was no intention for the proposed conference to deal with the rescue of European Jewry.

Waldman recommended to Proskauer that the AJC remain outside the conference. He called the planned meeting "a gang up on the American Jewish Committee", and saw it as another attempt by the American Jewish Congress to create an overall, elected body by which they could dominate American Jewry. He called Monsky "a Zionist stooge" and proposed threatening Weizmann with a pull out from the Jewish Agency Executive if he did not get the conference called off.[23] However the AJC could not isolate itself from the entire Jewish community. In April it agreed to participate in the conference on condition that the name be changed to the 'American Jewish Conference' (a name that supposedly sounded less nationalistic) and that it would not be bound by its decisions.[24] These conditions were agreed to by both sides. The only major groups that did not participate in the Conference were the Committee for a Jewish Army (which claimed that it was not a Jewish, but a non-sectarian organization) and the Revisionists. The Revisionists were allotted only one place at the Conference, not three as they demanded, and therefore decided not to participate.[25] The elections for the Conference were a sweeping victory for the American Jewish Congress and the Zionist Movement. Of the 379 elected representatives, 340 were members of Zionist organizations, though some of them had been elected on other slates.[26]

The AJC was not the only body worried that the American Jewish Conference might adopt a strong Zionist platform. The State Department, the U.S. Military and the President were equally concerned. President Roosevelt had always been considered as friendly to the Zionist cause. He had on many occasions expressed his opposition to the British White Paper and his support for the creation of a Jewish homeland. In private conversations with Rabbi Wise and Henry Morgenthau, Roosevelt had even spoken of the transfer of the Arab population from Palestine to provide room for the Jews, who could then create an independent state of their own.[27] But as with the rescue issue, FDR was not prepared to take any step that would lead to unnecessary conflict during the war – in this case with the British, the Moslem nations, the State Department and the U.S. Military. When approached for his aid by Zionist advocates he was ready to take minor steps, such as pressing the British government to abandon their stand of parity in the mobilization of Palestinian Jews and Arabs into the British Army,[28] or making ineffectual statements of support for the Zionist cause. However, he was not prepared to come to grips with the real problems of Palestine.

By 1942, Roosevelt accepted the view that support for the Zionist cause would lead to difficulties with the Arabs. Roosevelt was not only worried about its effect on the war effort but was equally concerned that it might endanger American efforts to obtain a foothold in the oil rich Middle East, which previously had been considered a British 'sphere of influence'. In a memorandum to Hull in July 1942, he told the Secretary of State that "we should say nothing about the Near East, or Palestine or the Arabs at this time [...] If we pat either group on the back, we automatically stir up trouble at a critical moment."[29] For the same reason he rejected a request by Felix Frankfurter to meet with Ben Gurion, explaining "the less said by everybody of all creeds, the better."[30]

In October 1942, Roosevelt sent Col. Harold Hoskins on a fact-finding mission to the Middle East to investigate the possibility of achieving some sort of an accord between the Jews and the Arabs. Hoskins' report, submitted in April 1943, was the basis for American policy on the Palestine issue until the end of the war. Hoskins reported that he did not believe in the possibility of a Jewish-Arab rapprochement. He recommended that no decisions be made on Palestine until after the war and even then only after consultations with all the parties concerned.[31] At their conference in Quebec, in August 1943, Roosevelt and Churchill (who also favored a Jewish state) decided that their governments would not consider the future of Palestine until the war ended.[32]

The War Department was the first to initiate pressure to prevent the American Jewish Conference from adopting a call for the creation of a Jewish state. In July, the Acting Secretary of War, Robert Patterson, wrote Hull that "Continued agitation in this country for the immediate establishment of a Jewish state in Palestine constitutes a grave danger to the United Nations war efforts" and he called on the State Department to discourage further agitation.[33] Hull responded by proposing to Roosevelt to gather a number of Jewish representatives, "especially discordant and vociferous elements", and tell them in plain language that if they did not refrain from further agitation, the government would publish Patterson's letter as well as a proposed joint statement by the British and American governments demanding all agitation to stop.[34]

In August, Nachum Goldmann reported to the Zionist leadership, that the State Department had asked him and Rabbi Wise to cancel the Conference, warning that if they persisted in their policy the Department would publish both the joint statement and Patterson's letter.[35] At Wise's request, Samuel Rosenman intervened and succeeded in preventing its publication. Wise feared that the dissemination of the declaration might make it seem that the Jews "put Palestine's interests above the victory of the United Nations." Yet Wise also warned Rosenman (knowing his words would be passed to the President) that the issuance of such a statement might change "the reverential attitude" of the Jews for Roosevelt.[36]

Rescue had not been on the proposed agenda of the Conference, and as late as July the American Jewish Congress did not envisage setting up a committee at the conference to deal with the question of how to save the surviving Jews of Europe.[37] They still saw the Joint Emergency Committee as the body to deal with rescue issues in the name of American Jewry. However, pressure in the Jewish community was increasing for the Conference, the most important war-time gathering of American Jewry, to address this problem as well. As far as the public could perceive: the Bermuda Conference had been a fiasco; the Joint Emergency Committee was silent; and only the Bergson Boys were maintaining a vociferous call for rescue. At the end of July the Bergsonites had organized a Rescue Conference attended by many outstanding American personalities and there was serious concern among the established organizations that they would upstage the American Jewish Conference.[38]

The Jewish Labor Committee was the first to demand that rescue not only be put on the agenda, but that it be dealt with as the very first item. On the eve of the conference *Congress Weekly* also called for "immediate rescue action" to be a principal topic on the agenda. In a rare criticism of the President by a Jewish body, the magazine attacked Roosevelt's oft-stated policy that the only solution for the tragic plight of European Jewry was "the final defeat of Hitler". It indicated that in order to guarantee that Jews remain alive so that they might be saved, the conference may have "to contradict the wishes of the highest authority of the land".[39] The intention, of course, was to the President.

Monsky, in his opening address at the Conference, convened in New York on August 29th, made relief and rescue efforts the first goal of the conference. Wise then proposed that the Conference appoint a delegation to meet with the President and present the demands of the American Jewish community, now represented almost entirely in the American Jewish Conference, "for action without further delay to rescue the remnants of European Jewry". "Further delay in rescue", Wise asserted, "would doubtless mean there would be no Jews to save". Wise also used the opportunity to restate his "unchanged faith in the deep humanity of the foremost leader of free men in the world today, Franklin Delano Roosevelt."[40] His words were chosen to cut off a growing militant attitude of some who were calling to "even criticize friends in high places" for their lack of action to rescue European Jewry.[41]

A rescue committee met during the conference and a rescue resolution was adopted by the Conference. The most important point of the resolution was a call to the American government to create a special intergovernmental agency which would be provided with the resources and armed with the authority to seize every opportunity to send supplies through appropriate channels, provide the means for Jewish self-defense [a new proposal], and coordinate and expand the work of rescue through the underground.[42]

The bleak atmosphere created in the wake of the Bermuda Conference bore heavily upon the Jewish organizations. There was no real enthusiasm in the discussion on rescue, and the resolution was passed "pro forma."

In reporting on the rescue resolutions the *Congress Weekly* recalled all the previous demands of the Jewish organizations from which nothing had emerged and noted that "the disparity between our words of pleading and their probable effect weighed heavily on the Conference."[43] This also was the feeling of many Jewish leaders that American Jewry had not responded to the crisis of their European brethren. Dr. Israel Goldstein admitted that American Jews had "not been stirred deeply enough [...] not risked [their] conveniences and [their] social and civic religion [...] in order to lay our troubles upon the conscience of our Christian neighbors [...] [only] a relatively small part of our people have taken part in our days of fast and prayer, and in our demonstrations."[44]

The main issue at the American Jewish Conference was the future of Palestine, though this, as well, was nearly averted. Unknown to most delegates, Rabbi Wise had agreed to postpone discussing a resolution on the establishment of a Jewish state until a second session of the Conference, to be held at a later date.[45] He had approved this compromise in order to maintain Jewish unity and prevent the American Jewish Committee and perhaps other non-Zionist groups, from leaving the Conference. Wise, who in the past had feared that unity of the Jewish organizations might stifle the actions of the American Jewish Congress, had now become a strong advocate of Jewish unity.

This change in Wise's approach was due, firstly, to the fact that the American Jewish Congress and the Zionists were the dominant elements at the Conference, and that his long-sought goal of creating a democratically elected body representative of American Jewry had been achieved. A year later Wise stated his readiness to disband the American Jewish Congress if the American Jewish Conference would act as the representative body of American Jewry, provided that other organizations would follow in suit.[46] Secondly, he felt the need for American Jewry to appear as a unified body in presenting Jewish and Zionist demands at a future Peace Conference. There was also the necessity of maintaining Jewish unity in order to pressure the administration for rescue action. Wise now believed that only if the Administration saw a strong, unified Jewish community demanding action something might be accomplished. In addition, since 1938 Wise had been moderating his stance and the gap in approach and tactics that had existed between him and the American Jewish Committee had considerably narrowed. Wise was now more concerned with strengthening the voice of moderation against new militant elements in the Jewish community – the Bergson group outside the Jewish establishment, and the Silver-Neumann group within.

Prodded on by Emanuel Neumann, Rabbi Silver rose to issue an appeal for the conference to adopt a resolution calling for the creation of a Jewish state. Second to Rabbi Wise, Abba Hillel Silver was the most powerful Jewish speaker and his militant stance struck a responsive chord among the delegates. They felt the world had stood by silently while European Jewry had been annihilated, and that the time had now come to demand a solution to the age-old Jewish problem. In what all described as a masterful speech, Silver obliquely attacked the President and Wise for offering no more than "the hope that the Atlantic Charter, and the Four Freedoms and victory will bring the healing of our people [...] We are again turning away from a history to dreams and to Apocalypses, which some of us amazingly choose to call realism and statesmanship."[47] At the end of Silver's speech the entire assemblage spontaneously rose to its feet and sang "Hatikvah", while only the three delegates of the American Jewish Committee remained seated.

Once Rabbi Silver's proposal was overwhelmingly adopted, Judge Proskauer recommended to the AJC that it leave the Conference. Some members of the Executive opposed withdrawal and sought a compromise with the Zionists, fearing that the break "would lead to a controversy [...] within the Jewish community that would be detrimental to the welfare of the Jews."[48] However, the AJC decided to withdraw from the Conference. This in turn led to the resignation of a number of its members and to bitter attacks on the Committee from much of the Jewish community and press.[49]

The American Jewish Committee was now almost totally isolated from the Jewish community, but the following year, in an attempt to recoup its prestige it opened up its membership; organized local chapters; expanded its staff; and began to recoup its strength. Still a force to be reckoned with, it began a battle against Zionism in the Jewish community. It also attempted to influence the policy of the American government. Concerned about the effect that the Palestine resolution might have on the status of American Jewry, Morris Waldman informed the State Department that "the resolution on Palestine did not, in fact, represent the majority viewpoint of American Jewry."[50] In January 1944, Waldman notified the State Department that the AJC was about to begin a campaign against Zionism in the Jewish community and guaranteed the officials that the majority of American Jews, now mostly native-born, "were good Americans who were not likely to be carried away by notions of extreme Jewish nationalism." He also used the opportunity to express his distress that "alien members" of the World Jewish Congress had been allowed to enter the U.S., implying that it might be a good idea to have them deported.[51]

Though the American Jewish Conference had been an overwhelming success for the Zionists, the attempts at Jewish unity were a failure. The in-fighting between the Zionists and non-Zionists, and between the establishment organizations and the Bergson group, had become even bitterer. The American Jewish Conference survived for a number of years more, though the soul had gone out of it. Structurally and financially it was unprepared for the tasks that it had set for itself. Rabbi Wise lost interest in the Conference, and left the umbrella organization in the hands of Louis Lipsky. Wise felt that it "muzzled" him, and he preferred working within the framework of the 'Congress movement' where his views still held sway.[52]

Once the American Jewish Committee had withdrawn from the Conference, the American government viewed that body as just another Zionist organization. The attempt to create a framework to speak in the name of the entire American Jewish community and to exert pressure upon the American government, had failed. At the international conference in San Francisco in 1945, at which the United Nations Organization was established, the American Jewish community was represented by delegations from both the American Jewish Conference and the American Jewish Committee.[53]

The Conference had set up a rescue committee and intended that it would take over the Jewish community's unified rescue efforts. That, however, meant the dismemberment of the Joint Emergency Committee. At the first meeting of the JEC after the Conference, the proposal to disband resulted in a tie vote between the four non-Zionist and the four pro-Zionist organizations. To break the deadlock the Hadassah Women Zionists were now permitted to join the JEC, just long enough to vote for its dissolution at the very next meeting.[54] That now left the American Jewish Committee outside of the unified Jewish rescue efforts. The Zionists were probably not perturbed that the AJC would not be on the new Rescue Committee but were concerned that if the AJC was not involved Joint would not support the Committee's work. Without the vast funds of Joint, the Rescue Committee could do very little. Thus they attempted to bring the two groups into the Rescue Committee without obligating them to join the American Jewish Conference.[55] Neither group agreed to the request and once again the attempt to create a unified American Jewish rescue effort came to naught. The Agudas Israel intent on creating an anti-Zionist bloc and perhaps, hoping to benefit from the financial support of Joint for its own rescue activities, proposed the formation of a non-Zionist rescue committee composed of the liberal American Jewish Committee, the orthodox Agudas, and the socialist Jewish Labor Committee (which in 1944 also left the Conference when a pro-Communist organization was permitted to join).[56] But nothing evolved from that plan either. In the last years of the war the Agudas Israel and the JLC maintained close ties on rescue matters.

What brought an ultra-Orthodox group and a militantly secular, pro-Bundist organization to cooperate one with another? Perhaps it was their common opposition to Zionism, or their strong Jewish roots and the Yiddish language that was often used by both. Or perhaps it was the special ties that both these groups maintained with Polish Jewry. What typified both these groups was their daring to act, even without government permission, and a readiness to carry out, what in war-time America, were considered illegal acts.

Though the efforts to create a unified and effective rescue program had failed, the Zionists, now under the militant leadership of Rabbi Silver, decided to press ahead with their plans for a Jewish state. In December, the newly created local chapters of American Zionist Emergency Committee (AZEC) convened an emergency conference in Cleveland where they decided to pressure Congress to adopt a resolution calling for American support for the creation of a Jewish state.[57] In January 1944, AZEC drafted a resolution to be presented to Congress but Rabbi Wise and Dr. Goldmann opposed the decision. One of the reasons expressed in the committee for the urgency in introducing the resolution was the fear that the Bergson group might again "steal the show" by lobbying Congress for such a resolution.[58]

The State Department, concerned that this proposal might actually pass in Congress, enlisted the support of the military to oppose the resolution, knowing that it would be difficult for the Zionists or the U.S. Congress, to oppose the wishes of the Army in time of war. General George Marshall, Chief of Staff of the U.S. Army, wrote Hull opposing the resolution and warning that a conflict between Jews and Arabs would mean "retention of troops in the affected areas [...] and would probably interfere seriously with arrangements now being made to procure Arabian oil for the use of our combat forces."[59] The new, combined pressure of the State Department and the War Department led some in the AZEC to reconsider the wisdom of their decision, though Rabbi Silver stood firm. He termed the War Department's statement part of a pattern by the military, and warned that "if we yield now we shall have to yield all along the line."[60]

In March, Rabbis Wise and Silver managed to arrange a meeting with the President with the intent of persuading him to support the establishment of a Jewish state after the war. The rabbis came away from the meeting believing that the President had agreed and that it was only a matter of timing as to when he would announce his support. Roosevelt did permit Wise and Silver to release a statement in his name stating that "when future decisions are made full justice will be done to those who seek a Jewish national home."[61] However, in a conversation with Henry Wallace, Roosevelt told his Vice-President that he had warned the Zionist leaders that their demand could lead to "a Holy Gehad" and the death of hundreds of thousands. Wallace, who was well acquainted with the deceptive tactics of the President, confided in his diary that "The President certainly is a waterman. He looks in one direction and rows the other with the utmost skill".[62] Wallace was correct in his judgment, for in the following months the President did everything possible to prevent the Congress from adopting the proposal.

Though both Wise and Silver wanted the U.S. to adopt a firm stand in favor of a Jewish State, they differed as to the tactics. Wise, as usual, was confident that Roosevelt would remain true to his pro-Zionist stance, and he therefore wanted to avoid antagonizing the President, especially in 1944, an election year. Silver, a Republican, would not rely only on the goodwill of the President and he pressed for a Senate resolution, despite the vigorous opposition of Roosevelt. Silver was critical of the role of the Zionist Movement during the war claiming that it had "placed too strong an emphasis on solving the refugee problem and not enough on our political goals."[63]

In October 1944, with the change in the war situation, the War Department withdrew its opposition.[64] In November, Silver succeeded in getting the resolution supporting the creation of a Jewish state introduced into the Senate by Sen. Wagner (a Democrat) and Sen. Taft (a Republican, and a close friend of Silver). FDR was infuriated with the Zionists for pushing the resolution in Congress. The State Department convinced the Senate Foreign Relations Committee not to bring the issue to a vote. The resolution was finally passed in Congress in December 1945, more than a year later.[65]

❖ ❖ ❖

A month before the American Jewish Conference, another major conference was held in the same hotel in New York, this one called by the 'Bergson Boys'. However, 'The Emergency Conference to Save the Jews of Europe', as its name implied, did not seek to solve the problems of Jewry in the post-war world. It had only one issue on its agenda – to rescue those Jews who still might be saved.

CHAPTER 11

The Joint Emergency Committee to Save the Jews of Europe

(a) *"Make a noise and create a fuss"*

("It is so easy to make a noise and create a fuss [...] when one has neither responsibility or standing") – Pierre van Paasen upon breaking with the Bergsonites, 4/44.)

Until the Bermuda Conference convened in April 1943, it was not at all clear whether rescue, in the sense of extricating Jews from the hands of their Nazi murderers and alleviating their suffering, was really the paramount goal of the Committee for a Jewish Army, despite Bergson's decision in November 1942. In March 1943, an article entitled "Has the Idea of a Jewish Army Been Abandoned?" appeared in *The Answer*, the organ of the CJA. The editor, Gabriel Wechsler, attempted to allay the fears of their supporters who suspected that "the demand for a Jewish Army has been shunted into the background because of new demands [of the CJA]."[1] Wechsler emphasized that his organization still insisted that

> During the progress of the war, the creation of a Jewish Army must of necessity be the primary demand of the Jewish people [and] more important than the rescue of as many Jews as possible by transporting them to safety, is the problem of staying Hitler's murderous hand, of creating a force large enough, strong enough, to force him to give up his determined campaign of annihilation.[2]

At this stage the Bergsonites still presumed that a Jewish Army could force the Nazis to terminate their campaign of murder. However, many in the American Jewish establishment saw the struggle of the CJA as nothing more than 'a publicity gimmick', to exploit the situation in order to promote the Irgun delegation and to advance Zionist goals.[3] The fact was that two out of the three Wechsler proposals (that certainly represented the views of his organization) were seen by many as bids aimed only at furthering Zionist aims. Wechsler recommended: a) The establishment of a Jewish Army composed of 200,000 Palestinian and Stateless Jews. Such an army would send commando units to attack Germany, and "Jewish pilots would bomb Germany in reprisal raids." b) The appointment of an "inter-governmental commission of military experts whose task it would be to devise the methods of stern action that will be used to stop the murdering hands of the German assassins." c) Transferring the Jews of occupied-Europe to Palestine. If a need arose to transfer some of the Jews to a temporary haven, then "[re]settlement in Palestine should be pledged to those who offer haven."[4]

However, by the eve of the Bermuda Conference a shift had taken place in the stand of the CJA, and it was already clear that now their primry demand was for the creation of a commission that would work to rescue the remaining Jews. On the day the conference opened in Bermuda, a full-page ad, paid for by the CJA, appeared in leading U.S. papers, addressed to "The Gentlemen at Bermuda". It proposed the creation of a United Nations (as yet, not an American) rescue agency, and called for "action, not 'exploratory' words", as was implied in the State Department announcement.[5]

After the Conference the CJA was among the first to react to the pitiful results of Bermuda, even though its decisions had not yet been published in full. On May 5, it placed an ad in the *N.Y. Times* in which it labeled the Bermuda Conference "a cruel mockery". The ad was a strong attack on the failings of the Conference as a whole, though the CJA placed the blame mainly upon Britain who, it charged, prevented rescue "fearing that public opinion will demand that these refugees be admitted to Palestine." Once again it called for the creation of an inter-governmental agency which would attempt to deal with the problem of refugees, even though such a decision had already been taken at Bermuda where it was decided to revive the Intergovernmental Committee on Refugees.[6]

Though the ad did not refer specifically to any member of the delegation, Sen. Lucas perceived it as a personal attack upon himself. Stung to the core, he rose to defend the actions of the U. S. delegation at Bermuda. Numerous Senators from both parties attacked the 'Bergson Boys' for the unauthorized use of their names in support of the ad. Senators Taft, Truman and others, including

Edwin Johnson,[7] sent letters complaining that their names had been used without their consent to attack British and American representatives to the Bermuda Conference.[8] They also explicitly directed the CJA never to use their names in their ads. Adolph Sabath, a Jewish Congressman from Chicago, wrote the CJA that its actions "amply explain and justify the refusal of the responsible organizations to sanction its work."[9]

The Bergsonites, at first, did not grasp the dire situation that they had gotten into. Eri Jabotinsky (son of the Revisionist leader) wrote to Sen. Johnson that he was very pleased with the Senate debate for Lucas' attack of rage "showed that we scored a hit."[10] But when Bergson realized that all he had built over the past two years was about to collapse, he expressed his regrets to those offended and claimed that the ad had been misconstrued.[11] Despite the resignation of some important personalities, the Bergsonites maintained their militant efforts and continued to achieve many successes in their publicity campaign.

What was the reason for their exceptional accomplishments, achieved in so short a period of time? According to a member of the Irgun delegation, the secret of their success was because "The idea was so dramatic, so new, so different [...] The idea was so simple and as usual, the simple things are the ones that impress people."[12] But from the apprehensive reports of the Jewish leaders, it is apparent that the main reason for the 'Bergson Boys' success was that they simply filled a vacuum in the Jewish community. Many Jews, far removed from embracing the Revisionist ideology, were nevertheless pleased to see one group stand up, without equivocating, and forthrightly demand the rescue of European Jews. These people were not aware at that time of the rescue actions of the Jewish leadership. Nor did they really know what the 'Bergson Boys' were actually achieving with their provocative shouting. However, even the simple act of shouting was a catharsis for them. And if it was possible to save the life of a Rumanian Jew for the paltry sum of $50, as the CJA ads had proclaimed in a "dramatic" and "simple" manner, would any Jew not lend his support? As a result, large amounts of money flowed into their coffers. These funds were not used for rescue, but were plowed into even greater publicity campaigns. The more the CJA publicized, the more the money poured in.

The publicity campaign and the dramatic activities of the Irgun delegation attracted wide circles of the American public. According to Ben Hecht, one of its most ardent supporters, the group obtained support mostly from non-Jewish circles.[13] Not just people on the Right, nor only Jews that leaned toward the activist line of the Revisionists were drawn to the group. Surprisingly, liberals Jews such as Max Lerner, the political commentator, and non-Jews such as Secretary Ickes, and even pronounced left-wingers such as Joe Brainin and Pierre Van Paasen, actively supported the 'Bergson Boys'. Things got to the point that the FBI even began an investigation to determine whether the organizations sponsored by the 'Bergson Boys' were not actually part of a communist conspiracy [!].[14]

Bergson succeeded also in attracting people from the other side of the political spectrum. Conservatives and isolationists, such as Senator Edwin Johnson and Sen. Guy Gillette, and publisher William Randolph Hearst, were loyal supporters of Bergson, and worked energetically for the Emergency Committee to Save the Jews of Europe. Some claim that Hearst's support of the Irgun delegation was not out of 'love for Mordechai', but rather from 'hatred of Haman'. According to them, the isolationist Hearst despised Britain and therefore he endorsed the Irgun which were fighting the British.[15]

Whatever were the reasons of the isolationists, the fact that Bergson was able to forge so wide a coalition – from Van Paasen to Hearst – was an impressive achievement for Bergson's tactics. However Bergson's success also created problems for the CJA. His feat in obtaining the support of former isolationists, who were among President Roosevelt's most vociferous opponents, succeeded only in enraging the President, who already was disturbed by their ads. Roosevelt made certain that the Jewish establishment be made aware of his desire to be rid of Bergson and his associates.[16] Both the American Administration and the Jewish establishment blackballed Bergson, hindered his activities and attempted to expel the Irgun delegation from the U.S., or at least to have them inducted into the Armed Forces so as to neutralize their activities.[17]

Despite his success in mobilizing mass support for his organizations, Bergson had great difficulty in maintaining the adherence of many important personalities whose backing he had obtained. Some of them left his committees when, as they claimed, they "wisened up" and "realized" who Bergson was, and what was the "real" purposes of his organizations.[18] Others left under pressure of the Jewish establishment, which did everything possible to break the Bergsonites, who were growing in strength, achieving influence and threatening the position of the Jewish leadership.[19] These resignations, generally accompanied by public denunciations of the 'Bergson Boys' and much commotion in the press, further sullied the image of what appeared as a deeply divided Jewish community.

These resignations, generally accompanied by public denunciations of the 'Bergson Boys' and much ado in the press, further sullied the image of what appeared as a deeply divided Jewish community. Less known were the conflicts within the Irgun delegation. Probably out of deep loyalty developed in their underground past, the members of the delegation kept their complaints about the leadership of Bergson within their own circle. Ari Ben-Eliezer disagreed with Bergson's ideological deviations. That possibly was one of the reasons for his return to Palestine in 1943.[20] Yaakov Ben Ami accused Bergson of running the organization like a military unit, and as though he was commander. He also accused Bergson of being responsible that many important people were leaving the organization, and that "We exist in the air without a base – [only] names on letterheads."[21] Matters reached the point that Ben Ami notified Bergson that he was glad to be drafted into the army, since he felt that it was a convenient way for him to withdraw from the organization.[22] The CJA representative in England, Jeremy Halperin, also complained bitterly about Bergson's leadership,[23] and there were others in the delegation with similar criticisms of him.

Bergson acted with energy and imagination, was not tied to dogmas and attempted to adapt himself to conditions in America and to the constantly changing climate of the war. Bergson's lack of dogmatism was shown in the ideology that he and Samuel Merlin (a close associate) developed regarding the status of American Jewry. Bergson pondered the question of how best to persuade American Jewry to support an outright struggle on behalf of Europe's Jews. He claimed that the reason for the general apathy of the American public to the Holocaust was because they mistakenly believed that influential American Jews, close to the Administration, were looking out for Jewish interests. If they were not doing anything for European Jewry, the public deduced, it was because there was simply nothing that could be done.

But, Bergson reasoned, the real motive why Jews were not acting stemmed from their fear to admit that they belonged to the Jewish people, for then their loyalty to the United States would be questioned. He concluded that American Jewry must be told that they really are Americans and that only their origins are Jewish. As Americans, not as Jews, they must act to save European Jewry, for it is in the best American tradition to come to the aid of the underdog.[24] As to a Jewish state, Bergson said that American Jewry shouldn't be disturbed by accusations of 'dual loyalty', since the future Jewish state is intended only for the 'Hebrews' of Palestine and for the stateless Jews of Europe.

Such views were a complete reversal for one who considered himself a disciple of Jabotinsky. In the discussion of this new ideology in the CJA, Ari Ben-Eliezer, loyal to his Revisionist past, opposed Bergson's novel theory and stated that "we should not appease [American Jewry] with principles that will not create a nation or a state."[25] Most of the other members of the Irgun delegation viewed Bergson's philosophy only as a tactical step to win over influential and wealthy Jews. This new ideology of the 'Bergson Boys' proved to be of no avail in winning the support of the influential and establishment Jews, yet their influence in the general Jewish public continued to grow.

After the failure of the Bermuda Conference, the CJA decided to organize an assemblage of leading personalities: military and economic experts and authorities on the refugee problem. The purpose was to place the question of saving Jews on the public agenda and to propose practical plans for rescue. In its manifesto, the organizing committee presented, once more, a call to transfer Jews to Palestine and the need to form an Allied agency to deal with rescue. It is worth noting, that this time there was no mention of a Jewish Army.[26]

The Jewish establishment tried to foil Bergson's plans for the conference. Aside from their attempts to prevent Bergson from establishing himself, the mainstream organizations were furious with his call for a major assemblage just a few weeks before the American Jewish Conference was to convene. They believed that this was an attempt by Bergson to upstage the American Jewish Conference.[27] The fears of the Jewish leaders were well founded.

The Emergency Conference did attract important personalities and gained the attention of the press. Maurice Perlzweig warned Rabbi Wise that the "public effect [of the Emergency Conference] will be devastating."[28] A vast array of important political personalities, Secretary Ickes, former President Hoover; heads of the Trade Unions (William Green and Philip Murray); figures from the media, (William Randolph Hearst and William Allen White); and many other notables expressed their support. Some of them even took the time to play an active role in the Conference.

The Emergency Conference convened in New York during the week of July 20th to July 26th with 1500 participants. Many more attended the evening sessions open to the general public. This time the Bergsonites called for the establishment of an American rescue agency, with other nations cooperating, if they so desired. The emphasis was again placed on Palestine as the principal refugee haven. According to the Conference, 600,000 Jewish refugees could be absorbed there and an additional 150,000 could be sent to neutral states. There was also a demand to send relief to the starving Jews of Europe and a clear-cut statement that there was enough shipping available for the projected plans. In order to implement its program the Conference proposed that the Allies threaten to bomb the satellite countries.[29]

A permanent committee, 'The Emergency Committee to Save the Jews of Europe', was set up composed of well-known personalities. These people not only were prepared to lend their names to the struggle but also involved themselves in spreading news of the Holocaust and urging the government to aid in rescue. The achievements of the Emergency Conference were impressive in publicizing news of the massacres, compared with what had previously been the case. It drew extensive press coverage throughout the nation and it placed large ads in the papers in the sensational style that characterized the 'Bergson Boys'.[30] The most noteworthy achievement of the Conference in the field of publicity was winning the support of Hearst, who controlled a large number of newspapers across the U.S. He ordered his newspaper chain to write editorials supporting the Conference and its resolutions.[31]

In contrast to the public relations successes of the conference, the lobbying by the Emergency Committee in Washington bore meager results. The resolutions of the conference were sent to the President and to the Secretary of State, and a few important members of the Committee attempted to arrange a meeting with Roosevelt. Roosevelt handed the request over to Hull, who instructed Long to meet with Bergson and a representative of the committee, Ira Hirschmann, a business executive from Bloomingdale's.[32] Long listened to their pleas to establish a governmental rescue agency, and to send Hirschmann to Turkey and Bergson to Palestine to deal with rescue matters. Long politely replied that the State Department was already handling rescue issues, but that he was prepared to consider their request.[33]

All the attempts of Bergson and of others in the Emergency Committee to meet with FDR were unsuccessful. In August Bergson sent the resolutions to Eleanor Roosevelt, and asked her to bring them to the attention of the President. The President's wife was sympathetic, but balked at any steps that might embarrass the President. She did give Bergson's letter to her husband, who answered: "I do not think that this needs any answer at the time."[34] The Emergency Committee proposed meeting the President during his conference with Churchill in Quebec, in September 1943. However, Roosevelt's secretary informed them that the timing was inappropriate, and suggested that they meet with Roosevelt after his return – but that meeting never came about.[35]

In October, a few days before Yom Kippur, the Emergency Committee, in conjunction with the Union of Orthodox Rabbis, organized 400 Rabbis in a 'march' on Washington to publicize the sufferings of European Jews and to demand that the American government act to rescue them. The organizers hoped that the highlight of the 'march' would be a meeting with the President, a meeting bound to receive wide coverage in the press. The President's secretary, however, informed the rabbis that the President was unable to see them, because "of the pressure of other business." The President was actually free that day, but he deliberately attended a minor ceremony to avoid meeting the rabbis.[36] Wise, who had suggested to the President not to meet the delegation, exploited their humiliation in order to attack the 'Bergson Boys'. In an editorial that appeared in *Opinion*, Wise reproached the Bergsonites that "We are now at a new phase in Jewish life, namely, at the phase of propaganda by stunts [...] which is the essence of unwisdom."

Alluding to Bergson, Wise proclaimed that "They who set out to be leaders must bear themselves with a sense of responsibility."[37]

During the coming months the Emergency Committee began directing its criticism of the government more and more in the direction of the President. In a rally organized by them to honor the Danish and Swedish nations for their rescue of Jews, one of the speakers attacked both Roosevelt and the Prime Minister of Britain for their "lack of courage" in failing to prevent the destruction of the Jewish people.[38] An ad written by Ben Hecht and released by the Emergency Committee in November, also hinted at the callousness of the President toward the Jews who were being slaughtered.[39] Roosevelt was angered by these attacks and he did not need advice from the Jewish establishment to decide to rid himself of Bergson and his colleagues. In November, Samuel Rosenman reported to Nachum Goldmann that the President was infuriated with Bergson and wanted to get rid of him.[40] According to Kook's testimony, Roosevelt threatened to prevent the Zionist movement from functioning in the U.S. if Bergson did not desist from his actions.[41]

Roosevelt's threats fortified Wise and other Jewish leaders in their own desire to be rid of Bergson and his group. The Zionist leaders apprehensions over the success of the 'Bergson Boys' continued to grow and these were no longer limited only to the growing public support for the group's campaigns for a Jewish Army and rescue action. Now the Zionist movement feared that the Bergsonites could use their successes in America to become the predominant body in the Zionist struggle for a Jewish state, and this in the spirit of the ideology of the Irgun.

Not all members of the 'Bergson Boys' were content that the group had neglected the Zionist campaign and for a number of months had concentrated primarily on the struggle for rescue. However they all were aware that their success in rescue, and the connections they had established among the American public as a result of this struggle would be of great value when they returned to the struggle for a Jewish state. According to the ideological tenets that Bergson had propounded, that Jewish state was to be established only for 'Hebrews' living in Palestine and for stateless Jews in Europe. He, therefore, did not recognize the American Zionist movement as a representative of that future state.

The 'Bergson Boys' as Palestinians, presented themselves as the exclusive, legitimate representatives of the 'Hebrew nation'. In 1942, the Washington office of the 'Bergson Boys' already began to label itself 'The Embassy of the Hebrew Nation' in the U.S.[42] In a letter that Bergson sent to Gen. Hershey, head of the Selective Service, he depicted the Irgun delegation as the sole body speaking for the Hebrew people of Palestine and Europe and compared the delegation to the other governments-in-exile.[43]

In a letter written in May 1943, from Eri Jabotinsky to Arieh Altman (a Revisionist leader in Palestine) he wrote that the delegation was now forming a new organization to strive for a Jewish state and it was using the rescue struggle "as an entering wedge... It will be an organization of the friends of Great Zionism" (i.e. of the Revisionist views).[44] A letter by Yaakov Ben Ami to Kook in August 1943, sent to all the activists of the organization, warned that the State Department was about to betray the Zionist issue and in his opinion, it was time to establish the 'League for a Free Palestine' and "our boys should give up all other work and devote themselves to this job."[45] Indeed, in September 1943, Bergson sent a bulletin to all CJA activists which informed them that the organization was about to be disbanded and would reorganize under the name, 'American League for a Free Palestine'.[46]

We can see, therefore, that though the 'Bergson Boys' did indeed mobilize a public campaign for rescue, they did not relinquish their struggle for their primary goal – the establishment of a sovereign, Jewish state. It was Bergson who persuaded the Irgun delegation to channel much of their forces to the struggle for rescue, but the members were aware that their new-found public status, a result of their stubborn battle for rescue, would serve them well in their future struggles. That is what the Zionist leadership feared when it decided in November, 1943 to begin a public campaign against the various organizations of the Bergsonites in order to bring about their dissolution.[47]

In 1944 the dispute between the Jewish establishment and the 'Bergson Boys' exacerbated when the Irgun declared a revolt against Britain (which was still battling Nazi Germany) and began waging terrorist attacks. That same year the Bergsonites opened an 'Embassy' of the 'Hebrew Nation' in Washington and pronounced itself as the 'Government-in-Exile' of "The Jews of Palestine and the Stateless Jews of Europe". Only they, they declared, are permitted to speak in the name of the 'Hebrew Nation'. They stated that the Jewish Agency for Palestine, the World Jewish Congress and sundry other Jewish organizations pretend to speak for all world Jewry, but that it is essential to clearly differentiate between 'Hebrews', who belong to a specific national and political entity – the 'Hebrew Nation' – and between the Jewish people, which is an intangible religious or cultural entity having no political status whatsoever. [48]

What the Jewish organizations had feared had become a reality! A group of six Palestinian Jews, who had not been elected by anyone, declared themselves to be the representatives of what they defined as the 'Hebrew Nation' – the Jewish Yishuv in Palestine, and European Jewry which was facing extermination under German occupation.

❖ ❖ ❖

The Bergson Boys made a distinctive contribution to rescue during the Holocaust. Yet the organizations established by Bergson did not deal with rescue activities per se. However, faithful to the precepts of Jabotinsky, the Irgun delegation saw political work and propaganda – i.e. bringing the rescue issue before the public and the government – as its main task. Eri Jabotinsky testified after the Holocaust: "In summation, in that period I did not rescue anyone."[49] Ira Hirschmann expressed similar views.[50] Some claim that the 'Bergson Boys' were the major factor in establishing the War Refugee Board, the most significant American contribution to the rescue of European Jews. This will be discussed in a separate chapter.

CHAPTER 12

The Struggle for the Creation of A Rescue Agency

(a) The US Treasury Changes Course
"First You Must Set a Precedent"
– Dr. Nachum Goldmann to the WJC Executive -1943

By the end of 1942 most of the Jews of Poland and the Baltic countries had been murdered, and the Germans would not allow any intermediaries to aid those who still remained alive. Thus, Riegner and Lichtheim were correct in their evaluation that the best way to save Jews laid in the satellite nations in South Eastern Europe. These countries were not under the direct control of Germany. After the Axis defeat at Stalingrad (where two Rumanian divisions had been destroyed), the Rumanians sought to extricate themselves from the war. They believed a change in their policy towards the Jews would stand in their favor in negotiations with the Allies over conditions of surrender.

In December 1942, Radu Lecca, in charge of the Jewish problem in Rumania, approached the President of the Rumanian Zionist Federation, Mishu Benvenisti. He offered to release the remaining Jews of those who had been deported to Transnistria the year before. At the same time Lecca sent a representative to Constantinople (Istanbul) to make the identical proposal to the Zionist emissaries in Turkey. The plan was that Rumania would permit the remaining 70,000 Jews in Transnistria to depart for Palestine at the cost of 200,000 Lei each.[1] Because of the unstable rate of the Lei on the black market the amount being demanded was unclear. The CJA ad spoke of $50 a head but Dr. Goldmann reported to the WJC that the figure was actually $1000.[2] This estimate was closer to the truth – the rate was 142.85 Lei to the dollar.[3] Neither the Jewish leadership of Rumania, nor the Jewish Agency emissaries, were certain whether the Lecca proposal was genuine, but both agreed that the matter should be explored.[4]

After a while it became clear that there was no real basis for the Lecca plan. The German Ambassador in Bucharest, Manfred Von Killinger, after consulting with his superiors, ordered Lecca to back down.[5] If the Rumanian government had persisted in its plan against the will of their German masters, the scheme would still have come to naught. The Zionist emissaries had no possibility of obtaining the many ships needed for such a large-scale operation; the British would not have permitted so great a number of Jews to enter Palestine; and the German U-boat commanders in the Black Sea were ordered to torpedo boats carrying refugees.[6]

The German veto of the scheme was not yet known in the West, and so for another few months Jewish leaders in America and Palestine continued to deal with the offer. The British, meanwhile, informed the Jewish leadership in Palestine that it had rejected the Lecca plan, claiming that they would not participate in, what they called, blackmail.[7] Though by February the original Lecca plan was no longer valid, the continuing efforts of the American Jewish leaders to aid Transnistrian Jewry became the first breakthrough in the wall of rejection that surrounded the U.S. administration's stand on rescue of Jews.

The first knowledge of the Lecca plan reached America two months after it was first broached through a news report that appeared in the *N.Y. Times* on February 13th. In an article that appeared on page five, Cyrus Sulzberger, its correspondent in London, reported on the major points of the plan.[8] The information was probably provided by the British who hoped to frustrate the scheme by a premature disclosure. Chaim Weizmann immediately contacted Secretary Morgenthau and requested that he consult the President to ascertain if there was any real basis for the plan. If so, he should see what could be done to forward the scheme. Morgenthau did not hesitate and immediately phoned the President who suggested that he talk it over with Sumner Welles to check "whether it is possible to get 70,000 of these out". Welles' reaction to the news was "That's almost unbelievably good."[9]

The details of the Rumanian plan were intended to have reached the American Jewish leadership earlier. At a Zionist meeting where Goldmann reported the main points of the plan, he revealed that Moshe Shertok had sent them a cable on the subject a long time ago, but it had been delayed by American censors. Goldmann also disclosed that for two or three months previous, channels of information about what was happening to European Jews had been blocked. This was even before the State Department cabled Bern ordering them to cut off information. Goldmann told the assemblage that in meetings held between representatives of the Jewish Agency in Palestine and the British authorities regarding the Rumanian plan, the latter questioned its feasibility because it was contrary to the law forbidding trade with the enemy.[10] That February the State Department had issued a warning in the press against any attempts to negotiate with the enemy for rescue. The State Department held that the intent of the enemy in such negotiations was only to extort foreign currency to aid its war effort.[11]

When the CJA heard of the Transnistria plan they quickly placed an ad proclaiming that it was possible to save 70,000 Rumanian Jews for the mere sum of $50 a head. This ad angered the Jewish leadership who viewed it as irresponsible and bordering on fraud. Rabbi Wise, the emissaries in Constantinople and the Jewish Agency in Palestine, all agreed that if there was any real basis for the scheme it was essential that it be kept in secret. Publicity would only elicit German intercession and prevent the Rumanian government from implementing the plan. Wise, therefore, was quick to deny the existence of such a plan. He also advised the public not to send contributions for this purpose, and promised that if there were any real possibility for rescue, the Jewish organizations would guarantee that it be carried out.[12] The Jewish leadership also was infuriated with the CJA appeal for money that inferred that such an act would save Jewish lives. They saw this as a deception that would only strengthen the Bergsonites financially while endangering funds being raised for genuine rescue operations.[13]

Wyman and Medoff in their book, *A Race Against Death*,[14] state that the importance of the Transnistria Plan was that for the first time it showed that it was still possible to save Jews. But quite the opposite is the truth! This attempt once again proved that even when some country offered a plan to rescue Jews (in this case the Romanians), the Germans did not allow the plan to come to fruition. And it was they who determined the fate of European Jewry.

The plan for saving the Jews of Rumania was revived when on March 31st Rabbi Wise wrote Sumner Welles that Gerhardt Riegner had additional, important information pertaining to the Jews. Wise asked Welles to instruct the

American Consulate in Switzerland to obtain this information and pass it on to him.[15] Welles (though probably without being aware of it) had himself signed the State Department cable of February 10th ordering the Legation in Bern to stop sending information deriving from Jewish sources. He now, however, immediately instructed Harrison to fulfill Wise's request.[16] Harrison sent the State Department a summary of Riegner's report, adding his own opinion that in the future such messages should not be restricted, as ordered in the February 10th cable. He asked for permission to send messages from Riegner "in view of the helpful information which they may frequently contain."[17]

On April 20th, Riegner cabled Wise that there "were wide rescue possibilities" in Transnistria and France. The cable also revealed that the Germans had rejected the relief plans for Poland and the East proposed by the Red Cross. On the other hand, Riegner stated, the Germans would allow relief shipments to Theresienstadt and the Red Cross was already preparing the supplies. The cable also stated that further attempts were in progress to receive similar permission for "the labor camps in Upper Silesia" (i.e. Auschwitz). The most important element in Riegner's cable was his judgment that it was possible to place large sums of money at the disposal of rescue and relief without the need to transfer them to enemy territory. This could be done by depositing funds in blocked Swiss bank accounts. Wealthy Jews in Switzerland and France were prepared to provide money for rescue activities in their countries, on the condition that they be reimbursed from the blocked accounts after the war.[18]

The Bermuda Conference was in session at the time, and a mood of despair had overtaken the Jewish leadership as to their ability to move the Allied powers to act for rescue. Nonetheless they spared no effort, still hoping that their few friends in the Administration would help as best as they could. Rabbi Wise and Dr. Goldmann sought a meeting with Sumner Welles to present their pleas to implement the Riegner plan. On April 30th, the two met with Welles and requested that he recommend to the Secretary of Treasury (who was responsible for all transfers of funds) that he grant the World Jewish Congress a license to transfer a substantial amount of money to Switzerland for rescue and relief operations.[19] Welles sought the advise of the economic adviser of the

State Department, Herbert Feis, and he in turn, asked the opinion of Bernard Meltzer, the head of Foreign Funds in the State Department. By chance or not, both these officials were Jewish – the only Jews of that rank in the State Department. Meltzer met with Dr. Goldmann who filled him in on the details of Riegner's rescue proposals. Meltzer then sent a cable to Harrison requesting that he obtain from Riegner further clarifications.[20]

A month later came Harrison's reply, confirming the main points in Riegner's cable. In a discussion at State on June 14th (two and a half months after Wise's request to obtain the information from Harrison), the 'Long clique' opposed support for Riegner's plan claiming that it would result in funds falling into the hands of the enemy. In contrast, Feis contended that the matter had to be decided by the Treasury, and that State should deal only with the political aspects. Since the State Department's proclaimed stand was to support relief activities, Feis claimed, there was no reason for them to object to issuing the license.

Feis later testified that only Meltzer and he supported the proposal and insinuated that the opposition of the others stemmed from antisemitism. Feis insisted that the only people in the State Department prepared to support rescue and relief activities for the Jews, were Dean Acheson, Thomas Finletter and Donald Hiss. However these matters were not within their competence and therefore they were unable to influence the decision.[21] It is interesting to note that Feis did not include Assistant Secretary Adolph Berle among the rescue advocates though the 'Bergson Boys' considered him one of their most loyal supporters in the Administration. From some of Berle's statements, we know that Bergson was completely mistaken in his evaluation.[22]

At that meeting it was decided that Feis prepare a memo stating his views. That paper was presented to Secretary Hull and then sent to the Treasury Department. Monty Penkower mistakenly claims that this memorandum brought "Treasury for the first time officially into direct contact with the Final Solution."[23] However, since the very onset of the war the Treasury Department made decisions that were connected with the Holocaust. However, the Jewish organizations appealed many times to Treasury for licenses to send money, food, and other forms of relief to aid the Jews in Europe. Throughout most of 1942, these requests were consistently denied. These same Treasury officials, who later became staunch advocates of rescue, were among the most stubborn opponents of any attempts to deviate from the policies of the blockade while the war still tilted towards the Axis powers. They were resolute in their determination "to make the feeding of the civilians incumbent upon the enemy."[24] According to the testimony of the Treasury people "it was on this case [the request of the WJC to transfer funds to Switzerland – A.H.] that we changed Treasury policy."[25]

After a few more weeks in which nothing was done, Feis' memorandum led to a joint meeting of State and Treasury officials to discuss the Riegner plan. Reams led the State Department's battle against adopting the scheme. According to the description of a Treasury official present at the meeting, Reams "threw cold water on the proposal." Reams claimed that it was inconceivable to establish satisfactory arrangements with the Rumanians and that everything depended on German consent to transportation arrangements, which was impossible to obtain. The British, he claimed, would not agree to the proposal because the 'White Paper' permitted only 30,000 more Jews to enter Palestine; the Turks would not allow transit of Jewish refugees through their territory; and the American Military opposed transferring thousands of Jews to Africa. As against his assertions, the Treasury people claimed that there were precedents and it was possible to guarantee that the money sent would not fall into enemy hands.[26]

Throughout all those months the World Jewish Congress leadership did not relent in their efforts to convince the Administration to adopt the plan. In June James Wise met with John Pehle of Treasury and told him of a woman named Eidisen who was prepared to place at the disposal of the WJC in Geneva $100,000 (in French Francs) to be used for rescue, if refund was guaranteed at the end of the war.[27] Four days later he returned to Treasury accompanied by Nachum Goldmann. The two explained that it was possible, for a sum of $170,000, to bribe Rumanian officials to permit the exodus of 70,000 Jews to Palestine, and this with no money falling into enemy hands.

The Treasury people, O'Connell (Legal adviser) and Pehle (head of the Foreign Funds Division) were in no hurry to adopt the plan. On the contrary, in a memorandum sent to Secretary Morgenthau they indicated the many problems involved in the scheme. They insisted that the financial arrangements proposed by the WJC, which included paying ransom, were not satisfactory and were contrary to government policy. They also claimed that the plan required extensive contact in enemy territory and that, too, was against stated government policy.[28] However, in the following weeks the Treasury people concluded that, despite the problems, they would support the WJC request. The Legal Counsel of the Treasury Department, Randolph Paul, explained his stand in a memorandum sent to Morgenthau. He stated that the "Trend, due to the change in the war, is towards liberation and relief operations should now be undertaken for this purpose [rescuing Jews], even if the enemy obtains certain limited benefits thereby."[29]

On July 16th, the day after the interdepartmental meeting, the Treasury sent State its agreement in principle to grant the WJC a license to transfer funds to Switzerland for rescue.[30]But they still needed the State Department's assent to activate the plan. To overcome the difference of opinion between the two departments, it was necessary for the President to intervene. Fortunately, and entirely by chance, Rabbi Wise was scheduled to meet the President on July 22nd. Ever since the failure of the Bermuda Conference, the Joint Emergency Committee had been trying to reach the President to present him with the rescue proposals of the Jewish organizations, hoping he would accede to their appeals. Wise's first request to meet with the President "as early as possible" was sent on April 28th, but received no reply for two weeks, and when it arrived, was negative.[31] In the following two months all attempts to arrange a meeting were unsuccessful, until, at last, the date was set for the end of July.

In his autobiography, 'Challenging Years', Wise claims that at the meeting he asked the President to permit smuggling Jews out from Poland to Hungary by payments sent to Switzerland.[32] Wise's request was made in an apologetic tone, indicating his self-abnegation in his relationship with the President. "I hesitate to bring the following [matters] to your attention", he said. "Even if you found that you couldn't comply with the extraordinary request I am about to make, you will understand and forgive". According to Wise, after FDR heard the request he did not hesitate but immediately replied: "Stephen, why don't you go ahead and do it". Wise states that, on the spot, Roosevelt phoned Morgenthau and told him "This is a very fair proposal that Stephen makes about ransoming Jews out of

Poland into Hungary."[33] We have no other evidence indicating that Wise spoke about bringing Jews out of Poland. Yet it is quite possible that he raised the subject of Poland, for at that time there was a lot of smuggling across borders. Whether or not Poland was discussed it is certain that they spoke about rescuing Jews from France and Rumania and that the President consented to the plan.

At that meeting Wise asked the President to condemn Nazi crimes against the Jews and warn the perpetrators in clear terms, to stop the killings. Wise saw a condemnation and warning coming from the recognized leader of the Allies as an important means of staying the hands of the murderers, especially in the satellite countries.[34] Despite continued pleas to the President, Wise could not induce the President to make such a public statement. In reply to Wise's requests, the President claimed that in the past he had "publicly denounced these barbaric crimes [...] I intend again in suitable occasion to revert publicly to this subject."[35] Roosevelt did not find the "suitable occasion" for seven more months. Yet, when the Foreign Ministers of the 'Big 3' issued a condemnation of Nazi war crimes in October 1943, the word 'Jewish' was missing from the long list of peoples suffering under the Nazi rule. Even the people of Crete were included in the roster.[36]

The day after the meeting, Wise wrote the President a letter of thanks for his sympathetic attitude, and for consenting to transfer funds to Switzerland for rescue activities in Rumania, France and Slovakia. This is the first time that Slovakian Jews were mentioned in this connection.[37] On July 29th, Morgenthau wrote Wise that the Treasury Department had informed State that it supported the World & American Jewish Congress plan and that "Treasury is prepared to take the necessary action to implement that proposal". Morgenthau also added a personal note to his letter and apprised Wise that "I do want you to know that we, too, are deeply concerned about the Jewish victims of Hitler."[38] Two weeks later Morgenthau wrote the President that he had already notified Wise that his Department would issue a license to the WJC, and that it was already arranged with Secretary of State Hull.[39] In light of Morgenthau's letter, Roosevelt informed Wise on August 14th that the matter was arranged and now all that remained to be done was to exchange a few cables with the American Legation in Bern to clarify some details.[40]

Secretary of the Treasury Morgenthau with President Roosevelt

The way was now open to initiate an important plan that offered the possibility of saving Jews. The project envisaged the transfer of funds to Europe to finance the shipment of food to Jews in Nazi-occupied countries. It was clear that the money would also be used to smuggle Jews out of France and to bribe Rumanian officials to permit Jews to leave their country.[41] The World Jewish Congress saw the scheme as a breakthrough in the barrier to rescue, and hoped to extend it to other areas of occupied Europe and to other rescue projects that might arise in the future. No one could imagine that after the plan had received the blessings of the President and the Secretary of Treasury and the agreement of Hull, it would be postponed for another few months because of the deliberate delaying tactics of State Department officials.

While the State Department officials procrastinated over the license, the Jewish organizations continued in their efforts to seek additional ways of funding rescue operations in Europe. In August, Dr. Joseph Schwartz, Joint's representative in Europe, met in Palestine with Eliyahu Dobkin, of the Jewish Agency, to discuss funding rescue activities. The two agreed that Joint would cover some of the costs of bringing and absorbing Jews in Palestine, thereby freeing Jewish Agency funds which could then be used for rescue operations in Europe. Schwartz was agreeable to this arrangement, for by freeing funds to be used for rescue Jewish Agency emissaries were prepared to execute important illegal operations which Joint was not prepared to carry out because it would have endangered its legal status.[42] Besides, Schwartz explained, Joint could not transfer funds directly to occupied territories because of the American government's adverse attitude. He suggested that "Joint is ready to put at the disposal of people who are ready to put in money in occupied countries, money which will be paid in America after the war." Schwartz declared that "The Joint Distribution Committee Executive is prepared to do such acts in conjunction with the Jewish Agency."[43]

At a meeting with Breckinridge Long on September 16th, Nachum Goldmann attempted to attain a new approach to the funding of rescue operations. Goldmann left that meeting feeling that he had received far-reaching promises from the Assistant Secretary. But as usual in all matters pertaining to the rescue of Jews Long had only led Goldmann on by the nose. At that meeting Goldmann had proposed that one way to save Jews was by sending food parcels through the International Red Cross. Since the situation was fluid, Goldmann contended, and one could not know when an opportunity might arise, he requested from Long that the U.S. and Britain place at the disposal of the IRC a substantial sum of money, since such large amounts were not available to the Jewish organizations. When asked about the sums involved, Goldmann mentioned ten million dollars of which the Jewish organizations would provide a total of two million.

Long told Goldmann that he would recommend granting the license to the Jewish organizations and agreed on principle that the Allied governments would also give their share, four million dollars each from the U.S. and Britain. The only difficulty, as stated by Long, was that no money remained in the President's 'Emergency Fund', and so there would be no choice but to ask Congress to appropriate the necessary funds. Long speculated that such a procedure could be "a long-drawn process". At the same time, Goldmann complained about British procrastination and bureaucracy which hindered the possibility of rescuing the Balkan Jews. Long agreed with Goldmann that the British were not acting properly, but rationalized that "the U.S. couldn't tell the British how to run their business."[44]

When Goldmann reported this to the Joint Emergency Committee, it decided not to wait for government funds but rather place its own resources at the disposal of the Red Cross, assuming that the Administration would agree. Joint's representative claimed that his organization had for a long time tried to transfer funds to the Red Cross but was unsuccessful. The Red Cross had told them that they were uncertain if they could use this money because of Hitler's opposition to aiding the Jews.[45] Joseph Hyman informed Long that the JEC had requested Joint to transfer funds to the Red Cross for food parcels to the Jews of Europe and that Joint was prepared to immediately forward $100,000 for this purpose. A decision regarding a larger sum (two million dollars) would take a while longer, he said. He also informed Long that he had been told that Turkey would provide 250 tons of provisions for the Jews if the Red Cross would expedite the matter.[46]

Goldmann's plan to create a fund in the hands of the Red Cross to use whenever the opportunity arose was very timely. When in December, Goldmann again raised the issue, Long divulged that the Intergovernmental Committee on Refugees (that supposedly had begun to function) agreed to the plan in principle, and was now asking the Red Cross for concrete proposals. Goldmann told Long that he knew the Red Cross had already forwarded such plans to the IGCR and to the American Legation in Switzerland. Long asserted that he hadn't heard of such plans but when they arrived there would be no difficulty to fund them. "There is no need for Jewish money", he told Goldmann, "as it is the obligation of the government [to provide the funds]." Long also claimed that there was no need to worry any longer about the Jews in Transnistria for they were already being returned to Rumania. He revealed to Goldmann that the Rumanian government had approached the U.S. authorities about terms of surrender, and had been told that the American attitude would be determined, among the rest, by Rumanian treatment of the Jews in Transnistria.[47]

Long's tale about the ten million dollars that were purportedly intended for rescue and relief was a complete fabrication. When Arieh Tartakower of the WJC, visited Britain in 1945, he discussed the issue with Herbert Emerson, the British director of the IGCR. Emerson stated unequivocally that the ten million dollar fund had never existed nor had the British government ever promised to contribute four million.[48] The story Long had told Goldmann that no money remained in the Emergency Fund, was also a total deceit. Treasury officials who checked the matter in January, 1944 clearly asserted that money did exist in the fund.[49]

Throughout the second half of 1943, many new channels for rescue began to open up. Not only the satellites realized that Germany was about to lose the war and were searching for ways to extricate themselves from the conflict but also the neutral nations began to free themselves from Nazi threats and were now readier to collaborate in the rescue of Jews.

At the end of September, 1943, information arrived that the Germans were about to deport Danish Jewry to extermination camps. When Wise received the news he hastened to the State Department to obtain assistance in saving the Jews of Denmark. On October 1st, Wise and Goldmann wrote Long that the Germans were preparing to deport Danish Jews and that the Swedes were ready to absorb them, if Germany agreed. They asked State to approach the Swedish government to open the gates of their country to the Jews.[50] Hillel Storch, the WJC representative in Stockholm also attempted to influence the Swedish government to cooperate in the rescue of the Danish Jews. The State Department acquiesced to the WJC request and encouraged the Swedish government to absorb all Danish Jews who would be permitted to leave their country.[51] Swedish radio stations broadcast the news that Sweden was prepared to accept Danish Jews. The Danish people and the Danish underground smuggled the Jews to Sweden in fishing boats. This was one of the most outstanding rescue stories during the Holocaust and it succeeded in saving nearly all of Danish Jewry.[52] It is not certain how much the WJC intervention affected this remarkable rescue. This feat demonstrates to those who claim that the American Jewish leadership did nothing to save European Jewry, one of the many examples of the continual efforts of the Jewish organizations to influence the American government to act for rescue.

Riegner had proposed his plan for the rescue of French and Rumanian Jews in the early spring of 1943. In the middle of the summer the American Administration had given the plan its blessings, but fall arrived, and nothing had been accomplished. On November 6th, Harrison wrote the State Department that the British Commercial Attaché in Switzerland was opposed to granting a license, maintaining that the Allies had decided against ransom payments to rescue Jews and that the money might fall into the hands of the enemy.[53] Three weeks later the new Under-Secretary of State Edward Stettinius Jr. (Sumner Welles was forced to resign when a number of Congressmen were about to divulge the fact that he was a homosexual) ordered Harrison not to heed the British opposition but to grant the WJC a license for transfer of funds.[54] Stettinius did this despite the continuing opposition of the State Department clique that consistently had prevented rescue attempts. The day before Stettinius' letter had arrived, Reams wrote a memorandum in which he proposed that the Department not support the granting of licenses, because "We are granting to a special group of **enemy aliens** [my emphasis-A.H.] relief measure which in the past we have denied to Allied people."[55]

This time, however, the issue of rescue of Jews was no longer only in the domain of the State Department, which had blocked any feasible plan for rescuing Jews from the Nazi inferno. This time the Treasury Department was also involved. Now, when the Treasury people saw that nothing was progressing despite the fact that it had already been agreed upon for quite a while, they began to hold a series of meetings to pressure the State Department and succeeded in bringing the issue to a successful conclusion. The intervention of Treasury in the matter of the WJC license opened wide the granting of other licenses for the transfer of funds. It also led in the end to the decision to remove rescue and relief out of the State Department and place it under the aegis of a new agency to be created specifically for this purpose.

(b) The War Refugee Board Established

"The bull has to be taken by the horns"
(Josiah DuBois at a meeting of the Treasury staff– 12/43)

The War Refugee Board (WRB) was the most significant U.S. Government undertaking established to save Jews during the Holocaust. It is therefore important to examine the reasons that brought about its establishment. An examination of these factors might shed some light on the question often debated today: Which policy should the American Jewish organizations have adopted to best induce their government to act for the rescue of European Jewry?

If it is true, as the 'Bergson Boys' claimed then[56] and as David Wyman and others claim today,[57] that the Gillette-Rogers resolution introduced in Congress at the initiative of the 'Bergson Boys' was the major factor that led to the creation of the WRB, then, perhaps, those who claim that a more aggressive public policy on the part of American Jewry could have impelled the American government to rescue Jews are justified in their criticism. However, if the actions of the Treasury Department were the decisive factor,[58] then, perhaps the Jewish organizations were correct in their policy of avoiding bitter conflict with the Administration. And if the World Jewish Congress' claim that the activities of Bergson actually caused the postponement of the creation of the WRB by several months,[59] then, perhaps, the Jewish establishment was justified in maintaining that the 'grandstanding' activities of the 'Bergson Boys' did not help, but rather hindered, rescue.

The first indication to the Treasury that the State Department was acting with undue delay in all that related to rescue of Jews, was a phone call Herbert Lehman (appointed by Roosevelt to head the American relief agency) made to Secretary Morgenthau on September 15, 1943. Lehman informed him that two cables which Morgenthau had sent two weeks earlier, instructing State Department representatives in Switzerland and in China to issue licenses to the WJC and to Joint enabling them to borrow money for the purpose of rescue, were never sent. He told Morgenthau that he had done all in his power to have the cables sent, but was unsuccessful.[60] Morgenthau immediately phoned Cordell Hull and told him that if the cables had not been sent and he had not been notified, he saw this as a "discourteous [act] to me." Hull promised that the cables would be sent the same day.[61]

Morgenthau no longer trusted the people at State to implement agreements and so asked his assistant, Randolph Paul, to report to him how the license issue was progressing. On November 2nd, Paul told Morgenthau that: a) The cables had not been sent until September 28th. b) The legation in Bern had cabled on October 10th, asking for specific instructions from the State Department to fulfill the Treasury's request. Harrison also informed his superiors that the British opposed granting the licenses. (The State Department had not informed Treasury of all these measures and Paul received this information from Lehman's office.) c) On October 26, the State Department cabled Harrison ordering him to grant the license to the WJC. (Long wanted to avoid a confrontation with Treasury since he knew the President supported it on this issue). d) The British Ministry of Economic Warfare (that opposed the licenses) had itself made a similar transaction – they had transferred funds to the British citizens living on the Channel Islands, which were then under German occupation, without previously consulting Washington.[62]

After three more weeks passed without any progress, Morgenthau assembled his senior assistants to discuss, what they termed, the 'Jewish Evacuation Plan'. At the group's first meeting on November 23rd, all participants agreed that since the Allies were well on the road to victory, Treasury should issue permits to finance rescue activities, as long as they would not benefit the enemy. There were many complaints voiced against the attitudes of both the State Department and the British. Morgenthau claimed that the people at State were not interested in rescue, "and [that] only by my happening to be Secretary of Treasury and being vitally interested [...] I can get it done."[63]

In all subsequent Treasury staff meetings dealing with rescue, it was not Morgenthau who took the most forceful stand. Yet at that first meeting he made clear to his subordinates that he wanted the matter resolved in a positive manner and that his Department would proffer all possible assistance to the Jews of Europe. However, Morgenthau's assistants did not act on the matter simply because it was the wish of their superior. The people at Treasury who dealt with rescue, especially Randolph Paul, John Pehle and Josiah DuBois Jr., were all Christians and liberals with deep humanist convictions who enthusiastically became involved in the attempt to save Jews. They wholeheartedly and courageously attempted to bring about a change in the attitude of their government to the problem.

At the following meeting, DuBois, Counsel for the Foreign Funds Division, was the most resolute in expressing his view that it was incumbent upon Treasury to confront the State Department about the permits. Morgenthau however, tried to avoid the conflict. He hoped that a direct approach from him to Hull would suffice to overcome the obstacles raised by State Department officials.[64] He complained to Hull that three-and-a-half months had already passed since the Treasury had agreed to grant the permits to the WJC, but so far, nothing had been done. Morgenthau asked for Hull's "assistance [...] in order to expedite the matter."[65] Two weeks later Hull informed Morgenthau, that according to Leland Harrison, the WJC plan meant bribing Rumanian officials and this "involved the danger that it would be converted into an instrumentality for benefitting those who are persecuting the Jews." Hull claimed that the British were opposed to the plan and they had requested Harrison not to issue the permits until they could discuss the matter with the Treasury Department in Washington.[66]

The Treasury staff attempted to obtain more information about the reasons for the delay in granting the licenses. To that end DuBois met with Bernard Meltzer. Meltzer, no longer with the State Department, had enlisted in the U.S. Navy and thus felt free to relate to DuBois what had transpired within the State Department. He described how the Department had dealt with the WJC request and accused the 'Long group' of opposing the licenses. He also told DuBois that the British Embassy in Washington had heard of the WJC plan from Nachum Goldmann long before, yet they had never once asked the U.S. government to consult with Britain before deciding upon it.[67]

The Treasury staff heard DuBois' report on December 13th, and decided to ask for further clarifications. At that meeting Pehle proposed setting up a committee in Switzerland to supervise the funds transferred to Geneva and to guarantee that they not fall into enemy hands. The committee was to be composed of a WJC representative; Saly Mayer, Joint's agent in Switzerland; and a representative of one of the international organizations: The Red Cross, YMCA, or the Quakers. The internal conflicts between the Jewish organizations now reached the attention of the Treasury Department. Pehle reported that he had discussed the matter with the Joint and was informed that they were not prepared to sit on a committee with the World Jewish Congress. Morgenthau ordered Pehle to tell Joint that they would have to sit with everybody "and no damned nonsense about it."[68]

On December 15th, Hull received a cable from John Winant, U.S. Ambassador to Britain, containing a letter sent him by the British Ministry of Economic Warfare. It raised the standard British objections to granting permits, namely their concern that they might actually succeed in freeing Jews and consequently the British would be obliged to care for them. The letter spoke drily of the Foreign Office being "concerned with the difficulty of disposing of any considerable number of Jews should they be rescued from enemy-occupied territories." They based their objections on the problem of finding ships to transport the refugees and the difficulty "of finding accommodations in the countries of the Near East for any but a small number of Jews." They claimed that it would be "almost impossible to deal with 70,000," though Riegner's plan never mentioned so large a number, at least not in the first stage of the scheme.[69] The British note incensed the Treasury people. Ansel Luxford claimed that British inaction was condemning the Jews to death. Randolph Paul defined the British in legal terms: "The law calls them para-delicto, of equal guilt."[70]

The British attitude strengthened Treasury's resolve to issue the permits. The following two meetings of the Treasury staff took place on a weekend, the first on a Saturday night and the second on a Sunday, indicative of the seriousness with which they viewed the issue. If this is compared to the attitude of the people at State, who generally let weeks pass between their dealings with matters relating to rescue of the Jews, the extent of the change that had evolved once the Treasury Department entered the scene becomes apparent.

At the Saturday night meeting, DuBois was again the most adamant in his stance that "the bull has to be taken by the horns," and the issue of rescuing Jews should be taken out of the State Department and placed with an agency "that is willing to deal with it frontally." He contended that we "don't know what to do with the Jews so we let them die." Pehle agreed with DuBois and proposed that the President establish a committee of prominent personages sympathetic to the rescue of Jews. Only Morgenthau still hesitated. He suggested that before turning to the President they should first consult with Hull and ascertain whether he would cooperate.[71]

The idea of setting up an American commission to deal with the 'refugees', as opposed to the impotent Intergovernmental Committee on Refugees, was not new. In addition to plans of the Jewish organizations and the 'Bergson Boys', it had also been proposed by Oscar Cox, Advisor to the Lend-Lease Authority, in June 1943. Cox's proposal was rejected by the State Department. State claimed that the IGCR was already working on rescue and if the American government created a special agency it would only interfere.[72] The proposal to establish an American rescue agency received new impetus when the 'Bergson Boys' attempted to obtain such a resolution in Congress. The decision to procure an American rescue agency had been taken at the 'Emergency Conference' in July, but in meetings of the 'Emergency Committee' with administration officials, they were unable to convince the government. Therefore they persuaded their friends on Capitol Hill to introduce a resolution in Congress, though even if they succeeded in getting such a resolution passed, it was not in the authority of Congress to establish an agency, but only to recommend it to the President.

On November 9th, Senator Guy Gillette (D-Iowa) proposed a resolution calling on the President to create "a committee of diplomatic, economic and military experts to formulate and effectuate a plan of immediate action designed to save the surviving Jewish people of Europe."[73] In the House of Representatives Will Rogers Jr. (D-Cal.) and Joseph Baldwin (R-N.Y.) introduced a similar resolution. Sol Bloom, chairman of the House Committee on Foreign Affairs, agreed to open hearings immediately. The historian, Monty Penkower, believes that Bloom agreed to cooperate in order to rectify the bad impression his words about the Bermuda Conference had made on the Jewish community.[74] On the other hand, David Wyman claims that Bloom only appeared to be cooperating and that his real intention was actually to hinder the resolution.[75] As a matter of fact, Bloom wanted the President himself to order the creation of a rescue agency and thereby avoid a debate in Congress.[76] He later declared publicly that he would support the resolution when it came to a vote.[77]

As part of the hearings, Breckinridge Long testified before closed doors. Wyman sees this as a plot by Bloom to block the resolution.[78] Wyman's criticism is misdirected, for it was quite evident that Long, who was responsible for all refugee matters, would appear before the committee. It was not surprising that Bloom condescended to the State Department's request that Long's testimony be given behind closed doors for the discussion revolved around issues about which the less said in public, the better. Long's testimony was aimed at answering the critics of the State Department's rescue policy. He did not attack the proposed resolution but implied that the creation of a rescue agency would be interpreted as a vote of no confidence in the State Department and the IGCR.[79]

Long surprised his audience when he revealed that "since the Hitler regime began to persecute the Jews and until today" the U.S. had absorbed 580,000 refugees.[80] This number genuinely impressed the members of the Committee but Long was also quick to calm the fears of the restrictionists by stating that, "aside from a few generous gestures," it was all done within the framework of the immigration laws and quotas.[81] As to the ability of the Intergovernmental Committee to deal with rescue, Long divulged the decisions supposedly taken by which the IGCR had been granted authority "to do whatever they can, within and without Germany and the occupied territories."[82] Long's testimony so impressed the committee members (even Congressman Will Rogers Jr., who had initiated the resolution in the House, avoided attacking Long's statement during his testimony[83]) that Bloom requested Long to permit publication of the facts to demonstrate the extent to which the American government had acted to save Jews.[84] It appeared that Long had achieved his goal and that Congress would now consent to leave the rescue issue in the 'good hands' of the State Department and the IGCR.

However like Balaam who came to curse and found himself blessing, Long's testimony achieved the exact opposite of what he had intended. After his testimony appeared in the press (his astonishing statement made the front page of the *N.Y. Times* [85]), little time elapsed before the Jewish organizations exposed Long's fabrications. The American Jewish Conference issued statistics, which clearly proved that the number of Jewish refugees who had entered the U.S.

since 1933 did not exceed 210,732, only 36% of the figure stated by Long.[86] Long's contention as to the authority vested in the IGCR was also debunked in a matter of weeks. The Jewish Telegraphic Agency cabled the IGCR offices in London to confirm Long's testimony in Congress. On December 22nd the *JTA Daily Bulletin* revealed that the IGCR had categorically stated that it had not been granted authority to negotiate with the enemy.[87] Long's testimony boomeranged. He was attacked by the Jewish organizations and Congressman Celler demanded he resign. According to Celler, either Long was completely ignorant about matters under his jurisdiction, or else he was a liar.[88]

The day after Long's appearance before the House committee, Rabbi Stephen Wise testified as representative of the Jewish organizations affiliated with the American Jewish Conference. Before Wise's appearance, the American Jewish Conference held a number of meetings to clarify its stand on the resolution. At the first meeting, they decided in favor of a rescue resolution, but opposed the one initiated by Gillette and Rogers. This was probably due to their desire not to enhance the prestige of the 'Bergson Boys'. Instead of the resolution proposed in Congress, they suggested organizing well-known non-Jews to pressure the State Department to activate the IGCR as an effective body.[89]

At the final discussion held a few days prior to Wise's appearance before the Committee on Foreign Affairs the Jewish leaders expressed their differing views. Rabbi Irving Miller reported on attempts to establish a committee of important personalities, which had been decided on at the previous meeting. He named several who had already agreed to join – but the successes were negligible. He asserted that the Gillette-Rogers resolution was a step in the right direction but lacked a few important elements. In particular he felt that a demand be made to open the gates of Palestine to the Jewish refugees. If it proved impossible to add this, he favored supporting the resolution anyway. Herman Schulman of the American Jewish Congress supported the resolution as it stood – without any additional demands. Nachum Goldmann believed that the Palestine issue should not be pressed unless it was certain that it would be adopted. However, it was the activist Zionist line, under the leadership of Rabbi Abba Hillel Silver that carried the day. Silver demanded that the Palestine issue be appended to the resolution. He claimed that "rescue and free immigration to Palestine are logically one and inseparable." The decision was taken to include the demand to open the gates of Palestine.[90]

It was precisely this proposal, which appeared a logical coupling of the demand for rescue with the Zionist appeal for free immigration to Palestine that the Irgun delegation opposed. Bergson had decided to heed the advice of friends in Congress and not combine the two.[91] It was the opinion of those Congressmen, that to include opening the gates of Palestine, which was seen as an attempt by the Zionists to hitch a ride on the rescue issue, would endanger the resolution. In all probability those Congressmen were correct in their judgment. Two months previous, an internal Treasury Department memorandum presented a similar evaluation about the danger of mixing the two issues. That memorandum stated that the Emergency Conference "had injected the Zionist issue into the rescue question," and therefore "It would seem doubtful whether it can be expected that organization is going to accomplish any real results."[92]

Before the House committee, Wise presented the position decided upon. He avoided opposing the Gillette-Rogers resolution but did say that it was inadequate, since it did not include any concrete proposals and lacked a demand to open the gates of Palestine.[93] The journal of the American Jewish Congress was less circumspect in opposing the resolution. An article in the December 10th issue of *Congress Weekly* attacked Bergson's Emergency Committee as a body that had "no inkling of public responsibility." It clearly opposed the resolution in Congress.[94] The differences over the question of rescue reached a new low with the Jewish establishment's tasteless attacks on the resolution appearing before the American Congress.

By the time Congress dispersed for the Christmas recess, the resolution had already been shunted aside in the House Committee. On the other hand, the Senate Foreign Relations Committee decided not to hold hearings but to debate the resolution before the full Senate when it reconvened at the end of January. In the meantime the Treasury continued debating rescue but these discussions no longer revolved solely around the question of issuing a license to the WJC. They were now discussing rescue on a much larger scale.

Treasury's pressure on the State Department proved effective and on December 18, Long instructed the American Legation in Bern to issue the license the WJC had requested in April.[95] Months of feverish activity had been needed, a direct request to the President and massive intervention by the Treasury Department, in order to obtain a license for only $25,000. On the same day that Long sent his instructions to Harrison, Hull sent a cable to the U.S. Ambassador in London instructing him to notify the British that their opposition to granting the license "is incompatible with the policy of the U.S. Government and of previously expressed British policy as it had been understood by us."[96]

The view had crystallized in the Treasury not to be content only with obtaining the permit for the WJC, but to propose to the President the establishment of an American rescue agency. It received added stimulus at the staff meeting on December 19, when Oscar Cox, who had been invited to participate, proposed creating a committee composed of Morgenthau, Leo Crowley (head of the Federal Economic Agency) and the new Under-Secretary of State, Edward Stettinius Jr. He viewed the three as people who sympathized with the attempts to rescue Jews. Several times during that meeting Cox stated unequivocally that creating a rescue agency had already been discussed with the President, that Roosevelt had agreed, and that only the State Department remained opposed. As to the legislative initiative of Gillette and Rogers, Cox alleged that those who supported it were all adversaries of the President.[97] Wyman is mistaken in his evaluation that at this stage Morgenthau still opposed the creation of a rescue agency. What Morgenthau did want, knowing that the State Department was the main obstacle to the establishment of a rescue agency, was to meet with Hull in the hope of convincing him to join the initiative of the Treasury Department.[98]

In preparation for Morgenthau's meeting with Hull on the 20th, two memoranda were prepared at his request. One contained a summary of the State Department's inept handling of rescue and of their sabotaging of the license issue. The second memorandum, prepared by DuBois, contained sensational revelations about the State Department's suppression of information about the Holocaust. While investigating the handling of the Riegner plan, DuBois had chanced upon a reference to cable #354, which the State Department had sent to the U.S. Legation in Bern. When DuBois requested to see the cable he was told that it contained nothing pertinent to Treasury and refused to show it to him. DuBois 'smelled a rat', and asked Donald Hiss, a friend in the State Department, to obtain the cable for him. Though all State Department officials had been forewarned not to allow the cable to fall into the hands of Treasury, Hiss took the risk and allowed DuBois to read it (the State Department officials were convinced that it was a Jew, Riegelman, who had passed the cable on to the Treasury). Cable #354 of February 10th referred to a previous cable #482, and instructed Harrison not to accept "reports submitted to you for transmission to private persons in the U.S." When DuBois read cable #482, in which Gerhardt Riegner forwarded to Wise information about the massacre of Jews, the policy of the State Department during the entire previous period became clear to him.[99] Randolph Paul was irate when he heard what DuBois had uncovered. He charged that "This movement to let the Jews be killed is an underground movement [...] in the State Department."[100]

When Morgenthau and his assistants arrived at the meeting with the people from State, Hull presented them with a copy of the stern note he had sent to the British. Long also surprised them by announcing that two days previously, he had sent instructions to Switzerland to issue the license. In an attempt to clear himself and his department of all blame, Long told the Treasury staff that the State Department several times had endeavored to help Jews flee from Occupied-Europe but that the Germans always prevented these attempts. In answer to Morgenthau's complaints about the State Department's attitude toward the rescue of Jews, Hull blamed it on his subordinates and claimed that "I don't get a chance to know everything that is going on." Morgenthau requested Hull to let him see cable #354. Long did send Morgenthau a copy of the cable but all reference to cable #482 had been deleted from it.[101]

The continuing deceit of the State Department was too much for Morgenthau and his staff. It was decided to bring the matter before the President. Pehle, DuBois and Paul were given the task of preparing a memorandum for the President, which would detail all their findings of the State Department actions concerning the rescue of Jews. They were also asked to draft a Presidential directive for the establishment of an American governmental rescue agency. The Treasury people, well-experienced by then, decided that in the meantime they would act on their own and bypass the obstacles obstructing the rescue of Jews.

On December 18th Randolph Paul informed Morgenthau that Joint had requested a permit to borrow money in China to bring relief to 10,000 needy Jewish refugees stranded in Shanghai. They needed more than $25,000 a month. Paul recommended that Morgenthau approve the permit and not notify either the State Department or Britain so as to avoid delays. Morgenthau agreed to the scheme.[102] Two weeks later the Treasury again issued a permit to Joint, this time for $200,000 to arrange for the 'evacuation' of Jews from France and to "sustain and safeguard their lives pending evacuation." The Treasury took this step also without notifying either the State Department or Britain.[103] Aid to Jews in their hour of need was now taking a serious form. The license to the World Jewish Congress for $25,000 was the first breach in the wall that had prevented attempts to rescue the Jews of Europe.

The Treasury staff renewed discussions on January 13th in preparation for the meeting with the President on Sunday, January 16th. The atmosphere at the meeting was replete with feelings of anger and shame over the policies embraced by the U.S. while Jews were being slaughtered by the Germans. It was reported at that meeting that a WJC request to evacuate 4000 Jews from the Italian island of Rab which had been liberated by the Americans, had been turned down by the military with the excuse "that to take such action might create a precedent"[104] The island with all the Jews there was later recaptured by the Nazis. Morgenthau responded to that news by declaring that "the [U.S.] attitude to date is no different from Hitler's attitude."[105]

At that meeting the memorandum to the President was presented to Morgenthau. It asserted that the stated policy of the government was "to work out programs to save those Jews and other persecuted minorities of Europe who could be saved," but that the State Department officials who were responsible for implementing this policy were not fulfilling their duties. The report stated that many people no longer view this failure "as a product of simple incompetence," but "They see plain Anti-semitism motivating the actions of these State Department officials and, rightly or wrongly, it will require little more in the way of proof for this suspicion to explode into a nasty scandal."[106]

The report concentrated on two incidents, which exemplified State's approach to matters of rescue. The first story detailed the many delays in granting the license for the WJC, despite the fact that the President and the Secretary of Treasury had agreed to the plan. The second account related the "Suppression of Facts Regarding Hitler's Extermination of the Jews in Europe" and the attempts to prevent such information from reaching the U.S. The report summed up that "the matter of rescuing Jews from extermination is a trust too great to remain in the hands of men who are indifferent, callous and perhaps even hostile [...] Only a fervent will to accomplish, backed by persistent and untiring effort can succeed where time is so precious."[107]

The meeting of the Treasury staff on January 15th was devoted entirely to discussing how best to present the subject to the President. Before the meeting Morgenthau and Samuel Rosenman, Roosevelt's political advisor, held one last telephone conversation. Morgenthau had kept contact with Rosenman concerning his moves on the issue and now asked Rosenman for his opinion. Rosenman, as usual, was sensitive about emphasizing the Jewish issue. A few days earlier when Morgenthau had suggested to him that he and Ben Cohen (another Jewish advisor of the President) be present at the meeting with Roosevelt, Rosenman expressed his doubts. He questioned whether it was wise for three Jews to attend the meeting called to discuss the fate of European Jewry.[108] Rosenman now told Morgenthau that the memorandum was good, but suggested that a paragraph be added clarifying that the plan "applies to Poles and Greeks and all willing to get out." Otherwise the President was liable to get the impression "that this is purely Jewish." Rosenman was quick to add that "Of course the Jewish problem probably is 99% of it," but Roosevelt might want to present it as a general matter.[109]

At the last moment Treasury got wind of a new State Department scheme to prevent the removal of refugee problems from their control. Their proposal called for the creation of a committee composed of various governmental departments senior officials to be headed by Howard Travers, Chief of the Visa Division and in the past one of the strongest opponents of rescue in the State

Department.[110] This plan was probably connected with Congressman Bloom's idea to prevent debate on the Gillette-Rogers resolution out of fear that it would develop into an attack on Roosevelt and his administration. Instead of the Gillette-Rogers resolution, Bloom favored Hull himself taking the initiative to create such an agency.[111] For a month the State Department, and especially Breckinridge Long, had been trying to rectify the situation, knowing that their previous activities had been uncovered and they were about to become targets for criticism. Therefore the State Department issued the WJC license on December 17, and Hull sent a strong note to the British criticizing them for their inflexible attitude towards rescue.

In the Treasury discussion Morgenthau raised the political considerations for establishing a rescue agency. He stated that perhaps the most important argument to present to the President was that shortly Congress itself might act on the issue. "When you get down to the point" Morgenthau contended, "this is a boiling pot on the Hill [Congress]." John Pehle, however, opposed presenting the case on a political basis. He believed that an effective rescue agency must be established and that they should not be satisfied with merely another gesture whose only purpose was to silence Roosevelt's critics, and win Jewish support. Pehle promptly responded that: "There is one danger in using too much of that political thing and that is that what is done here must be more than a symbol to satisfy and stop Congressional action."[112] From the minutes of that meeting it is not exactly clear how it was decided to present the matter to the President. However the protocol of the meeting with Roosevelt on the following day does not indicate that the establishment of the War Refugee Board was presented as a political maneuver whose purpose was to prevent criticism of the Administration from reaching the halls of Congress.

The remainder of the meeting was devoted to clarifying a number of items relating to the methods by which the rescue agency would function, when, and if, it was established. Morgenthau suggested that the agency should be headed by a well-known Jew (he did not mention who). The Treasury people endorsed the idea, but Ben Cohen (who had helped draw up the Executive Order) doubted whether this would be wise. As to financing the agency, Cox informed the Treasury staff that if it needed, the money could be obtained from the President's Emergency Fund, the same fund that Long had told Goldmann was completely depleted. At any rate, Cox stated, he had already clarified the matter with several organizations and private individuals and if necessary they were prepared to place the funds at the disposal of the rescue agency.[113]

The Treasury people met with the President on January 16th. Morgenthau was there with two of his assistants, Paul and Pehle. Roosevelt met them alone. Morgenthau submitted a copy of the memorandum prepared by his staff but the President did not read it. Its original title "Report to the Secretary on the Acquiescence of This Government in the Murder of the Jews" had been changed by Morgenthau to the less sensational title "A Personal Report to the President."

Morgenthau's presentation of the facts was very critical of the State Department. He explained that Treasury "had uncovered evidence indicating that not only were people at the State Department ineffective in dealing with this problem, but that they were actually taking action to prevent the rescue of Jews." In order to demonstrate to the President that it was really possible to save Jews, Morgenthau gave the example of his father (Henry Morgenthau Sr.), who as Ambassador to Turkey in the First World War had succeeded in evacuating many Armenians, thereby saving their lives. Morgenthau endeavored to prove to the President that humanitarian acts such as these were in the best American tradition.

Pehle reported to the President the essence of the Treasury revelations concerning the activities of the State Department. Roosevelt listened attentively and commented only that it appeared to him that the best possibilities for rescue were to transfer people from the Balkans to Turkey and from Western Europe across the borders to Spain and to Switzerland. Roosevelt refused to accept Treasury's criticism of Long. He justified Long's actions as due to his having turned sour after Rabbi Wise convinced him to admit a large number of refugees among whom, he found later, were many 'undesirables'. Morgenthau attempted to correct the President, and claimed that Secretary of Justice Biddle had stated that only three Jews among those permitted to enter the U.S. had been classified as "undesirables." Roosevelt still believed Long's version.

As to the main item on the agenda, the establishment of an American rescue agency, Roosevelt did not hesitate. He apparently was aware of all the arguments in favor of such an agency and had decided, prior to the meeting, to support the move. However, he thought it essential that Secretary of War Henry Stimson be on the committee but he saw no need for Crowley to be a member. It is not known whether Roosevelt's reason for changing the makeup of the committee was objective, or an attempt to add someone who would cool Morgenthau's enthusiasm. Roosevelt requested the Treasury people to meet with Stettinius and Rosenman to work out the details. He promised that Stettinius was favorable to the matter at hand (an indication that obviously he had already discussed it with him).[114]

That afternoon the Treasury people met with Rosenman and Stettinius. Despite Roosevelt's defense of Long, Morgenthau again accused the Assistant Secretary and his associates in the State Department of "deliberately obstructing the execution of any plan to save the Jews." He asserted that there was a need for immediate, bold action "if this government was not going to be placed in the same position as Hitler and share the responsibility for exterminating all the Jews of Europe." Stettinius was shocked by the facts as presented by Pehle but claimed that he was not surprised by Long's conduct, for Long had also failed in his handling of the prisoner-of-war exchange. Stettinius notified Morgenthau and Pehle that in reorganizing the State Department he had taken these matters out of Long's hands and transferred them to Adolph Berle. However, Stettinius was quick to warn them that they should not be elated with these changes because Berle "might even be worse than Long." Stettinius also felt that Stimson should be on the board and not Crowley. It appears that Roosevelt and Stettinius determined their position beforehand and that it was Stettinius who had helped to persuade the President to agree to the Treasury proposal. Morgenthau proposed that John Pehle head the new agency, and Stettinius and Rosenman concurred.[115]

On January 22, 1944 President Roosevelt signed Executive Order #9417 directing the establishment of the 'War Refugee Board', with John Pehle as acting Executive Director. The order stated that the U.S. government's objective was "to take all measure in its authority to rescue the victims of oppression in immediate threat of death and to provide those victims with all aid consistent with the successful prosecution of the war." The Order instructed the Board to develop and implement measures for: "a) the rescue, transportation, maintenance and relief of the victims of enemy oppression, and b) the establishment of havens of temporary refuge for such victims."[116]

Two and a half years after the Germans began their campaign to liquidate European Jewry and a year and a half after the plan had become known in Washington, there was finally established an American agency whose purpose was to prevent the Nazi from annihilating the Jewish people.

War Refugee Board. Secretary of State Hull,
Secretary of Treasury Morgenthau, Secretary of War Stimson and John Pehle

CHAPTER 13
Attempts To Save the Remnant

"Time is of the essence"
– John Pehle at a meeting of the WRB

What was the main factor that led President Roosevelt to establish the War Refugee Board? Was it the result of the Treasury's initiative, as Arthur Morse claimed nearly 45 years ago? Or perhaps Roosevelt acted only to prevent the passage of the Gillette-Rogers resolution in Congress, as David Wyman and Rafael Medoff claim today? The two initiatives, that of the Treasury and that of Gillette-Rogers, were simultaneous and served only to strengthen each other. Therefore, the real question is which of the initiatives might have achieved the objective of creating a rescue agency without the aid of the other? Even more important is the question: What type of agency would have been created, and with what authority, as a result of the various initiatives? We should also ask why Roosevelt agreed to establish the WRB at this date and whether more energetic action by the Jewish organizations might have brought the U.S. Government to support rescue activities at an earlier date, as Wyman claims.[1]

Wyman contends that the Gillette-Rogers proposal played the central role in the creation of the WRB. He bases this on the words of Secretary Morgenthau at the Treasury staff meeting: "There is a pot boiling over on the Hill" and Morgenthau's opinion that they should concentrate on this point with the President. However, Wyman does not mention Pehle's reply to the Secretary in which he opposed presenting the case as a political tactic to prevent an embarrassing situation for the President.[2] The minutes of the meeting with Roosevelt show only that the issue was presented on its merits and not as a political maneuver. The Treasury people spoke solely about the activities (and lack of activity) of the State Department and of the urgent need to take the matter of rescue out of the hands of State and transfer it to people who would be willing to act.

There is also a contradiction in Wyman's contention of the importance of the Gillette-Rogers proposal in establishing the WRB. Wyman himself claims that during all the years of the Holocaust, the American Congress was, at best, indifferent to the fate of European Jewry and at worst, actually hostile to rescue. In his final chapter Wyman notes "Few in Congress, whether liberals or conservatives, showed much interest in saving European Jews. Beyond that, restrictionism, especially opposition to the entry of Jews, was strong on Capitol Hill."[3] If the atmosphere in Congress was as described by Wyman (and his description is accurate), how can Wyman write that such a body would pass a resolution, especially one 'with teeth', whose intention was to impel the government to rescue? It is especially surprising since Congress always suspected that rescue of Jews would be accompanied by efforts to allow additional refugees to enter the United States. Congress was totally opposed to such a development. It is possible that as a result of the Gillette-Rogers proposal, Congress would have passed another vacuous resolution, like the one passed in the Senate in March 1943, condemning Nazi atrocities against the Jews.[4] Certainly such a resolution would not have obligated the President to establish the Board, much as the Senate resolution in March did not obligate the American delegation to the Bermuda conference to act decisively for rescue.

Roosevelt, however, had many means to prevent passage of the resolution had he wanted to scuttle it. Wyman himself tells of the fate of the pro-Zionist resolution introduced in Congress in January 1944, at the initiative of the American Zionist Emergency Committee. That proposal, supported by many in Congress, was put off when the War Department, at the request of the State Department and with the President's blessings, intervened. The War Department asked Congress to postpone the issue claiming that it would have a negative effect on the prosecution of the war.[5] Medoff devotes a number of pages in his book to prove how worried were some leading Democrats that Roosevelt's attitude to Zionism would cost him dearly in the upcoming Presidential elections in November.[6] However, Medoff does not indicate that Roosevelt easily won the election. Nor does he relate that Roosevelt garnered more than 90% of the Jewish vote, despite his negative position on the pro-Zionist resolution. FDR had no need to fear losing the Jewish vote.

If Congressional support for American rescue action for the Jews was really concrete and not just empty talk, why then does Wyman write "that Congressional indifference toward the European Jews ruled out the possibility of appropriations for rescue programs," including funding the WRB?[7] If there truly existed a broad consensus in Congress in favor of the Board, why didn't those same Congressmen appropriate the necessary funds so that it could fulfill its functions? A few months later, many Congressmen opposed the 'Free Ports' plan in which fewer than 1000 refugees (not all Jewish) were brought to the U.S. on a temporary basis. If such was the case, what was the change in the attitude of Congress that would have impelled it to create an effective War Refugee Board?

It is difficult to accept the views implied by Wyman, Medoff and Bergson that Congress had now become an enthusiastic supporter of rescue and that it was only the Administration, headed by President Roosevelt that stood passively aside and acceded only to the pressures of the Legislature. It is true that during 1943 a change had occurred in the temper of the American public concerning the issue of rescue and this was mirrored in the attitudes of their representatives on the Hill. The change was a result of: the turn in the tides of war; the deeper understanding of the war's ideological basis; and the partial success in making news of the Holocaust general knowledge and explaining its meaning.

As to the last point, the 'Bergson Boys' contributed much with their sensational ads, their impressive pageant and the well-publicized Emergency Conference. However, there is a tendency to minimize the role of the other Jewish organizations in this same matter. The Jewish organizations were the main source of information regarding the fate of European Jewry (the 'Bergson Boys' never issued any information they obtained on their own). The December, 1942 'Day of Mourning', the mass demonstration at Madison Square Garden, the many other rallies held in New York and other major American cities, and Wise's constant requests to the press that they write about and respond to the news, all contributed to altering the atmosphere among the American public and its attitude to the fate of European Jewry.

Though the Jewish organizations opposed the legislative initiative of the 'Bergson Boys', in effect it was they who breathed new life into it when it appeared about to falter. This occurred after Long's testimony before the House Foreign Affairs Committee. According to Wyman, "Long convinced the committee that the United States and the Intergovernmental Committee were already doing everything humanly possible to save Jews." From Long's testimony it could be understood that the U.S. had been extremely generous in allowing refugees to enter her borders and that the IGCR had ample authority to deal with the problems of rescue. Therefore, Long implied, there was no need to set up a rescue agency.

Wyman states that, "Long's testimony crippled the Rescue Resolution" and the House committee decided to postpone debate.[8] When Sol Bloom, the confidant of the State Department, publicized Long's testimony in order to demonstrate the many efforts of the State Department to rescue Jews, it was the Jewish organizations who caught Long in his lies and succeeded in turning the tables on him. The American Jewish Conference immediately pointed out the inaccuracies in Long's statement regarding the number of Jewish refugees who had found refuge in the U.S. They widely disseminated the true statistics which were in the hands of the World Jewish Congress.[9] It was also the JTA that investigated and uncovered the fact that Long had not told the truth when he stated that the IGCR had been authorized to negotiate with the enemy in order to rescue Jews.[10] Not only the Treasury people had grasped the devious ways of the State Department regarding rescue of Jews. In the revelations by the Jewish organizations, the tactics of Long had become clear to everyone and his machinations were used to attack him and undermine his authority.

From all the above, it is difficult to believe that the initiative of the 'Bergson Boys' in Congress could have, on its own, brought about the War Refugee Board with the authority that was granted it had not the Treasury people acted, at the same time and on their own initiative to achieve that same goal. Would the WRB have been established only at the initiative of the Treasury without the political pressures of Congress? The relevant material points to a positive reply. There is no documentary evidence indicating that Roosevelt was influenced by political factors, or that such reasons had been presented to him. All claims that they determined his stand are merely conjectures. It is not even clear that Roosevelt was aware of the discussions in Congress surrounding the Gillette-Rogers Resolution. During the entire Congressional debate on the resolution, Roosevelt was not even in the United States – from November 13th and for a period of five weeks, he travelled to the Cairo and Teheran Conferences; visited his commanders at the fronts and attended other diplomatic meetings.[11] Nor is it clear how much the House committee hearings caught the attention of either the general public or the politicians, until Long's testimony was shattered by the Jewish organizations. On December 18, more than five weeks after Gillette and Rogers began their initiative even Secretary Morgenthau barely knew anything about the matter when someone mentioned it at a staff meeting.[12]

There is reason to believe that when the Treasury people, with the influential Secretary Morgenthau at the forefront, presented their clear and firm case to the President, he would have acquiesced to their request even without the political initiative in Congress. On the one hand, Roosevelt realized that they had 'explosive' material and that if the facts became known, they could discredit the administration. On the other hand, according to the testimony of Oscar Cox and others, Roosevelt had previously agreed to support the establishment of such an agency.[13] By this time the Allies had already gained a military advantage, thus Roosevelt could believe that creating a rescue agency would not endanger the matter most crucial to him – a speedy victory. In addition, the atmosphere in the U.S. had changed sufficiently for the President to feel that such a step held no political liability. Secretary of War Henry Stimson, one of the three Cabinet members on the Board, acknowledged in his diary: "Morgenthau, on whose initiative the President had formed the committee."[14]

Therefore we may conclude that it was primarily the Treasury's initiative that led to the establishment of the Board and that the resolution which was proposed by the 'Bergson Boys' perhaps aided the Treasury to gain the President's approval but was not essential in achieving the decision. Inasmuch as the Treasury initiative resulted from actions initiated by the World Jewish Congress (the request for a license to transfer funds and Riegner's cable with information about the Holocaust), this organization must be credited, at least in part, with the achievement. In addition, according to Morgenthau's testimony, it was Rabbi Wise (President of the WJC) who first made the Secretary aware of the Holocaust and prepared to act to save Jews, the most important expression of which was his struggle to establish the War Refugee Board.[15]

What of the claim that Roosevelt had previously agreed to the creation of the Board and that only the initiative of Bergson prevented him from taking the step? It appears that there is no basis for this contention and that it was only a part of the Jewish establishment's attacks on the 'Bergson Boys'. We do have the statement of Cox that Roosevelt had already agreed to support the creation of the agency, but that does not mean that Roosevelt would have promoted such a step without the pressure exerted by the Treasury. It is not logical to believe that the President would have postponed the establishment of the Board only because of the Gillette-Rogers proposal. On the contrary, if Roosevelt did follow those moves in Congress, and if he really wanted to create a rescue agency, he would have stolen the thunder from Congress and announced the establishment of the WRB before the hearings began. Since he did not act to do this, we may assume that his support for the plan was still amorphous and had not solidified into a concrete decision until the Treasury staff met with him, presented their accusations, and asked him to support the creation of such an agency.

❖ ❖ ❖

It is not the intention of this work to deal in depth with the activities of the War Refugee Board. However, as the WRB was the major expression of the U.S. intention to save Jews during the Holocaust, it is appropriate to examine how it performed and to view some of its accomplishments. Immediately upon its establishment on January 22, 1944 Pehle and his assistants began at once to act energetically. The Treasury people concluded that they had first to overcome the delaying, bureaucratic red tape, and that time was of the essence if they were going to save Jews.

On January 25th, Secretary Hull cabled all U.S. diplomatic missions instructing them to cooperate with the WRB and "forestall the plot of the Nazis to exterminate Jews." They were ordered that "communications should be made freely available" for the use of organizations requesting to forward information concerning the fate of European Jewry, or proposing rescue plans.[16] Pehle also appointed, as expeditiously as possible, direct representatives of the Board to the main centers of neutral Europe. Ira Hirschmann, who was connected with the 'Bergson Boys', was sent to Turkey in February, 1944. Pehle viewed the key possibility for rescue, the transfer of Balkan Jews to a haven in Palestine. This would require the aid of Turkey. Hirschmann's main task was to convince the Turks to ease restrictions for the transfer of Jews through their territories and to obtain ships to move Jews from Black Sea ports to Turkey. Despite his efforts on the latter problem, and the assistance of American governmental agencies, Hirschmann was unable to achieve his goal. The Bulgarians and the Turks not only hesitated to lease their boats for this purpose but the Germans also threatened to torpedo refugee ships.[17]

Hirschmann, with the aid of the American Ambassador in Ankara, Laurence Steinhardt, succeeded in overcoming some of the bureaucratic problems and the many obstacles that the Turks and the British had placed before the refugees who managed to flee the Balkans. The American claim that they were responsible for the success in bringing Jews from the Balkans angered the Jewish Agency emissaries, the real initiators and executors of this project. Moshe Shertok asked Nachum Goldmann to let it be known, without offending the WRB, that "not one single refugee owes his escape to the Board's initiative or action," and that only through the activities of the Jewish Agency were Jews rescued in the Balkans.[18]

Pehle also managed to place his representatives in Switzerland, England, Portugal, Sweden, North Africa and Italy. These agents were drawn mainly from among the various relief organizations already at work in the field and consequently were well acquainted with the problems of rescue. An example of the positive attitude of the WRB agents was Roswell McClelland in Switzerland, the Quaker representative there. McClelland, energetic and devoted, did not hesitate to employ illegal methods if it would help save Jews.[19] Pehle also tried to send his representatives to the Soviet Union and to Egypt, but was unsuccessful. He was also unable to place an agent in Spain because of opposition by the American Ambassador, Carlton J. Hayes, who was not favorable to the Jews and did not approve the idea of the Board, nor would he cooperate with it.[20]

One of the surprising aspects of the WRB was its readiness to carry out illegal acts. As opposed to the legalistic approach of the State Department which demanded that all rescue activities be done "by the book," Pehle understood there was no other way to block the German plot except by unconventional and 'illegal' methods. Hirschmann testified that before he left for Turkey he was instructed by Pehle "to get the job done no matter how." Pehle made it clear that "he was ready to countenance any means, even unorthodox [ones]."[21]

Aryeh Kubowitzki also reported to the American Jewish Congress that the great change in the rescue front during the first half of 1944, resulted from the approach of the Board: "that there is no way of doing rescue work in a legal way."[22] McClelland established contacts with the undergrounds of Western Europe and agreed to forging papers and paying bribes in order to smuggle Jews into Switzerland.[23] Under the influence of the WRB the U.S. government changed directions and now pressured Latin American governments to honor the passports and documents issued by their consuls in Europe without the permission of their governments, so as to prevent the deportation of Jews to the extermination camps.[24]

By these actions the WRB implemented the proposals presented to them by the World Jewish Congress. Immediately after the formation of the WRB, Pehle approached the Jewish organizations and other relief agencies and asked them to forward proposals for rescue. The WJC presented him with a detailed program for rescue and relief. Apart from the already familiar plans that they had advanced i.e., sending food parcels; encouraging the neutrals to take in refugees; warning the perpetrators; etc., the WJC proposals now included, and even emphasized, the use of illegal activities. In the preface to the proposal presented to the Board, the WJC wrote that

> If the purpose of the War Refugee Board is to be fulfilled, customary procedures must be superseded. The rescue of the Jews from the clutches of the Nazis now falls for the most part within the sphere of underground activities, and commando and guerilla warfare.

The WJC plan projected four types of underground activities: a) Hiding Jews, which they labeled "the simplest, speediest and least expensive rescue." To achieve this it was necessary to encourage local populations to conceal Jews; to transfer funds to support Jews in hiding; and to provide them with false documents. b) Smuggling Jews over the borders to neutral countries, or to Germany's satellites, where they faced less danger than in countries directly under German control. c) Distributing Latin American passports to Jews in

Occupied-Europe. d) Transferring funds to the undergrounds to be used for "bribing German officials and inducing them to halt deportations." The plan included a proposal that these funds be used by the Jewish undergrounds also to prepare for self-defense, in case of need.[25]

The WRB fulfilled the first three points to the best of its ability. The fourth point obviously referred to the 'Europa Plan', the negotiations between Rabbi Weismandel and Gizi Fleischman from Slovakia with the S.S. representative Dieter Wisliceny. These negotiations revolved around a scheme to pay ransom to the S.S. in exchange for halting the deportation of Jews. The plan appeared in 1944 and 1945 in various forms as the 'Eichmann Plan' ('Goods for Blood'), and also as the negotiations between Saly Mayer, Joint's representative in Switzerland and the S.S. envoy Kurt Becher. In the 'Eichmann Plan' the WRB, as opposed to all other sectors in the Administration, favored negotiating with Germany, though they, too, opposed furnishing the Germans with any war materiel. In their opinion, as long as the Allies and Germans continued talking about the release of Jews, at least some Jews, candidates for deportation, would be kept alive.[26] According to Ira Hirschmann, Roosevelt also subscribed to this position. Hirschmann states that in June 1944, he was sent back to the Mid-East to handle matters in the 'Eichmann Plan'. Before leaving, Morgenthau brought him to a meeting with the President who instructed him "keep talking[...] While you talk these people still have a chance to live."[27] However, eventually Roosevelt deferred to British and Soviet opposition. On June 20th, Hirschmann and Steinhardt received official instructions to desist from further involvement in the affair.[28]

Pehle turned to the Jewish organizations not only for advice on methods of action but also asked them to finance the WRB, almost entirely. The Jewish organizations had hoped that with the formation of the Board the Administration would take upon itself funding rescue operations on an extensive scale. The World Jewish Congress recalled Long's promise to grant ten million dollars for rescue activities. This sum was never placed at the disposal of the Jewish organizations, and now they were being asked to finance a legitimate government agency. The WJC approached other Jewish organizations to establish a common front against the government's request for financing rescue operations.[29] Representatives of Joint and of the United Jewish Appeal met with representatives of the Board to convince them that the government should provide the maximum sum possible. According to Wyman, the reason for Pehle's stand was his hesitation in asking Congress to appropriate rescue funds.[30]

The Jewish organizations' request was rejected and they bore the major burden of the Board's cost. The WRB did not even use all the paltry sums it received from the government. At the end of the war it returned more than half of the amount to the Treasury. On the other hand, various Jewish organizations contributed about $20 million to defray the costs of the WRB. Of this, Joint's share was $15 million.[31] These funds, contributed by the Jewish organizations, were used not only to finance the rescue of Jews but also covered the costs of other WRB activities not even connected with Jews.[32]

The Board and its field representatives supported as best as they could all the 'small rescue' activities, such as stealing across borders; hiding Jews etc. However, Pehle's view was to pursue 'large rescue', i.e.: pressure the satellite countries (where most of the surviving Jews were to be found) to stop harming Jews. This policy held the best hope of saving Jews not in the hundreds but, perhaps, in the tens of thousands. This scheme was most clearly expressed in a partially successful attempt to save the 800,000 Hungarian Jews after Germany occupied the country on March 19, 1944.

Ever since the formation of the Board, Pehle and his colleagues tried to get Roosevelt to issue a stern condemnation of the Nazi crimes against the Jews that would include a warning that those responsible would be brought to justice after the war. Even at this late date the State Department opposed issuing such a warning. It asserted that it would only strengthen the Germans in their resolve to exterminate the Jews and to prolong the war. State also repeated that such a warning would strengthen the claim that the U.S. was fighting the war only for the sake of the Jews.[33] Under pressure of the WRB, and particularly through the direct intervention of Morgenthau, the President did issue the warning on March 24th, five days after the Germans entered Hungary.

The President's statement related in general to all war crimes committed by Germany and Japan, but this was the first time that Roosevelt specifically cited the fate of the Jews. He condemned the "wholesale systematic murder of the Jews of Europe" and defined it as "one of the blackest crimes of all history."

He warned all those taking part in those crimes that they would be punished severely after the war. As for Hungarian Jewry that had fallen into the clutches of the Germans, Roosevelt stated that it "would be a major tragedy" if those Jews "should perish on the very eve of triumph over the barbarianism which their persecution symbolizes."[34]

After the Germans began expelling Hungary's Jews in May 1944, the WRB started an energetic campaign to stop deportations. It requested the neutral nations, the Vatican and the Red Cross to send special envoys to Hungary in the hope that their presence would help frustrate the German plans. The request was fulfilled in large part and today we are aware of the roles played by these envoys, such as the Swiss Consul Charles Lutz or the Swedish diplomat Raoul Wallenberg, in rescuing tens of thousands of Hungarian Jews.[35]

Throughout the war there were many who called upon the U.S. to threaten to bomb the cities of Germany if it did not halt its murder of Jews. Opinion was split, even among rescue advocates, whether such a threat would actually help or hurt the Jews. Therefore it was not included in the 12 point program presented by the Joint Emergency Committee.[36]But all agreed that to threaten the satellites, who were seeking to extricate themselves from the war, could only be helpful. From 1943 onward this threat was perhaps the best way to defeat the plans for the 'Final Solution'.

The bombing of Budapest by the U.S. Air Force and parallel appeals by the Vatican and others, convinced the Hungarian Regent, Miklos Horthy, to halt the deportation of Jews on July 7th. At this stage of the war, Horthy feared the Allied threats more than the reaction of the Germans, for it was quite clear to him that they were losing the war. Later Horthy declared his readiness to allow the departure of every Jewish child, as well as Jewish adults who held certificates of entry to Palestine.[37] Under pressure from the WRB, the American and British governments, after much apprehension, agreed to the Horthy offer. In a joint communiqué the two Allied nations stated that they accept the offer of the Hungarian government "and will make arrangements for the care of such Jews leaving Hungary who reach neutral or United Nations territory, and also that they will find temporary havens of refuge where such people may live in safety."[38] This was perhaps the statement most sympathetic to the Jews, with the most commitment to rescue, that was issued by the Allies throughout the war. But the statement was of no avail, for the Germans overthrew Horthy and replaced him with a Hungarian Fascist who continued to cooperate with the S.S. in annihilating Hungarian Jewry.

The War Refugee Board represented an important change in the U.S. government's attitude toward rescue. It is difficult to estimate the number of Jews saved through its efforts. However, the number certainly was not large in proportion to the one or two million Jews who were killed in the last 16 months of the war. Wyman estimates the number of Jews rescued through the activities of the WRB as about 200,000.[39] However Yehuda Bauer claims that figure to be highly exaggerated. As opposed to Wyman's claim that Wallenberg (who was sent to Budapest at the initiative of the WRB) succeeded in saving tens of thousands of Budapest's Jewry, Bauer maintains that Wallenberg had only 4500 Swedish documents which he distributed among the Jews of Budapest. The tens of thousands of additional documents that were distributed were forged by members of the 'Chalutz' underground in Budapest. Bauer cites as well the fact that the source for financing Wallenberg's activities was not the WRB but rather funds of the Joint.

The reason more were not saved was not because of lack of effort, lack of desire or lack of initiative by the WRB. Nor was it due to lack of authority granted the Board. The Executive Order establishing the WRB specifically stated that its task was

> to take all measures within its power to rescue the victims of enemy oppression ... [and that] It shall be the duty of the heads of all agencies and departments [of the U.S. government] to supply or obtain for the Board such information and to extend to the Board such supplies, shipping and other specified assistance and facilities as the Board may require in carrying out the provisions of this Order.

The Board also was granted authority to accept aid or money from private individuals and from organizations.[40] The main reason that the Board did not save more Jews was because to the very end the Germans were determined to attain their 'solution' to the 'Jewish problem' once and for all – and the Jews were in their hands. But there were also other reasons, not connected with Germany and its policy that also prevented the Board from achieving maximum effectiveness in its struggle for rescue.

Firstly, the WRB did not receive financial support from the government but was forced to rely on funding from the Jewish organizations which were limited in their resources. Secondly, the Board was not composed, as planned, of the three senior Cabinet ministers – Morgenthau, Hull and Stimson. The last two sent their representatives – Stettinius and John McCloy – to represent them at meetings. Undoubtedly, the non-participation of Hull and Stimson weakened the ability of the Board to take far-reaching decisions. Only Morgenthau continued to exert his full influence on the President and to stand firmly behind the decisions of the Board. The State and War Departments continued to oppose many of the Board's plans, such as bombing Auschwitz and the railroad lines leading to the camp. The absence of these two cabinet officers indicated the lack of importance that they themselves still placed on rescue of the Jews. Stimson, in general, was not very sympathetic to Jews. He once explained to Pehle the reasons for his opposition to Jewish immigration to the U.S. as due to the traits and behavior of the Jews.[41]

A third factor that limited the work of the WRB was its inability to induce the other Allies to cooperate. The British, despite public opinion at home that favored rescue, not only did not establish an agency parallel to the WRB, but continued to carry out acts that hindered the rescue activities of the Board.[42] This was especially true in regard to all attempts to bring Jews from the Balkans to Palestine which was the main rescue route.[43] The Soviet government, as well, would not collaborate, thereby limiting the maneuverability of the Board.

The fourth factor that hindered the rescue activities was the government bureaucracy that still continued raising barriers in the way of those attempting to rescue. Even so strong an advocate of rescue as Myron Taylor attempted to block the first momentum of the WRB when he demanded that the Board coordinate its steps with the IGCR, of which he was the nominal U.S. representative.[44] If the WRB had yielded, it would be remembered today only as a pale shadow of that pathetic intergovernmental committee which did nothing to fulfill its task of saving Jews.

The small staff at the WRB was a group of sincere individuals, diligent in their endeavors to overcome bureaucratic obstacles and prepared to use unorthodox methods in their attempt to rescue Jews. But not everything was in its power. Proof of that can be seen in the attitude of the U.S. censors toward attempts by the Jewish organizations to send cables dealing with rescue. In August 1944, seven months after the establishment of the Board, an exchange of letters between the World Jewish Congress and the chief censor shows that there was no change in the U.S. attitude to rescue and that the machinations of the State Department of 1943 were again reappearing.

On August 1st Kubowitzki sent urgent cables to Europe in connection with attempts to rescue Hungarian Jewry. Two weeks later the Censor returned these cables to the WJC claiming that it could not authorize them and they should approach the War Refugee Board. The Board responded immediately to the request and asked the State Department to send the cables. They were dispatched on August 28th, four weeks after they had been written. Kubowitzki complained to the authorities that "the damage is irreparable."[45] In those same days 12,000 Jews were being sent every day to the gas chambers of Auschwitz from which they never returned.

The controversy over the possibility of bombing the gas chambers at Auschwitz – and the railway lines leading to the camp – continues to this day. There are some historians who claim that the possibility was real and could have been effective,[46] while others maintain that the mission was not feasible, and that even if it were carried out it would not have achieved its purpose of stopping the killing process.[47] Today both views are only matters of conjecture and neither can be proven as true. What concerns us in this study is not the question of whether the bombings could have achieved a measure of success, but rather what was the attitude of the U.S. Department of War to the request made by the various Jewish organizations to bomb Auschwitz, and was this attitude part of the general attitude of indifference to the fate of the Jews and an unwillingness to divert resources to rescue attempts that characterized the U.S. Administration policies throughout the war?

In early 1944, the War Department determined its policy as regards rendering military aid to rescue as follows:

> It is not contemplated that units of the armed forces will be employed for the purpose of rescuing victims of enemy oppression unless such rescues are the direct result of military operations conducted with the objective of defeating the armed forces of the enemy.[48]

In keeping with this policy, when pressured by Jewish organizations and by the WRB to bomb Auschwitz, the Assistant Secretary of War John McCloy wrote to Pehle on July 4th, 1944:

> The War Department is of the opinion that the suggested air operation is impractical. It could be executed only by the diversion of considerable air support essential to the success of our forces now engaged in decisive operations.[49]

At one point, McCloy wrote to Kubowitzki at the World Jewish Congress that "There has been considerable opinion to the effect that such an effort [bombing Auschwitz], even if practicable, might provoke even more vindictive [!] action by the Germans".[50] Did McCloy really not understand what was transpiring in Auschwitz?

Two standard arguments were used by the War Department and by both the U.S. Air Force and the RAF for not bombing Auschwitz: Their first reason was their claim that the camp could not be reached by Air Force bombers. [51] This blatant untruth has long been disproved by most everyone. Beginning in May 1944, planes based in Italy were capable of reaching the area of Auschwitz and beyond. In August, bombers from the 15th Air Force bombed the factories surrounding Auschwitz, just a few miles from the gas chambers.[52]

The second argument, that "It could be executed only by the diversion of considerable air support essential to the success of our forces" was also shown to be a matter of priorities, which did not include the rescue of Jews among them.

During the Polish uprising in Warsaw in August-September 1944, more than 100 U.S. Air Force bombers were sent to drop supplies to the insurgents, though it was already obvious that the revolt was doomed, and most of the supplies parachuted in would actually fall into the hands of the Germans. The fleet of bombers was committed to the mission for 8 days.[53]

The WRB at first accepted the arguments of the War Department and did not pressure the Air Force to bomb Auschwitz. However, in due time Pehle went along with the request of the Jewish organization and he too petitioned the War Department to carry out the bombing mission, which was fully in keeping with the President's order given when establishing the War Refugee Board. The request was unsuccessful.

❖ ❖ ❖

How is one to evaluate the contribution of the War Refugee Board to the rescue of European Jewry? The very fact of the establishment of the Board was evidence that at last, the American government had acknowledged that the need to save Jews was one of its goals in the war against Nazism. The small group of people who stood at the head of the WRB, as well as those in the field who acted in its name were energetic, devoted and wise. They represented the best in the American tradition of humanitarianism and aid to the oppressed. But they were few. One can not escape the conclusion, shared by Pehle and his associates, that the War Refugee Board was set up too late, received insubstantial support, and therefore was unable to accomplish much.[54]

CHAPTER 14
Conclusion

"A living organism cries out"
– Leib Joffe, A Zionist leader

Many years passed before historians and world opinion attempted to deal seriously with the role of the witness to the Holocaust. The perspective of time has enabled us, perhaps, to consider the subject more objectively and has afforded us the opportunity to delve into pertinent archives of that period. However writing history at a distance of time from when the events occurred has many pitfalls as well. There is the difficulty of understanding the thinking and actions of the participants and the danger of anachronistically judging them by values and attitudes that were not relevant, nor prevalent, at the time that those events were occurring. Jacob Katz has defined the role of the historian:

> to present the choices and dilemmas of people [who acted in the past] [...] he has to ignore his own knowledge and instead depict, interpret and judge their actions exclusively on the basis of motives that could enter their consciousness.[1]

Many authors who have written about the role of the United States, its government and its Jewish community, as witnesses to the destruction of European Jewry, have often proved themselves incapable of understanding the times, and are judging the responses of people then by values, attitudes and conditions that may be valid today but were not pertinent to the period under discussion. A picture has been formed, that appears to be fairly widespread today, of an American Jewish community unconcerned about the fate of their brethren in Europe, and except for holding a few protest rallies "the American Jewish leadership did nothing."[2]

A portrayal has also been presented of an American president, once revered by the Jews of America, who had in effect become almost an accomplice in the destruction of European Jewry. A professor of history describes Roosevelt's attitude as "sinisterism". He claims that "Roosevelt and the British acted in such a manner as to prevent the rescue of European Jewry [... and] enabled the Nazi Germans [...] to slaughter six million Jewish men, women and children."[3] This view does not do justice to historical realities. It appears to justify the opinion held by many Nazi leaders, as expressed by Goebbels in his diary, that: "At the bottom, however, I believe both the English and the Americans are happy that we are exterminating the Jewish riff-raff."[4]

In retrospect it is apparent that while Nazi Germany put a high priority on its intention to exterminate European Jewry, the U.S. government was equally intent on avoiding charges that it was fighting the war "to save the Jews." This, it felt, would be playing into the hands of Nazi propaganda and would weaken the nation's determination to fight. Nor would the government allow rescue efforts to interfere in any way with its primary goal: achieving a speedy and total victory. However, the march to victory was considerably slower than the pace of destruction and as a result six million Jews were murdered before the Nazi regime collapsed in the ashes of Berlin.

The American Administration's Response to the Holocaust

Why was America so slow to respond to news of the Holocaust? Why were its efforts at rescue so disproportionate to the fanatical German determination to destroy all of European Jewry? Were most Americans secretly pleased with Germany's murderous liquidation of the Jews as the Nazi leaders believed? It appears that the U.S. government responded hesitantly to the news of the Holocaust, firstly, because the information was so unbelievable that it was unwilling to think that such events were actually occurring. The unpredictable acts of the Germans, which had no precedence in history, and the trickery, deceit and camouflage implemented by the murderers, hampered news of the massacres from reaching the West and being absorbed. If the Nazi concealment of their true intentions succeeded for so long a time to deceive their victims in the ghettos and concentration camps, why then is it not understandable that people removed by thousands of miles from the atrocities had difficulty in fathoming the reality of the slaughter?

To understand the tragedy one needed verified information and that in itself was a serious problem that many still do not grasp. Not only did the information have to be obtained, but it also had to be understood and internalized before any action could be taken. The news was so terrifying, with no analogies in past history, that people were simply unable to overcome the cognitive barriers. Skepticism regarding the liquidation of the Jews remained until the very end of the war. This difficulty to fathom the news of the killings was critical, for without convincing the public as to what was actually happening to the Jews of Europe, it was impossible to pressure both Congress and the Administration to act for rescue. In fact, quite the opposite occurred. The State Department's desire not to inform, nor arouse the public, served as a brake on all attempts to rescue Jews.

There was no awareness then of the special suffering of the Jews, nor of the meaning of the Holocaust in the broader terms of the war as a struggle against the Nazi *weltanschaung*. The world was fighting a bitter struggle to the very end. Undeniably, Jews were suffering much in that war but, so Americans thought, were countless others. Every American had been taught General Sherman's aphorism that "War is Hell." There was a general feeling that the war was one immense atrocity perpetrated by the Germans and Japanese in all the occupied nations, and that the Allies, in effect, could do nothing to alter that fact. Stephen Wise was aware of that reality when in summing up a successful rally he concluded: "in time of war it is very difficult to get people excited, generally speaking, about atrocities."[5] However, the question still remains open, could stronger public pressure have changed the administration's attitude towards rescue?

In the U.S. people believed that the only hope that could be offered to all the suffering populations was to end the war as quickly as possible. Nothing short of that could be of any significant aid. Millions of Soviet citizens had been killed and for more than ten years the Chinese had been writhing under the Japanese invaders. What was so special about the Jewish suffering? Just because the Jews were demonstrating and demanding government action was not reason enough, so they believed, to single them out for particular help. The Jews, they felt, were always bemoaning their lot. The endless Jewish delegations to Washington asking for government assistance to ease the misery of their brethren in Europe more often exasperated the bureaucrats than spurred them to action. Breckinridge Long complained that "An unproportional amount of time of the department is wasted on those moaners."[6] In a deliberation held by the World Jewish Congress in June 1943 regarding what tactics they should use, Kubowitzki opposed continuing the demonstrations claiming that they were ineffectual; public opinion in any case was apathetic and "Roosevelt was very irritated with the many mass demonstrations that were held in the past few months."[7]

Many world leaders would not deal with the Jews as a people apart. To a degree this was an expression of a liberal, emancipatory approach by those statesmen who saw the Jews as an integral segment of their various nations. To respond in any other manner meant playing into the hands of Hitler and acquiescing in the Nazi view that placed the Jews outside the framework of the nations in which they lived. General Sikorski, the Prime Minister of the Polish Government-in-Exile, explained to Kubowitzki that the reason for not referring to the Jews specifically in the St. James declaration on Nazi atrocities was because if they had made mention of Jews "it would imply a recognition of the [Nazi] racial theory."[8] Secretary Hull used the opportunity of the 25th anniversary of the Balfour Declaration to state that in the post-war world Jews should be guaranteed full rights of citizenship wherever they resided.[9] Unwilling during the war to deal with Zionist demands for a sovereign state in Palestine and aware that public opinion in most countries precluded resettling Jews there after the war, the proclaimed policy of the U.S. government remained one of returning Jews to 'their homes' at war's end. But this emancipatory philosophy was not the main reason for concealing the fact of specifically Jewish suffering.

There were political reasons as well. Recognition of the uniqueness and extent of Jewish suffering would expose the Allies to pressure to aid these victims. The U.S. government feared that the war would be labeled as a 'war to save the Jews'. Nor would it entertain the idea of bringing Jewish refugees to a haven in the U.S. since they knew that this would create an uproar both in Congress and among the public. The British government feared that recognition of the Jews as a separate people would entail opening the gates of Palestine to Jewish refugees and allowing the Jews to attain sovereignty there. Therefore, the Allies generally discouraged singling out the problem of the Jews, and resorted to using the euphemism of 'political refugees' whenever referring to the Jewish question.

The American public did not respond with moral outrage to the Holocaust nor did it demand of its government to save the Jewish victims of Nazism. Their indifference was due, in part, to a lack of awareness as to what was happening; in part to an overwhelming concern for their own soldiers and to the developments on the war-front; and, in part, to a prevailing prejudice against Jews. If American Jewry was disliked by their American neighbors, those same Americans certainly would neither make an effort, nor make any sacrifices, to save Jews in foreign lands. Yet to claim that the American public was actually pleased with the German version of a 'Final Solution' to the Jewish problem is a far cry from the reality. A dislike of Jews was fairly widespread among Americans; discriminating against Jews was acceptable by many; but to actually deport them, incarcerate them, torture them and incinerate them, went against the moral grain of most Americans. True, a sixth of Americans polled agreed that Hitler was doing the right thing to the Jews, but most were opposed, and even those who favored the Nazi policy were probably unaware that Germany was actually murdering the Jews. Antisemitism in America ebbed dramatically after the war and has remained at a low level ever since.[10] Auschwitz has become a symbol for most Americans of the depths into which humanity had sunk.

America did not rush to help European Jews facing destruction, basically because it did not feel obligated to do so. America traditionally had cut itself off from events in Europe and saw its participation in the First World War as an aberration of this policy. Its involvement in World War II was not of its own choice but was forced upon America by the Japanese attack at Pearl Harbor. Most Americans perception of the war was that of a national conflict to guarantee America's security, and not as an ideological struggle against Nazism and its racial theories. Americans were fighting the war for the defense of their country, not for the safety of others – certainly not for the lives of European Jews. If, at times, America took into consideration the needs of other peoples, it did so because the political realities of an Allied coalition required it to do so, not because a humanitarian spirit moved it to act. The Jewish people were not a sovereign nation at that time, nor were they Allies, except as citizens of their respective countries. If Stalin could cynically ask how many divisions the Pope (spiritual leader of hundreds of millions of Catholics) has, how much more so could one question the military significance of sixteen million powerless and nationless Jews in the war against Germany. The historian Shlomo Aronson described the condition of world Jewry as being in "a triple trap": they were trapped between the murderous acts of the Nazis on the one hand and their need to support the Allies in their struggle on the other, and by the Allies inability to influence the Germans to desist from the killings, and by their reluctance to act.[11]

Openly aiding Jews appeared more as a liability to the Allies than as an advantage. The Jews of America, and of Europe, stood firmly in the anti-Nazi camp no matter how Jews were treated, for no other option was open to them. While Nazi ideologists firmly believed that international Jewry dominated decisions of the Allies, those same Allies, as the historian Monty Penkower put it, "consigned [the Jews ...] to one category: expendable."[12] The lack of options is the most blatant expression of the condition of the Jewish people at that time.

Nor was America prepared to aid others if the situation did not force it to do so. In 1943, a cyclone, and subsequent tidal waves, destroyed crops in Western Bengal, and India appealed to the United States for emergency food shipments to save the local population. The American government did not even reply. Two to three million Indians died in the ensuing famine.[13] In the midst of the war the journalist Vernon McKenzie summed up what he felt was the American public attitude to the Holocaust. "Is there room in bewildered minds", he asked, "obsessed by personal problems, to ponder about the fate of remote individuals?"[14] Could an ethnic minority influence the decisions of the Administration in a specific direction to the degree that such policy would not serve the direct interests of the United States? This question is particularly relevant in times of war and more so when the issue relates to people who are not even citizens of the country. The historian Henry Feingold claims that no other group of victims, apart from the Jews, has assumed that a nation has an obligation to foreign citizens. For Jews, such expectations from government are "an integral part of Jewish political culture", and it is a view, he claims, particular only to the Jews.[15]

It was this belief that a world conscience existed which could be aroused to save European Jewry that led Shmuel Zygelboim, a Bund member of the Polish National Council in London, to commit suicide in the hope that "perhaps by my death I shall contribute to breaking down that indifference [of the world to the liquidation of the Jews]."[16] Zygelboim's death went almost totally unnoticed. It was also this faith of American Jewry in the humanitarian spirit of the New Deal administration that led many Jews to assume that the American government was doing everything possible to save European Jewry. In March 1943, a leading Rabbi in Baltimore wrote Judge Proskauer of his opposition to carrying out demonstrations, since "evidence has already been given of the desire on the part of the State Department and our authorities to do what can be done."[17]

Both Helen Fein[18] and David Wyman[19] counter Feingold's claim that the possibilities of ethnic minorities to affect U.S. policy are very limited. They describe how, in 1941, the Black leader, A. Randolph Philips, threatened to organize a protest march of Blacks on Washington to demand equal rights. As a result of his threat, the Fair Employment Practices Commission was established. This is used by the two authors to prove that a minority can achieve results by use of political and mass pressure. However, the comparison presents a number of difficulties. These were Black Americans, citizens of the United States, and therefore the problem was solely an internal American affair. Such was not the case regarding European Jews during the Holocaust. In addition, Phillip's threat was made in 1941, before the U.S. became embroiled in the hostilities. Nor did the Commission develop into a very powerful agency. Roosevelt granted it limited funds and few powers. Its endeavors to end discrimination were often ignored, and a number of its reports were suppressed in order to avert controversy,[20] much as were the Riegner and Lichtheim reports later.

Another instance of ethnic political pressure is presented by the historian Rafael Medoff who relates the example of the Polish-Americans. Medoff attempts to make an important case of the fact that during the Polish revolt in Warsaw in 1944 Roosevelt sent supplies to the rebels. According to Medoff, this was due to pressure exerted by the Polish-American community in the United States, and he claims that had American Jewry acted similarly it, too, could have achieved similar results.[21] Medoff does not mention the fact that Roosevelt, under pressure by Stalin not to act, sent the supplies only when the battle was already lost, and even then dispatched only a small amount, most of which fell into the hands of the Germans. More than that, Roosevelt's decision was not a result of pressure by the Polish minority in the United States, but rather of pressure exerted by Churchill.[22] It must be emphasized that the Presidential election campaign was in full swing at that time, yet Roosevelt did not yield to the Polish-American demands calling for clear cut action to aid the rebels in Poland. Roosevelt, nevertheless, succeeded in holding his own among the Polish-American voters.[23] In citing the actions of Polish-Americans as an example which should have been emulated by American Jews, one should remember the fate of Poland at the Yalta Conference in which Roosevelt played a leading role.

Under the conditions of war, when all their contacts with Europe were maintained only through government channels, American Jews were unable to conduct an independent rescue policy. Without government support the hands of America's Jews were bound. There was little that they could have achieved on their own in the way of rescue without mobilizing the support of their government. Had they attempted to act contrary to the wishes of the Administration they would have gained little and endangered any possibility of attaining the government's support for rescue. The very existence of the Jewish organizations might have been threatened had they persisted in 'illegal acts' during the time of war. That certainly was the case in regards to the World Jewish Congress which was not an American organization, and most of whose leaders, were alien residents.

What options were open to the U.S. Jewish community to impel their government to act? Most government officials were at best, apathetic to the fate of the Jews and at worst, antagonistic to them and to their organizations. As in bureaucracies the world over, American officialdom was insensitive to moral and humanitarian issues. Some indicate this as one of the main reasons for the lack of an American response to the events of the Holocaust. Breitman and Kraut state that "Bureaucracy works by precedence, and in general limits itself to the tasks for which it is designated."[24] But in the case of the Jews, the role of American officialdom extended well beyond the limits of apathy. As shown above, many in the Administration were not only callously indifferent to the idea of rescue but even sabotaged plans that had already been decided upon. This was especially true of the State Department. It formed a veritable barrier to Jewish rescue efforts. Breckinridge Long did all he could to prevent Jews from entering the United States and sabotaged rescue efforts during the time he was responsible for dealing with the problem.

Peter Novick in his book, *The Holocaust in American Life*,[25] which deals mainly with the collective memory of the Holocaust in America, attempts to justify the Administration's handling of the rescue issue. Novick criticizes historians and Jewish leaders for using the terms 'complicity', 'accomplice', 'abandonment' in describing the role of the Administration in matters of rescue. However, as we have noted, it was the Treasury officials (all of them non-Jews), who in their report to the President in January 1944, had initially entitled it "Report to the President on the Acquiescence of This Government in the Murder of the Jews." The Legal Counsel of the Department Randolph Paul described the Allies policy as "para-delicto, of equal guilt."[26] Novick never mentions the policies of the State Department, such as their attempts to hide news of the exterminations of the Jews from the Jewish organizations and the public.

Could American Jews have turned to the American public, especially to intellectuals and to religious leaders, to call for a rescue effort? As we have seen they did attempt to do this. They organized rallies and demonstrations and frequently appealed to the press and to important personalities. But even the startling ads and the dramatic pageant of the 'Bergson Boys' did not arouse the general public. In the summer of 1943, a certain change did come about in the American attitude to the Holocaust. This was due, mostly, to the fact that as time went on, individuals began to grasp that something horrendous was actually happening to European Jews. The striking victories of the Allies also alleviated the fears that had gripped the public at the outset of the war. They could now devote time and some thought, to matters other than victory. But even then they did not prod their government to undertake rescue activities.

Perhaps the Jews should have turned to the members of Congress to pressure their government to initiate rescue, much as the AIPAC lobby does today? If those who claim that the War Refugee Board was established as a result of the Gillette-Rogers proposal are right, then perhaps the Jewish organizations should have placed their confidence in Congress. But, as shown above, the

Gillette-Rogers proposal played only a secondary role in establishing the Board. Even if the proposal had been adopted in Congress, it would have been nothing more than the same 'policy of gestures', which the FDR is accused of having embraced. Even after the WRB was created Congress was not prepared to appropriate it the necessary funds, and, as well, most Congressmen opposed the 'Free Ports' plan. Therefore, it was not likely that the Jewish organizations could have expected the American Congress to produce a positive change in U.S. rescue policy. Wyman himself claims that "Few in Congress, whether liberals or conservatives, showed much interest in saving European Jews."[27]

American Jews were powerless to move their country to demand rescue because all options were closed to them. They could not execute an independent rescue policy; the public and Congress were indifferent to the fate of the Jews; and many government officials were hostile to the issue. What else was there for the Jewish organizations to do but to turn to the President, who, they believed, had been so favorable to them? They hoped that the 'great humanitarian' and leader of the alliance fighting the Nazis would heed their request and act to save the Jews of Europe.

Franklin Delano Roosevelt and the Holocaust

We have recounted the reasons for the great faith American Jews placed in Roosevelt. It is important again to emphasize, that in effect, no other option was open to them apart from their role of patron-client with President Roosevelt. Roosevelt did not do much to save the Jews of Europe. Today he is accused of executing "policies [which] endangered European Jews."[28] A number of historians even see Roosevelt's position on the question of rescuing Jews as resulting from anti-semitism. Medoff claims that this attitude FDR absorbed from his beloved mother, Sarah. In a new book published this past year, *FDR and the Jews*, the historians Breiman and Lichtman, negate this contention and point out that Roosevelt's father "counseled his son about the immorality of anti-semitism and his contempt for it." His mother "made friends with Jews and engaged in charitable work for Jewish causes." [29]

In truth, Roosevelt was in all probability a 'gentlemanly' anti-Semite that was prevalent in the circle that he grew up-the upper classes of WASPs, and at times he did make some anti-Semitic remarks. On the other hand-when elected President- Roosevelt appointed many Jews (some 15% of his appointees)[30] to leading positions in his administration. For that he paid a high political price. Perhaps, a reason for the bitter criticism leveled by Roosevelt's detractors is because Roosevelt symbolizes the connection of Jews with the Democratic Party and with a liberal political outlook. Many today assail that connection and outlook, and attempt to prove that such an approach was wrong from the outset. Despite all this criticism, the truth is that Roosevelt, though he did not do much, did more to rescue Jews than any other leader at that time. However, expectations from Roosevelt were apparently so great that today anger is primarily directed toward him. In Britain the public was, perhaps, more sympathetic to the idea of rescue but during the war the British government did less than the American government to rescue Jews. Britain barred the gates of Palestine, a well-suited haven for the Jews of Eastern Europe. Nor did Britain establish any agency like the WRB for rescue. Neither did the Soviet Union deal at all with rescue, nor Canada, nor the Latin American countries.

The little that was done in the U.S. to save Jews was done primarily at the initiative, or with the agreement, of the President, and the Jewish leaders were well aware of this. It was Roosevelt who initiated the Evian Conference, and it was he who encouraged the resettlement of Jews before the war. In 1938 Roosevelt combined the immigration quotas of Germany and Austria. Between the years 1937-1940, 83,000 German and Austrian Jews were admitted to the U.S. and, in addition, after 'Kristallnacht', Roosevelt permitted 15,000 Jews who were in the country on visitor's visas to remain.[31] He did this contrary to the views of the public, and of Congress who were overwhelmingly opposed to increasing immigration. Wyman, himself, writes that in this act FDR "was treading the outer limits of Congressional toleration." [32] He also was active in swaying Britain to abstain from closing immigration to Palestine after the outbreak of Arab riots in 1936. The historian H.W. Brands believes that the isolationists in Congress were not willing to rescue European Jewry and that at the heart of the isolationist philosophy lay the belief that the problems of other nations and peoples should be solved by themselves.[33] It appears that it was Roosevelt who at times decided to allow Jewish organizations to send food parcels to European Jews despite the blockade. When he heard of the purported Rumanian proposal concerning the Jews of Transnistria, Roosevelt agreed to investigate the offer and, if possible, bring it off. In July 1943, the President agreed to transfer funds to Switzerland for rescue operations in Rumania and France. In so doing he opened the first serious avenue for extending aid to the Jews. In January, 1944 Roosevelt agreed to the creation of the WRB. In August he consented to absorb refugees in the 'Free Port' at Oswego.

A very interesting contention actually appears in an interview by Rafael Medoff with Benzion Netanyahu, the father of the Prime Minister, who for a time during the war was close to the 'Bergson Boys'. In order to prove that intervention by the president to act for rescue could have been of importance, Professor Netanyahu pointed out that already at the onset of the Arab revolt in 1936, Britain had weighed the possibility of issuing a 'White Paper' that would limit Jewish immigration to Palestine. The plan was put aside until 1939 as a result of Roosevelt's intervention with the British at the request of Rabbi Wise. Netanyahu, relying on the historian Melvin Urofsky, claimed that in those ensuing three years 50,000 European Jews arrived in Palestine thereby being saved from the Holocaust. Justice Brandeis wrote Rabbi Wise: "you have performed a marvelous feat. Nothing more important has happened to us since [receiving] the mandate."[34] From Netanyahu's telling it appears that Roosevelt contributed significantly to saving of a large number of Jews.[35]

It is obvious that the American and Allied victory in the war saved many Jews from death, however, at times there were steps taken by Roosevelt during the war itself, not motivated by a desire to save Jews but rather to prevail over the enemy army, and they too contributed to rescue. Such was his decision to ship tanks and cannon (just coming off the line in America) to the British Army, which stood before their critical battle at El-Alemein. Had Rommel succeeded in piercing the British line he would have captured Egypt within a few days, and afterwards Palestine as well. In a speech to Parliament on December 12, 1942 Churchill publicly thanked FDR stating the emergency equipment sent to Egypt played a major role in the victory of the 8th Army. As a result of Rommel's defeat the more than half million Jews of Palestine were saved from the fate of their fellow Jews in Europe.[36]

Why did FDR not do more to rescue Jews? In my opinion, there were four main reasons: a) Roosevelt concentrated on winning the war, and relegated issues he thought to be of secondary importance to others. b) He believed it was impossible to do much in the matter of rescue and that only a speedy victory could save Jews. c) In the pursuit of victory he attempted to maintain a consensus at home, and in the world, preserve the alliance of the 'Big Three.' d) The political realities in the U.S. severely limited his ability to maneuver on the issue of rescue.

Roosevelt stood at the head of his nation at the most crucial trial in the history of the world. Opposed were totalitarian and aggressor nations seeking to dominate the whole universe and to effectuate their 'New Order'. Until the end of 1942, the Axis powers caused the Allies defeat after defeat, and there was serious concern that they would actually attain their goal. The President's worries turned to only one direction – to guarantee the security and existence of his country. To achieve this, Roosevelt was prepared temporarily to waive many social and economic issues dear to him. Torn, at all times, between being a leader with lofty ideals, or an astute politician attune to the facts of 'realpolitik', Roosevelt, more than once, waived his principles in order to hasten victory.

Roosevelt commiserated with the agony of the Jewish victims of Nazism but was not prepared to take steps to rescue them if he suspected that this would hinder the war effort. He believed that as long as the war continued, the fate of the Jews was in the hands of the Germans, and this fact basically could not be altered. Salvation would come to the Jews only through an Allied victory. The faster the victory could be won, the better it would be both for the world and for the Jews. The handling of the Jewish problem he entrusted to the State Department, mainly in the hands of Breckinridge Long and his close circle of officials. Perhaps he acted in this manner because it was convenient for him that the barbs of criticism as to the failure of rescue would be directed against them and not against his self. Long, who was an anti-Semite and a zealous nativist, did everything that he could do to prevent Jewish refugees from entering the United States and later sabotaged rescue efforts.

We must also keep in mind the political atmosphere in which Roosevelt was operating. On the surface it appeared that his stature as President of the

U.S. and leader of the free world fighting Nazism was unchallengeable. The unprecedented fact that Roosevelt was elected to the presidency four times made him seem to be a strong leader, stoutly supported in all his acts. However, though he had many admirers – so too were his enemies numerous. In the years most critical to the rescue of European Jewry, Roosevelt faced the most hostile Congress in all his years in office. His biographer, J. MacGregor Burns, wrote that "The President moved in an atmosphere of conflict – of political bitterness, industrial discord, racial tension, press opposition, Democratic party defections – and of an enmity against him so intense and persistent that for a parallel in Britain we would have to go far back."[37] Could the President have acted against the public's wishes, clashed with Congress and still remained an effective leader of the nation? When conflict arose between his role as moral leader in the war against Nazism and his role as political leader of the American people, FDR yielded to the greater pressure. In addition, Roosevelt had to take in to consideration the positions of America's allies. Clarence Pickett, a member of the Quakers, wrote in his memoirs, that a State Department official told him that FDR tried in 1943 to convince Churchill to permit him to deviate from the Blockade agreement for humanitarian reasons. Churchill replied that they should not damage the priority given to military considerations.[38]

If public opinion was opposed to opening the country to Jewish refugees, or to fighting the 'war for the Jews', Roosevelt was not prepared to openly challenge those views which were widely held by the public. For those reasons the President was unwilling to take further steps to save the Jews of Europe, but rather walked a tightrope so as not to arouse neither the wrath of the public nor the hostility of Congress, against himself. Democracy, which generally provides Jews with a sense of security, in this case limited the ability of the President to work for rescue. Throughout the years of the war, Roosevelt zealously preserved his political assets in order to work for goals that to him were more urgent than rescuing Jews.

The Possibilities of Rescue

What possibilities of rescue were open to the President? The best opportunity for saving Jews was in the period preceding the war. If at that time the nations of the world had opened their gates to Jewish refugees seeking a haven, many more would have later been spared the cruel fate awaiting them in Europe. But in the United States the public was opposed to permitting more refugees to enter their country. Had the President attempted to augment the number of immigrants permitted to enter, it would, in all probability, only have caused Congress to limit immigration still further.

During the war, a plan was proposed by Yitzchak Greenbaum, the Bergsonites and others, to bomb the cities of Germany as retaliation for killing Jews and to warn the Nazis that if they persisted in injuring Jews then the Allies would continue to bomb the cities of Germany. This, however, was not a feasible scheme. The Air Forces of Britain and of the United States were by then bombing Germany for their own strategic reasons and the Germans were already accusing the Jews that they were to blame for those bombings. On the contrary, they threatened that if the bombings did not cease, Germany would retaliate and liquidate the Jews of Europe.[39] How then was it possible to threaten the Germans with the destruction of their cities, if, in any case, they saw the Allied bombings as a Jewish plot and accordingly threatened to retaliate against the Jews? Had the Allies made such a threat it would have meant that if Germany would stop killing Jews then the Allies would have to cease their bombings. The Allies would not agree to such a step as they saw the bombing of German cities; the destruction of Germany's industrial base; and the spreading of terror and demoralization among the civilian population as a prime strategy in their war to vanquish Germany. The Jewish organizations in the United States also realized that this plan was not feasible, and therefore it was not included among the 12-point proposal they had submitted to the American government on the eve of the Bermuda Conference.

However, the Axis satellites could have been threatened with bombings. From the beginning of 1943, this threat might have influenced them to stop cooperating with the Germans in the destruction of Jews. The bombing of Budapest in July 1944, led Horthy to halt the deportation of Jews.[40] In the summer of 1944 it was possible, as well, to bomb the killing instillations at Auschwitz and the railroad lines leading to there, as the Jewish organizations requested. This appeal was not implemented.

The proposal of the Joint Emergency Committee to open negotiations with the Germans for the release of all Jews under their control was also not realistic. The Jewish organizations almost immediately realized this and in their first letter to the State Department after the Bermuda Conference they did not revert to the proposal. The Germans were not prepared to discuss this proposition and until the very last stages of the war they turned down any attempt to interfere with their policies to eliminate all the Jews. What was left for the Allies to do? Appeal to the humanitarian instincts of the Nazis? Offer all sorts of benefits, such as Eichmann proposed? These proposals could not be met by the Allies because it would have threatened the wartime coalition with the Soviet Union, which feared that the West might reach a separate peace with Germany. Was it really possible for millions of refugees to reach the borders of Europe and then transfer to places of refuge at a time when the fiercest battles known to mankind were being waged? The Allies assumed that Germany was more likely to eject the Jews in order to embarrass the Allies and create difficulties than they could believe that Germany intended to destroy all the Jews of Europe in gas chambers.

What could have been done was to pressure the Axis satellites to desist from harming the Jews of their countries and permit at least some of those who faced immediate danger of falling into the clutches of the Germans to leave their countries. It was especially possible to appeal for the release of children. Feelers were made but they failed. There was an American plan in 1942 to bring to the US 5,000 Jewish children from France. In 1943 the British also proposed allowing 5.000 Jewish children from Bulgaria to enter Palestine. These plans failed because, among other reasons, of the bumbling bureaucracy of various government departments. These officials saw no need to exploit a chance opportunity to expedite the rescue of Jews. If more pressure had been exerted earlier on the satellites and if opportunities for rescue had been handled more expeditiously, perhaps tens of thousands of Jews might have been saved.

The proposal of the Jewish organizations to create havens of safety in the neutral countries of Europe and to provide guarantees of financial aid, supplies and assurances that at war's end the refugees would be removed from their countries, was a plausible scheme and held out the possibility of saving thousands of Jews. Until the end of 1942 the neutrals feared Germany's threats and were concerned about their own security. But from 1943 on, they were more amenable to Allied requests. Perhaps if the Allies had acted energetically, guaranteeing the needed supplies, they might have achieved greater results. The United States did do some things along this line, but had the President turned to Congress to appropriate the large funds required for this activity, it appears that his request would have been rejected.

The neutral nations of Europe were prepared to absorb a limited number of refugees but when the numbers went beyond this it was necessary to remove the surplus refugees. The United States headed the war-time coalition and was the country least affected by the hardships of war. Therefore, it bore the primary responsibility to provide an example to other nations. In February 1943, Joseph Schwartz reported to Joint that he had been told by the governments everywhere in Europe that "We are ready to do our share, but what is the United States prepared to do? If the United States shows its willingness, we will not be far behind."[41] In 1943, the U.S. was capable of absorbing, at the very least, the number of refugees permitted under the immigration quotas. Ships that could transport the survivors to safety were also available. A gesture of this sort would have influenced other countries and America could have proclaimed to the world its readiness to rescue Jews. But in reality the President feared the reaction of Congress and the public, and did not act on this matter until he opened the 'Free Port' in Oswego in the summer of 1944. Even then he took only a rather hesitant and limited step. He also attempted to obscure the Jewish aspect of his action. A year passed before the decision taken at Bermuda – to remove the Jewish refugees from Spain to North Africa – was implemented. Yet, even then, only 630 refugees were moved into the Fedalla camp in Morocco.[42]

Were the plans of the Jewish organizations to send food to the Jews of Europe feasible? Could they have reduced the starvation which was decimating so many victims? Until the summer of 1942, most parcels sent to European Jews did reach their destinations. These parcels were not a solution for the mass starvation but could have alleviated the suffering to some degree. The appalling condition of the Jews of Poland was known early in the West. In light of these conditions the Allies should have relaxed the boycott restrictions in order to permit food parcels to be sent the Jews of Europe. The government offices continued to create difficulties. Even when it was possible to send food to the inmates at Theresienstadt, the various agencies obstructed the consignment.

A possibility existed to send money to the Jews via channels of the underground. It was also feasible to mobilize rescue funds from local sources if the Jewish organizations were permitted to deposit money in closed bank accounts in Switzerland. However until Roosevelt approved the Riegner-Lichtheim proposal in July, 1943 the U.S. government prevented such measures. They even notified the Jewish organizations that it was illegal and threatened punishment for such acts. The money could have mitigated the suffering of Jews and may have helped save some. The funds could have been used to pay gentiles to hide Jews; to organize a Jewish underground; to smuggle Jews across the borders. At times it was also possible to bribe officials. Sending money had another aspect in addition to concrete rescue: it would have signaled the Jews of Europe that the world had not forgotten them.

The United States could have pressured Latin American countries to honor the visas and passports that their consuls had sold to Jews in Europe. It was even possible to enlarge this practice and send additional papers to thousands more Jews. The Germans generally honored these papers and kept their holders in separate camps for transfer as long as the issuing countries recognized them. When the Germans learned that the papers were specious, they sent their holders to extermination camps. Only in May, 1944 did the Latin American countries recognize the validity of these papers, but unfortunately for many, it was already too late. American pressure on Latin American governments, as requested by the Jewish groups, could have brought an earlier recognition of these documents validity and thus saved more lives.

No serious effort was made to warn the German people and their collaborators to desist from participating in the murder of Jews. In the summer of 1942, it was decided to establish a 'War Crimes Commission', but it did not meet until December, 1943 and then only at the insistence of Britain.[43] The United States hesitated to create such a commission, and even after its establishment America did not support its own representative, Herbert Pell. His views concerning the punishment of Nazi war criminals were unpopular in the State Department.[44] It was also possible, in diverse ways, to warn the Jews about the fate awaiting them and to appeal to the non-Jewish population to hide them.

The possibilities of saving Jews were limited, apart from those living in the satellite countries. Despite all the difficulties, it had been possible to save thousands, perhaps tens of thousands, by exploiting "the nooks and crannies and paths to rescue", that Menachem Bader had spoken of. However, until the creation of the War Refugee Board, there was practically no concern by government officials to save Jews. Had the Board been created a year earlier (after the meeting of the Jewish leaders with the President in December, 1942); and had it been granted larger funding and greater support; and had representatives been stationed at strategic spots around the world – such a body could have found the way to save many thousands of lives. Such a step would have indicated the United States' desire to save Jews, and would have spurred other countries and international organizations to increase their efforts.

What Did the Jewish Leadership Do

Today, a generation and more after the Holocaust, there is widespread criticism as to the lack of unity among the Jewish organizations during those fateful years. Today, with most major Jewish organizations members of the 'President's Conference', the Jewish public cannot understand why the community was so fragmented during the Holocaust years and why it could not unite around the most vital and urgent objective – saving the Jews of Europe. Many writers condemn the rift that existed among the Jewish organizations and claim, that if the Jewish leadership had acted with more wisdom, it could have overcome the disunity. Medoff concludes his book with the words of Rabbi Abba Hillel Silver who accused the Jewish leadership for its failure to save Jews. Silver claimed that it "was due to their lack of coordination, their working at cross purposes."[45] This criticism coming from Silver is strange, for throughout the Holocaust years he was not at all active in rescue. It was Silver who convinced the American Jewish Conference to call for the creation of a Jewish state, a resolution that caused a number of major organizations to leave the Conference, thereby destroying the then most serious endeavor to create Jewish unity.

The tragic truth is, that at the outbreak of the Second World War, the American Jewish community found itself without an agreed upon leadership. The chasm that rent the community was very deep. There were many petty quarrels and jealousies, and each organization zealously guarded its own domain. Yet, beneath the surface there were more serious reasons for the conflict. The gap between the wealthy German- Jewish community that leaned towards assimilation, and the Jewish masses from Eastern European who still maintained a national consciousness, was difficult to bridge. There were serious and bitter conflicts over their approaches to Zionism, and over the question: Who should represent the Jewish community before the Administration? Even rescue matters became a thorny issue. Should they appeal to the President, or should they demonstrate in order to create pressure? Should they work for rescue only through conventional and legal methods, or did the realities of the situation require illegal steps as the only way to achieve results? The world outlooks that rent the community also prevented it from achieving an agreed upon policy of action. Each organization accused the other that it was part of the Jewish problem. It is also not certain whether the attempts to create unity aided or hampered the struggle to save Jews. When they did reach an agreement, as happened at times, it was an agreement taken at the lowest common denominator.

For many months, from fall 1942 to summer 1943, the Jewish organizations (excluding the Bergsonites) succeeded in uniting to work for rescue. The American Jewish Congress went along in that course because it knew that the American Jewish Committee and Joint had more money and influence and that these were sorely needed to organize rescue programs. The AJC abandoned its traditional policies and met the other organizations part way when it participated in the March 1943 demonstrations, but remained a moderating factor in the more far reaching plans of other groups which wanted to arouse the public and put political pressure on the government.[46]

Could greater unity in the Jewish community have significantly changed the Administration's attitude to the issue of rescue? It is reasonable to assume that the answer is no. During the few months of the Joint Emergency Committee's existence the Jewish community acted in unity, organized many impressive demonstrations and presented the Administration with a clear and agreed upon plan of action. Yet, despite the joint action of the mainstream organizations they were unable to budge the American stand at the Bermuda Conference even one iota. From the meager results achieved there the Jewish organizations concluded that all the demonstrations and protests and unity had actually achieved nothing.[47]

It does not seem reasonable that American Jewry could have been able to overcome the widespread antisemitic prejudices in order to influence their government to rescue, even if they had been united. Nor could they allay the fear of many Americans that the main goal of their outcry about Jewish suffering in Europe was only to get more Jews into the country. The organizations were also unable to modify the prevailing view that Jews had too much political power in America and were determining its policies. James Dunn, the State Department's political advisor, warned his colleagues "That Jew Morgenthau, and his Jewish assistants like DuBois [sic], are trying to take over this place."[48]

Some critics cite the success of the American Zionist Emergency Committee in mobilizing America to support the creation of Israel as proof of what could have been accomplished if American Jewry had worked in unity; had improved its organizational ability; and had striven more fervently to rescue Jews.[49] Undoubtedly the efforts of the Zionist Emergency Committee contributed significantly to the political battle to establish the State of Israel. But the story of AZEC can prove just the opposite. The Zionists did manage to have Congress pass a resolution supporting the creation of a Jewish state – but not until December 1945, more than two years after the resolution had been adopted at the American Jewish Conference, and after several failed attempts.[50] Two more years were needed until the UN adopted its resolution on the partition of Palestine. In the matter of rescue, however, time was of the essence. It was inconceivable to drag out the rescue struggle for four years. Immediate action was necessary, even if it were on a more limited scale.

AZEC also worked in a different atmosphere from what had existed at the time of the struggle for rescue. The Congressional resolution calling for the establishment of a Jewish state was passed after the war because until then, political and military considerations throttled such action, much as they had operated to curb rescue. We have already noted that antisemitism declined dramatically after the war. When the extent of the killings and the methods by which the Jews were liquidated became known, America's attitude towards the victims of Nazism changed significantly. Americans commiserated with the remnants of Jewry and demonstrated their desire to help them reconstruct their lives. In addition, supporting the creation of the State of Israel and thereby opening the gates of Palestine to the Jewish refugees would also mean averting renewed pressures to absorb Jewish refugees in the U.S.

The 'Bergson Boys' and their Criticism of Roosevelt and the Jewish Leadership

Recently the debate has been renewed over the role of the 'Bergson Boys' and their contribution to the efforts to goad the American government to act for the rescue of European Jewry. At Yad Vashem a study day was held devoted to an evaluation of their activities. A debate was carried in a number of issues of *The Israel Journal of Foreign Affairs* in which historians discussed the question of rescue of European Jewry and which dealt, as well, with the criticism leveled by the proponents of the Bergsonites at the American government and the Jewish leadership for their lack of action during the Holocaust. Some claim that the Bergsonites were the only ones who acted energetically and accomplished the few results, which were attained in the field of rescue, and chiefly the most meaningful achievement – the creation of the War Refugee Board.

These views held by the supporters of Bergson have gained many adherents among the American Jewish community – in part because of American Jewry's feeling of shame for not doing enough to rescue; in part because American Jews have become more militant and have learned how to carry out a fight in the public sphere in order to obtain programs that are important to them; and for some, it appears, for political reasons – in order to sever the close connections, which continue to exist to this day, between American Jewry and the Democratic Party.

Are those criticisms justified? Undoubtedly the spectacular publicity campaign waged by the Bergsonites in the American press contributed greatly to the dissemination of knowledge of the Holocaust. Kook was right when he stated, that "we placed them [the news] on the American public agenda, providing the momentum for their movement from the dead pages to the news section and even to the front pages."[51] However, as we well know today, despite their publicity campaign the vast majority of Americans did not see, were not influenced nor did they absorb the import of the news. If the intent of those ads was to goad America to act for rescue, they did not achieve their purpose.

Every ad in the papers ended with a call to contribute money in order to rescue Jews such as the pretentious call to contribute $50 in order to save a Jew from Romania. Yet the Bergson Group, itself, did not engage in acts of rescue. The historian, Noam Penkower, claimed that the Bergson Group had a problem "in their inability to implement their plans [...] when it came time to realize these ideas, 'implementation had to be left to other hands. Action lay beyond the Bergsonites' capabilities.'"[52] We should also recall the words of a member of the group, Eri Jabotinsky, who confessed at war's end that "In summation, in that period I did not rescue anyone."[53] The historian of the Bergson Group, Judith Baumel, described the fund-raising campaign of the group as "an ever increasing spiral with a twofold purpose: to mold public opinion and to bring in donations, these to be utilized in turn to finance another advertising campaign to draw public attention to the issue and elicit still further contributions."[54]

Medoff criticizes harshly those who did not react to news of the Holocaust claiming that until the press conference of Stephen Wise in November 1942 they did not know nor did they comprehend that a Holocaust was transpiring. He rebukes Yehuda Bauer who had written "Information about the mass murders in the Soviet Union [in 1941] was not available to the Americans."[55] In a sarcastic tone Medoff replied "Not available? Perhaps if U.S. officials never read newspapers such as the *N.Y. Times* [...] numerous articles about mass-killings that were published in the United States in 1941, including reports of the Jewish Telegraphic Agency of the 'mass-shootings of Jews' in Minsk' [reported on July 7th]; 'the mass execution of the Jews in Bialystok' (July 18th); a slaughter by machine-guns of 4,200 Jews in Kamentz-Podolsk (October 2nd)"; and so forth.[56] However, for some reason, Medoff does not question why his protagonists in the Bergson Group also did not know about the extermination of European Jewry until Stephen Wise's press conference in November 1942. Bergson (Kook) related in later interviews that when he read about Wise's press conference that was the moment he identifies "as when the full import of the Final Solution hit him."[57] According to Bergson, the following evening he gathered the members of the group and demanded of his comrades to put aside all other work and harness themselves to a struggle for rescue, for that was now the urgent need. Yet, according to Ben-Ami, just a month previously at a special meeting held to discuss initial reports concerning the situation of European Jewry, both Merlin and Kook "refused to believe that such a thing was possible in the twentieth century."[58] It appears that Bergson, as well, still found it difficult to absorb the information (and we are talking already about late 1942 and not 1941!). Their decision to work for rescue was taken only at the end of 1942 and until then the group engaged only in the issue of establishing a Jewish Army and not at all with aid and rescue.

Nevertheless, as we have already noted, the Jewish leadership **did know** that many Jews were being murdered in occupied Europe, and that tens of thousands were dying of hunger, disease and cold, and since the beginning of the war they were already involved in dealing with government agencies and the International Red Cross in an endeavor to provide aid and attempt to rescue, however they were generally met with a wall of imperviousness and bureaucratic passivity. As long as it was permitted the organizations sent money and packages to the Jews who were living at death's door in the ghettos. Funds from the Joint were an important source of relief for the Jews, and the Joint was afterwards the main source of funding for the War Refugee Board.[59] The Jewish organizations also held public assemblies (long before the activities of the 'Bergson Group', who for some unfathomable reason had no knowledge of them) in an attempt to arouse public opinion to demand action. We should recall, among others, the rallies held: in Town Hall (May 1942); the gathering in Madison Square Garden (July 1942); the mass demonstration in Madison Square Garden (March 1, 1943) and the many demonstrations held subsequently in other cities.

An additional criticism which is leveled against the Jewish leadership, and mainly against Rabbi Stephen Wise, was their animosity toward the 'Bergson Group' and their attempt to obstruct its activities and even worked to have them expelled from the United States (they were foreign residents) or, at least, have them drafted into the American army in order to silence them. According to Kook, Roosevelt, who was angered by the attacks upon him in the group's publicity, threatened to prevent the Zionist Movement from operating in the United States if they themselves did not silence Bergson.[60] There was, however, an attempt by the Zionist leadership in 1942 to reach an agreement on cooperation with the Bergsonites, though Ben-Gurion, who was in America at that time, demanded as a condition for cooperation, that the Bergsonites would recognize the authority of the Zionist Movement for he feared their independent activities were akin to those of Irgun, as the Bergson Boys were Irgun's delegation in the United States. The Bergsonites did not agree to that condition and consequently Ben Gurion placed a veto on their collaboration with the Zionist Movement. Unfortunately that was the outcome (though Kook himself, admitted that he, as well, did not want to collaborate, fearing that they would be co-opted by the Zionist establishment).[61]

The members of the 'Bergson Group', in general, and Kook specifically, had a problem of accepting authority, even in their own 'home field'. In 1940, when Zev Jabotinsky, the leader of the Revisionist movement, arrived in America, he attempted to bend the delegation to his will, however without any success.[62] In addition, there was a rift between the Revisionist Movement in the United States and the 'Bergson Group'. When the group declared itself a "Government-in-Exile", Menachem Begin (who at that time commanded Irgun) was opposed to their action, yet nevertheless they went ahead. On a number of other issues the conflict between Kook and Begin intensified. In her important study of the 'Bergson Group', Judith Baumel maintains that 'whereas Begin viewed it [The Bergson Group] primarily as a public relations tool, for Kook the delegation was the intellectual vanguard for the Irgun as a whole"[63] It is not surprising that animosity existed between Bergson and Begin. According to Ben-Ami "They [the Irgun leadership] resented that Peter Bergson and others [in the delegation] [...] were receiving such a buildup which appeared to smack of personal ambitions for the future."[64] Even amidst the group there existed much tension from which the members were barely able to hold back until, after the war, Bergson was replaced as head of the delegation and Merlin was appointed in his place.

In summing up, aside from their success in disseminating news of the Holocaust, the 'Bergson Group' (and both Wyman and Medoff, as well) claim that they were the factor which brought about the creation of the War Refugee

Board. I have already addressed myself extensively to this assertion (see chapter 12). If they contributed to the creation of the Board, their contribution was marginal. At the best, Congress would have called for the establishment of the Board, and declarations of this sort in the past by the Congress calling for action to aid European Jewry remained just that – declarations on paper. The authority to establish the Board rested solely in the hands of the President and he made the decision in the wake of the Treasury Department report, which was an outcome of Stephen Wise's initiative with Morgenthau and Roosevelt, who the critics continue to defame.

❖ ❖ ❖

Though it may be possible to explain the reasons why the American Jewish leadership acted as it did, yet it is still difficult to understand and explain the restrained response of the general Jewish public to the horrendous news from Europe. The demonstrations, the mass-meetings, the drive for financial contributions reached hundreds of thousands of Jews in the United States – but the American Jewish community numbered over five million at that time.

One of the reasons why the Jewish leadership did not act more forcefully during the Holocaust was because it did not feel that the Jewish community would support it in its endeavors. Why were so many silent? Perhaps, like all other American citizens the Jews were mainly concerned with what was happening on the battlefields of the war and were more worried about the well-being of their loved ones serving in the Armed Forces (more than some five hundred thousand American Jews served in the Armed Forces during the Second World War). They, too, faced the cognitive problem of an inability to grasp the events in Europe. However, by the end of 1942, enough information about the fate of Europe's Jews had arrived in the U.S., and this should have aroused and warned them. True, even if they had cried out, they could not have induced the shapers of American policy to change their attitude toward rescue, but this fact is not enough to justify the silence of many. In 1939, during the very first days of the war, Chaim Greenberg had already grasped the dilemma of Jewish powerlessness. "What's the point of talking any longer", he questioned.

"We've said it all. In Germany only one language is understood – the language of threat backed by real power. Yet we know we have nothing with which to back up our threats. [...] Perhaps we should arouse the conscience of the world?" he pondered. "But the world knows very well what is happening to us", he continued, "and it is too cowardly to do anything for our rescue if it entails any kind of risk, or threatens even the least of its interests. [...] We talk for we have no other weapons in our arsenal."[65] Greenberg concluded that though he was aware that nothing of value would come from his outcry, he felt that he must assert himself and not give the world the impression that the Jews feel that they are lost.

A similar sentiment was expressed by Arieh Kubowitzki in 1942 when he turned to Stephen Wise and demanded that the World and American Jewish Congresses "must do something. Even if we don't succeed, we must try."[66] There is a value in action even if it does not achieve immediate results. At times these acts are undertaken as a moral response and as an internal need and they become a symbol for future generations. For ages the strength of the Jewish people, dispersed among the nations and persecuted throughout much of their history, lay in their mutual responsibility, obligations and the sense of a common fate.

"And Mordecai rent his clothes, and put on sackcloth with ashes, and went out into the midst of the city, and cried with a loud and bitter cry." (Esther, Ch. IV, 1). The Zionist leader, Leib Joffe, demanded that the Jews of America protest "even if it won't help [...] because a living organism cries out when in pain."[67] At times there is a need to shout, simply because it is impossible to remain silent.

❖ ❖ ❖

In the aftermath of the Second World War people at last began to understand what befell the Jews of Europe. There was a fervent belief and a hope that the Holocaust would be a turning point in world history, and that in the wake of the most immense failing that humanity has ever known there would be a determination that never again would the world allow such atrocities to be repeated. In the wake of the Holocaust the United Nations adopted a 'Convention on the Prevention and Punishment of the Crime of Genocide'

(1948) which required member governments to act when such deeds occur. Yet in practice, as we well know, genocide has occurred again and again. In the past few decades alone there have been massive genocides in Cambodia, Bosnia, Rwanda and Darfur and immense killings still go on in the Congo, but neither the governments of the world nor the United Nations did much to prevent the slaughter of innocent civilians. 'Never Again!' has become an empty slogan.

Samantha Power, the United States Representative at the UN, has bitterly rebuked world governments for their indifferent and opportunistic reactions to acts of genocide. In an article written in the journal *Dissent*, she admonished "the United States and its allies [who] have wholeheartedly endorsed the pledge 'never again', while tolerating unspeakable atrocities that have been committed in clear view [...] because their vital national interests were not considered imperiled by mere genocide."[68] However it is not only governments but the general public, as well, that react to the crime of genocide indifferently. People around the world don't want such infamous crimes to happen, yet they are not prepared to act, to do practically anything in order to prevent such acts from occurring.

We have to ask ourselves, do we, the bystanders, also share, at least morally, the responsibility for the acts of genocide. If we choose the easy way of silence or the expedient path of compromise and enable such acts to occur, do we, in effect, stand on the side of the perpetrators? The bible commands us: "Neither shalt thou stand idly by the blood of thy neighbor." (Leviticus, 19, 16).

ABBREVIATIONS IN NOTES

The following is a list of abbreviations used in the notes:

AJA	American Jewish Archives.
AJCL	American Jewish Committee Library.
AJCongL	American Jewish Congress Library.
AJH	American Jewish History.
AJHQ	American Jewish Historical Quarterly.
AJHS	American Jewish Historical Society.
AJYB	American Jewish Year Book.
AJHQ	American Jewish Historical Quarterly.
BBA	B'nai Brith Archives.
BLDiary	Breckinridge Long Diary.
BLMSS	Breckinridge Long Papers.
CW	Congress Weekly.
CZA	Central Zionist Archives.
FDRL	Franklin D. Roosevelt Library.
FRUS	Foreign Relations of the United States
HadA	Hadassah Archives.
HMD	Henry Morgenthau Diaries.
JDCA	American Joint Distribution Committee Archives
JF	Jewish Frontier.
JLCA	Jewish Labor Committee Archives.
JPSA	Jewish Publication Society of America.
JSS	Jewish Social Studies.
JTA	Jewish Telegraphic Agency.
LA	Labor Archives.
LDBMSS	Louis D. Brandeis Papers.
L of C	Library of Congress.
MTMSS	Myron Taylor Papers.
MZ	Metzudat Ze'ev.
NA/SD	National Archives, State Department Files.
NA/TD	National Archives, Treasury Department Files.
NYT	New York TimesNew York Times.
OF	Office Files (FDRL).
OH	Oral History.
PSCMSS	Palestine Statehood Committee Papers (Yale U, Sterling Library).
PPF	President's Personal Files (FDRL).
PWWII	Problems of World War II & Its Aftermath, Part 2, The Palestine Problem.
VMI	George C. Marshall MSS, Virginia Military Institute.
WaMS	Morris Waldman Papers (YIVO).
WJCA	World Jewish Congress Archives.

WiseMSS	Stephen S. Wise Papers.
YM	Yalkut Moreshet.
ZANY	Zionist Archives, New York.

ABBREVIATIONS OF COMMITTEES

AC	Administrative Committee
EC	Executive Committee
GC	Governing Council
NB	National Board
OC	Office Committee
SC	Sub-Committee

ABBREVIATED NAMES AND TITLES

AK	Arieh Kubovy (Leon Kubowitzki)
AT	Arieh Tartakower
BC	Bermuda Conference
BL	Breckinridge Long
CH	Cordell Hull
DA	Dean Acheson
FDR	Franklin D. Roosevelt
FF	Felix Frankfurter
GR	Gerhardt Riegner
HAW	Henry A. Wallace
HM	Henry Morgenthau Jr.
IG	Israel Goldstein
JP	Joseph Proskauer
JWW	James Waterman Wise
LDB	Louis D. Brandeis
LS	Libby Schultz
MP	Maurice Perlzweig
MT	Myron Taylor
MW	Maurice Waldman
NG	Nachum Goldmann
PB	Peter Bergson
SIR	Samuel I. Rosenman
Sof S	Secretary of State
SW	Stephen S. Wise

ENDNOTES

PREFACE

1 Peter Novick, *The Holocaust in American Life*, (Boston & New York, 1999), Chapter 5.

2 Arthur Morse, *While Six Million Died*, (New York, 1967).

3 See: Yehuda Bauer, *American Jewry and the Holocaust*, (Detroit, 1981); Richard Breitman & Alan Kraut, *American Refugee Policy & European Jewry* (Bloomington,, 1987); Henry L. Feingold, *The Politics of Rescue*, (New York ,1970); Saul S. Friedman, **No Haven for the Oppressed**, (Detroit., 1973); Rafael Medoff, *The Deafening Silence, American Jewish Leaders and the Holocaust*, (New York, 1987); Monty Noam Penkower, *The Jews were Expendable*, (Urbana, 1983); David S. Wyman, *The Abandonment of the Jews*, (New York, 1984).

4 See: Moshe Gottlieb, "The Anti-Nazi Boycott in the American Jewish Community" (Ph.D. dissertation, Brandeis Univ.,1967); Haskel Lookstein, "American Jewry's Public Response to the Holocaust 1938-44", (Ph.D. dissertation, Yeshiva Univ., 1979); Also Isaac Neustadt-Noy, "The Unending Task: Efforts to Unite American Jewry from the American Jewish Congress to the American Jewish Conference", (Ph.D. dissertation, Brandeis Univ., 1976).

5 Seymour Maxwell Finger, ed., *American Jewry During the Holocaust*, (American Jewish Commission on the Holocaust, March 1984).

6 Elie Wiesel, "Telling the Tale", *Dimensions*, vol. II, no. 3 (Spring, 1968).

7 Ibid., 11.

8 Elie Wiesel, *A Jew Today*, (New York, 1978) 191-192.

9 Alan M. Dershowitz, *Chutzpah*, (Boston, 1991), 298.

10 See, most specifically: Medoff, *The Deafening Silence*.

11 David S. Wyman, *The Abandonment of the Jews*, (New York, 1984).

12 Wiesel, Tale, 11.

13 Medoff, *The Deafening Silence*, 162-67.

14 See note 11.

15 Novick, *The Holocaust in American Life*, 2.

16 Wiesel, "Tale", 11

CHAPTER 1

1 Arthur Goren, *New York Jews and the Quest for Community*, (New York, 1970).

2 Samuel Halperin, *The Political World of American Zionism*, (Detroit, 1961), 58.

3 Melvin I. Urofsky, *A Voice that Spoke for Justice*, (Albany, 1982), 126.

4 Lloyd P. Gartner, "The Mid-Passage of American Jewry, 1929-45", 5th Annual Feinberg Memorial Lecture, Univ. of Cincinnatti, 5/13/82, 10.

5 Charles H. Stember, *Jews in the Mind of America,* (New York, 1966), 55.

6 Ibid., 54, 82.

7 Ibid., 92.

8 Bauer, American Jewry, 40.

9 Friedman, No Haven, 28.

10 Stember, Mind, 113.

11 Ibid., 121.

12 J. David Valaik, "American Catholics, Anti-Semitism, and the Spanish Civil War", *Journal of Church and State*, Vol. XIII, no. 3, Autumn, 1971, 476.

13 Wayne S. Cole, *Roosevelt and the Isolationists*, (Lincoln, 1983), 465.

14 Ibid., 308

15 Edward S. Shapiro, "The Approach of War: Congressional Isolationism and Anti-Semitism", AJHQ, Vol. LXXIV, no.1, 9/84, 64.

16 Stember, Mind, 128.

17 Ibid.

18 See for example, Milton Persitz, "Jews in Government Service", CW, 3/20/42, 7-8.

19 Deborah E. Lipstadt, *Beyond Belief: The American Press and the Coming of the Holocaust* (New York, 1986), 65

20 Milwaukee Journal, 3/30/38, Quoted in Lipstadt, Belief, 92.

21 Barry Rubin, "Perils of a Jewish Diplomat: Ambassador Laurence Steinhardt, 1940-45" AJH, LXX, 3/81, 335.

22 Friedman, No Haven, 50.

23 Henry A. Wallace, *The Price of Vision: The Diary of Henry A. Wallace,* John M. Blum, ed., (Boston, 1973), 5/22/43, 210-11.

24 FRUS, Casablanca Conference, 1/17/43, FDR-Gen. Nogues talk, 608-09.

25 LofC, Diaries of Harold Ickes, 11/7/43, 8337.

CHAPTER 2

1   Gottlieb, Boycott, 37.

2   Melvin I. Urofsky, Voice, 128.

3   Gottlieb, Boycott, 39.

4   Ibid, 44.

5   Ibid, 38.

6   See for example: Voss, Servant, Rosenau (Baltimore) to SW, 186.

7   WA, Box 107, 5/5/33, SW to Anita Cohen.

8   Elizabeth E. Eppler, "The Rescue Work of the World Jewish Congress During the Nazi Period", in *Rescue Attempts During the Holocaust,* (Jerusalem, 1977), 48-49.

9   Arthur Hertzberg, ed., *The Zionist Idea,* (New York, 1981), 519.

10 NYT, 3/28/33.

11 Voss, Servant, 4/15/33, SW to Judge J. Mack, 184.

12 Noy, Unending Task, 85.

13 Naomi Cohen, *Not Free to Desist,* (Philadelphia, 1972), 163.

14 Ibid., 164.

15 Gottlieb, Boycott, 74.

16 AJCongA, EC, 2/1/44.

17 Morris Frommer, "The American Jewish Congress: A History 1914-50", (Ph.D. dissertation, Ohio State Univ., 1978), 340-41.

18 WA, Box 92, SW to Max Kopstein, 1/29/42.

19 Edwin Black, *The Transfer Agreement,* (New York, 1984), 380.

20 Avraham Barkai, *Hakalkalah Hanazit,* (Tel Aviv, 1986) (Hebrew), 16.

21 Ibid., 142.

22 Gottlieb, Boycott, 439.

23 Opinion, 6/33, 20.

24 WA, Box 95, 6/10/34, M. Waldman to AJC.

25 Bauer, American Jewry, 26, Table # 1.

26 Ibid., 28, Table # 2.

27 David Wyman, *Paper Walls, America and the Refugee Crisis 1938-1941,* (Univ. of Mass., 1968), 221.

28 Stephen S. Wise, *The Challenging Years,* (New York, 1949), 237.

29 Wyman, Paper Walls, 4.

30 Ibid., 69-70.

31 Sheldon M. Neuringer, "American Jewry and U.S. Immigration Policy, 1881-1953",
(Ph.D. dissertation, Univ. of Wisconsin, 1969), 222.

32 Wyman, Paper Walls, 69.

33 Friedman, No Haven, 25.

34 Stember, Mind, 145-146.

35 Wyman, Paper Walls, 210.

36 Feingold, Politics, 335, n. 39.

37 David Wyman, Paper Walls, 24.

38 Neuringer, Immigration Policy, 216, n. 6.

39 Wyman, Paper Walls, 3-4.

40 Ibid.

41 Frommer, AJCong, 378.

42 Bauer, American Jewry, 29.

43 Feingold, Politics, 335, n. 39.

44 Lipstadt, Beyond Belief, 57.

CHAPTER 3

1 See in: Bauer, American Jewry, Table 1 (26), Table 2 (28).

2 Lipstadt, Beyond Belief, 87-88.

3 Feingold, Politics, 23.

4 Lipstadt, Beyond Belief, 91.

5 Ibid, 3/26/38, FDR to FF, 90.

6 WA, Box 65, 5/16/38, Minutes of 1st Meeting of PACPR.

7 Feingold, Politics, 99.

8 Friedman, No Haven, MT to SD, 66.

9 Lipstadt, Beyond Belief, 18-19.

10 Ibid., 98-99.

11 Feingold, Politics, 41-42.

12 David Brody, "American Jewry, the Refugees and Immigration Restrictions (1932-42)",
PAJHS, 6/56, 228.

13 Wyman, Abandonment, 8.

14 Friedman, No Haven, 83.

15 Morse, Six Million, 140.

16 Ibid., 130.

17 Neuringer, Immigration Policy, 237, n. 43.

18 WA, Box 109, 3/30/38, SW to FF.

19 Friedman, No Haven, 91.

20 Ibid., 93.

21 Shapiro, Congressional Isolationism, 55.

22 Friedman, No Haven, 95-96.

23 Leo V. Kanawada, *Franklin D. Roosevelt's Diplomacy and American Catholics, Italians and Jews,* (Ann Arbor, 1982), 121.

24 Wyman, Paper Walls, 38.

25 Haskel Lookstein, Were We Our Brother's Keepers? 66.

26 Wyman, Paper Walls, 33-34, 37.

27 Neuringer, Immigration Policy, 229, n. 32.

28 Feingold, Politics, 102-03.

29 Friedman, No Haven, 90.

30 Henry Feingold, *A Midrash on American Jewish History,* (Albany, 1982), 210.

31 Feingold, Politics, 96.

32 Wyman, Paper Walls, 61-62

33 Brody, Immigration Restrictions, 240

34 Feingold, Politics, 124-25.

35 Ibid.

36 Opinion, editorial, 3/39, 6.

37 See for example: Ibid, 12/38, "America Has Spoken", 10-11.

38 Feingold, Politics, 49.

39 Wyman, Paper Walls, 52.

40 Gottlieb, Boycott, 353-54.

41 Wyman, Paper Walls, 56.

42 Feingold, Politics, 73.

43 Gottlieb, Boycott, 354.

44 See the views of Louis Lipsky in: Bet-Zvi, Hazionut HaPost-Ugandit, 233.

45 Feingold, Politics, 74.

46 Ibid, 73.

47 Haskel Lookstein, *Brother's Keepers*, 40 and 224, note 9.

48 Harold Ickes, The Secret Diaries of Harold L. Ickes: vol. 3: The Lowering Cloud, 1939-41, (New York, 1954), 12/3/38, 510.

49 WA, Box 104, 11/18/38. AJCong Statement at Meeting of GJC.

50 Gottlieb, Boycott, 39.

51 Voss, Servant, 3/29/33, SW to Mack, 182-183.

52 Ibid.

53 WA, Box 104, 11/18/38. AJCong Statement at Meeting of GJC.

54 Medoff, Deafening, 55.

55 Urofsky, Voice, 245.

56 Medoff, Deafening, 60.

57 Lookstein, Brother's Keepers, 58, note.

58 WA, Box 104, GJC, Statement of AJCong, 11/18/38.

59 Seymour M. Lipset & Earl Raab, *The Politics of Unreason*, (New York, 1970), 163.

60 Ibid, Chapter V.

61 William E. Leuchtenberg, *Franklin D. Roosevelt and the New Deal, 1932-40,* (New York, 1963), 276.

62 WA, Box 118, SW to D. Niles, 10/7/36.

63 Ibid., 249-50.

64 Leonard Baker, Brandeis and Frankfurter, (New York, 1984), 355.

65 Shabtai Tevet, Kinat David, Vol. III, (Jerusalem, 1987), (Hebrew) 319.

66 WA, Box 106, 7/19/39, SW to LDB.

67 Ibid, Box 91, 9/21/39, SW to MP.

68 Penkower, Expendable, 39.

69 Ibid., 32.

70 Ibid., 150.

71 Ibid., 53-54.

72 . ZANY, OC, 3/13/42.

73 Wyman, Paper Walls, 221.

74 Robert Dallek, *FDR and American Foreign Policy, 1932-1945,* (New York, 1979), 446.

75 Fred Israel, ed., *The War Diary of Breckinridge Long,* (Lincoln, 1966), XIX.

76 Ibid., XXIV.

77 Ibid., 4/11/40, 78.

78 Ibid., 9/24/40, 133.

79 Ibid., 9/4/41, 216.

80 Ibid.

81 Ibid., 10/3/40, 134.

82 Feingold, Politics, 142.

83 Israel, Long Diaries, 11/13/40, 151.

84 Ibid., 4/2241, 196.

85 Ibid., 1/13/42, 243.

86 Ibid., 9/18/40, 131.

87 WA, Box 65, Minutes of 40th Meeting of PACPR, 9/12/40. and Minutes of 41st Meeting of PACPR, 10/30/40.

88 Wyman, Paper Walls, 201.

89 Voss, Servant, 9/17/40, SW to O. Nathan, 242.

90 Gottlieb, Boycott, 373.

91 WJCA, 265, Box 1, 11/3/39, Interview GR and NG with Nicholson (ARC).

92 Ibid.

93 Ibid., 8A, EC, 2/27/41.

94 Ibid., 8A, AC, 10/26/41.

95 Bauer, American Jewry, Chapter 3.

96 Ibid, 33.

97 141. JDCA, EC, 10/22/42, J.Willen.

98 WJCA, Box 8A, AC, 3/26/44, J. Tennenbaum.

99 YIVO, Waldman MSS, 5/2/44, Memorandum on WJC.

100 WJCA, OC, 10/44, AT.

101 Ibid, AC, 10/29/40, J. Lestchinsky.

102 Ibid, SC of AC, 10/23/40, AK.

103 Ibid, 8A, AC, 10/8/40, NG.

104 Ibid, 82, Box 3, 11/20/42, AT to AK.

105 AJHS, AJCong, AC, 6/23/44, I. Miller.

106 Hilberg, Destruction, 174.

107 WJCA, 101A, J. Robinson to SW, 2/26/43.

108 Ibid, File 216A, Correspondence of NG with Nicholson (ARC), 11/3/39.

109 Ibid, 216A, Relief Committee, 2/4/42.

110 Ibid, File 265, Meeting NG & GR with Nicholson (ARC), 12/13/39.

111 Bauer, American Jewry, 99.

112 Yisrael Gutman, *The Jews of Warsaw, 1939-1942,* (Bloomington, 1982), 64.

113 Ibid.

114 Ibid, 94-95.

115 Ibid, 99.

116 Ibid, 99.

117 WJCA, Box 266, AT to SW, 7/23/42.

118 Goldberg Commission, 32.

119 Penkower, Expendable, 123.

120 Bauer, American Jewry, 97-99.

121 Ibid, 99.

122 Sherwood, Roosevelt and Hopkins, 273.

123 WA, Box 91, British Embassy (Washington) to MP, 6/14/41.

124 Ibid., 4/2/41, E. Henriques to WJC-British Section.

125 WA, Box 91, SW to MP, 5/9/41

126 Ibid.

127 Penkower, Expendable, 124.

128 WJCA, 8A, AC, 10/26/41.

129 Ibid.

130 Bauer, American Jewry, 36.

131 NASD, 851.48/420, 4/18/41, P. Baerwald (JDC) to CH.

132 Bauer, American Jewry, 95.

133 Efraim Zuroff, "Rescue Priorities and Fund-Raising Issues During the Holocaust", AJH, Vol. XVIII, 10/79, 311.

134 Ibid, 314.

135 Penkower, Expendable, 123-24.

136 Ibid, 124.

137 Christopher Browning, *The Final Solution and the German Foreign Office,* (New York, 1978), 85.

138 Gutman, The Jews of Warsaw, Table, 142.

139 WJCA, File 266, N. Schwalb (Geneva) to AT, 12/16/41.

140 Penkower, Expendable, 124.

141 WA, Box 92, MP to SW, 1/27/42.

142 LofC, BL, Box 209, Minutes of Meeting of SD, TD, BEW, British Embassy, 3/4/42.

143 Bauer, American Jewry, 39.

CHAPTER 4

1 Sherwood , Hopkins, 507 .

2 Leuchtenberg, New Deal, 312.

3 Ibid, 217-18.

4 Ibid, 230.

5 Sherwood, Hopkins, 128.

6 Leuchtenberg, New Deal, 312.

7 Burns, Soldier, 41.

8 Dallek, Foreign Policy, 267.

9 Ibid, 530.

10 Burns, Soldier, 120.

11 Ibid, 331.

12 Sherwood, Hopkins, 272-273; Burns, Soldier, 86-88.

13 Sherwood, Hopkins, 445.

14 Burns, Soldier, 467.

15 Blum, V for, 16.

16 Ibid, 46.

17 Burns, Soldier, 469.

18 Blum, V for, 190.

19 Burns, Soldier, 468.

20 Ibid, 463.

21 Blum, V for, 255.

22 Dallek, Foreign Policy, 335-336.

23 Ibid, 336.

24 Burns, Soldier, 381.

25 Sherwood, Hopkins, 695-96

26 Stember, Mind, 132.

27 Naomi Cohen, Not Free, 188.

28 See for example: Leib Yoffe, *Ktavim, Iggerot V'yomanim*, (Jerusalem, 1964), (Hebrew), L. Jaffe to NG, 7/22/43.

29 LofC, BL MSS, Box 203, Bermuda Conference, Meeting of U.S. delegation, 4/25/43, 63.

30 Ibid, Ickes Diaries, 9/19/42, 6993.

31 Ibid, 9/29/44, 9224.

32 FDRL, Francis Biddle MSS, Minutes of Meeting of the Cabinet, 11/20/42.

33 Congress Weekly, "Timely Topics", 11/12/43 and 11/19/43.

34 Friedman, No Haven, 174.

35 Blum, V for, 20.

36 Stember, Mind, 116-18.

37 Blum, V for, 174.

38 Cole, Isolationists, 465.

CHAPTER 5

1 Raul Hilberg, *The Destruction of European Jewry* (New York, 1973), 619.

2 Sara Shner-Nishmit, „Traunung", *Dapim LeCheker Hashoah*, 4, (Haifa, 1985), 55.

3 WJCA, 266, AK to Weismann (Lisbon), 3/7/44.

4 Ibid, JTA Bulletin (London), 8/25/44.

5 Lipstadt, Belief, 4.

6 Wyman, Abandonment, 75

7 Stember, Mind, 141.

8 Lipstadt, Belief, 159-60.

9 CW, ed., 3/20/42, 3.

10 JLCA, Part III, Section 2, Bund report.

11 Jan Karski, *Story of a Secret State,* (Boston, 1944).

12 Interview with Mencham Bader August 1987

13 Penkower, Expendable, 96.

14 NYT, 7/4/42, 4.

15 Wyman, Abandonment, 47-48.

16 NA SD, 740.001 16EW39/ 527, Statement at Press Conference, E. Frischer, 6/29/42.

17 NYT, 11/25/42, 10.

18 Lipstadt, Belief, 152-53.

19 As to the attitude of the Vatican, see: Penkower, Expendable, 95-95; as to the attitude of the ICRC see: Meir Dworzecki, "The International Red Cross and its Policy Vis-a-Vis the Jews in the Ghettoes and Concentration Camps in Nazi Occupied Europe" in *Rescue Attempts during the Holocaust*, Y. Gutman & E. Zuroff, eds., (Israel, 1977).

20 CW, 2/27/42, 8-9.

21 See, for example, the minutes of the Office Committee of the "Farband" 8/31/42 on how best to publicize the news received in the Riegner cable. Archion Haavodah 24 (73).

22 Wyman, Abandonment, 64.

23 Lipstadt, Belief, 17.

24 Novick, Refugee Policy, 23.

25 Lipstadt. 155.

26 Marie Syrkin, "What American Jews Did During the Holocaust", *Midstream,* Vol. XXVIII, 10/82, 8.

27 William L. Shirer, *The Rise and the Fall of the Third Reich,* (New York, 1960), 952.

28 New York Times,11/25/42, 17

29 *Davar,* 6/25/42, 1.

30 L of C, Ickes MSS, file 375, Ickes to SW, 12/31/42.

31 L of C, Ickes MSS, file 375, Ickes to SW, 12/31/42.

32 TIME, 10/9/89. no. 41, 37.

33 Lipstadt, Belief, 170 and 170n.

34 Ibid, 228n.

35 Ibid, 269.

36 Bauer, American Jewry, 39.

37 Cantril, PO, 383.

38 Oral History, Testimony of Ceszka Borokowski (Niesky).

39 Karski, Secret State, 322.

40 Novick, Refugee Policy, 24.

41 Lipstadt, Belief, 141.

42 Ibid, 181.

43 NYT, 8/8/43.

44 Judith Doneson, The Holocaust in American Film (Philadelphia, 1987), 55.

45 AJHS, AJCong MSS, AC of AJCong, 6/23/44, A. Kubowitzki.

46 Lipstadt, Belief, 252.

47 Wyman, Abandonment, 62.

48 Ibid, 364, n. 4.

49 87. ZANY, ECZA, OC, 4/17/42.

50 Alex Grobman, "What Did They Know: The American Jewish Press & the Holocaust". AJH, LXVIII, 10/79, 338.

51 CW, 5/29/42 SW speech at War Emergency Conference

52 WJCA, EC 2/3/42

53 Opinion, 11/41 ed. 7

54 Shabtai Bet Zvi, Hazionut Hapost-Ugandit, 44.

55 NYT, 5/18/42, 4.

56 Lipstadt, Beyond Belief, 161.

57 YIVO LZOA Box 9 Folder 106 BG at League for Labor Palestine 5/29/42.

58 WA, Box 106, 5/34/34, Memo of Meeting of SW, Strook, M. Waldman with L. Brandeis.

59 YIVO LZOA Box 9 Folder 106 BG at League for Labor Palestine 5/29/42.

60 JLCA, Reel III, Section 2, contains copy of the Bund Report that reached the U.S.

61 Ibid.

62 Unity, 161

63 WJCA, U 185A, Box 4, AK to SW et al, 8/21/42.

64 Ibid, 18A, Box 1, Greenbaum.

65 CW, ed., 6/26/42, 3.

66 Ibid, ed., 7/10/42 .

67 Ibid.

68 AJCong, GC, 7/17/42.

69 ZANY, OC, 7/22/42.

70 JDC, Emer AC, 6/30/42.

71 N. Cohen, 240.

72 NA SD, 862.4016/2224, J. Edgar Hoover to A. Berle, 5/5/42.

73 Ibid, 862.4016/2229, H. Johnson (Stockholm) to SofS, 7/16/42.

74 Ibid, 867n20/121 1/2, W. Murray to S. Welles, 7/24/42.

75 Ibid.

76 Ibid, 740.00116 EW39/527 1/2, Harrison (Bern) to SofS, 8/3/42; and Hull to Tittman (Vatican), 8/4/42.

77 C W, FDR Message to MSG, 7/24/42.

78 L of C, Ickes Diaries, 7/14/42, 6814-15.

79 WJCA, 18A, Box 1, I. Greenbaum to NG, 6/17/42.

80 NA SD, 740.00116EW39/528, RBR to PTC and JWR, 8/42.

81 WJCA, U-185A, Box 4, AK to SW et al, 8/21/42.

82 Ibid, 185A, Box 4, AK to SW et al, 8/26/42.

83 Ibid, Letter from Caplan and Boraisha, 8/28/42.

84 NA SD, 862.4016/2234, Cable #3697, 8/11/42 from Bern.

85 Ibid, 862.4016/2234, H. Elting (Geneva) to Sect'y of State, 8/10/42.

86 Ibid, 862.4016, Cable #3697, 8/11/42 from Bern.

87 Ibid, 862.4016/2235, Memo of E. Durbrow, 8/13/42.

88 Penkower, Expendable, 64.

89 Interview with Maurice Perlzweig, 11/25/85.

90 Archion Avodah, (73) 24 III, Minutes of OC and minutes of Central Committee, Farband, 8/31/42.

91 Ibid.

92 Ibid.

93 YIVO, LZOA, Box 9, Folder 106.

94 NA SD, 840.48 Ref/3080, SW to Welles, 9/2/42.

95 Voss, Servant, SW to FF, 9/4/42, p.248.

96 Penkower, Expendable, p.68.

97 NA SD, 740.00116EW39/570, Rosenheim to FDR, 9/3/42.

98 Wyman, Abandonment, pp. 45-46.

99 Penkower, Expendable, p. 68.

100 Ibid., pp. 67-68.

101 Wiesel, Telling, p. 11.

102 Richard Breitman & Alan M. Kraut, *American Refugee Policy & the Jews of Europe*, (Bloomington: Indiana Univ. Press, 1987), p. 280, n. 27.

103 Penkower, Expendable, p. 70.

104 Ibid, pp. 68-69.

105 WA, Box 113, SW to Fanny Korn, 9/9/42.

106 Voss, Servant, SW to FF, 9/4/42, pp. 248-49.

107 Sherwood, Hopkins, p. 631.

108 Voss, Servant, SW to FF, 9/16/42, p. 251.

109 OH, 44 (56) A, G. Riegner.

110 ZA ,S5-354, Appendix to Members of ECZA for meeting 9/24/42.

111 WA, Box 92, M. Perzweig memo 10/6/42.

112 Finger, Goldberg Commission, p.14.

113 WJCA, U-185, Memo AK to SW et al, 9/29/42.

114 ZA, Z5-354, R. Lichtheim to A. Lourie (ECZA), 9/15/42.

115 Voss, Servant, SW to FF, 9/16/42, p. 250-51.

116 Penkower, Expendable , p.71.

117 NA SD, 740:00116EW39/597A, Welles to Taylor (Bern), 9/23/42.

118 Ibid, /600A, Welles to Bern, 10/5/42.

119 Ibid, 862.4016/2233, Cable to American Legation, Bern 8/17/42, not sent.

120 Ibid, /2238, Barou and Easterman to Wise, 9/1/42.

121 Ibid, /2242, Paul Squire (Geneva) to Sect'y of State, 9/28/42.

122 Ibid, EW/599, Harrison to Sect'y of State, 9/26/42.

123 Ibid, EW/601, Harrison to SS, 10/7/42.

124 Wyman, Abandonment, p. 50.

125 NA SD, EW/605, Harrison (for Tittman) to SS, 10/16/42.

126 Ibid, EW/726, Report from the Vatican, 11/23/42 (arr 1/12/43).

127 L of C, M. Taylor file, #1, Memorandum for the President and the S of S, 10/20/42.

128 Ibid.

129 Penkower, Expendable, pp.72-73.

130 WJCA, 184A, Box 1, File 53, Aide-Memoire rc'd by WJC, 11/24/42.

131 Wise, Challenging, pp.275-76.

132 NYT 11/25/42.

CHAPTER 6

1 Feingold, Politics, p. 170.

2 JF, 11/42, p. 3.

3 Lipstadt, Beyond Belief, pp. 180-82.

4 NYT, 11/25/42, p. 10.

5 Lipstadt, Beyond Belief, p.183.

6 Ibid, p.184.

7 Urofsky, Voice, p. 320.

8 WJCA, U185, Box #1, Minutes of Meeting on the European Situation, 11/5/42.

9 YIVO, Waldman Papers, Box 47, 12/30/42.

10 Ibid, Minutes of Meeting of SC of Special Conference on European Affairs, 11/30/42.

11 Lipstadt, Beyond Belief, p. 277.

12 Ibid, p. 71.

13 WA Box 68, SW to FDR, 12/2/42

14 AJCong, AC, Memorandum Submitted to the President of the United States 12/8/42. This was read to the President.

15 Ibid, Memorandum Submitted to the President of the United States. 12/8/42. This was submitted in writing.

16 JLCA, Part III, Section 2, Report on the Visit to the President, 12/8/42.

17 JTA, 12/9/42.

18 Lipstadt, Beyond Belief, p.186.

19 WJCA, U185, Minutes of the Planning Committee, 12/17/42.

20 NA SD, 740.00116EW39/712, Biddle to S of S, Submits report of the Polish Foreign Minister, 12/17/42.

21 Ibid, /694. Reams Memo, 12/9/42.

22 Ibid.

23 Penkower, Expendable, p. 91.

24 Penkower, Expendable, p. 91.

25 WJCA, U185, Cable from Ben-Zvi, Berlin, Greenbaum et al to AJCong, 11/10/42.

26 ZA, S5/687, Lichtheim to Greenbaum, 10/8/42.

27 AJCongL, GC, 11/12/42.

28 A description of the meetings of the JA representatives with the people who had arrived in Palestine in the civilian exchange, and the subsequent response of the JA Executive can be found in Bet-Zvi, Hazionut, pp. 68-72.

29 HadA, H. Szold cable, rc'd 11/26/42, Read at meeting of NB, 12/6/42.

30 ZANY, ECZA, OC, 12/6/42.

31 HadA, NB, 12/9/42.

32 WJCA, U185, Box # 1, Memorandum submitted by M. Weisgal, 12/10/42.

33 AJCongL, GC, 12/10/42.

34 ZANY, ECZA, OC, Report of NG, 12/11/42.

35 Ibid, ECZA, OC, 12/22/42.

36 HadA, NB, 1/6/43.

37 Ibid, T. Pool to H. Szold, 1/13/43.

38 Wyman, Abandonment, p. 64.

39 Ibid, p. 95.

40 Wiesel, "Telling the Tale", p. 11.

41 Medoff, Deafening, p. 160.

42 Ibid ,p. 178.

43 Ibid, p. 98.

44 Ibid, p. 116.

45 Wyman, Abandonment, p. 330.

46 Bulletin of Council of Jewish Federations and Welfare Funds, 1/12/44.

47 Harvey Klehr, *Communist Cadres,* (Stanford: Hoover Institute Press, 1978), p. 41.

48 Medoff, Deafening, p. 116.

49 Wyman, Abandonment, p. 14.

50 Lipstadt, Beyond Belief, p. 149.

51 Emanuel Celler, *You Never Leave Brooklyn,* (N.Y.: John Day, 1953), pp. 90-92.

52 Newsweek, 11/30/42, p. 11 in Wyman, Abandonment, p. 57.

53 Wyman, Abandonment, pp. 56-57.

54 Ibid, p. 8.

55 Ibid, p. 136n.

56 Dallek, Foreign Policy, p. 446.

57 Friedman, No Haven, p. 206.

58 LofC, BL, Box 202, Ref. File, BL Memo, 10/5/42.

59 Burns, Soldier, p. 607.

60 NYT, 11/24/42, p. 11.

61 WJCA, 265, JWW to AT, 8/31/42.

62 Wyman, Abandonment, p. 329.

63 Medoff, Deafening, p.106.

64 OH, 5 (22) Hei, Interview with Dr. I. Goldstein, p. 17.

65 Celler, Brooklyn, p.12.

66 Alon Gal, "Characteristics of American Zionism", Symposium held at the Hebrew U., 1985.

67 Leuchtenberg, New Deal, p. 332.

68 Stember, Mind, p. 121.

69 Ibid, p. 127.

70 Lawrence H. Fuchs, editor, *American Ethnic Politics*, (N.Y.: Harper & Row, 1968), p. 53.

71 Stephen Sharot, Judaism, *A Sociology,* (London: Newton, Abbots, David & Charles, 1976), Chapter III.

72 See the results of the U.S. Presidential elections of the past few years.

73 Fuchs, Politics, p. 101.

74 Fein, Accounting, p. 181.

75 Henry Feingold, "Could America Have Done More?" p. 310.

76 ZA, S25/296, Protocol of meeting of the Zionist Actions Committee, 2/2/43.

77 Moreshet Archives (Givat Haviva, Israel), D. 1.730.1, M. Bader to Heini (Bornstein).

CHAPTER 7

1 See for example: NYT, "Extinction Feared by Jews in Poland", report by Henry Shoskes, 3/1/42.

2 WA, Box 92, MP to SW, 2/2/42.

3 NA SD, 868.48/3188, Kohler Memo on Chronology of Relief to Greece, 2/22/43.

4 Penkower, Expendable, p. 124.

5 LofC, BL, Box 199, Memo of W. Murray, 8/22/41.

6 NA SD, 868.48/3363, BL memo on meeting with Charles Taft (War Relief Board), 9/23/42.

7 LofC, BL, Box 194, P. Alling to BL, 1/29/43.

8 JDCA, EC, 5/20/42.

9 Ibid, EC, 4/15/42.

10 Ibid, EC, 5/20/42.

11 See for example: Penkower, Expendable, p. 147.

12 NA SD, 868.48/3188, Kohler memo on Chronology of Relief to Greece, 22/2/43, and /3363, BK memo on meeting with C. Taft, 9/23/42.

13 WJCA, File 108, EC, 3/26/42.

14 Ibid, U54, AK to SW et al, 6/25/42.

15 Penkower, Expendable, p. 124.

16 LofC, BL, Box 209, Memorandum of conversation between BL, D. Acheson, NG & JWW, 9/29/42.

17 LofC, BL, Box 209, BL Memo, 5/8/42.

18 NA SD, 860.48/775, Memo On Sending Food to Enemy-Occupied Territories, 9/24/42.

19 Ibid, J. Kealey to BL, 5/2/42.

20 NA TD, RG056, R. Paul to HM. 9/1/42.

21 NA TD, RG 056, H.D. White & R. Paul to HM, 10/742.

22 LofC, BLD, 10/1/42, p. 283.

23 Ibid.

24 LofC, BL, Box 204, File FDR, FDR to David Morris, n.d.

25 JDCA, EC, 10/22/42.

26 Ibid.

27 LofC, BL, Box 209, BL Memo to S. Welles, 10/25/42.

28 Ibid, BL Memo, 12/2/42.

29 Ibid, BL Memo, 12/8/42.

30 NA SD, 860.48/775 4/5. J. Pehle to S. Welles, 12/11/42.

31 Ibid, 4/28/43.

32 JDCA, EC, 10/27/43.

33 YIVO, Waldman File, JEC, 9/24/43.

34 WA, Box 91, MP to AT, 12/12/41.

35 WJCA, 108, WJC (Geneva) to WJC (N.Y.), 4/20/43.

36 Ibid, 265, L. Osborne to JWW, 4/8/43.

37 Penkower, Expendable, p. 127.

38 Ibid.

39 LofC, BL, Box 203, Confidential Memo on Topics for Agenda at Bermuda Conference. n.d.

40 Wyman, Abandonment, p.139.

41 WJCA, 267, AT to SW, 7/23/42.

42 Ibid.

43 Ibid.

44 Ibid., AT to J.C. Foulis, 6/25/43.

45 Penkower, Expendable, p. 224

46 Dworzecki, The IRC, p. 92.

47 WJCA, 265, M. Peter (ICRC) to AT, 7/10/43.

48 Dworzecki, The IRC, p. 91.

49 WJCA, 265, JWW to AT, 8/31/42.

50 Ibid, AK to NG, 2/1/43.

51 Ibid, AT to AK, 2/9/43.

52 Ibid, AK to SW et al, 4/23/43.

53 Ibid.

54 Ibid, Peters to AT, 7/10/43.

55 Ibid, AK to SW, 12/17/43.

56 Ibid, N. Davis (ARC) t0 Dr. S. Kantor (WJC), 10/20/43.

57 Ibid, Peter (ICRC) to AT, 12/17/43.

58 Ibid, Memo of conversation between M. Peter and AK, 1/5/44.

59 Dworzecki, IRC, p. 94.

60 Ibid, pp. 84-85.

61 Gutman, Jews of Warsaw, p.197.

62 OH, 5 (22) H, Interview with Dr. I. Goldstein, p. 19

CHAPTER 8

1 CW, 12/18/42, p. 3.

2 NASD, 811.4016/518, MW to Welles, 1/28/43.

3 Ibid., CH to Welles, 1/30/43.

4 MZ, chet/3/3/23, Speech of Rep. Emmanuel Celler in the House of Representatives, 12/7/42.

5 Reconstructionist, "Save Jews Now!", Vol. 10, no. 2, 3/5/43, p. 24. Celler in the House of Representatives, 12/7/42.

6 Jewish Frontier, Chaim Greenberg, "Bankrupt!", 2/12/43

7 Ibid

8 Yoffe, Igarot, Letter to Dr. Hantke, 3/2/43.

9 Stember, Mind, pp. 116-18.

10 Ibid., p. 132.

11 AJCL, Report of Annual Conference of AJC, 1/31/43.

12 Ibid.

13 Stember, Mind, p. 141.

14 YIVO, Waldman MSS, JEC, 3/29/43.

15 See for example: OH, Testimony of Zesha Borokowski (Niesky).

16 See for example: ZANY, ECZA, 1/28/43.

17 Dallek, Soldier, pp. 335-38.

18 WJCA, 8A, AC, 1/25/43.

19 Lookstein, Brothers' Keepers, pp. 138-39.

20 ZANY, ECZA, OC, 12/22/42.

21 Hadassah, NB, 1/6/43.

22 Yale, PSC MSS, Reel 1, Merlin to Ziff, 4/23/43.

23 Hadassah, N.B., 6/1/43. Notes submitted 2/3/43.

24 Interview With Author and Hill Kook 8/15/83.

25 NASD, 862.4016/2256A, Welles to SW, 2/9/43.

26 Ibid., 860c4016/644 1/2, Durbrow Memo, 1/25/43.

27 FDRL, Book 688, II, DuBois Memo to HM, 12/18/43.

28 Ibid., Meeting on Jewish Evacuation, 1/15/44.

29 Cohen, Not Free, p. 240.

30 CW, "Challenge to Humanity", 2/26/43.

31 NYT, 2/26/43, p. 14.

32 Lipstadt, Beyond Belief, p. 199.

33 CW, 3/5/43, p. 4.

34 Ibid., p. 1.

35 Ibid., p. 16.

36 Medoff, Deafening Silence, p. 106.

37 Ibid 110-11.

38 Lipstadt, Beyond Belief, p. 199.

39 NYT, 3/3/43, p. 22.

40 Wyman, Abandonment, p. 95.

41 Lipstadt, Beyond Belief, p. 205.

42 See for example: Signatories to ad in NYT, "A Proclamation on the Moral Rights of the Stateless and Palestinian Jews", 12/7/42.

43 MZ, chet/1/3, "Proposals for the Establishment of the Committee for a Jewish Army, (n.d.).

44 Ibid, Bulletin of CZA, #134, 12/31/42, Report of National Conference.

45 Ibid.

46 NYT, 2/8/43, "Action Not Pity!", p. 8.

47 Current Biographies, "Edwin C. Johnson", 12/46, p. 287.

48 MZ, chet/ 3/1/1, Goals and Methods.

49 Bauer, Diplomacy, pp. 84-93.

50 MZ, chet 3/2/6, Bulletin # 74, 9/15/42, Quotes a Zionist named Harry Greir.

51 Ibid, chet 3/2/6, Bulletin #43, 8/6/42.

52 .ZANY, ZOA, EC, 11/16/42.

53 Ibid., ECZA, 12/2/42.

54 MZ, chet 3/3/38, A. Lourie to G. Wechsler, 1/6/42.

55 Ibid, G. Wechsler to A. Lourie, 1/14/42.

56 Yale, PSC MSS, Reel 1, G. Wechsler (CJA) to A. Lourie (ECZA), 12/9/42.

57 See for example: Yale, PSC MSS, Reel 1, P. Bergson to W. Ziff, 6/29/43.

58 Ibid., W. Ziff to L. Germain, 8/23/39.

59 WA, Box 104, SW to Rabbi Morton Berman, 5/5/42.

60 Interview with Hillel Kook.

61 Ibid.

62 MZ, chet 3/3/17, Bergson (?) to J. Halperin, 2/9/44.

63 Yale, PSC MSS, Reel 1, P. Bergson to Shapiro (AZEC), 1/13/44.

64 See Bulletins of CZA, MZ, chet 3/2/6. Until March, 1943 there are practically no references made to the Holocaust, and even after that date the subject is barely touched upon until July.

65 Answer, Vol. 1, no. 1, 4/43, p. 15.

66 Medoff, Deafening Silence, p. 105.

67 WJCA, U54, AK to SW et al, 6/25/42.

68 CW, 12/18/42.

69 Ibid., 12/25/42.

70 NYT, 12/7/42. p. 14.

71 MZ, chet 6/2/3, Bulletin # 134, 12/31/42, Report on Decisions of the National Convention.

72 NYT, 2/8/43, p. 8.

73 Ibid., 2/16/43, p. 11.

74 MZ, chet 3/5/56, Bulletin, 2/5/43.

75 Wyman, Abandonment, p. 92

76 Ben Hecht, *A Child of the Century*, (N.Y.: Simon & Schuster, 1954), pp. 556-58.

77 FRUS, 1943, 1:134.

CHAPTER 9

1 FRUS, 1943, 1:134.

2 Wyman, Abandonment, pp. 104-05.

3 David Engel, *In the Shadow of Auschwitz; The Polish Government-In-Exile & the Jews; 1939-45*, (Chapel Hill: Univ. of N.C. Press, 1987), p. 200.

4 LofC, BL, Box 202, Refugee Movement File, Memo of BL to A-L/B, VD, SD, 1/25/43.

5 BL Diary, p. 316.

6 Penkower, Expendable, p. 104.

7 LofC, BL, Box 202, Refugee Movement File, Draft of reply to Foreign Office, 2/22/43.

8 FDRL, PSF, CH to British FO, 2/25/43.

9 Irving Abella & Harold Troper, *None is Too Many*, (Toronto: Lester & Orpen Dennys Ltd., 1983), pp. 130-31.

10 Ibid..

11 ZA, S25/1504, NG to E. Kaplan, 1/11/43.

12 WJCA, U-185, Box 82, AC, 2/27/43

13 WA, Box 93, Libby Schultz to SW, 3/29/43.

14 AJCA, JP to Rabbi Gerstenfeld, 3/25/43.

15 Ibid., JP to Rabbi Lazaron, 3/25/43.

16 WA, Box 93, LS to SW, 3/29/43.

17 Ibid., MW to members, 3/25/43.

18 AHS, AJCong, SW to E. Kaufmann (GJC), 1/8/43.

19 WJCA, 82, Box 3, MP, 6/3/43.

20 JDCA, EAC, 3/30/43.

21 YIVO, Waldman Files, JEC, 3/29/43.

22 Ibid.

23 Ibid.

24 LofC, BL, Box 202, Refugee File, BL Memo to Welles, 3/20/43.

25 NASD, 740.0016EW39/858, CH to SW, 4/14/43.

26 Waldman MSS, JEC, 4/10/43.

27 YIVO, Waldman MSS, JEC, Program for Rescue of Jews from Nazi-Occupied Europe, 4/14/43.

28 Ibid., Emergency SC of JEC, 3/4/43.

29 Ibid., Program for Rescue, 4/14/43.

30 LofC, BL, Box 202, Refugee File, BL Memo to Welles, 3/20/43.

31 Ibid., BL to SW, 4/20/43.

32 Wyman, Abandonment, p. 108.

33 Ibid., p. 109.

34 LofC, BL, Box 203, n.d. (4/43?).

35 Ibid.

36 Penkower, Expendable, p. 108.

37 YIVO, Waldman MSS. JEC, 4/18/43.

38 LofC, BL Diaries, 4/20/43.

39 Wyman, Abandonment, p. 111.

40 LofC, BL, Box 203, Minutes of the Bermuda Conference, Morning Session, 4/20/43, p. 1

41 Ibid.

42 FRUS,1943, II, 3/27/43, pp.38-39.

43 AJCA, JP to S. Bloom (Bermuda), 4/16/43.

44 LofC, BL, Box 203, Minutes of BC, 4/20/43, Morning Session, p. 4.

45 Ibid.

46 Ibid., p. 5.

47 Ibid., pp. 6-8.

48 Wyman, Abandonment, pp. 335-36.

49 Ibid., p. 335

50 LofC, BL, Box 203, Minutes of BC, Morning Session, 4/23/43, p.10.

51 Ibid., 4/24/43, Morning Session, p. 7.

52 Ibid., 4/21/43, Afternoon Session, p. 7a.

53 Ibid., 4/22/43, Morning Session, pp. 7-8.

54 Ibid., 4/25/43, Meeting of U.S. Delegation, Morning Session, p. 4.

55 Ibid., p. 5.

56 Ibid., p. 23.

57 Ibid., p. 25.

58 Ibid., p. 53.

59 Ibid., p. 59.

60 Ibid., p. 63.

61 Ibid., p. 77.

62 Ibid., Summary of Recommendations, Chapter 7.

63 FRUS, 1943, I, 5/19/43, pp. 183-84.

64 Celler, You Never Leave, p. 87.

65 Lipstadt, Beyond Belief, p. 213.

66 Ibid., pp. 213-15.

67 LofC, BL Diaries, p. 307.

68 Ibid., p. 316.

69 LofC, BL, Box 203, Ref. Mov't File, Alexander (VD) to BL, 5/7/43.

70 Ibid., CH to FDR, 5/7/43.

71 Penkower, Expendable, p. 117.

72 LofC, BL, Box 203, Ref Mov't. File, CH to FDR, 5/743.

73 Penkower, Expendable, p. 121.

74 FDRL. OF, FDR to MT, 7/7/43.

75 Wyman, Abandonment, p. 139.

76 Ibid.

77 Burns, Soldier, p. 447.

78 Opinion, 6/43, p. 5.

79 ZANY, ECZA, OC, 6/1/43.

80 WJCA, U-185, Special Committee on the European Situation, 6/23/43.

81 ZANY, ECZA, 5/3/43. Also: Aaron Berman "American Zionism and the Rescue of European Jewry", AJH, Vol. LXX, 3/81, p. 319.

82 AJCA, Shulman Draft, 5/21/43.

83 Ibid., JP to Shulman, 5/24/43.

84 NASD, 548.g1/149. SW et al to Welles, 6/1/43.

85 JDCA, EC, 6/16/43.

86 Ibid.

87 AJCA, JP to A. Held, 6/9/43.

88 AZA, S25/1504, NG to Shertok, 6/3/43

89 NASD, 862.4016/2280, Harrison (Bern) to CH, 7/29/43.

90 NATD, Paul to HM, 8/21/43.

CHAPTER 10

1 Black, Transfer Agreement, p. 352.

2 Bet Zvi, Post-Uganda, pp. 458-459.

3 Halpern, Political World, pp. 231-32.

4 Doreen Bierbrier, "The American Zionist Emergency Council: An Analysis of a Pressure Group", AJHQ, Vol. LX, no. 1, 9/70, p. 100.

5 Halpern, Political World, p. 32.

6 Ibid, p. 38.

7 Wyman, Paper Walls, p. 33.

8 Howard M. Sachar, *A History of Israel,* (N.Y.: Alfred A. Knopf, 1976) p.189.

9 Mordechai Friedman, "Zionei Artzot Habrit v'Hatzalat Yehudei Europa B'shnot Ha'shoah", YM, #42, 12/86, pp.115-116.

10 ZANY, AZEC, sundry meetings of AZEC & OC, 1942-43.

11 Bierbrier, AZEC, p. 87.

12 ZANY, ECZA, 5/3/43.

13 Ibid.

14 AJCL, Proskauer File, 3/19/40, J. Willen to A. Strook.

15 AJCA, EC, 7/23/42.

16 AJCA, EC, 12/6/42.

17 Ibid.

18 AJCA, JP to MW, 4/29/42.

19 NASD, 811.4016/518, Welles to CH, 1/30/43.

20 Lookstein, Brother's, p. 133.

21 Halpern, Political World, p. 149.

22 Lookstein, Brother's, p. 134.

23 YIVO, Waldman MSS, MW to JP, 2/7/43.

24 AJCA, AC, 4/9/43.

25 Noy, The Unending Task, p. 273.

26 Halperin, Political World, pp. 231-32.

27 HMD, 12/3/42, pp. 519-20.

28 WA, Box 68, SW to AHS, 5/15/41.

29 NASD, 867n.01/1812, Memo FDR to CH, 7/7/42.

30 Baker, Brandeis &, p. 392

31 FRUS, Vol. IV, 4/20/43, Summary of Hoskins' Report, pp. 782-85.

32 FRUS, Vol. IV, 4/20/43, Summary of Hoskins' Report, pp. 782-85.

33 FDRL, OF, 3186, Patterson to CH, 7/26/43.

34 Ibid, CH to FDR, 7/30/43.

35 ZANY, OC, 8/12/43.

36 FDRL, SIR, Container 4, SW to SIR, 8/24/43.

37 AJCongL, Joint EC of W&AJCong, 7/8/43.

38 WA, Box 92, MP to SW, 6/18/43.

39 CW, 8/20/43, p. 4.

40 Opinion, 10/43, p. 11.

41 ZANY, Box XXXVII, AJConf, 8/29/43, IG.

42 Lookstein, Brother's, p. 168.

43 CW, 9/24/43, p. 6

44 ZANY, XXXVII, AJConf, 8/29/43, IG.

45 Urofsky, Voice, p. 338.

46 AJCongL, EC, 6/13/44.

47 Noy, Unending, pp. 316-17.

48 AJCA, AC, 10/4/43.

49 Ibid, 11/9/43.

50 NASD, 867n.01/1897, Conversation Murray, et al (SD) with MW (AJC).

51 LofC, BL, Box 200, Meeting of MW with Near East Division, 1/10/44.

52 AJHS, AJCong, AC, 6/23/44.

53 Noy, Unending, p. 321.

54 YIVO, Waldman MSS, JEC, 11/5/43.

55 JDCA, EC, 11/17/43.

56 YIVO, Waldman MSS, JEC, Rosenheim (A-I) to JP, 10/28/43.

57 M. Orion, "Manhiguto Shel Harav Abba Hillel Silver B'zirah Ha'yehudit Amerikait, 1938-49," (Ph.D. Dissertation, Heb. U., 1982), p. 132.

58 ZANY, AZEC, 1/3/44.

59 VMI, Marshall MSS, Box 89, File 44, Marshall to CH, 2/7/44.

60 ZANY, AZEC, 2/28/44.

61 Ibid, 3/13/44.

62 Wallace Diaries, 3/10/44, p. 313.

63 ZANY, AZEC, 5/1/44.

64 Cyrus Adler & Aaron Margalith, *With Firmness in Right,* (N.Y.: AJC,1946), p. 401.

65 Wyman, Abandonment, pp. 173-174.

CHAPTER 11

1 Answer, "Has the Idea of a Jewish Army Been Abandoned?", Vol. 1, no. 1, 3/43, p. 15.

2 Ibid.

3 Lookstein, Brothers', p. 137.

4 Answer, "Has the Idea", p. 22.

5 Wyman, Abandonment, p. 111.

6 Answer, "To 5,000,000 Jews in the Nazi Death-Trap Bermuda Was a Cruel Mockery", Vol. 1, no. 3, 5/43, p. 17.

7 Yale, PSC MSS, Reel1, Sen. E. Johnson to PB, 5/8/43.

8 Ibid., Sen. R. Taft to CJA, 5/17/43.

9 Ibid., Rep. A. Sabath to CJA, 5/17/43.

10 Ibid., E. Jabotinsky to Sen. E. Johnson, 5/6/43.

11 Ibid., PB to Sen. E. Johnson, 5/7/43.

12 OH, 4 (67) G, Interview with Dr. Raffaeli.

13 Ben Hecht, A Child of the Century, p. 546.

14 NASD, 867n20/180, J.E. Hoover to Berle; also /202, J. E. Hoover to Berle 5/25/43.

15 Lipstadt, Beyond Belief, p. 276n.

16 Penkower, "The Bergson Boys", p. 294.

17 AJA MSS, no. 9, SW, NG to SW, 8/5/43.

18 See for example: Yale, PSC MSS, Reel 11, Statement of Van Paasen in "Protestant", 4/44.

19 WA, Box 99, Memo of Interim Committee of AJConf.

20 Yale, PSC MSS, Reel 1, EC of CJA, 4/25/43.

21 MZ, chet/3/5/53, Ben Ami (LA) to PB, 10/2/43.

22 Ibid.

23 Ibid, chet/ 3/3/17, Y. Halperin (London) to PB & S. Merlin, 6/12/44 & 6/24/44.

24 Yale, PSC MSS, Reel 1, EC of CJA, 4/25/43.

25 Ibid.

26 Answer, "Emergency Conference to Save the Jews of Europe", Vol. 1, no. 4, 6/43, pp. 10, 19.

27 WA, Box 99, Memo of Interim Committee of AJConf.

28 WA, Box 92, MP to SW, 6/18/43.

29 Penkower, Expendable, p. 135

30 Yale, PSC MSS, Reel 4.

31 Wyman, Abandonment, p. 147.

32 NASD, 840.48ref/4435, "Pa" Watson to CH, 8/30/43 & CH to Max Lerner, 9/1/43.

33 LofC, BL, Box 202, Ref File, BL minutes of meeting with PB and Ira Hirschmann, 9/1/43.

34 Wyman, Abandonment, p. 148.

35 NASD, 840.48ref/4443, PB to S. Early, 8/23/43.

36 Wyman, Abandonment, pp. 152-53.

37 Opinion, 11/43, editorial, p. 4.

38 Wyman, Abandonment, p. 154.

39 NYT, 11/5/43, p. 14.

40 Penkower, "Bergson Boys", p. 294.

41 OH, 14 (33), Interview with Hillel Kook (Peter Bergson).

42 MZ, chet/3/5/58.

43 Yale, PSC MSS, Reel 1, PB to Maj. Gen. Hershey, 6/18/43.

44 MZ, chet/ 3/3/22, A. Jabotinsky to A. Altman (Jerusalem), 5/3/43.

45 Yale, PSC MSS, Reel 1, Y. Ben Ami to PB, 8/13/43.

46 MZ, chet/ 3/2/6, Bulletin # 24, 9/17/43.

47 ZANY, ECZA, 11/15/43.

48 "Declaration of the Hebrew Committee for National Liberation", JTA, 18.6. 1944.

49 OH, 13 (33), Interview with E. Jabotinsky, 8/18/68, p.10.

50 Yale, PSC MSS, Reel 10, Statement by I. Hirschmann, 11/14/44.

CHAPTER 12

1 Ephraim Ophir, «Haim Nitan Haya L'hatzil 70,000 Yehudim MiTransnistria?» YM # 33, 6/82, p. 115. (Hebrew).

2 WJCA, U 101 A, Box 84, AC, 2/27/43.

3 Ophir, "Haim Nitan", p. 121, fn., n. 26.

4 Dina Porat, "Chelka Shel Hasochnut B'Yerushalayim B'maamatzim L'hatzalat Yehudei Europa B'shanim 1942-1945," (Ph.D. Dissertation, Tel Aviv U., 1983), p. 156 & p. 161(Heberw)

5 Ophir, "Haim Nitan", p. 164.

6 Porat, "Hasochnut", p. 170.

7 Ibid, p. 163.

8 NYT, 2/13/43, p. 5.

9 FDRL, HMD, Book 609, Phone conversation HM & S. Welles, 2/15/43.

10 ZANY, Box VIII, ZOA, EC, 2/20/43.

11 Porat, "Hasochnut", p. 162.

12 CW, 2/26/43.

13 WA, Box 99, Memo of Interim Committee of AJConf.

14 David Wyman and Rafael Medoff, *A Race Against Death: Peter Bergson, America and the Holocaust* (New York, 2000).

15 NASD, 862.4016/2266, SW to S. Welles, 3/31/43.

16 Ibid., Welles to Atherton, 4/5/43.

17 Ibid, Harrison to S of S, 4/20/43.

18 Ibid.

19 Penkower, Expendable, p. 128.

20 FDRL, HMD, Book 688, Part I, Memo of DuBois of meeting with B. Meltzer, 12/9/43.

21 Ibid.

22 NASD, 867n.01/1964, Brandt to Gray, 8/6/43.

23 Penkower, Expendable, p. 129.

24 NATD, RG 056, R. Paul to HM, 9/1/42.

25 FDRL, Book 688, Part I, 11/23/43.

26 FDRL, HMD, Box 688, Part I, Paul to HM, 8/12/43.

27 WJCA, File 41, JWW memo, 6/28/43.

28 NATD, RG 056, O'Connell & Pehle to HM, 7/1/43.

29 FDRL, HMD. Book 688, Part I. R. Paul to HM, 8/26/43.

30 Wyman, Abandonment, p. 180.

31 FDRL, PPF, 3292, SW to FDR, 4/28/43.

32 Wise, Challenging, pp. 277-78.

33 Ibid.

34 WJCA, Box 266, SW to Gen. Watson, 8/17/43.

35 WA, Box 66, FDR to SW, 8/20/43.

36 Penkower, Expendable, p. 121.

37 FDRL, OF 3186, SW to FDR, 7/23/43.

38 NATD, RG 056, HM to SW, 7/29/43.

39 FDRL, HMD, Book 688, Part I, HM to FDR, 8/11/43.

40 FDRL, OF 3186, FDR to SW, 8/14/43.

41 WJCA, 266, S of S to American Legation (Bern) 12/13/43.

42 Bauer, American Jewry, p. 185.

43 ZA, S-26 1080. Resume of discussion between Schwartz (JDC) and Dobkin (JA), 8/4-7/43.

44 WJCA, File 41, Minutes of meeting NG & BL, 9/16/43.

45 YIVO, Wa MSS, JEC, 9/24/43.

46 NASD, 840.48ref/4556, J. Hyman to BL, 10/6/43.

47 WJCA, File 41, Notes of conversation between BL & NG, 12/9/43.

48 Ibid., AT to NG (from London), 1/16/45

49 FDRL, HMD, Book 693, 1/13/44.

50 NASD, 840.48ref/10-143, SA & NG to BL, 10/1/43.

51 ZANY, Z51216, SW to M. Weisgal, 10/26/43.

52 Penkower, Expendable, pp. 266-67.

53 NASD, 862.4016/2292, Harrison to S of S, 10/6/43.

54 Ibid., Stettinius to American Delegation in Bern, 10/26/43.

55 Ibid., Reams to Matthews, 10/25/43.

56 Yale, PSC MSS, Reel 6, "A Year in the Service of Humanity", 8/8/44.

57 Wyman, Abandonment, pp. 204-05.

58 See for for example: Breitman & Kraut, American Refugee Policy, Chapter 9. The authors do not attribute much importance to the initiative in the House of Representatives.

59 See for example: Baruch Zuckerman's statement in the Central Committee of the Farband, Labor Archives, 1/26/44.

60 FDRL. HMD, Book 688, Part I, Telephone conversation Lehman to HM, 9/15/43.

61 Ibid., HM to CH, 9/23/43.

62 Ibid., Paul to HM, 11/2/43.

63 Ibid., Meeting on Jewish Evacuation, 11/23/43.

64 Ibid., Meeting on Jewish Evacuation, 11/24/43.

65 Ibid., HM to CH, 11/24/43.

66 Ibid., Book 685, CH to HM, 12/6/43.

67 Ibid., Book 688, Part II, DuBois Memo on meeting with B. Meltzer, 12/9/43.

68 Ibid., Meeting on Jewish Evacuation, 12/13/43.

69 Ibid., Book 688, Part II, Winant (London) to CH, 12/15/43.

70 Ibid., Meeting on Jewish Evacuation, 12/17/43.

71 Ibid., Meeting on Jewish Evacuation, 12/18/43.

72 Wyman, Abandonment, pp. 183-84.

73 MZ, chet/ 3/3/23, Gillette Resolution in the U.S. Senate, 11/9/43.

74 Penkower, Expendable, p. 137.

75 Wyman, Abandonment, pp. 194-95.

76 Lucy Davidowicz, "American Jews and the Holocaust", NYT Magazine, 4/18/82, p. 112.

77 Wyman, Abandonment, p. 195.

78 Ibid.

79 House of Representatives, Extract from Hearings before the Committee on Foreign Affairs, "Rescue of Jewish and Other Peoples in Nazi-occupied Territories",78th Congress,1st Session, 11/26/43, (Washington:GPO,1943), p. 32.

80 Ibid., p. 23.

81 Ibid., p. 23.

82 Ibid., p. 34.

83 See W. Rogers questioning, HofR, Hearings, 48 & ff.

84 Penkower, Expendable, pp. 138-39

85 NYT, 12/11/43, p. 1.

86 Interim Report of Rescue Commission of the American Jewish Conference,1944,Appendix I.

87 JTA Bulletin, 12/22/43, p. 1.

88 Wyman, Abandonment, p. 198.

89 ZANY, Box XXXVII, EC, AJConf, 11/6/43.

90 Ibid., Interim Committee of AJCon11/23/43.

91 Wyman, Abandonment, p. 199.

92 FDRL, HMD, Book 688, Part I, Paul & Pehle to HM, 9/3/43.

93 House of Representatives, "Problems of World War II", Hearings before the Committee on Foreign Affairs, Wise testimony, pp. 217-47.

94 CW, "Timely Topics", 12/10/43.

95 FDRL, HMD, Book 688, Part II, Meeting on Jewish Evacuation, 12/20/43.

96 Ibid.

97 Ibid., 12/19/43.

98 Ibid., 12/18/43.

99 Ibid., DuBois Memo, 12/18/43.

100 Ibid., Meeting on Jewish Evacuation, 12/20/43.

101 Ibid.

102 Ibid., Book 106, R. Paul to HM, 12/18/43.

103 Ibid., Book 688, Part II, R. Paul to HM, 1/3/44.

104 Ibid., CH to American Embassy (London), 1/3/44.

105 Ibid., Meeting on Jewish Evacuation, 1/13/44.

106 Ibid, Personal Report to the President, 1/26/44 p. 2.

107 Ibid, p. 9.

108 Ibid., Phone Conversation, HM & SIR, 1/13/44.

109 Ibid., Phone Conversation, HM & SIR, 1/15/44.

110 Ibid., Meeting on Jewish Evacuation, 1/15/44.

111 Ibid., ibid.

112 Ibid., ibid.

113 Ibid., ibid.

114 FDRL, HMD, Memorandum for the Secretary's Files, 1/16/44.

115 Ibid., ibid.

116 JTA Bulletin, 1/24/44, pp.1-2.

CHAPTER 13

1 Wyman, Abandonment, p. 205.

2 FDRL, HMD, Book 688, Part II, Meeting on Jewish Evacuation, 1/15/44.

3 Wyman, Abandonment, p. 316.

4 Ibid, p. 95.

5 Ibid., pp.172-73.

6 Medoff, Deafening Silence, pp. 176-80.

7 Wyman, Abandonment, p. 317.

8 Ibid., pp. 195-97.

9 CW, 12/24/43, pp. 16-17.

10 JTA, 12/22/43, p. 1.

11 Sherwood, Roosevelt and Hopkins, pp. 776 ff.

12 FDRL, HMD, Book 688, Part II, Meeting on Jewish Evacuation, 12/18/43.

13 Ibid., 12/19/43, also WJCA.

14 LofC, Stimson Diaries, Meeting of War Refugee Committee, 1/26/44.

15 Voss, Servant, p. 249.

16 FDRL, HMD, Book 696, Jewish Evacuation Meeting, 1/25/44.

17 Porat, "Sochnut", p. 170.

18 WJCA, 41, M. Shertok to NG, 6/2/44.

19 Wyman, Abandonment, pp. 231-34, & Bauer, American Jewry, p. 407.

20 Wyman, Abandonment, p. 211.

21 Wyman, Abandonment, p. 211.

22 AJHS, AJCong, AC, 6/23/44.

23 Wyman, Abandonment, p. 232.

24 WJCA, 266, J. Pehle to SW, 6/21/44.

25 Ibid., 125A, "Program of General Measures of Relief and Rescue of Jews", submitted to WRB by WJC, 3/3/44.

26 Bauer, American Jewry, pp. 395-96, p. 412.

27 Hirschmann, Caution, p. 172.

28 Porat, "Sochnut", p. 205.

29 WJCA, 8A, EC, 2/10/44

30 Wyman, Abandonment, p. 213.

31 Bauer, American Jewry, p. 407.

32 Ibid., pp. 404-05.

33 Breitman and Kraut, American Refugee Policy, pp. 194-196.

34 NYT, 3/25/44, pp. 1, 4.

35 See, for example: Per Anger, With Raoul Wallenberg in Budapest, (N.Y.: 1981).

36 See: YIVO, Waldman Files, "Program for the Rescue of Jews from Nazi-Occupied Europe", submitted to the Bermuda Refugee Conference by the JEC, 4/14/43.

37 Penkower, Expendable, p. 196.

38 Eppler, "The Rescue Work", p. 67.

39 Wyman, Abandonment, p. 85.

40 Breitman & Kraut, American Refugee, p. 191; Wyman, Abandonment, p. 209.

41 LofC. Stimson Diaries, Reel, 3/4/44.

42 Wyman, Abandonment, pp. 212-13.

43 WJC, Unity, p.186.

44 Wyman, Abandonment, p. 214.

45 WJCA, File 41, WJC cables to Representatives in England & Sweden, 8/1/44; AK to L. Spiegler (Washington).

46 See for example: Wyman, Abandonment, chapter 15.

47 See for example: Novick, 54-58.

48 Quoted in: Wyman, Abandonment, 291.

49 Quoted in: Saul Friedlander, The Years of Extermination (New York, 207), 627.

50 Quoted in: Wyman, Abandonment, 296.

51 Ibid, 297.

52 Ibid, 299

53 Ibid, 306.

54 Ibid, 287.

CHAPTER 14

1 Jacob Katz, "Was the Holocaust Predictable?", in The Holocaust as Historical Experience, Yehuda Bauer & Nathan Rotenstreich eds., (New York, 1981), p. 27.

2 Moshe Lifshitz, Toldot Am Yisrael, p. 241.

3 Herbert Druks, The Failure to Rescue, (New York, 1977), p. 98.

4 Louis Lochner, (ed.), The Goebbels Diaries, 1942-1943, (New York, 1948), December 12, 1942, p. 241.

5 Voss, Servant, SW to L. Bakstansky (London), 9/29/42, p. 251.

6 Quoted in: Bernard Wasserman, "The Myth of Jewish Silence", Midstream, vol. XXVIII, no. 4, (June, 1984), p. 13.

7 WJCA, U 185, Advisory Committee on European Jewish Affairs, 6.23.1943.

8 Unity, pp. 160-161.

9 Penkower, Expendable, p. 298.

10 Stember, p. 210.

11 Shlomo Aronson, Hitler, the Allies and the Jews, (Cambridge, 2004).

12 Penkower, Expendable, p. 300.

13 Burns, p. 381.

14 Lipstadt, p. 269.

15 Henry Feingold, "Did American Jewry Do Enough During the Holocaust?", B.G. Rudolph Lecture, Syracuse Univ., 4/84, Pamphlet Form, p. 2.

16 Wyman, *Abandonment*, p. 123.

17 Lazaron to Proskauer, AJCA, 24.3.1943.

18 Helen Fein, *Accounting for Genocide*, (N.Y.,1979), p. 179.

19 Wyman, *Abandonment*, p. 78.

20 Burns, *Soldier*, pp. 124, 421, 462.

21 Medoff, *Deafening*, pp. 167-72.

22 Wyman, *Abandonment*, p. 306.

23 Burns, *Soldier*, p. 535.

24 Breitman and Kraut, *American Refugee Policy,* p. 9.

25 Peter Novick, *The Holocaust in American Life* (Boston & New York, 1999).

26 FDRL, HMD, Book 688 II, p. 61.

27 Wyman, *Abandonment*, p.316.

28 Medoff, p. 181.

29 Richard Breitman & Allan J. Lichtman *FDR and the Jews*, (Cambridge, Mass., 2013)Pag 8-9

30 Ibid p.316.

31 Wyman, *Paper Walls*, p. 211.

32 Ibid, p. 211.

33 H.W. Brands, *Traitor to His Class*, (New York, 2008), p. 633.

34 Urofsky, *A Voice*, p. 284.

35 Medoff, "Interview with Ben Zion Netanyahu, *Jerusalem Post*, 3.5.2012.

36 Robert Morgenthau and Frank Tuerkheimer, "How FDR Helped Save Jews of the Holy Land", *Jewish Daily Forward*, 12.10.2011.

37 Burns, *Soldier*, p. 497.

38 Quoted in Breitman, *Official Secrets*, p. 193.

39 *NYT*, 6.13.1942, p. 7.

40 Bauer, *American Jewry*, p. 404.

41 JDCA, EC, 10.2.1943

42 Wyman, *Abandonment*, p. 117.

43 Penkower, *Expendable*, p. 99.

44 Wyman, *Abandonment*, pp. 257-259.

45 Medoff, pp. 187-188.

46 YIVO, Waldman MSS, Proskauer to Rabbi Gerstenfeld, 25.3.1943.

47 ZANY, S25/1504, N. Goldmann to Shertok, 3.6.1943.

48 Breitman and Kraut, *American Refugee Policy*, p. 192.

49 See foe example: Wyman, *Abandonment*, p. 172

50 Walter Laquer, *A History of Zionism* (New York, 1978), p. 554.

51 Quoted in: Judith Tydor Baumel, *The "Bergson Boys" and the Origins of Contemporary Zionist Militancy*, (Syracuse, 2005), p.130.

52 Quoted in ibid, pp. 247-248.

53 Institute of Contemporary Jewry, Oral History, 13 (33), Interview with Ari Jabotinsky, 10.8.1968, p. 10.

54 Baumel, *The "Bergson Boys"*, p. 104.

55 Yehuda Bauer, "How to Misinterpret History", *The Israel Journal of Foreign Affairs*, vol. VI, no. 3, p. 139.

56 Rafael Medoff, "What Did They Know and What Could They Have Done? More on the Allied Response to the Holocaust", *The Israel Journal of Foreign Affairs*, vol. VII, no. 1, p. 113.

57 Baumel, *The "Bergson Boys"*, p. 19.

58 Ibid, p. 113.

59 See Yehuda Bauer's book: *American Jewry and the Holocaust.*

60 Oral History, Interview with Hillel Kook, OH 14 (33).

61 Ibid.

62 Baumel, *The "Bergson Boys"*, p. 25.

63 Ibid, p. 235.

64 Ibid, ibid.

65 Hayim Greenberg, *The Inner Eye, Selected Essays*, (Shlomo Katz, ed.) (New York, 1964), p. 182.

66 WJCA, 185A, Kubowitzki to Wise and others, 21.8.1942.

67 Leib Joffe, *Ktavim* (Hebrew), p. 205.

68 Samantha Power, "Raising the Cost", *Dissent*, 1.4.2002.

BIBLIOGRAPHY

ARCHIVES

In Israel

1 – Central Zionist Archives – Jerusalem
   Various correspondence; Protocols of meetings of the Jewish Agency Executive and of ECZA

2 – Labor Archives – Tel Aviv
   "Farband" Archives

3 – Moreshet Archives – Givat Haviva
   Correspondence of Menachem Bader in Constantinople

4 – Metzudat Ze'ev – Tel Aviv
   Archives of the CJA; Emergency Committee to save the Jewish People of Europe.

5 – Yad Va'shem Archives – Jerusalem
   Chaim Barlas File; Chaim Pazner File

In the United States

1 – American Jewish Archives – Hebrew Union College, Cincinnatti, Ohio.
   AJCong MSS; S. Bloom MSS; L. Brandeis MSS; S. Dickstein MSS; Stephen Wise Archives; WJC Archives.

2 – American Jewish Committee Library – N.Y.
   Minutes of Executive Committee; Selected Correspondence.

3 – American Jewish Congress Library – N.Y.
   Minutes of Meetings of AC, EC, OC, GC.

4 – American Jewish Historical Society Archives – Brandeis U., Waltham, Mass.
   AJCong Archives; Institute for Jewish Affairs MSS.

5 – American Jewish Joint Distribution Committee – N.Y.
   Minutes of Meetings of A.C., E.C., Emergency AC.

6 – B'nai Brith Library – Washington, D.C.
   Minutes of Central Administrative Board.

7 – Franklin Delano Roosevelt Library – Hyde Park, N.Y.
   Official Files (OF), President's Personal Files (PPF), President's Secretary's Files (PSF).

8 – Hadassah Archives – N.Y.
Minutes of NB; Selected Correspondence; Youth Aliyah Files.
9 – Jewish Labor Committee Archives – N.Y.
Microfilm of Documents from the Holocaust, Reels 1-3.
10 – Lehman Library – Columbia Univ., N.Y.
James MacDonald MSS.
11 – Library of Congress- Washington, D.C.
Emmanuel Celler MSS, Harold Ickes MSS & Diaries, Henry L. Stimson MSS, Myron Taylor – MSS, Henry Wallace MSS., Breckinridge Long MSS.
12 – National Archives- Washington, D.C.
State Department Archives; Treasury Department Archives.
13 – Sterling Library- Yale Univ., New Haven Conn.
Palestine Statehood Committee MSS.
14 – VMI Archives, Lexington, Va.
George C. Marshall Papers.
15 – Yeshiva Univ. Archives – N.Y.
Vaad Hatzalah MSS.
16 – YIVO Archives – N.Y.
Joint Emergency Committee MSS; Labor Zionist Org. of America MSS; Joseph Tennenbaum MSS; Morris Waldman MSS.
17 – Zionist Archives – N.Y.
Minutes of Meetings of AZEC & ECZA; Selected Correspondence; Zionist Organisation of America

B. INTERVIEWS

1- Interviews that the author conducted with Maurice Perlzweig (25/11/85), and with Hillel Kook (15/7/82).

2- Oral History Department – Institute of Contemporary Jewry, Hebrew University, Jerusalem: Czeshka Borokowski; Nachum Goldmann; Israel Goldstein; Ari Jabotinsky; Hillel Kook; Alex Hadani; Louis Levinthal; Gerhardt Riegner.

C. PAPERS AND JOURNALS

Davar and Ha'aretz; CongressWeekly; Jewish Frontier;
New York Times; Newsweek; New Republic; OPINION; Reconstructionist; Time.

D. BOOKS

Abella, Irving & Troper, Harold. *None is too Many*. (Toronto: Lester & Orpen Dennys Ltd., 1983).

Adler, Cyrus & Margalith, Aaron. *With Firmness in Right*. (N.Y.: AJC,1946).

American Jewish Committee. *American Jewish Year Book,* 1942-1943, Vol. 44.

Anger, Per. *With Raoul Wallenberg in Budapest*. (N.Y.: 1981).

Aronson, Shlomo. *Hitler, the Allies and the Jews*, (Cambridge, 2004).

Baker, Leonard. *Brandeis and Frankfurter*. (N.Y.: Harper & Row,1984).

Barkai, Avraham. *Hakalkalah HaNazit*. (Tel Aviv: Sifriat Hapoalim, 1987) (Hebrew).

Bauer, Yehuda. *American Jewry and the Holocaust*. (Detroit: Wayne Univ. Press, 1981).

_____ *From Diplomacy to Resistance: A History of Jewish Palestine,* 1939-1945. (Philadelphia: JPSA, 1970).

Bauer, Yehuda & Rotenstreich, Nathan, eds., *The Holocaust as Historical Experience*. (N.Y.: Holmes& Meier Publishers, 1981).

Baumel, Judith Tidor. *Bein Ideologia V'Taamulah*. (Jerusalem: Magnes Press, 1999).

Bet Zvi, Shabtai. *HaZionut HaPost-Ugandit B'mashber Ha'shoah*. (Tel Aviv: Bronfman, 1977) (Hebrew).

Black, Edwin. *The Transfer Agreement*. (N.Y.: MacMillan, 1984).

Blum, John Morton. *Roosevelt & Morgenthau – A Revision & Condensation*, "From the Morgenthau Diaries". (Boston: Houghton Mifflin, 1970).

_____ *V Was for Victory*. (N.Y.: Harcourt Brace Janovich, 1976).

Breitman, Richard & Kraut, Alan M. *American Refugee Policy & European Jewry,* 1933-1945. (Bloomington: Indiana Univ. Press, 1987).

Breitman, Richard & Lichtman, Allan J. *FDR and the Jews*, (Cambridge, Mass., 2013).

Browning, Christopher. *The Final Solution and the German Foreign Office*. (N.Y.: Holmes & Meier Publishers, 1978).

Burns, James MacGregor. *Roosevelt: The Lion & the Fox*. (N.Y.: Harcourt, Brace & Co., 1956).

_____ *Roosevelt: The Soldier of Freedom*. (N.Y.: Harcourt, Brace & Janovich, 1970).

Cantril, Haley. ed., *Public Opinion, 1935-1946*. (Princeton: Princeton Univ. Press, 1951).

Celler, Emanuel. *You Never Leave Brooklyn, Autobiography of Emanuel Celler*. (N.Y.: John Day, 1953).

Cohen, Naomi. *Not Free to Desist.* (Philadelphia: JPSA,1972).

Cohen, Werner. "The Politics of American Jews" in *The Jews.* (Glencoe: Free Press, 1960).

Cole, Wayne S. *Roosevelt and the Isolationists.* (Lincoln: Univ. of Nebraska Press, 1963).

Cornwell, Elmer, Jr. *Presidential Leadership of Public Opinion.* (Bloomington: Univ. of Indiana Press, 1965).

Dallek, Robert. *FDR and American Foreign Policy, 1932-1945.* (N.Y.: Oxford Univ. Press, 1979).

Dallek, Robert. ed., *The Roosevelt Diplomacy & World War II.* (N.Y.: Holt, Rinehart & Winston, 1970).

Dinnerstein, Leonard. ed., *Anti-Semitism in the United States.* (N.Y.: Holt, Rinehart & Winston, 1971).

Doneson, Judith E. *The Holocaust in American Film.* (Jewish Publication Society, 1987.)

Druks, Herbert. *The Failure to Rescue.* (N.Y.: Robert Speller & Sons, 1977).

Engel, David. *In the Shadow of Auschwitz; The Polish Government-In-Exile & the Jews 1939-45.* (Chapel Hill: Univ. of N.C. Press, 1987).

Fein, Helen. *Accounting for Genocide.* (N.Y.: Free Press, 1979).

Feingold, Henry L. *A Midrash on American Jewish History.* (Albany: SUNY Press,1982).

_____ *The Politics of Rescue.* (N.Y.: Holocaust Library, 1970).

Finger, Seymour Maxwell. ed., *American Jewry During the Holocaust.* American Jewish Commission on the Holocaust, (March 1984).

Foreign Relations of the United States, 1939-1945. (Washington: GPO, 1956-1969).

Friedman, Saul S. *No Haven for the Oppressed.* (Detroit: Wayne State Univ., 1973).

Fuchs, Lawrence H., ed., *American Ethnic Politics.* (N.Y.: Harper & Row, 1968).

_____ *The Political Behavior of American Jews.* (Glencoe: Free Press, 1956).

Gilbert, Martin. *Auschwitz & the Allies.* (London: Michael Joseph/Rainbird, 1981).

Goldmann, Nahum. *The Autobiography of Nahum Goldmann.* Trans. by H. Sebba. (N.Y.: Holt, Rinehart & Winston,1969).

Goldstein, Israel. *My World As A Jew.* (N.Y.: Herzl Press, 1984).

Goren, Arthur. *New York Jews and the Quest for Community.* (N.Y. : Columbia Univ. Press, 1970).

Greenberg, Hayim. *The Inner Eye, Selected Essays*, ed. by Shlomo Katz. (N.Y.: Jewish Frontier Associates, 1964)

Grobman, Alex & Landis, Daniel. eds, *Genocide*. (Chappaqua: Russel Books, 1983).

Grusd, Edward *B'nai Brith--The Story of a Covenant*. (N.Y.: Appleton-Century, 1966).

Gutman, Yisrael. *The Jews of Warsaw, 1939-1942*. (Bloomington: Univ. of Indiana Press, 1982).

Halperin, Samuel. *The Political World of American Zionism*. (Detroit: Wayne Univ. Press,1961).

Hecht, Ben. *A Child of the Century*. (N.Y.: Simon & Schuster, 1954).

Hertzberg, Arthur. ed., *The Zionist Idea*. (N.Y. : Atheneum Press, 1981).

Hilberg, Raul. *The Destruction of European Jewry*. (Chicago: Quadrangle Books, 1961).

Hirschmann, Ira. *Caution to the Winds*. (N. Y.: David McKay Inc., 1962).

House of Representatives. *Extract from Hearings before the Committee on Foreign Affairs,* "Rescue of Jewish and Other Peoples in Nazi-occupied Territories", 78th Congress,1st Session, 26/11/43. (Washington: GPO, 1943).

_____. Problems of World War II. *Hearings before the Committee on Foreign Affairs* (Washington: GPO, 1976).

Ickes, Harold. *The Secret Diaries of Harold L. Ickes:* Volume III: The Lowering Clouds. (N.Y.: Simon & Schuster,1954).

Israel, Fred. ed., *The War Diary of Breckinridge Long*. (Lincoln: Univ. of Nebraska Press, 1966).

Janowsky, Oscar, ed., *The American Jews – A Composite Portrait*. (N.Y.: Harper & Bros., 1942).

Joffe, Leib. *K'tavim, Iggerot V'Yomanim*. (Jerusalem: Ha'Sifriah Ha'Zionit, 5724) (Hebrew).

Kanawada, Leo V. *Franklin D. Roosevelt's Diplomacy and American Catholics, Italians and Jews*. (Ann Arbor: Univ. of Michigan Research Press, 1982).

Karski, Jan. *Story of a Secret State*. (Boston: Houghton Mifflin Co.,1944).

Klehr, Harvey. *Communist Cadres*. (Stanford: Hoover Institute Press, 1978).

Laqueur, Walter. *The Terrible Secret*. (England: Penguin Books, 1980).

Leuchtenberg, William E. *Franklin D. Roosevelt and the New Deal*. (N.Y.: Harper & Row [Torchbook Edition], 1963).

Lipset, Seymour Martin & Raab, Earl. *The Politics of Unreason.* (N.Y.: Harper & Row, 1970).

Lipsky, Louis. *Memoirs in Profile.* (Philadelphia: JPSA, 1975).

Lipstadt, Deborah E. *Beyond Belief: The American Press and the Coming of the Holocaust.* (N.Y.: Free Press, 1986).

Lochner, Louis. (ed.), *The Goebbels Diaries, 1942-1943*, (New York, 1948)

Lookstein, Haskel. *Were We Our Brothers' Keepers?* (N.Y.: Vintage Books, 1985).

Medoff, Rafael. *The Deafening Silence, American Jewish Leaders and the Holocaust.* (N.Y.: Shapolsky Publishers, 1987).

Moore, Deborah Dash. *B'nai Brith & the Challenge of Ethnic Leadership.* (Albany: SUNY, 1981).

Morse, Arthur D. *While Six Million Died.* (N.Y.: Hart Publishing Co., 1967).

Patterson, James. *Congressional Conservatism & the New Deal.* (Lexington: Univ. of Kentucky Press, 1967).

Novick, Peter. *The Holocaust in American Life.* (Boston & New York: Houghton Mifflin Co, 1999).

Penkower, Monty Noam. *The Jews were Expendable.* (Urbana: Univ of Illinois Press, 1983).

Polenberg, Richard. *One Nation Divisible.* (England: Penguin Books, 1980).

Polier, Justine W. & Wise, James W. eds., *The Personal Letters of Stephen Wise.* (Boston: Beacon Press, 1956).

Porat, Dinah, *The Blue and Yellow Stars of David* (Cambridge, Mass., 1990).

Raphael, Marc Lee. *A History of the United Jewish Appeal: 1939-1982.* (Brown Univ: Scholars Press, 1982).

Ross, Robert W. *So It Was True: The American Protestant Press & the Nazi Persecution of the Jews.* (Minneapolis: Univ. of Minnesota Press, 1980).

Sanders, Ronald. *Shores of Refuge: 100 Years of Jewish Emigration.* (N.Y.: Henry Holt & Co., 1988).

Schlesinger, Arthur Jr. *The Imperial Presidency.* (Boston: Houghton Mifflin, 1970).

Sharot, Stephen. *Judaism, A Sociology.* (London: Newton, Abbots, David & Charles, 1976).

Sherwood, Robert E. *Roosevelt and Hopkins.* (N.Y.: Harper & Brothers, 1948).

Shirer, William L. *The Rise and the Fall of the Third Reich.* (N.Y.: Simon & Schuster, 1960).

Stember, Charles H. *Jews in the Mind of America.* (N.Y.: Basic Books, 1966).

Tevet, Shabtai. *David's Passion,* Vol. III. (Jerusalem: Shocken, 1987).

Tydor Baumel, Judith. *The "Bergson Boys" and the Origins of Contemporary Zionist Militancy,* (Syracuse, 2005).

Urofsky, Melvin I. *American Zionism from Herzl to the Holocaust.* (N.Y.: Anchor Press, 1976).

_____ *A Voice that Spoke for Justice.* (Albany: SUNY Press, 1982).

Voss, Carl Herman. ed., *Stephen S. Wise: Servant of the People, Selected Letters.* (Philadelphia: JPSA, 1970).

Wallace, Henry A. *The Price of Vision: The Diary of Henry A. Wallace,* John M. Blum, ed., (Boston: Houghton Mifflin Co., 1973).

Wasserstein, Bernard. *Britain & the Jews of Europe.* (London: IJA, 1979).

Weizmann, Chaim. *Letters & Papers of Chaim Weizmann,* Series A Letters, (Israel: University Press, 1975).

Weyl, Nathaniel. *The Jews in American Politics.* (New Rochelle: Arlington House, 1969).

Wischnitzer, Mark. *To Dwell in Safety.* (Phila.: JPSA, 1948).

Wise, Stephen S. *As I See It.* (N.Y.: Jewish Opinion Publishing Co., 1944.)

_____ *The Challenging Years,* (N.Y.: G.P. Putnam's Sons, 1949).

_____ editor, *Never Again!, Symposium.* (N.Y.: Jewish Opinion, 1943).

_____ *Servant of the People, Selected Letters,* ed. by Carl Herman Voss, (Phila: JPSA, 1970).

World Jewish Congress, *Unity in Dispersion.* (N.Y.: WJC, 1948).

Wyman, David. *Paper Walls, America and the Refugee Crisis 1938-1941.* (U. of Massachusetts Press, 1968).

_____ *The Abandonment of the Jews.* (N.Y.: Pantheon Press,1984).

E. DISSERTATIONS

Doneson, Judith E. The Holocaust in American Film. (Jewish Publication Society, 1987.

Friedman, Mordechai. "Hatguvah Ha'Politit-Ha'Ziburit shel Yahadut America L'Shoah B'Shanim 1939-1945." (unpublished Ph. D. dissertation, Tel Aviv University, 5745) (Hebrew).

Frommer, Morris. "The American Jewish Congress: A History 1914-50". (unpublished Ph.D. Dissertation, Ohio State Univ., 1978).

Gottlieb, Moshe. "The Anti-Nazi Boycott in the American Jewish Community". (unpublished Ph.D. Dissertation, Brandeis Univ., 1967).

Lookstein, Haskel. "American Jewry's Public Response to the Holocaust 1938-44". (Ph.D. Dissertation, Yeshiva University, 1979).

Neuringer, Sheldon M. "American Jewry and U.S. Immigration Policy, 1881-1953". (unpublished Ph.D. Dissertation, Univ. of Wisconsin, 1969).

Neustadt-Noy, Isaac. "The Unending Task: Efforts to Unite American Jewry from the American Jewish Congress to the American Jewish Conference". (Ann Arbor, 1977).

Orion, M. "Manhiguto shel Ha'Rav Abba Hillel Silver B'Zirah Ha'Yehudit-Amerikait 1938-1949", (unpublished Ph.D. dissertation, Hebrew University, 1982) (Hebrew).

Skolnick, Myron. "Anti-Semitism and the New Deal". (unpublished Ph. D. Dissertation, U. of Md., 1971).

Shapiro, David. "Binyana shel Moetzet Ha'Cherum Va'Zionit k'Zroah Ha'Peulah Ha'Ziburit M'dinit shel Ha'Zionut Ha'Amerikait, 1938-1944". (unpublished Ph. D. dissertation, Hebrew Univ., 5739) (Hebrew).

F. ARTICLES

A.J.Conf. "Interim Report of the Rescue Commission of the American Jewish Conference", 1944.

Bauer, Yehuda. "How to Misinterpret History", *The Israel Journal of Foreign Affairs*, vol. VI, no. 3.

Benedict, Ruth. "Reaction to Events Overseas", *American Jewish Year Book*, XLV.

Berman, Aaron. "American Zionism and the Rescue of European Jewry". AJH, Vol. LXX, 3/81.

Bierbrier, Doreen. "The American Zionist Emergency Council: An Analysis of a Pressure Group". AJHQ, Vol. LX, no. 1, 9/70.

Brody, David. "American Jewry, The Refugees and Immigration Restrictions (1932-42)". PAJHS, 6/56.

Current Biographies. "Edwin C. Johnson" & "Guy Gillette".

Davidowicz, Lucy. "American Jews and the Holocaust". *NYT Magazine,* 18/4/82.

Dinnerstein, Leonard. "Jews and the New Deal". AJH, 6/83.

Dworzecki, Meir. "The International Red Cross and its Policy Vis-A-Vis the Jews in the Ghettoes and Concentration Camps in Nazi-Occupied Europe" in Rescue Attempts During the Holocaust. (Jerusalem: Yad Vashem, 1977).

Eppler, Elizabeth E. "The Rescue Work of the World Jewish Congress During the Nazi Period", in Rescue Attempts During the Holocaust. (Jerusalem: Yad Vashem, 1977).

Eshkoli, Chava. "Tochnit Transnistria – Hizdamnut Hatzalah O Hona'a?". YM, 27 (Hebrew).

Feingold, Henry. "Courage First & Intelligence Second". AJH, 6/83.

_____. "Did American Jewry Do Enough During the Holocaust?" B.G. Rudolph Lecture, Syracuse U. 4/84.

_____. "The Failure to Rescue European Jewry". 450, 7/80.

_____. "Roosevelt & the Holocaust: Reflections on New Deal Humanitarianism".

_____. "Stephen Wise & the Holocaust", Midstream. 1/83, Vol. XXIX. Judaism, Vol. XVIII, no. 3, Summer, 1969.

Friedman, Mordechai. "Zionei Artzot Ha'Brit V'Hatzalat Yehudei Europa B'Snot Ha'Shoah". YM, #42, 12/86(Hebrew).

Gartner, Lloyd P. "The Mid-Passage of American Jewry, 1929-45". 5th Annual Feinberg Memorial Lecture, Univ. of Cincinnatti, 13/5/82.

Genizi, Haim. "American Interfaith Cooperation on Behalf of Refugees from Nazism, 1933-1945". AJH, Vol. LXI, 3/81.

Grobman, Alex. "What Did They Know: The American Jewish Press and the Holocaust, 1/9/39-17/12/42", AJH.Vol. LXVIII, 10/82.

Kaplan, Yonatan. "Peulot Ha'Hatzalah shel Ha'Etzel B'Artzot Ha'Brit". Yalkut Moreshet, 30, 11/80. (Hebrew).

Kubovy, Arieh. "Criminal State Vs. Moral Society". Yad Vashem Bulletin, no. 13, 10/43.

Laqueur, Walter "Jewish Denial & the Holocaust". Commentary, Vol. LXVIII, no. 6, 12/79.

Lazin, Frederick A. "The Response of the AJC to the Crisis of German Jewry, 1933-1939". AJHQ, Vol. LXVIII, 3/79.

Medoff, Rafael. "What Did They Know and What Could They Have Done? More on the Allied."

_____ "Response to the Holocaust," The Israeli Journal of Foreign Affairs, Vol. III no.1.

Morgenthau, Robert and Tuerkheimer, Frank. "How FDR Helped Save Jews of the Holy Land", Jewish Daily Forward, 12.10.2011. H.W. Brands, Traitor to His Class, (New York, 2008).

Ofir, Efraim. "Ha'im Nitan Haya L'Hatzil 70,000 Yehudim Mi'Transnistria?" YM, 33, 6/82(Hebrew).

Oral History, Interview with Hillel Kook, OH 14 (33).

Penkower, Monty Noam. "In Dramatic Dissent: The Bergson Boys". AJH, Vol. LXX, 3/81.

Pinsky, Edward. "American Jewish Unity During the Holocaust: The Joint Emergency Committee, 1943". AJH, 6/83.

Power, Samantha. "Raising the Cost", *Dissent,* 1.4.2002.

Response to the Holocaust", *The Israel Journal of Foreign Affairs*, vol. VII, no. 1.

Rubin, Barry. "Perils of a Jewish Diplomat: Ambassador Laurence A. Steinhardt, 1940-45" AJH. LXX, 3/81.

Shapiro, Edward S. "The Approach of War: Congressional Isolationism and Anti-Semitism". AJHQ, Vol. LXXIV, no. 1, 9/84.

Strum, Harvey. "The Fort Ontario Refugee Shelter, 1944-1946". AJHS, Vol. LXXIII, no. 4, 6/84.

Syrkin, Marie. "What American Jews Did During the Holocaust". Midstream, Vol. XXVIII, 10/82.

Urofsky, Melvin I. "Stephen Wise & his Critics". JF, 10/81, Vol. 48.

Valaik, J. David. "American Catholics, Anti-Semitism, and the Spanish Civil War". Journal of Church and State, Vol. XIII, no. 3, Autumn,1971.

Wasserstein, Bernard. "The Myth of Jewish Silence". Midstream, 7 & 8/ 80, Vol. XXVI, no. 7.

Wiesel, Elie. "Telling the Tale". Dimensions, vol. II, no. 3 (Spring 1968).

Zuroff, Efraim. "Rescue Priority and Fund-Raising as Issues During the Holocaust". AJH, Vol. XVIII, 10/79.

INDEX

www.ingramcontent.com/pod-product-compliance
Lightning Source LLC
Chambersburg PA
CBHW060000100426
42740CB00010B/1345